Learning Force.com Application Development

Use the Force.com platform to design and develop real-world, cutting-edge cloud applications

Chamil Madusanka

[PACKT] enterprise 88
PUBLISHING
professional expertise distilled

BIRMINGHAM - MUMBAI

Learning Force.com Application Development

First published: April 2015

Production reference: 1220415

Published by Packt Publishing Ltd.
Livery Place
35 Livery Street
Birmingham B3 2PB, UK.

ISBN 978-1-78217-279-6

www.packtpub.com

Credits

Author
Chamil Madusanka

Reviewers
Rakesh Gupta
Mrs. Zarna Chintan Naik
Rahul Sharma
Gautam Singh

Commissioning Editor
Owen Roberts

Acquisition Editor
Owen Roberts

Content Development Editor
Govindan K

Technical Editor
Bharat Patil

Copy Editors
Aditya Nair
Trishla Singh
Laxmi Subramanian

Project Coordinator
Shipra Chawhan

Proofreaders
Safis Editing
Maria Gould
Bernadette Watkins

Indexer
Priya Sane

Graphics
Arvindkumar Gupta
Abhinash Sahu

Production Coordinator
Arvindkumar Gupta

Cover Work
Arvindkumar Gupta

About the Author

Chamil Madusanka is a Salesforce.com-certified Force.com developer. He has been working on Force.com projects since 2011. He works as a developer on many custom applications built on Force.com and has also trained end users and new Salesforce developers at his current company (attune Lanka (Pvt) Ltd.) and former company (Sabre Technologies (Pvt) Ltd). He has authored *Visualforce Developer's Guide*, *Packt Publishing*.

Chamil won the Salesforce New Year Resolution 2013 challenge, which was rolled out by Salesforce. He is an active member of the Force.com community and contributes through various channels. He is passionate about Force.com and shares his knowledge of Force.com technologies through his blog (`http://salesforceworld.blogspot.com/`). He is a super-contributor on the Force.com discussion board and shares his knowledge and experience on Force.com by providing effective answers to developer questions. He is the initiator and organizer of the Sri Lanka Salesforce Platform Developer User Group. His contribution to the Sri Lanka Salesforce community has led to an increase in Salesforce competency in Sri Lanka.

He completed his BSc in computer science from the University of Colombo, School of Computing, Sri Lanka (UCSC). His areas of interest include cloud computing, semantic web technologies, and Ontology-based systems. Hailing from Polonnaruwa, an ancient city in Sri Lanka, he currently resides in Gampaha in the Western province of Sri Lanka. His interests include reading technology books and technology blog posts, and playing cricket. Chamil can be reached via twitter at `@chamilmadusanka`, Skype at `chamilmadusanka`, and e-mail at `chamil.madusanka@gmail.com`.

Acknowledgments

I would like to express my gratitude to many people who saw me through this book—to all those who provided support, read, and offered their comments, allowed me to quote their remarks, and proofread. I would like to thank Chandima Cooray, who introduced me to the Salesforce path and my gratitude to attune Lanka (Pvt) Ltd. for letting me continue the journey with Salesforce.

Their support and guidance has been a great strength when I started to work on Salesforce technologies. I would like to thank my family who supported and encouraged me, and accepted the moments when I was away from them. I would like to thank Packt Publishing for giving me the opportunity to write my second book.

I would like to thank Owen Roberts, Govindan K, and Bharat Patil from Packt Publishing for helping me throughout the process of completing this book. I would like to thank Rakesh Gupta, Mrs. Zarna Chintan Naik, Rahul Sharma, and Gautam Singh for their technical review of this book and for their valuable comments.

About the Reviewers

Rakesh Gupta is a Salesforce MVP, evangelist, trainer, blogger, and an independent Salesforce consultant. He is from Katihar, Bihar, and lives in Mumbai. He has been working on the Force.com platform since 2011. Currently, he is working as a Salesforce consultant and is a regular contributor to the Salesforce Success Community. He is the coauthor of *Developing Applications with Salesforce Chatter, Packt Publishing*. He is very passionate about Force.com and shares information through various channels, including his blog at http://rakeshistom.wordpress.com. He has trained almost 180 professionals around the globe and handled many corporate training events. He has 5x certifications in Salesforce. He works on all the aspects of Salesforce and is an expert in data migration, integration, configuration, and customization. He is the leader of the Navi Mumbai and Nashik developer user groups in India. He is also the initiator of the Mumbai Salesforce user group. He organizes meetings at regular intervals for the groups he is part of. He can be reached at rakeshistom@gmail.com or you can follow him on Twitter at @rakeshistom.

Rakesh is the coauthor of *Developing Application with Salesforce Chatter* and *Salesforce.com Customization Handbook* both by Packt Publishing. He is the author of *Learning Salesforce Visual Workflow, Packt Publishing*.

I would like to thank my parents, Kedar Nath Gupta and Madhuri Gupta, and my sister, Sarika Gupta, for supporting me at every step of my life. I would like to thank the author, project coordinators, and Packt Publishing for giving me this opportunity.

Mrs. Zarna Chintan Naik is a proprietor of YES CRM Consultants, a Salesforce.com consulting company based in Mumbai. YES CRM Consultants is primarily focused on Salesforce.com consulting, administration, and training services for clients based around the globe. Zarna and her team also have expertise in multiple AppExchange products, including Conga Merge, Clicktools, Rollup Helper, and Drawloop. Zarna herself holds multiple certifications: Salesforce.com Certified Administrator, Developer, and Sales & Service Cloud Consultant. She earlier worked for one of the leading Salesforce.com partners in USA.

I would like to thank my parents, in-laws, husband, sister, friends, and family for their continued support in my work.

Rahul Sharma has been working on Salesforce for the past 5 years and is a certified Force.com advanced developer. He helps community members in his free time and also participates in Challenges in Topcoder (previously known as Cloudspokes).

His interests are mainly in mobile and web development. He has also reviewed *Visualforce Developer's Guide*, *Packt Publishing*.

You can follow him on Twitter at @rahuls91221. He can be found on LinkedIn at http://in.linkedin.com/in/rahuls91221. You can find him on Salesforce developer at https://developer.salesforce.com/forums/ForumsProfile?communityId=09aF00000004HMGIA2&userId=005F0000003Fg9TIAS.

I would like to thank my friends and family for supporting me to perform reviews. A special thanks to Chamil and the team at Packt for giving me this opportunity. It was nice working with you!

Gautam Singh is a computer science engineer, blogger, online trainer, technical reviewer, and smiling human being. He is from Patna, Bihar and lives in Pune. He had been working with the platform since 2012 and from the very start has contributed to motivate and train a large number of homo sapiens in Salesforce and its certificates.

Currently, he works for Jade Global Inc. as a consultant. He holds the following Salesforce certifications: Certified Developer [DEV-401], Certified Developer [ADM-201], Certified Advanced Developer [ADM-211], and Sales Cloud Consultant, and is on course to complete the Salesforce Certified Advanced Developer [DEV501].

Gautam actively participates on the Salesforce discussion platform and currently holds the SMARTIE [Trusted Contributor] position on developer boards. You can follow Gautam through his active blog at http://singhgautam02.blogspot.in/.

In his spare time, Gautam is a backpacker who explores the beauty and heritage of India. If not with Salesforce, you can find him in discussions about dogs, of whom he is very fond.

You can follow him on Twitter at @retweetgautam and he can be found on LinkedIn at http://www.linkedin.com/pub/gautam-singh/24/657/244.

www.PacktPub.com

Support files, eBooks, discount offers, and more

For support files and downloads related to your book, please visit www.PacktPub.com.

Did you know that Packt offers eBook versions of every book published, with PDF and ePub files available? You can upgrade to the eBook version at www.PacktPub.com and as a print book customer, you are entitled to a discount on the eBook copy. Get in touch with us at service@packtpub.com for more details.

At www.PacktPub.com, you can also read a collection of free technical articles, sign up for a range of free newsletters and receive exclusive discounts and offers on Packt books and eBooks.

https://www2.packtpub.com/books/subscription/packtlib

Do you need instant solutions to your IT questions? PacktLib is Packt's online digital book library. Here, you can search, access, and read Packt's entire library of books.

Why subscribe?

- Fully searchable across every book published by Packt
- Copy and paste, print, and bookmark content
- On demand and accessible via a web browser

Free access for Packt account holders

If you have an account with Packt at www.PacktPub.com, you can use this to access PacktLib today and view 9 entirely free books. Simply use your login credentials for immediate access.

Instant updates on new Packt books

Get notified! Find out when new books are published by following @PacktEnterprise on Twitter or the *Packt Enterprise* Facebook page.

Table of Contents

Preface

Learning Force.com Application Development is a hands-on guide aimed at developing Force.com applications on the Force.com platform. As you read through the content, you will notice that this book focuses on a single real-world example. This book builds upon this example to help you understand and use the tools and features of the Force.com platform.

Cloud computing has made significant changes to the IT/software development industry. Cloud platforms are one of the important directions of cloud computing. Cloud platforms allow the developers to develop apps and run them on the cloud, including platforms for building on-demand applications and platforms as a service (PaaS). Salesforce.com has introduced the first on-demand platform, called Force.com.

What this book covers

Chapter 1, Getting Started with Force.com, introduces the Force.com platform and explains the design and development aspects of the Force.com platform. The sample application scenario and ERD are introduced at the end of this chapter.

Chapter 2, Building the Data Model, introduces the data model of the Force.com platform and explains about creating custom objects, custom fields, and the various data types of the Force.com platform.

Chapter 3, Building the User Interface, explains how to create custom applications, custom tabs, and customized page layouts. The overview of Visualforce will be there at the end of the chapter and that overview will link to *Chapter 8, Building Custom Pages with Visualforce*.

Chapter 4, Designing Apps for Multiple Users and Protecting Data, explains the security aspects of the Force.com platform. That means design considerations for Force.com applications, which are accommodating multiple users and the security framework of the Force.com platform.

Chapter 5, Implementing Business Processes, describes the capabilities of data validation rules and the ways of automating business processes with workflows and approval processes. The troubleshooting of automated processes are explained at the end of the chapter.

Chapter 6, Data Management on the Force.com Platform, describes typical data management operations and data management tools. There is a section to talk about the record IDs and a consideration of the object relationships in data management.

Chapter 7, Custom Coding with Apex, introduces custom coding on the Force.com platform. Apex controllers and Apex triggers will be explained with examples of the sample application. The Force.com platform query language and data manipulation language will be described with syntaxes and examples.

Chapter 8, Building Custom Pages with Visualforce, introduces Visualforce, the architecture of Visualforce, the advantages of Visualforce and the use of Visualforce. There are sections to describe Visualforce pages and Visualforce controllers with examples of the sample application. Finally, there is an explanation section on Visualforce custom components.

Chapter 9, Analytics as a Service with the Force.com Platform, introduces the reports and dashboard of the Force.com platform and analytical features of the Force.com platform.

Chapter 10, E-mail Services with the Force.com Platform, introduces the e-mail feature of the Force.com platform that allows the extension of the application out to a broader population of users, through the use of e-mails.

Chapter 11, Building Public Websites with Force.com Sites, introduces the Force.com sites that allow extending the application out into the broader population of users, through the use of the public website.

Chapter 12, Deploying the Force.com Application, introduces deployment methodologies that allow for the distribution of Force.com applications to other end users.

Appendix, Force.com Tools, explains Force.com tools by looking at the Force.com IDE.

What you need for this book

The prerequisites for the Force.com platform are:

- A basic knowledge of Internet/websites
- An overview knowledge of cloud computing

Who this book is for

This book is aimed at both beginners to Force.com development and developers who already have some experience with Force.com application development and are looking forward to taking your Force.com application development skills to the next level.

Conventions

In this book, you will find a number of styles of text that distinguish between different kinds of information. Here are some examples of these styles, and an explanation of their meaning.

Code words in text are shown as follows: "We can reference a static resource by name in page markup by using the $Resource global variable instead of hardcoding document ID."

A block of code is set as follows:

```
global class ProcessApplicants implements
  Messaging.InboundEmailHandler
{
global Messaging.InboundEmailResult
  handleInboundEmail(Messaging.InboundEmail email,
    Messaging.InboundEnvelope env)
{
Messaging.InboundEmailResult result = new
  Messaging.InboundEmailresult();
return result;
}
}
```

New terms and **important words** are shown in bold. Words that you see on the screen, in menus or dialog boxes for example, appear in the text like this: "Click on **Next**. Then you will get the last step called **Add custom related lists**".

> Warnings or important notes appear in a box like this.

> Tips and tricks appear like this.

Reader feedback

Feedback from our readers is always welcome. Let us know what you think about this book—what you liked or may have disliked. Reader feedback is important for us to develop titles that you really get the most out of.

To send us general feedback, simply send an e-mail to feedback@packtpub.com, and mention the book title via the subject of your message.

If there is a topic that you have expertise in and you are interested in either writing or contributing to a book, see our author guide on www.packtpub.com/authors.

Customer support

Now that you are the proud owner of a Packt book, we have a number of things to help you to get the most from your purchase.

Downloading the example code

You can download the example code files for all Packt books you have purchased from your account at http://www.packtpub.com. If you purchased this book elsewhere, you can visit http://www.packtpub.com/support and register to have the files e-mailed directly to you.

Errata

Although we have taken every care to ensure the accuracy of our content, mistakes do happen. If you find a mistake in one of our books—maybe a mistake in the text or the code—we would be grateful if you would report this to us. By doing so, you can save other readers from frustration and help us improve subsequent versions of this book. If you find any errata, please report them by visiting http://www.packtpub.com/submit-errata, selecting your book, clicking on the **errata submission form** link, and entering the details of your errata. Once your errata are verified, your submission will be accepted and the errata will be uploaded on our website, or added to any list of existing errata, under the Errata section of that title. Any existing errata can be viewed by selecting your title from http://www.packtpub.com/support.

Piracy

Piracy of copyright material on the Internet is an ongoing problem across all media. At Packt, we take the protection of our copyright and licenses very seriously. If you come across any illegal copies of our works, in any form, on the Internet, please provide us with the location address or website name immediately so that we can pursue a remedy.

Please contact us at copyright@packtpub.com with a link to the suspected pirated material.

We appreciate your help in protecting our authors, and our ability to bring you valuable content.

Questions

You can contact us at questions@packtpub.com if you are having a problem with any aspect of the book, and we will do our best to address it.

1
Getting Started with Force.com

Cloud computing has made significant changes to the IT/software development industry. Cloud platforms are one of the important components of cloud computing. Cloud platforms allow developers to develop apps and run them on the Cloud, including platforms to build on-demand applications and **platforms as a service (PaaS)**. Salesforce.com has introduced the first on-demand platform called Force.com.

This chapter introduces the Force.com platform and explains designing and developing applications on the Force.com platform. The sample application scenario and **Entity Relationship Diagram** (**ERD**) will be introduced at the end of this chapter. This chapter covers the following topics:

- Introduction to the Force.com platform
- Designing and developing applications on the Force.com platform
- Identifying building blocks of the Force.com platform
- The sample application

Introduction to the Force.com platform

Salesforce.com established the company as a Customer Relationship Management (CRM) product vender in 1999. The Force.com platform, which is known as Salesforce.com's platform as a service (PaaS) product, was launched in 2007. Force.com is a cloud computing platform that allows for developers to quickly build, share, and run custom business applications over the Internet. When we are developing applications on the Force.com platform, we don't need any additional hardware, additional software, and configuration and maintenance (database and hardware) efforts. The Force.com platform provides three default application categories, which include applications of Salesforce.com CRM. The main categories are as follows;

- **Sales cloud**: This is for the automated Sales processes of an organization. For example, from campaign management to lead capture and account to quote management, you can do everything related to Sales here. Sales cloud can be used for marketing, leads, opportunities, and maintaining new customers (Accounts and Contacts).

- **Service cloud**: This is used for any kind of support application such as call center, customer support desk, and so on. It helps the organization to manage their support on the cloud.

- **Chatter**: This is the collaboration tool of Salesforce CRM. It helps the organization to integrate back office work in to Salesforce.

The Force.com platform runs on Salesforce.com's infrastructures with the main architecture called multitenant architecture. For more details about multitenancy, read the *Key features of Force.com platform* subsection. The multitenant architecture allows us to build custom applications without purchasing hardware and software licenses and without having to worry about database maintenance. It provides a trusted, configurable and customizable, upgradable, able to integrate, and a secure platform to build our custom applications on.

Understanding the Force.com model

In traditional software development, we need to manage additional software and hardware, software licenses, networks, database configurations, and maintenance by ourselves. However, the Force.com platform provides these additional features in their cloud computing model. We need to pay only for the things we use, not for all the hardware and software. That's because we get the Force.com platform as a service.

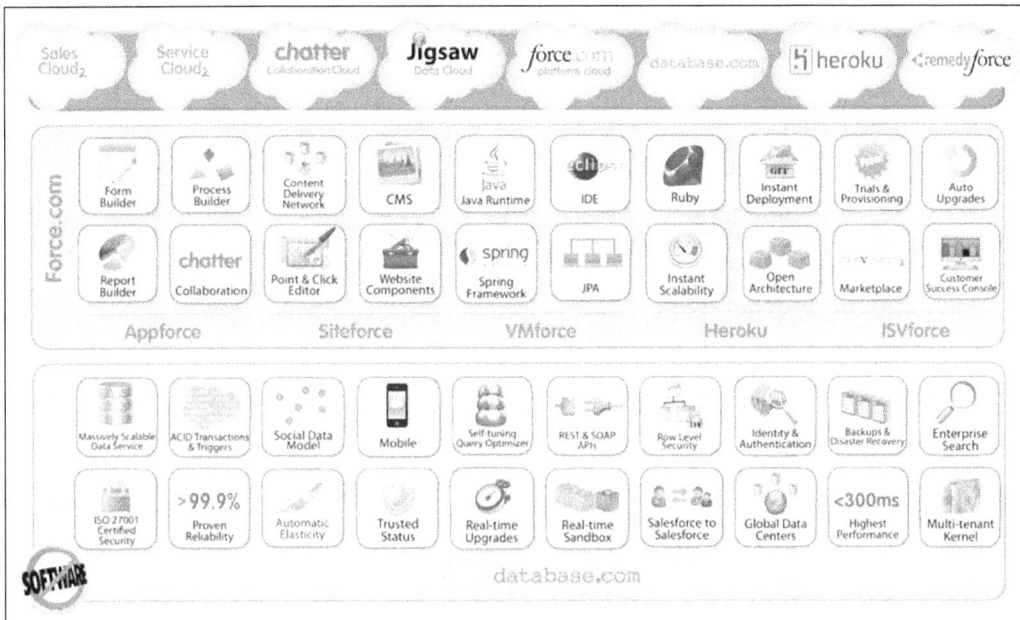

The architecture of the Force.com platform

The preceding figure shows the overview of the Force.com platform. The following table shows you the difference between the traditional platform and the Force.com platform.

Traditional Platform	Force.com Platform
Supply the core services of Database access	Form builder (build complete and standard UIs)
Supply Containers for logic	Process builder
Supply Containers for presentation	Logic and presentation as a service (Apex and Visualforce for custom developments)
Need to use other software to create our app	Fully functional reporting and analytical tools
Additional components to run the data center	Security
All of this will end up with additional expenditure	Sharing model
	Workflow and approvals
	Full support for the integrations with existing systems
	Full support for mobile devices
	Can access the platform through a web browser

Key features of the Force.com platform

The following are the key features of the Force.com platform:

- Multitenancy
- Application services
- Force.com metadata
- MVC architecture
- Programming language
- Integration
- Force.com sites
- AppExchange

Multitenancy

Multitenancy is the major technology of the Force.com cloud platform. It is used to share the IT resources in a secure and cost-effective way. Let's consider a real-world example to understand the multitenancy. Let's think about a luxury apartment complex with some facilities such as a playground, a swimming pool, and a gymnasium. This apartment complex has multiple owners. Everyone owns a separate apartment and every owner uses the shared playground, the shared swimming pool, and the shared gymnasium. These facilities are equal to a single, shared stack of hardware and software. The apartment is equal to the instance of a single client (a tenant). Therefore, a client has their own apartment with shared facilities and privacy.

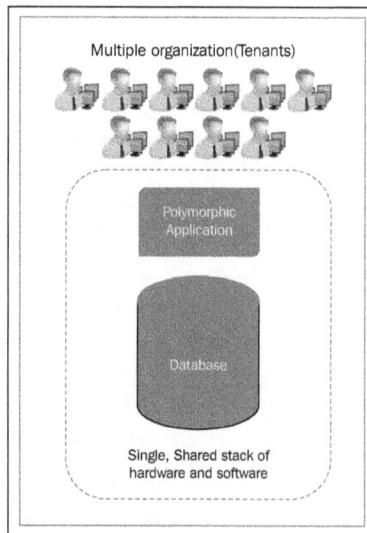

The multitenant architecture

There are some advantages of multitenancy, which are as follows:

- User satisfaction
- Cost reduction
- Automatic upgrades
- No maintenance
- Enhanced quality
- User retention
- Application providers can reach the hosted application
- Application providers can gather some information (such as errors and performance issues) of the application, which will be helpful to make further enhancements
- An error can be incurred from a particular tenant, but the solutions will be received by all the users who use the application

Application services

In traditional software development projects, we have to build or integrate various additional support applications such as login, validations, e-mail functions, reporting, UI, testing, and integrations. You had to repeatedly build these kinds of additional support applications in different projects. The Force.com platform provides the majority of support applications, which are most commonly needed in developing today's business application. For example, the Force.com platform has various features to automate your business process such as reporting, workflow and approvals, e-mail, user authentication, and integrations. These services are common to many software projects. Therefore, we can build applications with more functionality and within a short time period.

Force.com metadata

With multitenancy, we get secure, fast, reliable, customizable, and upgradable applications. When it comes to custom extensions by multiple tenants, we need to track and keep tenant-specific customizations without affecting the core application. The metadata-driven architecture takes care of that. After multitenancy, metadata-driven architecture is the second most important architecture in the Force.com platform. All the configuration, customization, and coding in the Force.com platform are defined and available as XML. It can be extracted and imported via a set of web services. Simply, metadata is data about data. The metadata-driven model provides the following advantages:

- Complex applications can be created by only using point-click developments (without any coding).

- A developer can build the application with the end user experience but the elements of the application are automatically translated to the metadata at creation time.

- Metadata provides a speedy development.

- Customization and extensions can be done without affecting the end user.

- Metadata can be used to construct an identical environment to use in another organization.

- Metadata can be used to assist version controlling.

- Metadata can be used for testing and troubleshooting by comparing multiple environments.

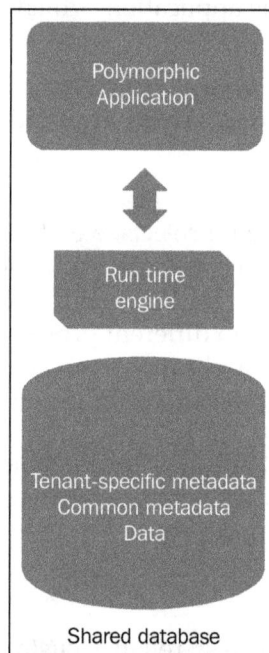

The metadata architecture of Force.com

The preceding figure shows the metadata-driven architecture of Force.com. It creates the separation between the runtime engine, the application data, and metadata. The polymorphic application includes database tables, relationships, UI elements, pages, classes, and so on.

MVC architecture

The Force.com platform uses the Model View Controller (MVC) architectural pattern for developing an application:

- **Model**: This defines the structure of the data. In Force.com, objects define the data model. Salesforce has designed the platform by mapping every entity to some object.

- **View**: This defines how the data is represented. In Force.com, page layouts and Visualforce pages come under this category.

- **Controller**: This defines the business logic. The rules and actions which manipulate the data control the view. In Force.com, apex classes, triggers, workflows, approvals, and validation rules are under this category.

Programming language

The Force.com platform provides its own set of programming language, mark-up language, query language, and search language.

Apex

Apex, the world's first on-demand language is considered as the programming language of the Force.com platform. Apex is object oriented and the syntax is similar to Java and C#. It allows developers to build the logic with the interaction of existing platform features. According to the MVC architecture, Apex falls into the controller because it is used to write the controller classes and triggers on the Force.com platform. Apex can be used to:

- Create custom controllers/Controller extensions

- Create triggers that are executed automatically in records such as insert, update, delete and undelete particular objects

- Access and invoke external web services

- Create batch jobs

Visualforce

Visualforce is an implementation of MVC architecture. In the Force.com platform, we can develop Force.com applications with custom objects and standard objects. Every object has a standard user interface with one or more page layouts. But we cannot use standard page layouts for complex requirements. Here, Visualforce comes into play.

Visualforce is a web-based user interface framework, which can be used to build complex, attractive, and dynamic custom UIs. Visualforce allows the developer to use standard web development technologies such as jQuery, JavaScript, CSS, and HTML5. Therefore, we can build rich UIs for any app, including mobile apps. We'll be discussing Visualforce with standard web development technologies and Visualforce for mobile in more depth later. Similar to HTML, the Visualforce framework includes a tag-based markup language.

SOQL

Salesforce Object Query Language (SOQL) allows us to fetch data from Saleforce objects. SOQL syntax is similar to SQL but simpler. For example, SOQL has the SELECT keyword but doesn't contain the INSERT or UPDATE keywords. It is different from SQL as SOQL doesn't have the JOIN keyword. SOQL can be used in Apex code and it provides a powerful feature to manipulate and process data in Apex code.

> Salesforce objects are similar to database tables. This will be explained in the next couple of chapters.

SOSL

Salesforce Object Search Language (SOSL) allows us to search your organization's data from Salesforce objects by specifying a text expression, scope of field to search, list of objects and fields to retrieve, and conditions to select rows in the source objects.

> SOQL is used to fetch data from a single object and SOSL is used to fetch data from multiple objects. More about SOSL and SOQL will be discussed in *Chapter 7, Custom Coding with Apex*.

Integration

The Force.com platform provides the facility to integrate with existing applications. There are various advantages of integrating, such as including external systems into our processes, syncing data from multiple sources, and accessing data in other systems. Using an open **Simple Object Access Protocol (SOAP)** web service, the Force.com API provides access to all the data stored in the application. There are integration benefits as follows:

- By using Force.com technologies, it takes less time to integrate than traditional integrations
- The Force.com platform-based API provides direct and low-level access to Salesforce application data and metadata

- There are many options to choose integration technologies and solutions that fit into their existing system
- Proven platform and integration

Force.com sites

Force.com sites allow us to create public sites using Salesforce.com data, Visualforce, and standard web technologies such as CSS, JavaScript, and jQuery. Force.com sites are directly integrated with the Salesforce organization and it doesn't require a user authentication using the Salesforce username and password. A Force.com site has the following features and benefits:

- Data from selected organizations can be exposed to the public through your own domain URL
- There are no integration issues because Force.com sites are hosted on Salesforce servers
- It can be built using Visualforce pages
- According to the requirement, you can enable or disable the user registration

AppExchange

With the preceding features, you can build different kinds of applications. But how can you publish and distribute these applications? AppExchange will do it for you. AppExchange is the place to submit your developed applications, which can be directly installed in the client's organization.

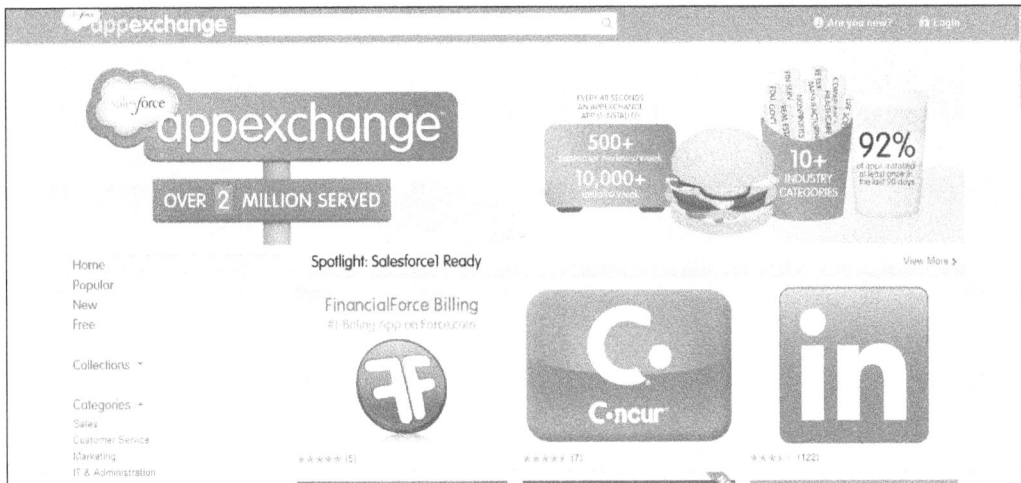

AppExchange – the destination for CRM and Force.com apps

Advantages of Force.com

When we use Force.com platform to build enterprise applications instead of traditional software development, we will gain the following advantages:

- We don't need to buy, install, maintain, and configure hardware and software.
- We can start customizations as soon as we buy the organization and user license.
- We can rapidly build and customize the applications on the Force.com platform.
- The Force.com platform has a simplified development model because it uses multitenant and metadata-driven architecture.
- It has the feature of instant scalability.
- Quarterly upgrades of Salesforce.com do not require any maintenance from the user.
- We can use or build multiple applications on a single platform. This is dependent on which Salesforce edition you are using. In Salesforce, the limitations change from edition to edition.
- This is a proven platform for business-critical applications.
- The Force.com platform is more secure and reliable. To learn more about security and trust visit `http://trust.salesforce.com/`.

Designing and developing applications on the Force.com platform

Before you start development on the Force.com platform, you have to do some ground work and have to learn about the data orientation of the Force.com platform, suitability of the application for the Force.com platform, the nature of the data underlying that application, and design the application for the Force.com application.

Signing up for a free developer edition account

The Force.com platform provides the development environments, tools, resources, and documentation, which can be used to develop applications. The Force.com tools will be described in *Appendix A, Force.com tools*. When we talk about development environments, free developer edition (DE) environment is the best option to develop with the latest technologies such as the Apex programming language, Visualforce markup language, and web services API.

> DE is free, and you can use it for learning purposes, although it comes with certain limitations.

Follow the steps to create a free developer account:

1. Go to `https://developer.salesforce.com/`.

2. Click on **Signup**.

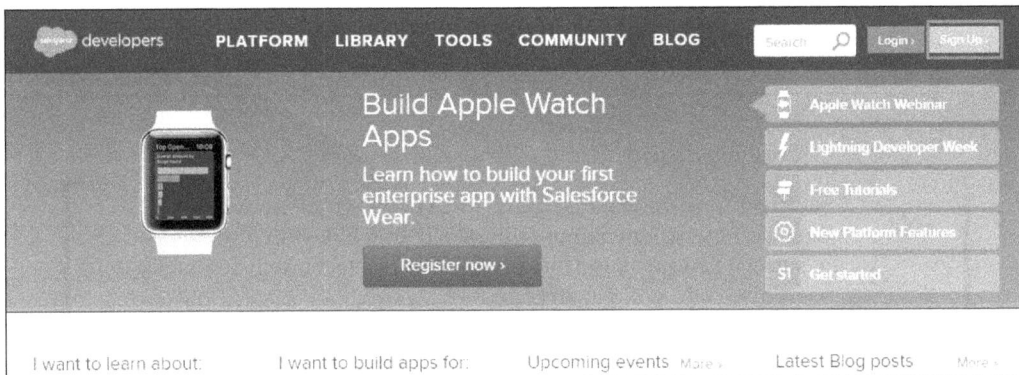

The developerforce web page

3. Then, you will get the following page and fill all the fields in the form.

The registration page

> Select a unique username in the form of an e-mail by which you
> will access your developer edition account. Salesforce allows you
> to select a unique name by default. If you select any pre-existing
> username, you will get an error.

4. Click on **Sign me up**.

5. An e-mail will be received including the link to specify your login credentials

Basic application design

When we design and build an application on the Force.com platform, we need
to be aware of the data that we are going to process underneath the application.
Good data design and good development practices can produce flexible and
efficient applications.

Types of applications suitable for Force.com

We cannot use the Force.com platform for any kind of application development. Therefore, we need to understand the apps that are better suited for the Force.com platform. There are four types of applications that are required to automate an enterprise process, which are as follows:

- **Data-Centric Apps**: Data-centric applications are the ones that have powerful databases. They are based on the structure and consistency data such as in database or XML files. They are centered on a database and with data-centric apps it is easy to control access and manage data, which are centered to the database. The Force.com platform is data-centric by its nature and it is a perfect platform to build and host data-centric apps.

- **Process-Centric Apps**: A process-centric app is based on automating the business process in the organization and multiple users can be involved in the process. The Force.com platform has many features that align with the features of process-centric applications such as the approval process, the workflow, and security and sharing models.

- **Content-Centric Apps**: These applications are intensely increasing the storage needs of on-demand performance. These kinds of applications have main functionalities such as version controlling, content management, and sharing.

- **Transaction-Centric Apps**: The main functions of these types of applications are focused on transactions such as banking systems, stock market-related systems, and online payment systems.

Data and process-centric apps are the most suitable application types for the Force.com platform. The following two figures explain to us how the data-centric and process-centric apps are the most suitable apps for the Force.com platform:

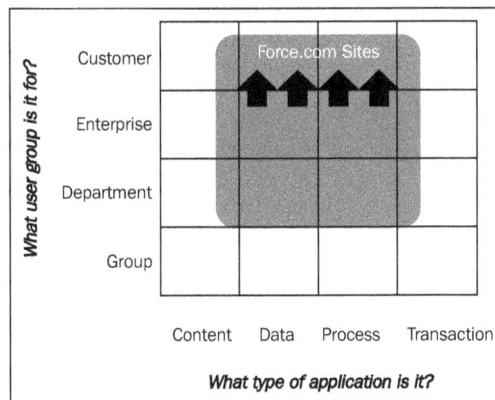

Types of apps that are a good fit for the Force.com platform

	Content	Data	Process	Transaction
Internet/ Portal	Marketing/Content websites	PRM	Account provisioning	Banking/Payment websites
Enterprise	Intranet Search	HR CRM PTO	Benefits Enrollment Expenses Mgmt Help desk Procurement	Payroll Financials Supply chain
Department	Project Portal Sharepoint	Time & Billing Project management	Recruiting Bug Tracking	Quickbooks
Group	File Share	Spreadsheet	Press Release approval	

Types of apps suitable for the Force.com platform

Design consideration

When we develop a system on the Force.com platform, we need to consider some facts about the design phase. As in traditional software development, identifying your stakeholders and business partners is the first thing you need to do. Then, you need to capture the business requirement from your stakeholders. By analyzing the captured requirement, you can identify the users of the applications and the security model of the application. The security model is the most important part of designing a Force.com application.

> Do not keep the defining of the security model of the Force.com application to the end. It will only increase the rework required of the application's designing and development.

Customization on the Force.com platform

In the design phase, we can consider the development method, which can be used to develop the particular application. There are two development target methods on the Force.com platform. They are as follows:

1. **Declarative Development**: This development can be done using point and click with zero coding. We can do declarative development via the browser. The declarative customizations require an understanding of the Force.com platform overview, but no coding knowledge. The developments and deployments can be rapidly done using the declarative development method.

2. **Programmatic Development**: Programmatic developments require coding skills and allow developments to extend beyond the declarative capabilities. For example, if we need to create a page with a wizard, we cannot fulfill that requirement with declarative development. We need to use programmatic development, such as Apex and Visualforce.

The following screenshot shows the Force.com development model. It illustrates the deviation development methods with the skills of the developer.

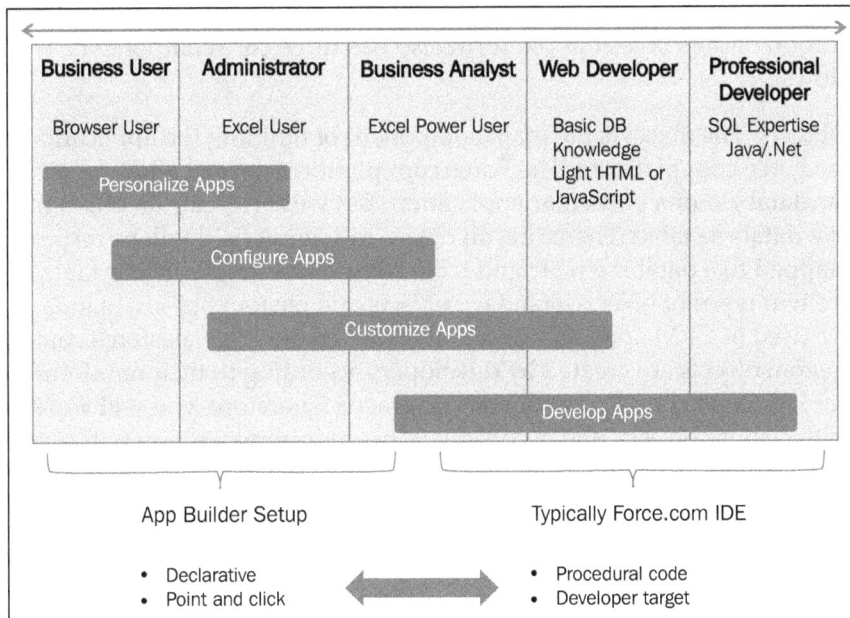

Business User	Administrator	Business Analyst	Web Developer	Professional Developer
Browser User	Excel User	Excel Power User	Basic DB Knowledge Light HTML or JavaScript	SQL Expertise Java/.Net

Personalize Apps

Configure Apps

Customize Apps

Develop Apps

App Builder Setup   Typically Force.com IDE

- Declarative
- Point and click

- Procedural code
- Developer target

Force.com development model

Most complete and robust solutions actually use a combination of declarative and programmatic solutions. Developers should understand how to develop using both declarative and programmatic features. The following table shows the advantages of declarative and programmatic customizations:

Declarative customizations	Programmatic customizations
Ease of development (more visual and quicker to do)	Can extend the capabilities of an application beyond standard functionalities
Ease of upgrade	More control and flexibility over the application
Ease of maintenance	

Identifying building blocks of the Force. com platform

Every application has some key components that are considered as the building blocks of the particular application. These building blocks define the application. An application of the Force.com platform also has three core components, which are as follows:

1. **Objects**: The object is the main component of building the application on the Force.com platform. The Force.com platform doesn't allow accessing the database of a particular application. But we can create an object instead of a database table. Therefore, an object and object field will be respectively mapped to a database table and table columns of the particular table. There are two types of objects: standard objects and custom objects. Standard objects are used in CRM applications and they are created by Salesforce.com. The custom objects are created by developers according to their requirements. This book is focused on Force.com development. Therefore, you will work more with custom objects, and according to the requirements, you will work with standard objects. For further details, refer to *Chapter 2, Building the Data Model*.

2. **Tabs**: These are the views of objects. We need to declare tabs if we want to insert data records in them. There are standard tabs that are created by Salesforce.com and custom tabs that can be created by developers. There are 3 types of custom tabs:

    1. **Custom object tabs**: On Force.com, when we create a custom object, a set of user interfaces are generated to add, edit, and view particular object records. These standard user interfaces can be bound to a custom object tab. While creating an object, it is asked at the bottom to launch the tab wizard, opening of which redirects us to the next page where we declare the tab of an object.

    2. **Custom web tabs**: These types of tabs are used to display external web applications or a web page in the Salesforce platform.

    3. **Visualforce tabs**: These types of tabs are used to bind and display a Visualforce page. More details about custom tabs will be described in *Chapter 3, Building the User Interface.*

3. **Application**: An application is a group of tabs that work as a unit to provide functionality. A Saleforce.com organization can have multiple applications. The users can switch between apps in an organization. Then we need to have a method to define the logical boundary of the app. The number of custom applications in a particular organization depends on the Salesforce edition of the organization.

More details about the custom app will be described in *Chapter 3, Building the User Interface.*

The sample application

Let's introduce the leave management application called eLeaveForce. In this application, an employee can request a particular type of leave and his/her manager can approve the leave. We will maintain the leave types and leave categories as reference data (user defined data). A holiday calendar will be maintained for this leave management application. You can use this application to learn about different elements and features of the Force.com platform.

The following is the E-R diagram of the eLeaveForce application, which we will create on the Force.com platform:

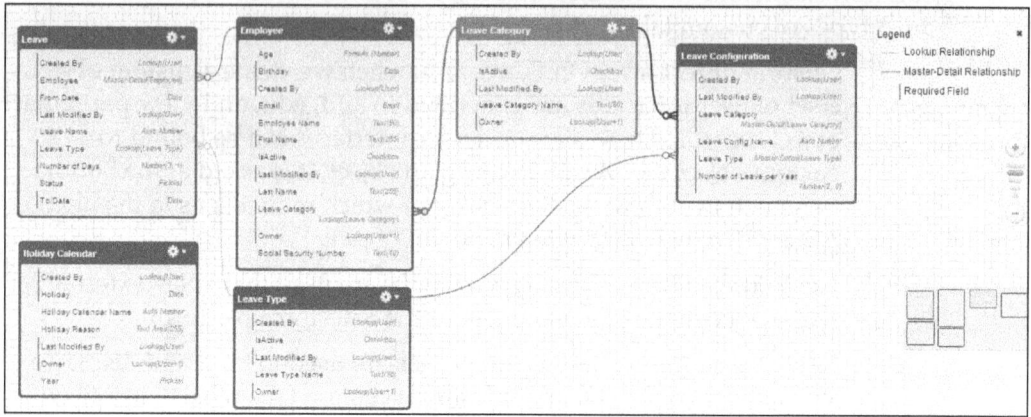

E-R diagram of eLeaveForce

In this section, you will capture an idea about the leave management application and the design of the eLeaveForce application. Later, you will learn about the Force.com platform in depth by using this sample application.

There are six custom objects for our leave management application. These six custom objects are used to track the data of the leave management app. They are as follows:

- Employee
- Holiday Calendar
- Leave (main leave object)
- Leave Type
- Leave Category
- Leave Configuration

According to the requirement, these objects are connected with relationships as illustrated in the E-R diagram. More details about custom objects and relationships will be described in *Chapter 2, Building the Data Model*.

When we define the security model of the application, we need to consider the built-in security features of the Force.com platform. More details about sharing and security models will be described in *Chapter 4, Designing Apps for Multiple Users and Protecting Data*.

Our leave management app has a few approval processes, such as getting the approval for the particular leave. Approval processes are considered in our design and will be implemented using the in-built workflow and approval processes. More details about workflow and approval processes will be described in *Chapter 5, Implementing Business Processes*.

We will use Visualforce pages and Apex to accomplish the requirements that can be fulfilled beyond the declarative developments. For example, a graphical view of the current status of the leave process will be displayed on a Visualforce page. More details about Apex and Visualforce will be described in *Chapter 7, Custom Coding with Apex* and *Chapter 8, Building Custom Pages with Visualforce*.

Summary

In this chapter, we became familiar with the Force.com platform by examining its key features and advantages. You have learned the design considerations of an application on the Force.com platform and development methods of the Force.com platform. We discussed the building blocks of a Force.com application. We also captured the scenario and the E-R diagram of the sample application, which is going to continue in the next chapter.

2
Building the Data Model

In this chapter, the data model of the Force.com platform will be introduced, which explains about creating custom objects, custom fields, and various data types of the Force.com platform.

This chapter covers the following topics:

- Creating objects
- Creating custom fields

Before we start building the data model on the Force.com platform, we need to log into our organization using the login credentials specified in *Chapter 1, Getting Started with Force.com*. You will see the Force.com home page (or landing page) for developers and administrators after you have logged on:

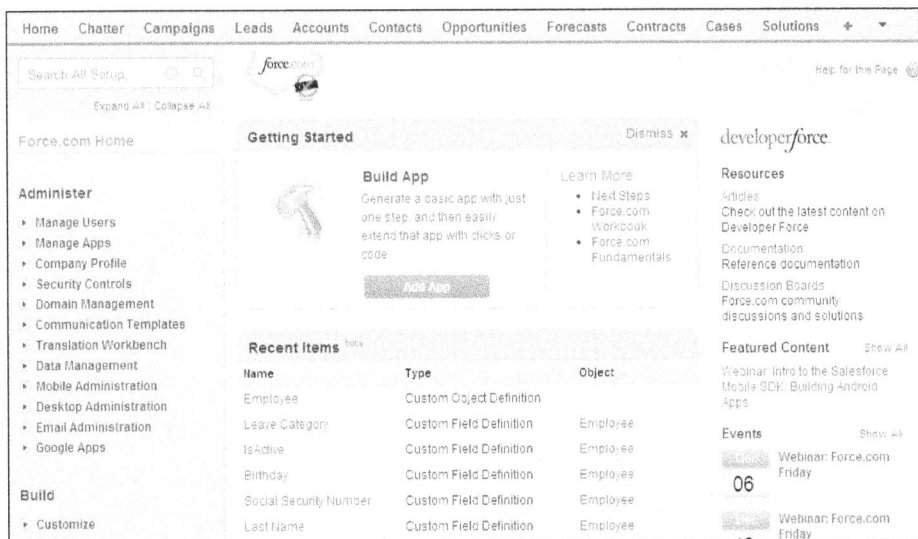

The Force.com home page

Creating objects

We have already introduced our leave management application, which we will continue looking at in future chapters. In the previous chapter, we introduced the objects as one of the building blocks of the Force.com platform. An object is a container used to store particular object data in the Force.com platform. By creating an object, we can create user interfaces to add/edit/view the records of a particular object. With the creation of an object, the Force.com platform provides us the related user interfaces to add, edit, and view records of the particular object.

> **Time saving feature**
>
> Create an object and gain a bunch of UI (standard pages) for various tasks such as add, edit, view, list view, and lookup view.

The objects of Salesforce.com have the following features:

- Configurable
- Relational
- Reportable
- Searchable
- Securable

There are two types of objects on the Force.com platform:

1. Standard Objects
2. Custom objects

Standard objects

The Force.com platform comes with a set of standard objects that are part of **Salesforce Customer Relationship Management** (**Salesforce CRM**). Standard objects are created by Salesforce.com. A standard object has a set of standard functionalities and properties, which are pre-defined and are Salesforce CRM-oriented. However, we can do customizations up to some extent and that customization is much less than custom objects. Let's consider the following example:

- Custom fields can be added to standard objects (custom fields will be described in the next few sections)
- Modify the existing pick list value
- Page layouts can be added

- Standard fields cannot be deleted
- Standard objects cannot be deleted

All the standard objects are categorized under the **Customize** link. The following screenshot shows the place where we can find the standard objects:

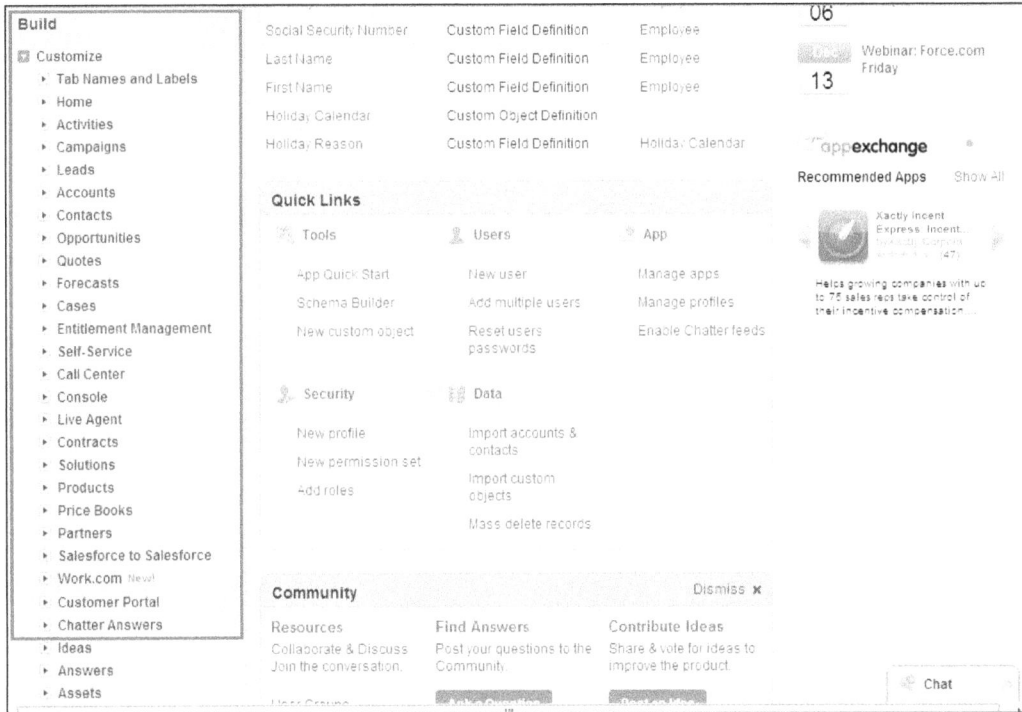

The standard objects are under the customize category

You can find the standard objects by navigating to **Setup** | **Customize**.

Custom objects

Custom objects are created by the developer according to the requirements of the application. The custom objects are more important building blocks because they can be created according to our requirements of the application. A custom object is more customizable than a standard object. A set of fields that are created in a custom object creation are called standard fields. All the other fields that are created by the developer according to the requirements are called custom fields. We will discuss more about fields in the next couple of sections.

All the custom objects are categorized under the **Create** link. The user can create custom objects through schema builder or the old fashioned way by clicking on the **New Custom Object** button. The following screenshot shows the place where we can find the custom objects.

You can find the custom objects by navigating to **Setup | Create | Objects**.

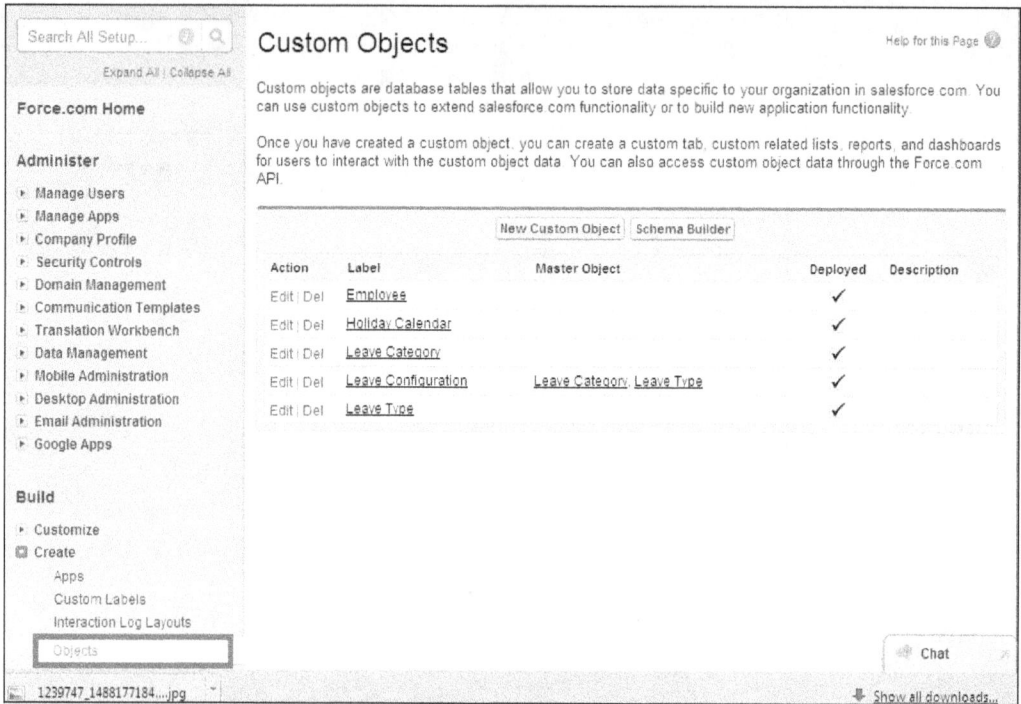

The custom objects are categorized under the Create category

[💡 The design of the data model behind an app is typically the biggest factor in its success or failure.]

Let's consider our leave management application and defined objects. According to the design, there are five custom objects for our leave management application. These five custom objects are used to track the date of the leave management application:

- Employee
- Holiday Calendar
- Leave Type
- Leave Category
- Leave Configuration

That's enough talk about objects for now. Let's go define one!

Although we have to create all of the preceding objects for the leave management app, let's create the `Employee` object as the example of creating a custom object. Use the following steps to create the `Employee` object:

1. Go to **Setup** | **Build** | **Create** | **Objects**.

2. Click on the **New Custom Object** button. You will see the following screenshot:

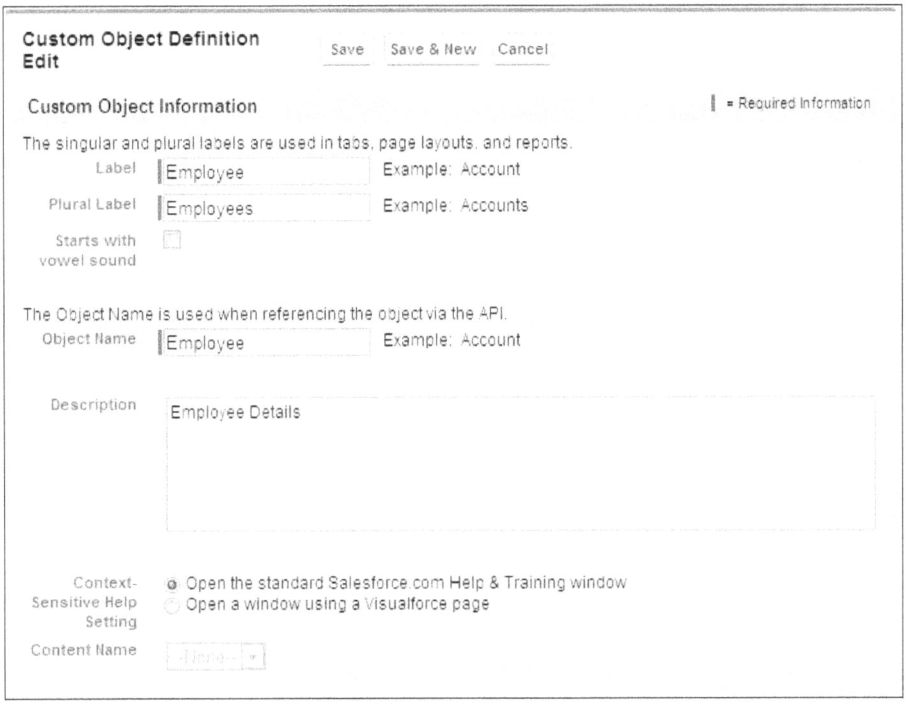

Custom Object Definition Edit	Save Save & New Cancel

Custom Object Information   ▌ = Required Information

The singular and plural labels are used in tabs, page layouts, and reports.

Label	Employee Example: Account
Plural Label	Employees Example: Accounts
Starts with vowel sound	☐

The Object Name is used when referencing the object via the API.

Object Name	Employee Example: Account
Description	Employee Details

Context-Sensitive Help Setting	⦿ Open the standard Salesforce.com Help & Training window
	⦾ Open a window using a Visualforce page
Content Name	--None--

The custom object definition create/edit page — upper section

The employee's object-related information is captured in the upper section of the object definition page.

The preceding screenshot shows the upper section of the object definition page. Let's see the information that is captured in this section. For ease of explanation, the screenshot of the object definition page has been divided into an upper section and a lower section. The content of the sections are as follows:

- **Label**: This is the label of the object definition page. This label is seen on page layouts and reports. Here we have used Employee as the label of this object.

- **Plural Label**: This label is used in the Salesforce object tabs. In this case, we have used Employees as the plural label.

- **Starts with a vowel sound**: Check whether the label **Starts with a vowel sound** should be preceded by "an" instead of "a".

- **Object Name**: The object name (otherwise API name) must be a unique name because it is used to refer to the object via the Force.com API. When the object name is accessed from the API, it will be appended with __c to the object name. For example, in the preceding screenshot, we have used Employee as the object name, and the API name will be Employee__c. This is automatically done by Force.com. This __c is the key to identify a custom object from a standard object. The standard objects don't have any __c suffix in their API name.

> The object name must be unique, should begin with a letter, should not include spaces, should not end with an underscore, and should not contain two consecutive underscores.

- **Context-Sensitive Help Setting**: There are two options to select the user help page. You can get the standard Salesforce help page by selecting the **Open the standard Salesforce.com Help & Training window** option or you can select a custom Visualforce page by selecting the **Open a window using a Visualforce page** option. From the **Open a window using a Visualforce page**, you can provide your own help page rather than using a standard Salesforce.com help window.

The lower section of the object definition page, including the record name label and format, the deployment status, and other value-added optional features will be captured. This is shown in the following screenshot of the lower section of the object definition page.

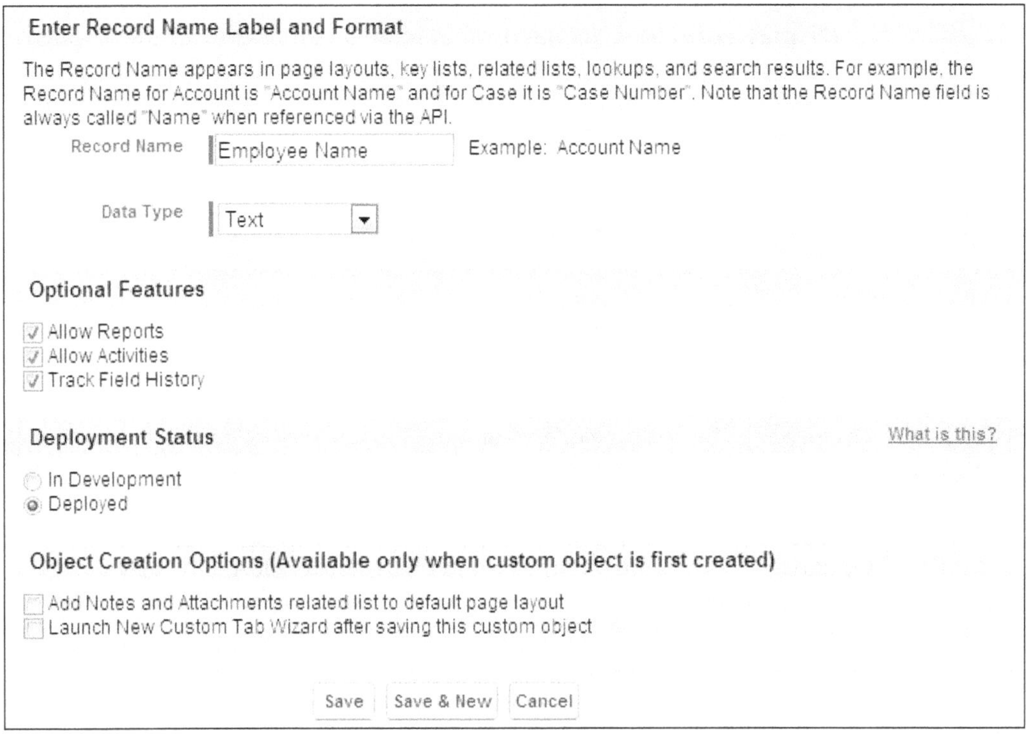

The custom object definition create/edit page—lower section

The lower section of the object definition page contains the following fields:

- **Record Name**: The record name is used everywhere the particular object records appear (such as page layouts, search results, list views, and related lists). We can specify the record name as our desire but the API name of the record can always be accessed as the name.

- **Data Type**: This field specifies the data type of **Record Name**. There are two options (text or autonumber) to select the data type of record name. If you choose the **Text** type, the end user must enter the record name for the particular object record. If you choose the **Auto Number** option, then you have to specify the following two additional fields:

  - **Display Format**: A display format allows you to control the format of the **Auto Number** field. A display format consists of the substitution variables described in the following table, plus any other characters you wish to include as a prefix or suffix. The following table shows the substitution variables in display format:

{0}	Required	This is the sequence number. One or more zeros enclosed in curly braces represent the sequence number itself. The number of zeros in the curly braces dictates the minimum number of digits that will be displayed. If the actual number has fewer digits than this, it will be padded with leading zeros. The maximum is 10 digits.
{YY} {YYYY}	Optional	This is the year. Two or four Y characters enclosed in curly braces represent the year of the record creation date. You can display 2 digits (for example, "04") or all 4 digits (for example, "2004") of the year.
{MM}	Optional	This is the month. Two M characters enclosed in curly braces represent the numeric month (for example, "01" for January, "02" for February) of the record creation date.
{DD}	Optional	This is the day. Two D characters enclosed in curly braces represent the numeric day of the month (for example, "01" to "31" are valid days in January) of the record creation date.

> If you modify the display format of an existing field, only records created after the change will be affected.

  - **Starting Number**: You can specify the starting number of the autonumber format. It will start the counting with that starting number. For example, if you use the display format of the Employee object as EMP-{0} and the starting number as 1, the Name field of Employee records will be populated with the value of EMP-1, EMP-2, EMP-3, so on.

- **Allow Reports**: This checkbox allows you to make the data of the particular object available for reporting.

- **Allow Activities**: This checkbox allows you to associate tasks and events related to the particular object records and the related lists for the activities will be added to the page layout.

- **Track Field History**: This checkbox allows you to track the records of the particular object when it changes the field value of the record. It will keep the old value, the new value, and the user who made the changes.

- **Deployment Status**: This is the option to deploy a particular object. The object will not be visible to any users (except to the users who have a system admin profile) until it is deployed.

When we are creating an object, there are two special options to select as **Object Creation Options**. They are available only when the custom object is first created and not available in modifying the custom object. The following options are available as **Object Creation Options**:

- **Add Notes and Attachments related list to default page layout**: This checkbox allows you to add the notes and attachment-related list to the particular object's page layout.

- **Launch New Custom Tab Wizard after saving this custom object**: This checkbox allows you to launch the new custom tab creation wizard after saving the particular object's definition. In this scenario, we don't select this checkbox. Tab creating will be discussed in *Chapter 3, Building the User Interface*.

After filling in the preceding details, click on the **Save** button. Now, we have created the Employee object and now we can create custom fields according to our requirements. Before that, let's get an idea about standard fields that are automatically created at custom object creation. The following are the standard fields that are system generated upon object creation:

ID: ID field stores the key, which uniquely locates each record. This unique key is system assigned and you cannot update this value. The ID field exists in every standard and custom object. But this field is not listed in the object definition page. The ID field is equivalent to the primary key of a relational database. Each key (ID value) has the following two versions:

- **15 digit**: This version is used in the Salesforce user interfaces and it contains case sensitive and base-62 strings.

- **18 digit**: This version is used in all API calls and is created by adding a 3-digit suffix to the 15-digit version. 18-character IDs are the case-safe version of Salesforce ID and it is used to safely compare the uniqueness by case-insensitive applications.

[💡 You cannot delete standard fields from the object.]

- **Name**: As we discussed in the object creation, there are two data type options: Text and Auto Number. The following table shows the difference between text and the autonumber data type options in the name field.

Text	Auto Number
User assigned value	System generated value
Not necessarily unique	Unique
Modifiable	Not modifiable
Required field	Required field

- **Owner**: This is a reference to the user or group of users (queue). The owner is granted additional privileges. Upon the record creation, the record creator will be assigned as the owner of the particular record but it can be changed later.

- **CreatedBy**: This is a reference to the user who created the particular record.

- **LastModifiedBy**: This is a reference to the user who last modified the particular record.

- **CreatedDate**: This is a DateTime field that contains the date/time that the record was created.

- **ModifiedDate**: This is a DateTime field that contains the date/time when the record was last modified.

[📝 The values of **CreatedBy/LastModifiedBy/CreatedDate/ ModifiedDate** are systematically assigned. These fields are also called as audit fields.]

You will learn more about the preceding data types in the next couple of sections. The following screenshot shows the `Employee` object details:

Custom Object				Help for this Page
Employee				

Standard Fields [4] | Custom Fields & Relationships [5] | Validation Rules [0] | Page Layouts [1] | Field Sets (BETA) [0] | Compact Layouts [1] | Search Layouts [4] | Buttons, Links, and Actions [8] | Record Types [0] | Apex Sharing Reasons [0] | Apex Sharing Recalculation [0] | Object Limits [10]

Custom Object Definition Detail   Edit   Delete

Singular Label	Employee	Description	
Plural Label	Employees	Enable Reports	✓
Object Name	Employee	Track Activities	
API Name	Employee__c	Track Field History	
		Deployment Status	Deployed
		Help Settings	Standard salesforce.com Help Window
Created By	Chamil Madusanka, 11/28/2013 7:27 AM	Modified By	Chamil Madusanka, 11/28/2013 7:34 AM

Standard Fields   Standard Fields Help ?

Action	Field Label	Field Name	Data Type	Controlling Field
	Created By	CreatedBy	Lookup(User)	
Edit	Employee Name	Name	Text(80)	
	Last Modified By	LastModifiedBy	Lookup(User)	
Edit	Owner	Owner	Lookup(User,Queue)	

Custom Fields & Relationships   New   Field Dependencies   Custom Fields & Relationships Help ?

Action	Field Label	API Name	Data Type	Controlling Field M

Object definition details and fields—Employee Object

In the same way as with the `Employee` object creation, create the `Holiday Calendar`, `Leave`, `Leave Type`, `Leave Category`, and `Leave Configuration` objects. According to the data type, we will create custom fields for these objects in the next couple of sections.

Creating custom fields

We have successfully created the Employee object with the standard fields. According to the requirements, we need more fields to store various types of data values. In the preceding sections, you have learned that a Salesforce object is analogous to a database table, in the same way as the Salesforce standard/custom field is analogous to a database table column. Normally, a **Database Management System (DBMS)** has a set of data types for the database table columns. The Force.com platform also provides a set of data types to define custom fields of Salesforce custom objects and selected standard objects. The following two figures show us a few data types in the Force.com platform:

Employee

New Custom Field

Help for this Page

Step 1. Choose the field type   Step 1

Next   Cancel

Specify the type of information that the custom field will contain.

Data Type

⦿ None Selected	Select one of the data types below.
○ Auto Number	A system-generated sequence number that uses a display format you define. The number is automatically incremented for each new record.
○ Formula	A read-only field that derives its value from a formula expression you define. The formula field is updated when any of the source fields change.
○ Roll-Up Summary ⓘ	A read-only field that displays the sum, minimum, or maximum value of a field in a related list or the record count of all records listed in a related list.
○ Lookup Relationship	Creates a relationship that links this object to another object. The relationship field allows users to click on a lookup icon to select a value from a popup list. The other object is the source of the values in the list.
○ Master-Detail Relationship	Creates a special type of parent-child relationship between this object (the child, or "detail") and another object (the parent, or "master") where:

- The relationship field is required on all detail records.
- The ownership and sharing of a detail record are determined by the master record.
- When a user deletes the master record, all detail records are deleted.
- You can create rollup summary fields on the master record to summarize the detail records.

The relationship field allows users to click on a lookup icon to select a value from a popup list. The master object is the source of the values in the list.

💬 Chat

The set of data types of Force.com platform — set 1

Checkbox	Allows users to select a True (checked) or False (unchecked) value.
Currency	Allows users to enter a dollar or other currency amount and automatically formats the field as a currency amount. This can be useful if you export data to Excel or another spreadsheet.
Date	Allows users to enter a date or pick a date from a popup calendar.
Date/Time	Allows users to enter a date and time, or pick a date from a popup calendar. When users click a date in the popup, that date and the current time are entered into the Date/Time field.
Email	Allows users to enter an email address, which is validated to ensure proper format. If this field is specified for a contact or lead, users can choose the address when clicking Send an Email. Note that custom email addresses cannot be used for mass emails.
Geolocation	(Beta) Allows users to define locations.
Number	Allows users to enter any number. Leading zeros are removed.
Percent	Allows users to enter a percentage number, for example, '10' and automatically adds the percent sign to the number.
Phone	Allows users to enter any phone number. Automatically formats it as a phone number.
Picklist	Allows users to select a value from a list you define.
Picklist (Multi-Select)	Allows users to select multiple values from a list you define.
Text	Allows users to enter any combination of letters and numbers.
Text Area	Allows users to enter up to 255 characters on separate lines.
Text Area (Long)	Allows users to enter up to 32,768 characters on separate lines.
Text Area (Rich)	Allows users to enter formatted text, add images and links. Up to 32,768 characters on separate lines.
Text (Encrypted)	Allows users to enter any combination of letters and numbers and store them in encrypted form.
URL	Allows users to enter any valid website address. When users click on the field, the URL will open in a separate browser window.

The set of data types of Force.com platform — set 2

As you can see, we have a set of data types to create custom fields for a custom object or a standard object.

Let's explore the data types of the Force.com platform under the seven categories. This categorization will be helpful for you to understand the usage of these data types. The following are the categories:

- Text data types
- Numeric data types
- Calendar data types
- Formatted text data types

- Calculation data types
- Limited option data types
- Relationship data types

Text data types

There are five text data types, which are used to create text type fields. The fields of text data types are used to store alphanumeric values. The following table depicts data types with their properties:

Data Type	Properties
Text	<ul><li>This allows the users to enter any combination of letters and numbers</li><li>It allows maximum 255 characters</li><li>A single line field is allowed</li></ul>
Text Area	<ul><li>This allows the users to enter any combination of letters and numbers</li><li>It allows maximum 255 characters</li><li>A multiple line field is allowed</li></ul>
Text Area (Long)	<ul><li>This allows the users to enter any combination of letters and numbers</li><li>It allows maximum 32,768 characters</li><li>Here, multiple lines are allowed</li></ul>
Text Area (Rich)	<ul><li>This allows users to enter formatted text, add images, and links</li><li>It allows maximum 32,768 characters</li><li>Here, multiple lines are allowed</li></ul>
Text (Encrypted)	<ul><li>It allows users to enter any combination of letters and numbers and stores them in encrypted form</li></ul>

> The value of an encrypted field is only visible to users that have the "View Encrypted Data" permission.

Let's see the creation of the text data type field of the `Employee` object. Use the following steps to create a text data type of a custom object:

1. Navigate to **Setup | Create | Objects**.

2. Click on **Employee**.

3. In the **Custom Fields & Relationships** related list, click on **New**.

4. Select the field data type (for this example, we select the **Text** data type) and click on **Next**.

5. Then you will get the following screen to fill in the field details:

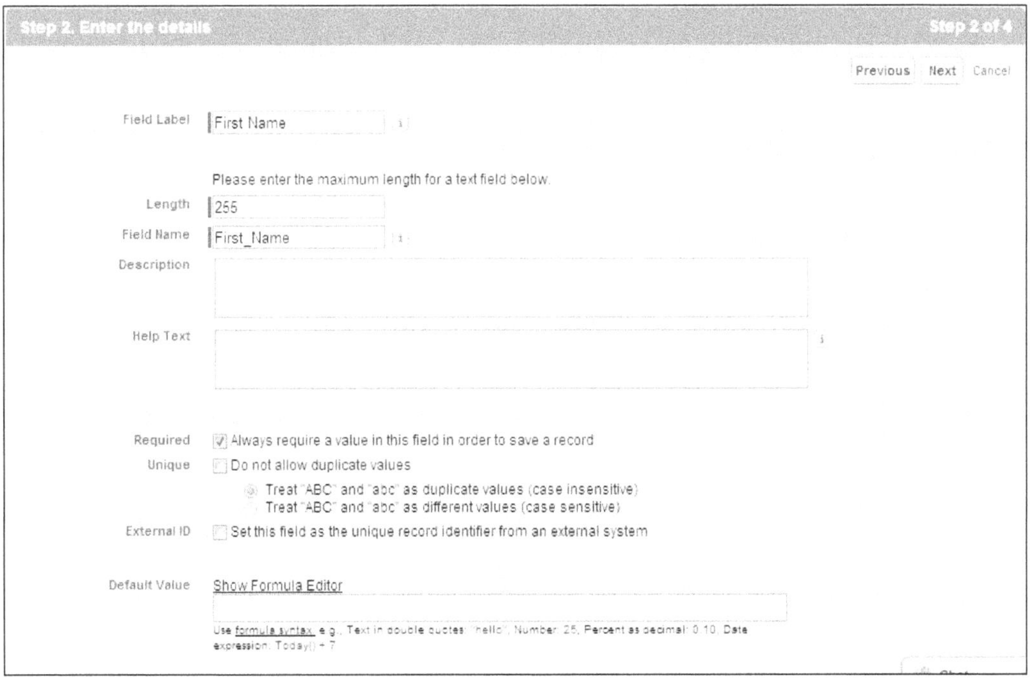

Enter text field type details

Following are the details to be filled:

- **Field Label**: This is the label to identify the particular custom field. Enter a label to be used on displays, page layouts, reports, and list views (First Name).

- **Length**: This is the maximum length of the particular text field. Refer to the preceding table for length limits of different text data types (255).

- **Field Name**: Normally, this will be autopopulated. The **Field Name** is an internal reference and is used for integration purposes such as custom links and the API. Be careful when changing the **Field Name** as it may affect existing integrations.

- **Description**: This is an option field. This will be helpful to understand the purpose of the custom field.

- **Help Text**: This is an optional field. This text displays on detail and edit pages when users hover over the Info icon next to this field.

- **Required**: If you tick this checkbox, this field always requires a value in order to save the record.

- **Unique**: If you tick this checkbox, duplicate values are not allowed here. There are two options to specify the case sensitivity.

- **External ID**: You can use this checkbox to set the particular field as the unique record identifier from an external system.

- **Default Value**: You can specify a default value here by entering any value or using a formula.

Click on **Next**. Then you will get step 3 of the custom field creation wizard with the title, Establish field-level security. For now, accept the defaults. We will discuss more about security of the Force.com platform in *Chapter 4, Designing Apps for Multiple Users and Protecting Data*.

Click on **Next**. Then you will get the last step of the text data type field creation with the Add to page layouts title. You can specify the page layout by adding the newly created custom field to the particular object's page layout.

Click on **Save**. Now, we have created the First Name custom field (Text type) in the Employee object.

Employee Custom Field		Help for this Page
First Name		
Back to Employee		

Validation Rules [0]

Custom Field Definition Detail   Edit   Set Field-Level Security   View Field Accessibility

Field Information

Field Label	First Name	Object Name	Employee
Field Name	First_Name	Data Type	Text
API Name	First_Name__c		
Description			
Help Text			
Created By	Chamil Madusanka, 11/28/2013 7:28 AM	Modified By	Chamil Madusanka, 11/28/2013 7:28 AM

General Options

Required	✓
Unique	
Case Sensitive	
External ID	
Default Value	

Text Options

Length	255

Validation Rules   New   Valid

Employee custom field — First Name

Numeric field data types

There are three numeric data types on the Force.com platform, which are listed in the following table:

Data Type	Properties
Number	• This allows users to enter the number • The leading zeroes are removed • The decimal places can be defined • The maximum length is 18 digits and 18 digits are shared among the length and the number of decimal places
Currency	• This allows users to enter a currency amount • It automatically formats the field as a currency amount • If you have enabled the multicurrency in your organization, your currency fields are automatically converted into your corporate currency in the view mode • The decimal places can be defined • The maximum length is 18 digits and the sum of the length and decimal places must be an integer less than or equal to 18
Percent	• This allows users to enter a percentage number • It automatically adds the percentage sign to the number

Let's see the creation of a numeric data type field on the Leave Configuration object. Use the following steps to create a text data type of a custom object:

1. Navigate to **Setup | Create | Objects**.
2. Click on **Leave Configuration**.
3. In the **Custom Fields & Relationships** related list, click on **New**.
4. Select the field data type (this time **Number**) and click on **Next**.

5. Then you will get the following screen to fill in the field details:

Step 2. Enter the details **Step 2 of 4**

Previous Next Cancel

Field Label | Number of Leave per Year i

Please enter the length of the number and the number of decimal places. For example, a number with a length of 8 and 2 decimal places can accept values up to "12345678.90".

Length | 2   Decimal Places | 0

Number of digits to the left of the decimal point

Number of digits to the right of the decimal point

Field Name | Number_of_Leave_per_Ye i

Description

Help Text

i

Required   ☑ Always require a value in this field in order to save a record

Unique   ☐ Do not allow duplicate values

External ID   ☐ Set this field as the unique record identifier from an external system

Default Value   Show Formula Editor

Use formula syntax: e.g., Text in double quotes: "hello", Number: 25, Percent as decimal: 0.10, Date expression: Today() + 7

Chat

Enter the numeric field type details

Fill in the following details:

- **Field Label**: This is the label to identify the particular custom field. Enter a label (`Number of Leave per Year`) to be used on displays, page layouts, reports, and list views.

- **Length**: You can define the maximum length of the particular number field. You can define the length up to 18.

- **Decimal Places**: You can define the decimal places to the particular number field. The sum of the length and decimal places must be an integer less than or equal to 18.

- **Field Name**: Normally, this will be autopopulated. **Field Name** is an internal reference and is used for integration purposes such as custom links and the API. Be careful when changing **Field Name** as it may affect existing integrations.

- **Description**: This is an optional field. This will be helpful to understand the particular custom field.

- **Help Text**: This is an optional field. This text displays on detail and edit pages when users hover over the Info icon next to this field.

- **Required**: If you tick this checkbox, this field always requires a value in order to save the record.

- **Unique**: If you tick this checkbox, duplicate values are not allowed here. There are two options to specify the case sensitivity. This field is not in currency and percent data types.

- **External ID**: You can use this checkbox to set the particular field as the unique record identifier from an external system.

- **Default Value**: You can specify a default value here by entering any value or using a formula.

Click on **Next**. Then you will get step 3 of the custom field creation wizard with the title, **Establish field-level security**. For now, accept the defaults. We will discuss more about the security of the Force.com platform in *Chapter 4, Designing Apps for Multiple Users and Protecting Data*.

Click on **Next**. Then you will get the last step of the number data type field creation with the **Add to page layouts** title. You can specify the page layout by adding the newly created custom field to the particular object's page layout.

Click on **Save**. Now, we have created the `Number of Leave per Year` custom field in the `Leave Configuration` object.

Calendar data types

There are two types of calendar data types in the Force.com platform. The fields of calendar data types are used to store date or date/time values.

Data Type	Properties
Date	• This allows users to enter a date value of pick a date from the popup calendar • This type doesn't contain the information about time
Date/Time	• This allows users to enter a date and time, or pick a date from the popup calendar • When users click on a date from the popup, that selected date and the current time are entered into the Date/Time field

Let's see the creation of a numeric data type field of the `Holiday Calendar` object. Use the following steps to create a date data type of a custom object:

1. Navigate to **Setup | Create | Objects**.
2. Click on **Holiday Calendar**.
3. In the **Custom Fields & Relationships** related list, click on **New**.
4. Select the field data type (this time **Date**) and click on **Next**.

5. Then you will get the following screen to fill in the field details:

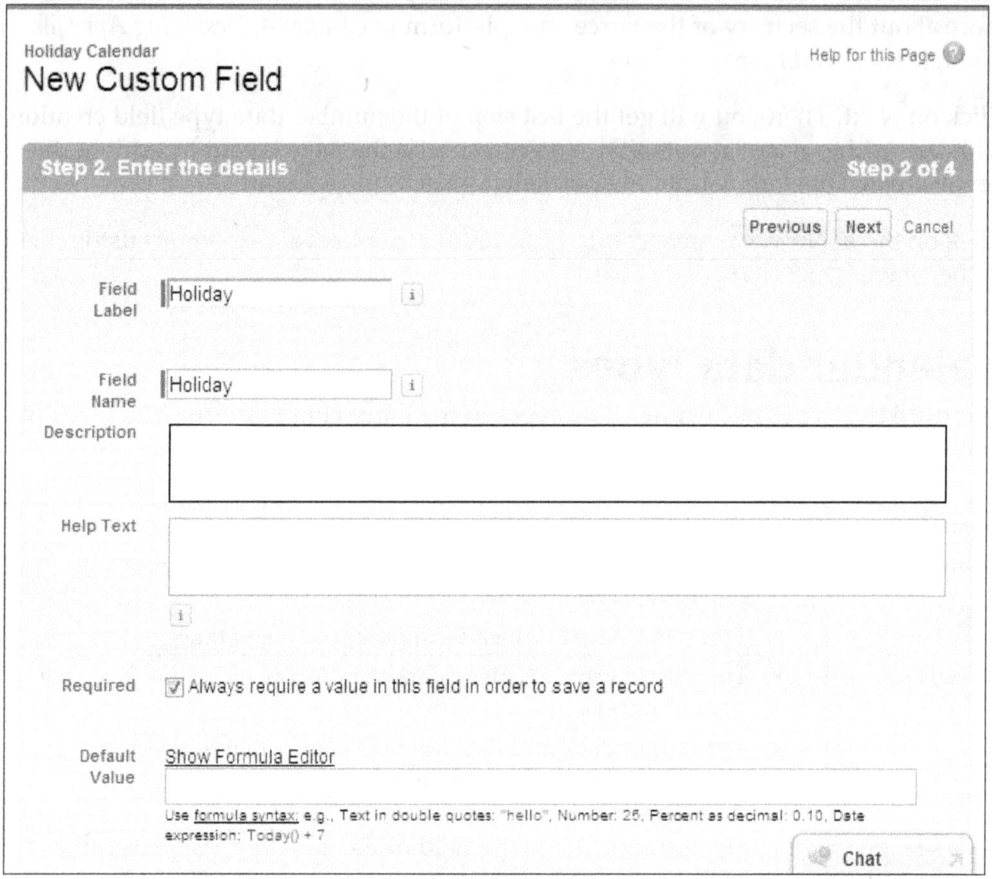

Holiday Calendar

New Custom Field

Help for this Page 🔘

Step 2. Enter the details   **Step 2 of 4**

Previous | Next | Cancel

| Field Label | Holiday | i |

| Field Name | Holiday | i |

Description

Help Text

i

Required   ☑ Always require a value in this field in order to save a record

Default Value   Show Formula Editor

Use formula syntax; e.g., Text in double quotes: "hello", Number: 25, Percent as decimal: 0.10, Date expression: Today() + 7

💬 Chat

Enter Date field type details

Fill in the **Field Label** as `Holiday`, and the **Field Name** will be autopopulated. We mark this field as required because this field always needs a date value in order to save a holiday calendar record. In such a scenario, when a user is trying to save the particular record without specifying a required field, an error will be fired.

Click on **Next**. Then you will get step 3 of the custom field creation wizard with the title **Establish field-level security**. For now, accept the defaults. We will discuss more about the security of the Force.com platform in *Chapter 4, Designing Apps for Multiple Users and Protecting Data*.

Click on **Next**. Then you will get the last step of the date type field creation with the title, **Add to page layouts**. You can specify the page layout by adding the newly created custom field to the particular object's page layout.

Click on **Save**. Now, we have created the `Holiday` custom field in the `Holiday Calendar` object.

Formatted text data types

We can categorize **Email**, **Phone**, and **URL** field types as the formatted text data types.

Data Type	Properties
Email	• This allows users to enter an e-mail address • This field type has in-built validation to ensure a proper e-mail format • If this field is specified for a contact or lead, users can choose the address when clicking on send an e-mail
Phone	• This allows users to enter any phone number • It automatically formats it as a phone number
URL	• This allows users to enter any valid website address • When users click on the field, the URL will open in a separate browser window • This field type has in-built validation to ensure a proper URL format

> Custom e-mail addresses cannot be used for mass e-mails.

Let's see the creation of a formatted data type field of the `Employee` object. Use the following steps to create an `Email` data type of a custom object:

1. Navigate to **Setup | Create | Objects**.
2. Click on **Employee**.
3. In the **Custom Fields & Relationships** related list, click on **New**.
4. Select the field data type (this time **Email**) and click on **Next**.

5. Then you will get the following screen to fill in the field details:

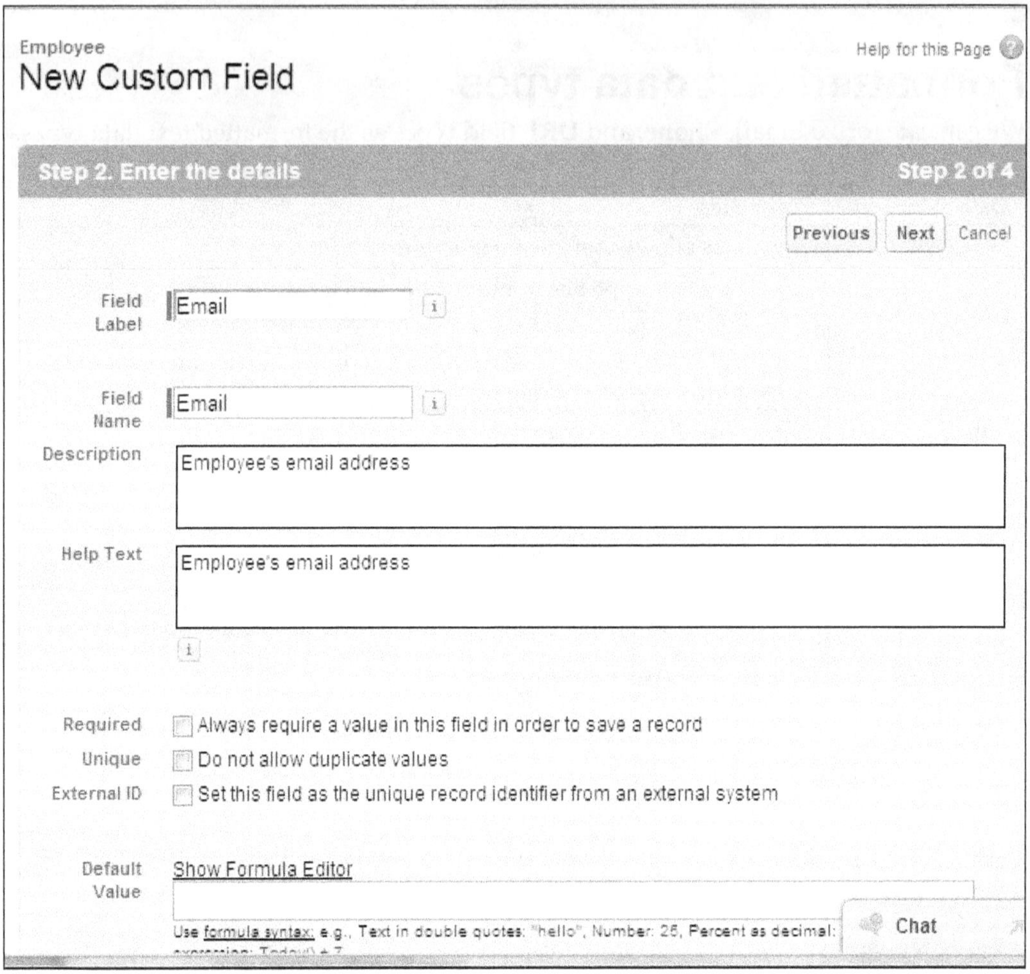

Employee
New Custom Field

Help for this Page

Step 2. Enter the details **Step 2 of 4**

Previous | Next | Cancel

Field Label | Email

Field Name | Email

Description | Employee's email address

Help Text | Employee's email address

Required | Always require a value in this field in order to save a record

Unique | Do not allow duplicate values

External ID | Set this field as the unique record identifier from an external system

Default Value | Show Formula Editor

Use formula syntax: e.g., Text in double quotes: "hello", Number: 25, Percent as decimal:

Chat

Enter Email data type details

Fill in the **Field Label** as Email, and the **Field Name** will be autopopulated.

Click on **Next**. Then you will get step 3 of the custom field creation wizard with the title of **Establish field-level security**. For now, accept the defaults. We will discuss more about the security of the Force.com platform in *Chapter 4, Designing Apps for Multiple Users and Protecting Data*.

Click on **Next**. Then you will get the last step of the Email data type field creation with the title of **Add to page layouts**. You can specify the page layout by adding the newly created custom field to the particular object's page layout.

Click on **Save**. Now, we have created the `Email` custom field in the `Employee` object.

Calculation data types

We can categorize the **Auto Number**, **Formula**, and **Roll-Up Summary** field types as the calculation data types in the Force.com platform.

Data Type	Properties
Auto Number	• This data type is a system-generated sequence number that uses a display format you define • The number is automatically incremented for each new record
Formula	• This data type is a read-only field that derives its value from a formula expression you define • The formula field is updated when any of the source fields change
Roll-Up Summary	• This data type is a read-only field that displays the sum, minimum, or maximum value of a field in a related list or the record count of all records listed in a related list • You cannot create this type of field on an object that is the master of a master-detail relationship. The master-detail relationship will be explained in the *Relationship data types* section

Let's create a formula field called `Age` for the `Employee` object. This field will return the employee's age that is calculated using the birth date and the current date. The following are the steps to create a formula field:

1. Navigate to **Setup** | **Create** | **Objects**.
2. Click on **Employee**.
3. In the **Custom Fields & Relationships** related list, click on **New**.
4. Select the field data type (this time **Formula**) and click on **Next**.

5. Then you will get the following screen to fill in the field details:

Step 2. Choose output type	Step 2 of 5

Previous | Next | Cancel

Field Label: Age   Field Name: Age

Formula Return Type

None Selected — Select one of the data types below.

Checkbox — Calculate a boolean value
Example: TODAY() > CloseDate

Currency — Calculate a dollar or other currency amount and automatically format the field as a currency amount.
Example: Gross Margin = Amount - Cost__c

Date — Calculate a date, for example, by adding or subtracting days to other dates.
Example: Reminder Date = CloseDate - 7

Date/Time — Calculate a date/time, for example, by adding a number of hours or days to another date/time.
Example: Next = NOW() + 1

Number — Calculate a numeric value.
Example: Fahrenheit = 1.8 * Celsius__c + 32

Percent — Calculate a percent and automatically add the percent sign to the number.
Example: Discount = (Amount - Discounted_Amount__c) / Amount

Text — Create a text string, for example, by concatenating other text fields.
Example: Full Name = LastName & ", " & FirstName

Options — Decimal Places 0 ▼ Example: 999

Choose the output type of the formula filed

Fill in the **Field Label** as Age, and the **Field Name** will be autopopulated.

Select the return type of formula field. For this field, we have selected **Number** as the output type. There are seven options to select the output type, which are as follows:

- **Checkbox**
- **Currency**
- **Date**
- **Date/Time**

- **Number**
- **Percent**
- **Text**

Define the decimal places for the field. (For this example, we don't need decimal places. So we set the value to 0.)

Click on **Next** and you will get the page to enter the formula you need to execute in this field.

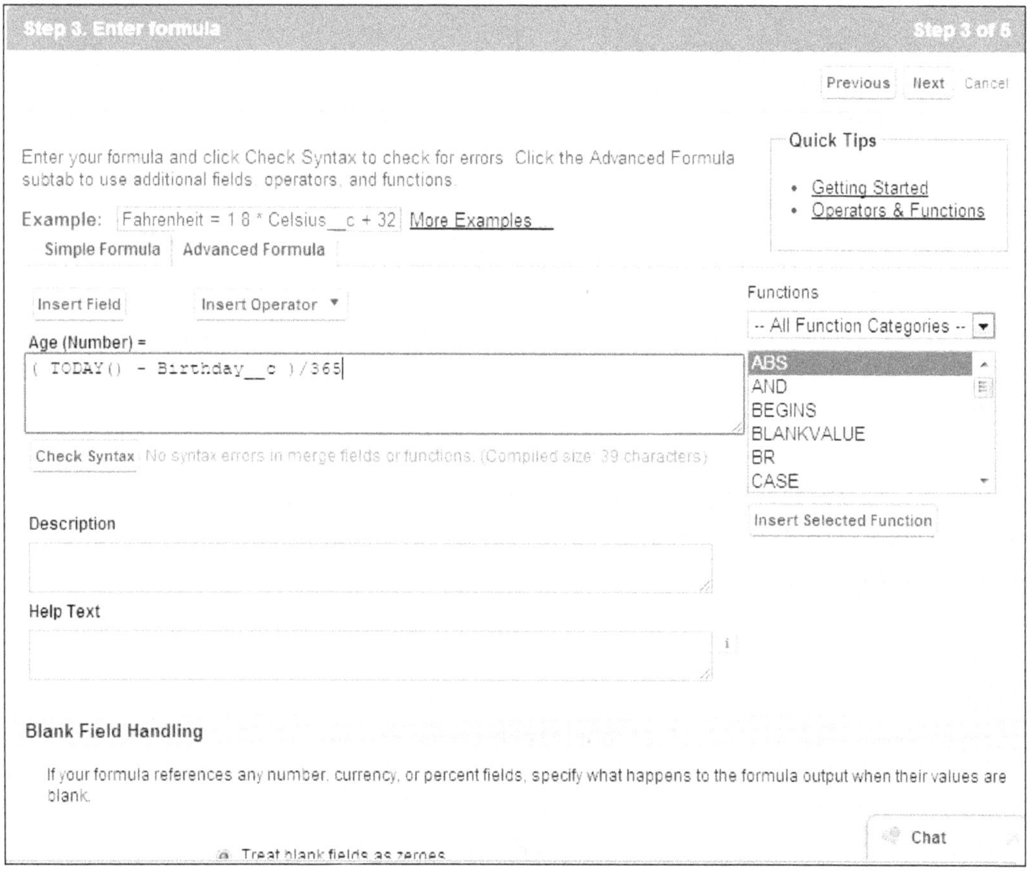

Enter formula of the formula field

You can enter your formula in the formula editor. There are **Simple Formula** and **Advanced Formula** editors. You can use them according to your requirements. We have used the advanced editor in this field creation. The Force.com platform provides a facility to check your formula before you save.

> A formula is more like an equation that performs a calculation at runtime. Depending on the context, the formula can use data and operations to calculate the new value of some other type. You can build your formula using the set of in-built functions. There are four types of functions. They are, **Date & Time**, **Logical**, **Math**, and **Text**.

Click on **Next**. Then you will get step 3 of the custom field creation wizard with the title, Establish field-level security. For now, accept the defaults. We will discuss more about the security of the Force.com platform in *Chapter 4, Designing Apps for Multiple Users and Protecting Data*.

Click on **Next**. Then you will get the last step of the formula field creation with the title, **Add to page layouts**. You can specify the page layout by adding the newly created custom field to the particular object's page layout.

Click on **Save**. Now, we have created the Age formula field in the Employee object. When you are viewing the particular employee record, the age will be calculated and viewed on the page.

Limited option data types

We can identify **Checkbox**, **Picklist**, and **Picklist (Multi-Select)** as limited option data types, which are explained in the following table:

Date Type	Properties
PickList	• This allows users to select a value from a predefined list
	• A single value can be selected
	• A maximum of 1,000 picklist values can be accommodated in a **Picklist** field
	• This type of field can be used to prevent spelling mistakes and grammatical errors by users

Date Type	Properties
Picklist (Multi-Select)	• This allows users to select multiple values from a predefined list • A maximum of 1,000 picklist values can be accommodated in a **Picklist** field • This type of field can be used to prevent spelling mistakes and grammatical errors by users
Checkbox	• This allows users to select a Boolean value • Select **True** for checked field • Select **False** for unchecked field

You can define dependent picklists in the Force.com platform. A dependent picklist has a controlling picklist. The controlling picklist controls the whole set of values in the dependent picklist. In other words, the selected values of the controlling picklist can change the values of the dependent picklist. There are two types of picklists, which are as follows:

- Standard picklist: This can only be the controlling picklist
- Custom picklist: This can be the controlling picklist as well as the dependent picklist

Let's create a **Picklist** field called `Year` for the `Holiday Calendar` object. This field contains the year values. The following are the steps to create a picklist field:

1. Navigate to **Setup** | **Create** | **Objects**.
2. Click on **Holiday Calendar**.
3. In the **Custom Fields & Relationships** related list, click on **New**.
4. Select the field data type (this time **Picklist**) and click on **Next**.

5. Then you will get the following screen to fill in the field details:

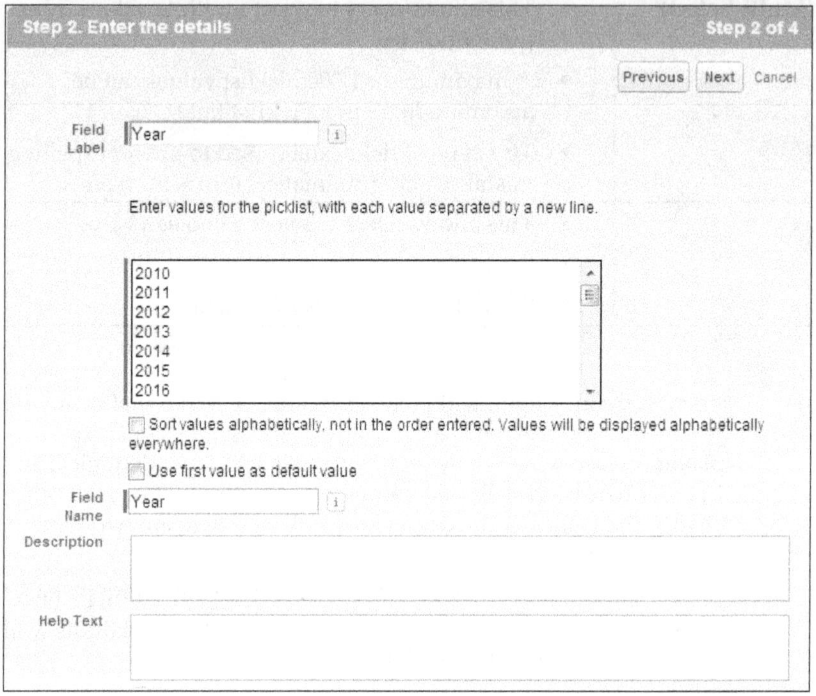

Step 2. Enter the details   **Step 2 of 4**

Previous | Next | Cancel

Field
Label | Year | i |

Enter values for the picklist, with each value separated by a new line.

```
2010
2011
2012
2013
2014
2015
2016
```

☐ Sort values alphabetically, not in the order entered. Values will be displayed alphabetically everywhere.

☐ Use first value as default value

Field
Name | Year | i |

Description

Help Text

Enter the details and values of the picklist field

Fill in the **Field Label** as Year, and the **Field Name** will be autopopulated.

Enter the year values to the picklist values' text area. According to the requirements, you can select that first value as the default value.

Click on **Next**. Then you will get step 3 of the custom field creation wizard with the title, **Establish field-level security**. For now, accept the defaults. We will discuss more about security of the Force.com platform in *Chapter 4, Designing Apps for Multiple Users and Protecting Data*.

Click on **Next**. Then you will get the last step of the picklist data type field creation with the title, **Add to page layouts**. You can specify the page layout by adding the newly created custom field to the particular object's page layout.

Click on **Save**. Now, we have created the Year picklist field in the Holiday Calendar object.

Relationship data types

In *Chapter 1*, *Getting Started with Force.com*, we have already discussed the ER diagram of the leave management application. There are a few relationships in the leave management app. The relationships play an important role in the Force.com platform. The Force.com platform provides two relationship data types to link two objects, which are listed in the following table:

Data type	Properties
Lookup Relationship	• This creates a relationship that links one object to another
	• The relationship field allows users to click on a lookup icon to select a value from a popup list
	• The other object is the source of the values in the list
	• The lookup field value can be mandatory or optional. It is up to the developer to decide according to the design
	• The relationship dependency between two objects can be defined as **Clear the value of this field. You can't choose this option if you make this field required** or **Don't allow deletion of the lookup record that's part of a lookup relationship**. Therefore, updating and deleting the child record depends on the particular relationship field definition
	• Two objects can have their own owners and sharing rules
	• There are maximum of 25 lookup relationships per child
Master-Detail Relationship	• This creates a special type of parent-child relationship between two objects
	• The relationship field allows users to click on a lookup icon to select a value from a popup list
	• The other object is the source of the values in the list
	• The relationship field is required on all detail records
	• The ownership and sharing of detail records is determined by the master record
	• When a user deletes the master record, all the detail records are deleted (cascade deleting)
	• You can create roll-up summary fields on the master record to summarize the detail records
	• A detail object can have a maximum of two master objects and both masters are required in the detail record

Both relationship types look almost the same on a page layout; both include a lookup field for the one side and a related list for the many sides. You will learn more about page layout in *Chapter 3, Building the User Interface*.

Special relationship types

Besides the lookup and master-detail relationships, there are two special relationship types in the Force.com platform. These types are created using master-detail and lookup relationships, which are as follows:

Self-Relationship	Many-to-Many Relationship
• This involves a lookup relationship to the same object. For example, the Employee object has a lookup field called Manager and Manager is an employee. Therefore, the Employee object has a lookup relationship to the Employee object • The user object has a special type of lookup relationship called Hierarchical Relationship • For example, a hierarchical relationship allows developers to create a Manager field on the User object to relate to another user	• This allows for the relationship of two objects in a many-to-many fashion • When modeling a many-to-many relationship, you use a Junction object to connect the two objects you want to relate to each other • A junction object is a custom object with two relationships • For example, in our sample, the leave management app, a `Leave Category` can have many leave types and a `Leave Type` can have many leave categories. Therefore, we have created the junction object called `Leave Configuration` to apply the many-to-many relationship between `Leave Type` and `Leave Category`

When creating a junction object, consider the following:
  • Name the object with a label that indicates its purpose
  • Use the autonumber data type to the Name field

> The junction object takes the initially created master as the primary master and uses the look and feel of the primary master. It also inherits the sharing model from the primary master. If any master record is deleted, the junction record is deleted.

Creating a lookup relationship field

Let's create a lookup relationship field called `Leave Category` for the `Employee` object. The following are the steps to create a lookup relationship field:

1. Navigate to **Setup** | **Create** | **Objects**.
2. Click on **Employee**.
3. In the **Custom Fields & Relationships** related list, click on **New**.
4. Select the field data type (this time **Lookup Relationship**) and click on **Next**.
5. Then you will see the page for step 2 (choose the related object). You have to select the other object to which the `Employee` object is related. Click on **Next**.
6. Then you will get the following screen to fill in the field details:

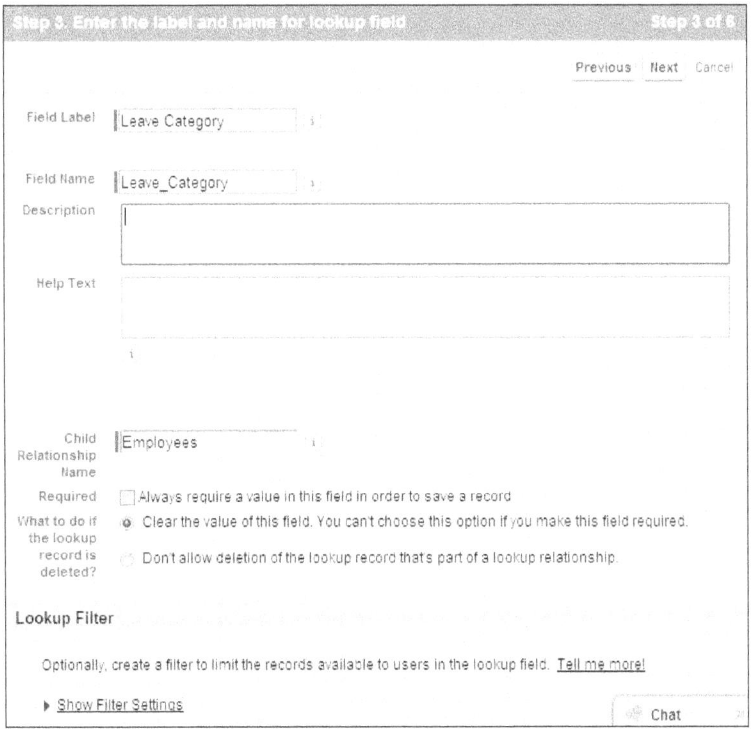

Enter the details of the lookup field

Fill in the **Field Label** as Leave Category, and the **Field Name** will be autopopulated.

- **Child Relationship Name**: The Child Relationship Name is an internal reference and is used for integration purposes. Be careful when changing the Child Relationship Name as it may affect existing integrations. This is an autopopulated field, but you can change/modify it.

- **Required**: If you tick this checkbox, this field always requires a value in order to save the record. This option was released in Summer '12. When the lookup field is optional, you can choose one of the following options:

    ° **Clear the value of this field**: If the referenced lookup record is deleted, this default option clears the value of the dependent lookup field. You can't choose this option if you make this field required.

    ° **Don't allow deletion of the lookup record that's part of a lookup relationship**: This option is used to restrict the deletion of the dependent lookup records by deleting the referenced lookup record.

- **Lookup Filter**: Optionally, you can create a filter to limit the records available to users in the lookup field. It helps to improve the productivity and the data quality of the lookup field. It can be made mandatory and fields can be compared to static values or to other fields. You can define informational messages to the lookup window.

Click on **Next**. Then you will get step 4 of the custom field creation wizard with the title, **Establish field-level security**. For now, accept the defaults. We will discuss more about security of the Force.com platform in *Chapter 4, Designing Apps for Multiple Users and Protecting Data*.

Click on **Next**. Then you will get step 5 of the lookup relationship field creation with the title, **Add to page layouts**. You can specify the page layout by adding the newly created custom field to the particular object's page layout.

Click on **Next**. Then you will get the last step called Add custom-related lists. Here, you can specify the title that the related list will have in all of the layouts associated with the parent. Also, you can select the page layouts that should include this field. The field will not appear on any pages if you do not select a layout in step 5.

Click on **Save**. Now, we have created the Leave Category lookup field for the Employee object.

You can convert relationships in the Force.com platform as follows:

- **Master-Detail Relationship** to a lookup relationship only if the master object doesn't have any roll-up summary field
- **Lookup Relationship** to a master-detail relationship only if the lookup field in all records contains a value

Creating a master-detail relationship field

Let's create a master-detail relationship field called Leave Type for the Leave Configuration object. When you are creating a master-detail relationship field, you can follow the same steps of creating a lookup relationship field. The only difference is the content of step 3. The following screenshot shows step 3 of creating a master-detail field:

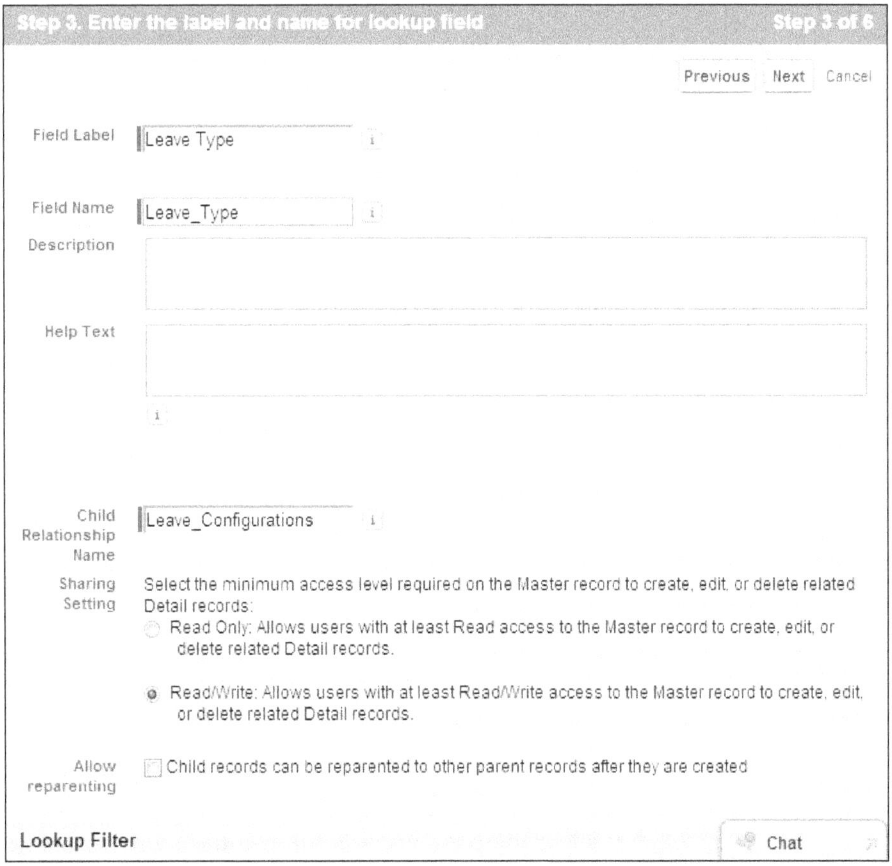

Enter the details of master-detail relationship field

> If the Master-Detail relationship is between the standard and the custom object, the custom object will always be the detail record.
>
> A master-detail can be multiple levels deep, parent-child-grand-children.
>
> If the master is a standard object: two multiple levels deep.
>
> If the master is a custom object: three multiple levels deep.

Fill in the **Field Label** as Leave Type, and the **Field Name** will be autopopulated.

- **Child Relationship Name**: The **Child Relationship Name** is an internal reference and is used for integration purposes. Be careful when changing the **Child Relationship Name** as it may affect existing integrations. This is an autopopulated field, but you can change and modify it.

- **Sharing Setting**: This setting is to select the minimum access level required on the Master record to create, edit, or delete related detail records. There are two options to select the minimum access level.

    ◦ **Read Only**: This allows users with at least read access to the master record to create, edit, or delete related detail records.

    ◦ **Read/Write**: This allows users with at least read/write access to the master record to create, edit, or delete related detail records.

- **Allow reparenting**: If you tick this checkbox, the child records can be reparented to other parent records after they are created.

- **Lookup Filter**: Alternatively, you can create a filter to limit the records available to users in the lookup field. It helps to improve the productivity and the data quality of the lookup field. It can be made mandatory and the fields can be compared to static values or to other fields. You can define informational messages to the lookup window.

Click **Next**. Then you will get the 4th step of the custom field creation wizard with the title of **Establish field-level security for reference field**. For now, accept the defaults. We will discuss more about the security of the Force.com platform in *Chapter 4, Designing Apps for Multiple Users and Protecting Data*.

Click on **Next**. Then you will get step 5 of the master-detail relationship field creation with the title, **Add to page layouts**. You can specify the page layout by adding the newly created custom field to the particular object's page layout.

Click on **Next**. Then you will get the last step called **Add custom related lists**. Here, you can specify the title that the related list will have in all of the layouts associated with the parent. You can also select the page layouts that should include this field. The field will not appear on any pages if you do not select a layout in step 5.

Click on **Save**. Now, we have created the `Leave Type` master-detail field for the `Leave Configuration` object.

Now, we have finished creating custom objects and custom fields. You can complete the data model (according to the ER diagram in *Chapter 1, Getting Started with Force.com*) of the leave management application using the knowledge we gain in this chapter. Use the following details of custom fields and particular data type to complete the data model of the leave management application:

1. Employee Object

Field Label	API Name	Data Type
Age	Age__c	Formula (Number)
Birthday	Birthday__c	Date
Email	Email__c	Email
First Name	First_Name__c	Text(255)
IsActive	IsActive__c	Checkbox
Last Name	Last_Name__c	Text(255)
Leave Category	Leave_Category__c	Lookup(Leave Category)
Manager	Manager__c	Lookup(Employee)
Social Security Number	Social_Security_Number__c	Text(10) (External ID)
User	User__c	Lookup(User)

2. Holiday Calendar

Field Label	API Name	Data Type
Holiday	Holiday__c	Date
Holiday Reason	Holiday_Reason__c	Text Area(255)
Year	Year__c	Picklist

3. Leave Category

Field Label	API Name	Data Type
IsActive	IsActive__c	Checkbox

4. Leave Type

Field Label	API Name	Data Type
IsActive	IsActive__c	Checkbox

5. Leave Configuration

Field Label	API Name	Data Type
IsActive	IsActive__c	Checkbox
Leave Category	Leave_Category__c	Master-Detail(Leave Category)
Leave Type	Leave_Type__c	Master-Detail(Leave Type)
Number of Leave per Year	Number_of_Leave_per_Year__c	Number(2, 0)

6. Leave

Field Label	API Name	Data Type
Employee	Employee__c	Master-Detail(Employee)
From Date	From_Date__c	Date
Leave Type	Leave_Type__c	Lookup(Leave Type)
Number of Days	Number_of_Days__c	Number(3, 1)
Status	Status__c	Picklist
To Date	To_Date__c	Date

Summary

In this chapter, we got familiar with the data model of the Force.com platform. You have learned about standard and custom objects and have created custom objects according to our sample leave management application. We have discussed various kinds of data types available in the Force.com platform and you learned to create those various data type custom fields. Finally, you learnt the object relationship that is an important topic for building data models on the Force.com platform.

3
Building the User Interface

In the previous chapter, you learned to build a data model of the leave management system. That means we built the underlying object and field structure of the application. Now we have the database. To store our application data, it needs some kind of user interface to add, edit, and delete records of a particular object. This chapter explains the methods for creating custom application, custom tabs, and customizing page layouts. In the Force.com platform, most of the UI designing and developing can be done using point-and-click controls. But the Force.com platform allows us to design and develop user interfaces beyond the standard UIs using Visualforce markup language. An overview of Visualforce will be discussed at the end of the chapter and that overview will link to *Chapter 8, Building Custom Pages with Visualforce*. This chapter covers the following topics:

- Creating an app
- Creating custom tabs
- Customizing page layouts
- Overview of Visualforce

Creating a Force.com custom application

When we are building an application using a client-server architecture, first we need to build the project and then we build the other components (such as classes and pages) within that project. Therefore, the project acts as the boundary of the application. Like a programming project, an application of the Force.com platform is a logical container for all of the objects, tabs, processes, and services associated with a given business function. A Force.com custom application consists of a name, a description, an ordered list of tabs, and optionally, a custom logo and a landing page. Therefore, a Force.com application can group different tabs and objects together to form a single business requirement. Users can switch between apps using the Force.com app drop-down menu at the top-right corner of every page.

Salesforce provides standard **Sales** apps such as **Call Center**, **Marketing**, and **Community**, among others. The following screenshot indicates the standard apps on the Force.com platform. You can customize the existing apps to match the way you work, or build new apps by grouping standard and custom tabs.

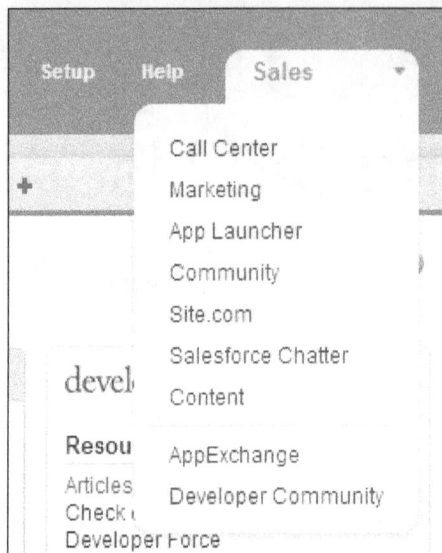

App selection area

Because the platform is continually evolving, you might find that the screenshots you see in this book vary slightly from what you see on your screen. These changes should be minor and shouldn't affect your understanding.

Let's start through the process of actually creating the leave management app now:

1. Log in to your Salesforce account.
2. Click on **Setup**.
3. Click on **Create** under the **Build** category.

4. Click on **Apps**. Then the following screen will be displayed:

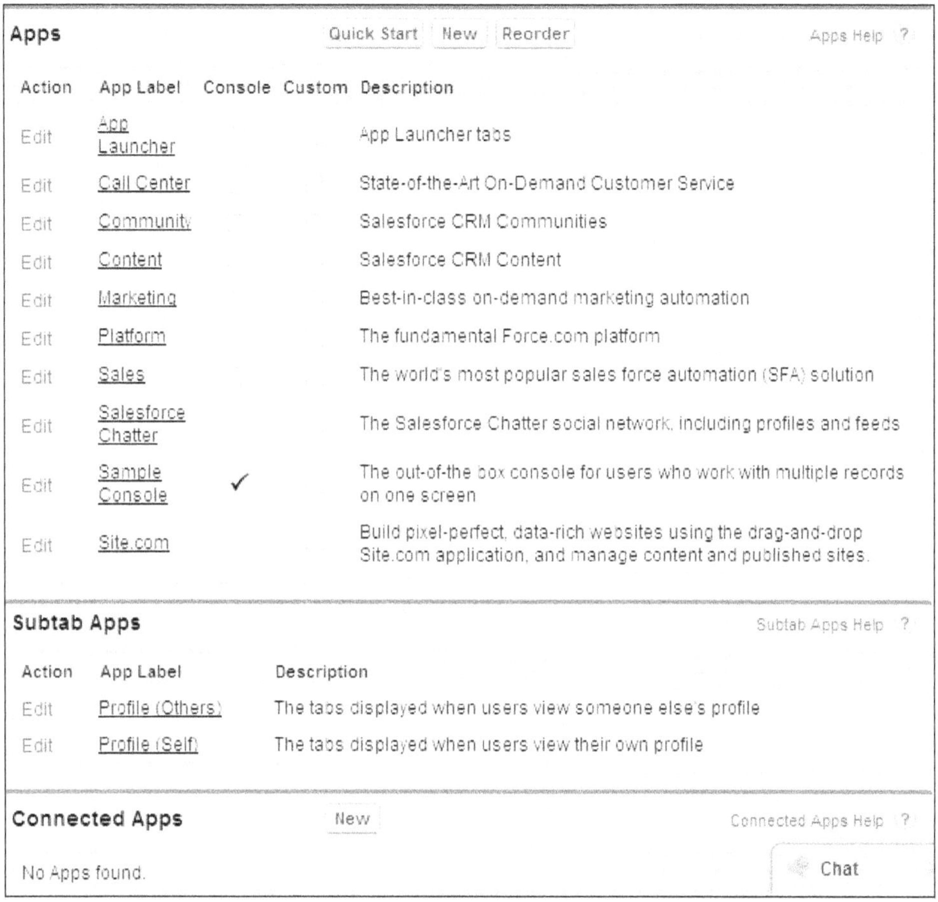

Apps		Quick Start	New	Reorder	Apps Help ?

Action	App Label	Console	Custom	Description
Edit	App Launcher			App Launcher tabs
Edit	Call Center			State-of-the-Art On-Demand Customer Service
Edit	Community			Salesforce CRM Communities
Edit	Content			Salesforce CRM Content
Edit	Marketing			Best-in-class on-demand marketing automation
Edit	Platform			The fundamental Force.com platform
Edit	Sales			The world's most popular sales force automation (SFA) solution
Edit	Salesforce Chatter			The Salesforce Chatter social network, including profiles and feeds
Edit	Sample Console		✓	The out-of-the box console for users who work with multiple records on one screen
Edit	Site.com			Build pixel-perfect, data-rich websites using the drag-and-drop Site.com application, and manage content and published sites.

Subtab Apps		Subtab Apps Help ?

Action	App Label	Description
Edit	Profile (Others)	The tabs displayed when users view someone else's profile
Edit	Profile (Self)	The tabs displayed when users view their own profile

Connected Apps	New	Connected Apps Help ?
No Apps found.		Chat

Manage apps on the Force.com platform

There are two ways to create an app, which are as follows:

- The **Quick Start** button: This creates an app with one custom object and associated tab
- The **New** button: This creates an app with a logo and existing tabs, and specifies the app's visibility for your profiles

In this book, we are going to discuss the use of the **New** button. You can try out the **Quick Start** button later.

5. Click on **New**.

6. If the Salesforce console is available, select whether you want to define a custom app or a Salesforce console. We will choose the custom app for the `leave management` app.

7. Click on **Next**.

8. Specify the **App Label** name as `eLeaveForce` for our `leave management` app.

> This label will appear as the app name in the app menu. The label can have a maximum of 40 characters. Spaces are allowed.

9. The **App Name** textbox will be autopopulated from the app label.

> The app name must be unique. This will be the unique name used by the API and managed packages. The name must begin with a letter and use only alphanumeric characters and underscores. The name cannot end with an underscore or have two consecutive underscores.

10. The **Description** field is optional. Even though the description is optional, it is a good idea to provide some description that will help identify the app directly.

New Custom App

Help for this Page

Step 2. Enter the Details   Step 2 of 5

Fill in the fields below to define the custom app.

Custom App Information | = Required Information

App Label	eLeaveForce	Example: HRforce, Financeforce, Bugforce
App Name	eLeaveForce [i]	
Description	Leave Management Application	

Previous Next Cancel

Enter custom app details

11. Click on **Next**.

12. In the 3rd step of creating an app, you can choose an image source for the custom app logo.

> To do so, choose an image file from the document library. The image format must be GIF or JPEG. The file size of a custom app logo must be smaller than 20 KB. (For comparison, the Salesforce.com logo is about 3 KB).
>
> To upload an image file, add a new document to the **Documents** tab. When the document is inserted, the externally available checkbox must be selected. You must save this image in a public folder, but not in a personal folder. This needs to be done before you attempt to create the app.
>
> Image dimensions should be a maximum of 300 pixels wide by 55 pixels high for best results. Larger images will be resized and may appear distorted.
>
> We recommend using an image with a transparent background.

Click on **Insert an Image**. Choose the image file from the document library.

13. Click on **Next**.

14. In the 4th step, you can choose the tabs to include in this custom app. After you add the tabs, you can choose the default landing tab. In the **Default Landing Tab** dropdown, choose the tab to be displayed when the user first navigates to this app. You cannot remove the **Home** tab from any app.

15. Click on **Next**.

16. In the 5th step, you can assign the application to profiles:

    1. Choose the user profiles for which this custom app will be visible in the Force.com AppExchange menu. You may specify this custom app as the default custom app of a profile, which means that new users who have the profile will see this custom app when they log in for the first time.

    2. If a custom app is set as the default for a profile, then you cannot make it invisible for that profile. Both the **Visible** and **Default** checkboxes will be read-only. A profile is a security feature that will be covered in *Chapter 4, Designing Apps for Multiple Users and Protecting Data*.

17. Click on **Save** to finish the wizard.

We just created the leave management application for our organization. Now, you can select the app from the Force.com app menu:

eLeaveForce is listed on the Force.com app menu

After you select the **eLeaveForce** app from the Force.com app menu, you will see the home page with the following header:

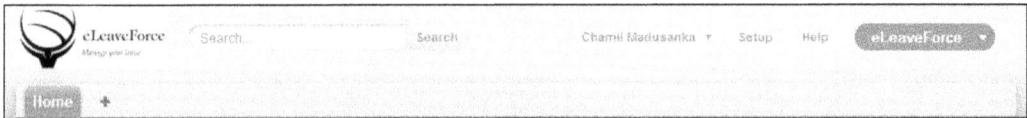

The header of the eLeaveForce app

Creating custom tabs

A tab is the main way to access the objects and Visualforce pages in the application. Without the tab, you will not be able to see object records. The tabs are positioned at the top of the page. You can create new custom tabs to extend Salesforce.com functionality or to build new application functionality. The tabs of standard objects are already defined by Salesforce.com. Therefore, we cannot edit or add standard object tabs. But we can hide or show the particular standard object tab to any custom application. When we come to adding tabs, we can create custom tabs in the Force.com platform. There are three types of custom tabs in the Force.com platform:

1. Custom object tabs

2. Visualforce tabs

3. The Web tab

Custom object tabs

These are the user interface for the custom application that you build in the Force. com platform. The look and feel of a custom object tab is similar to the standard tabs provided by Salesforce.com (such as accounts, contacts, and opportunities). These tabs can be used for viewing, editing, deleting, and adding a particular custom object data. The visibility of the buttons of edit, delete, add, and clone depends on the logged user's permission. Further details of security and permission will be discussed in *Chapter 4, Designing Apps for Multiple Users and Protecting Data*. The plural name of the object (which we give at the creation of the object) is taken as the tab name to display on the tab menu. Let's create a custom object tab for the Employee object:

1. Go to **Setup | Create | Tabs**.

2. Click on **New** which is under the **Custom Object Tabs** section. Then you see the following screenshot to create the custom object tab wizard.

> Currently, we can create tabs up to 100 in a developer edition.

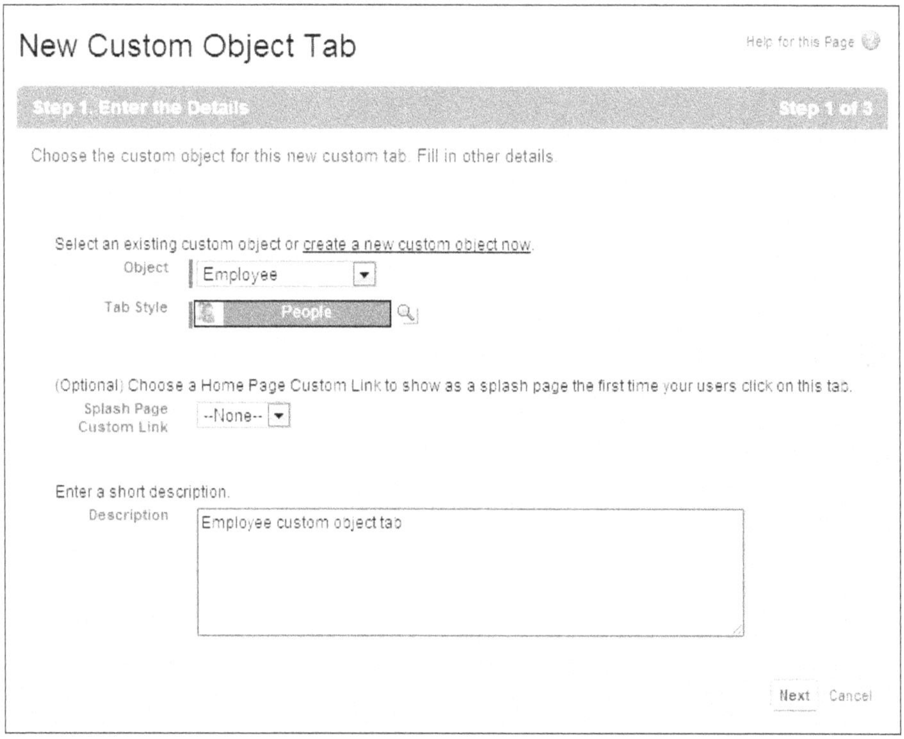

Enter the details of the new custom object tab

To get started, enter the following details:

- **Object**: Select the object that you want to create the custom object tab.

- **Tab Style**: This defines the unique color scheme and the icon to the custom object tab. This color scheme is used in every user interfaces (detail page, edit page, search results, and related lists) which are related to the particular object record. Click on the lookup icon to select the tab style. Then the following popup will be displayed. Then, you can select the tab style from the existing tab styles and you can create your own tab style by providing your color scheme and your own icon.

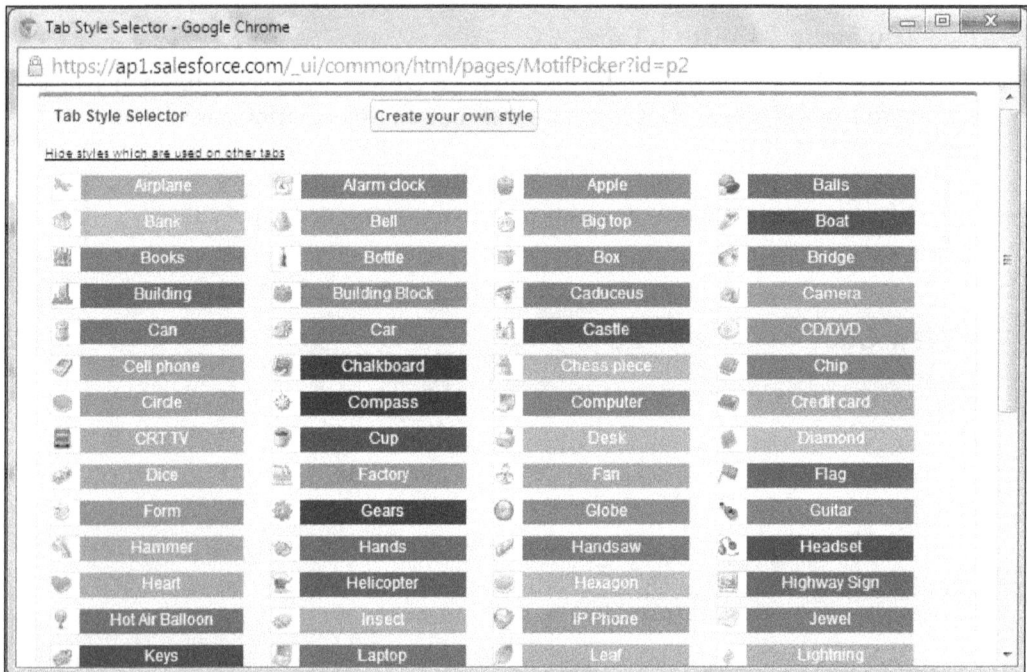

Selecting the tab style

> The icon should already be present in the documents tab at this stage.

- **Splash Page Custom Link**: Optionally, you can choose a **Home Page Custom Link** to show as a splash page the first time the user clicks on this tab.

- **Description**: You can enter a description of the custom tab.

- Click on **Next**. This step allows you to specify which profiles will be allowed to access this tab. A profile is a security feature that decides the components that can/cannot be seen by a particular user. We will discuss this further in *Chapter 4, Designing Apps for Multiple Users and Protecting Data*. Leave the default choice as is for now.

New Custom Object Tab

Help for this Page 🕮

Step 2. Add to Profiles   **Step 2 of 3**

Choose the user profiles for which the new custom tab will be available. You may also examine or alter the visibility of tabs from the detail and edit pages of each profile.

◉ Apply one tab visibility to all profiles [Default On   ▼]
◯ Apply a different tab visibility for each profile

Profile	Tab Visibility
Authenticated Website	Default On ▾
Contract Manager	Default On ▾
Custom: Marketing Profile	Default On ▾
Custom: Sales Profile	Default On ▾
Custom: Support Profile	Default On ▾
Customer Community Login User	Default On ▾
Customer Community User	Default On ▾
Customer Portal Manager Custom	Default On ▾

Assigning security to a tab

- Click on **Next**. This step allows you to specify which application will use this tab by default. Therefore, you can choose the eLeaveForce custom app for which the new custom tab will be available. You can also examine or alter the visibility of tabs from the detail and edit pages of each custom app.

Step 3. Add to Custom Apps	Step 3 of 3

Choose the custom apps for which the new custom tab will be available. You may also examine or alter the visibility of tabs from the detail and edit pages of each Custom App.

Custom App	Include Tab
Platform	☐
Sales	☐
Call Center	☐
Marketing	☐
Sample Console	☐
Authenticated Website User	☐
High Volume Customer Portal User	☐
App Launcher	☐
Community	☐
Site.com	☐
Salesforce Chatter	☐
Content	☐
eLeaveForce	☑

☑ Append tab to users' existing personal customizations

💬 Chat

Including a tab in the existing applications

- Select **Append tab to users' existing personal customizations**. This will automatically append the new tab permission to the particular user without customizing the user's personal settings.

- Click on **Save**. Now, you can see that the newly created tab is listed and the new tab has been created. Click on the tab and you will see the following screen:

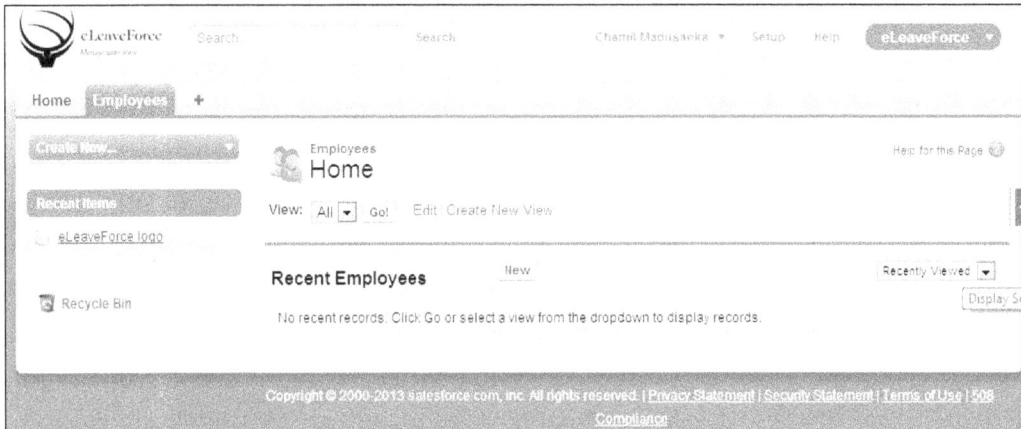

Visualforce tabs

These types of custom tabs are used to display a Visualforce page. The behavior and the look and feel of a Visualforce tab is similar to a standard Salesforce.com tab like the tabs of **Contacts**, **Accounts**, and so on. To create a Visualforce tab, select an existing Visualforce page or create a new one. The fields and page layout are part of the page definition.

Let's create a Visualforce tab in the `eLeaveForce` application. Suppose we have created a Visualforce page (assume that the page name is `SampleVisualforceTab`) to show the creation of the Visualforce tab. You will learn to create and develop the Visualforce page later in this chapter and in *Chapter 8, Building Custom Pages with Visualforce*.

To create a Visualforce tab, perform the following steps:

1. Go to **Setup | Create | Tabs**.
2. Click on the **New** button under the Visualforce tabs section. You will see the following screenshot:

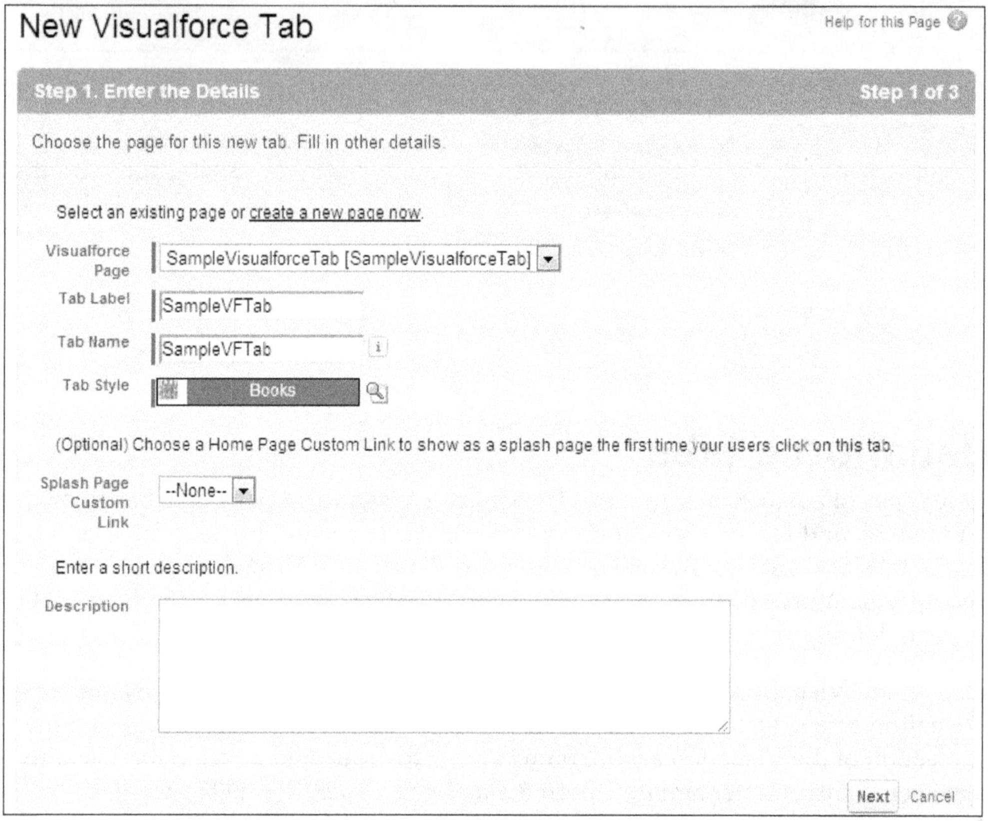

New Visualforce Tab

Help for this Page

Step 1. Enter the Details   Step 1 of 3

Choose the page for this new tab. Fill in other details.

Select an existing page or create a new page now.

Visualforce Page	SampleVisualforceTab [SampleVisualforceTab]
Tab Label	SampleVFTab
Tab Name	SampleVFTab
Tab Style	Books

(Optional) Choose a Home Page Custom Link to show as a splash page the first time your users click on this tab.

Splash Page Custom Link	--None--

Enter a short description.

Description	

Next   Cancel

Enter the details for creating a Visualforce tab

Fill in the following details:

- **Visualforce Page**: Select the Visualforce page you want to associate with a tab. In this case, we select the SampleVisualforceTab page.
- **Tab Label**: This label is taken as the tab name to display on the tab menu.

- **Tab Name**: This is automatically populated. You can modify the populated tab name. The unique name is used by the API and managed packages. The name must begin with a letter and use only alphanumeric characters and underscores. The name cannot end with an underscore nor can it have two consecutive underscores.

- **Tab Style**: The tab style is the same as the custom object tab creation.

- **Splash Page Custom Link**: Optionally, you can choose a home page custom link to show as a splash page the first time the user clicks on this tab.

- **Description**: Optionally, you can enter a description of the custom tab.

Click on **Next**. This step allows you to specify which profiles will be allowed to access this tab. We will discuss this further in *Chapter 4, Designing Apps for Multiple Users and Protecting Data*. Leave the default choice as it is for now.

Click on **Next**. This step allows you to specify which application will use this tab by default. Therefore, you can choose the custom apps for which the new custom tab will be available. You may also examine or alter the visibility of tabs from the detail and edit pages of each custom app.

Click on **Save**. Now, you can see that the newly created Visualforce tab is listed and the new tab has been created.

The Web tab

This is the third type of custom tab that is used to display web content or applications embedded in the Salesforce.com window. Using a web tab, a user can quickly access any web content that they frequently use without leaving the Salesforce application. For example, you can create web tabs for expense reporting, travel management, company intranet pages, Salesforce.com partner solutions, e-mail, and so on. Web tabs enable you to make Salesforce.com a true portal for your users, thereby increasing productivity and accelerating user adoption. Let's create a web tab for the eLeaveForce app. Perform the following steps to create a web tab:

1. Go to **Setup** | **Create** | **Tabs**.

2. Click on the **New** button under the **Web Tabs** section. You will see the following screenshot:

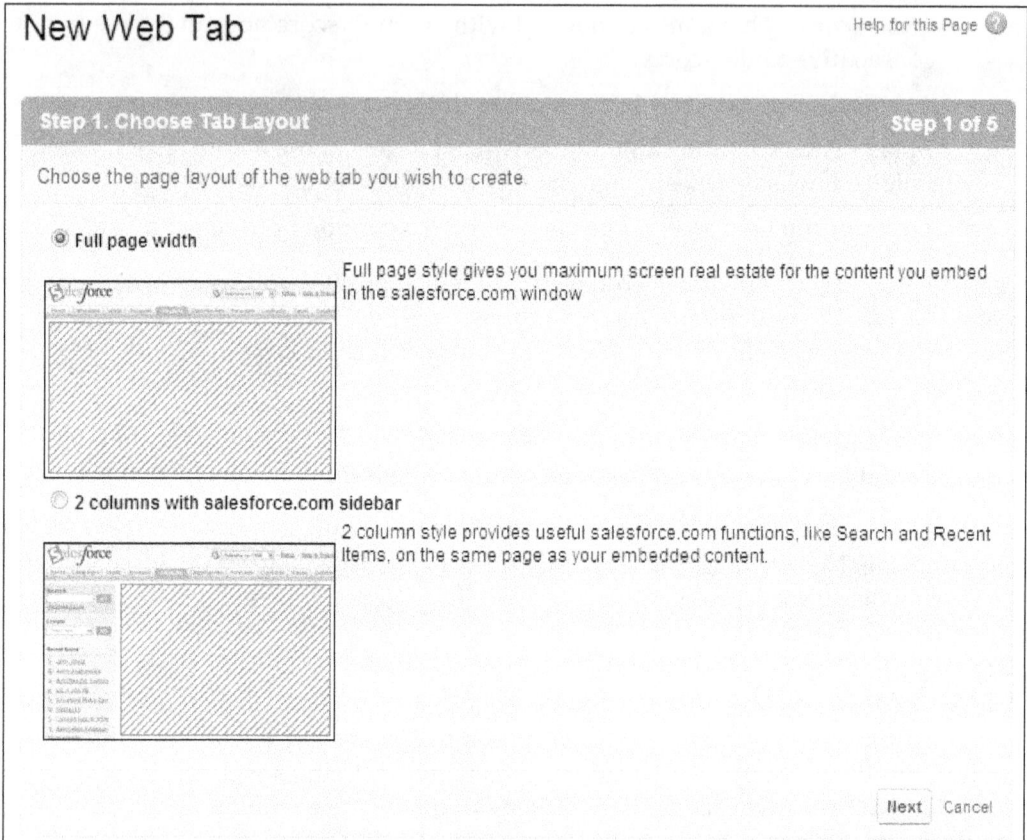

New Web Tab

Help for this Page

Step 1. Choose Tab Layout   Step 1 of 5

Choose the page layout of the web tab you wish to create.

◉ Full page width

Full page style gives you maximum screen real estate for the content you embed in the salesforce.com window

○ 2 columns with salesforce.com sidebar

2 column style provides useful salesforce.com functions, like Search and Recent Items, on the same page as your embedded content.

Next   Cancel

Creating a web tab

3. You have two options to select the type of web tab either **Full page width** or **2 columns with salesforce.com sidebar**. In this case, we select the **2 columns with salesforce.com sidebar** option. Then click on **Next**.

4. In this step, you can define the content and display properties of the web tab. Same as other tab types, you can specify the **Tab Label**, **Tab Name**, **Tab Style**, **Splash Page Custom Link**, and **Description**. The only different property is Content Frame Height (pixels). That property defines the height of the frame.

5. Then click on **Next**. You will see the following screenshot as part of step 3:

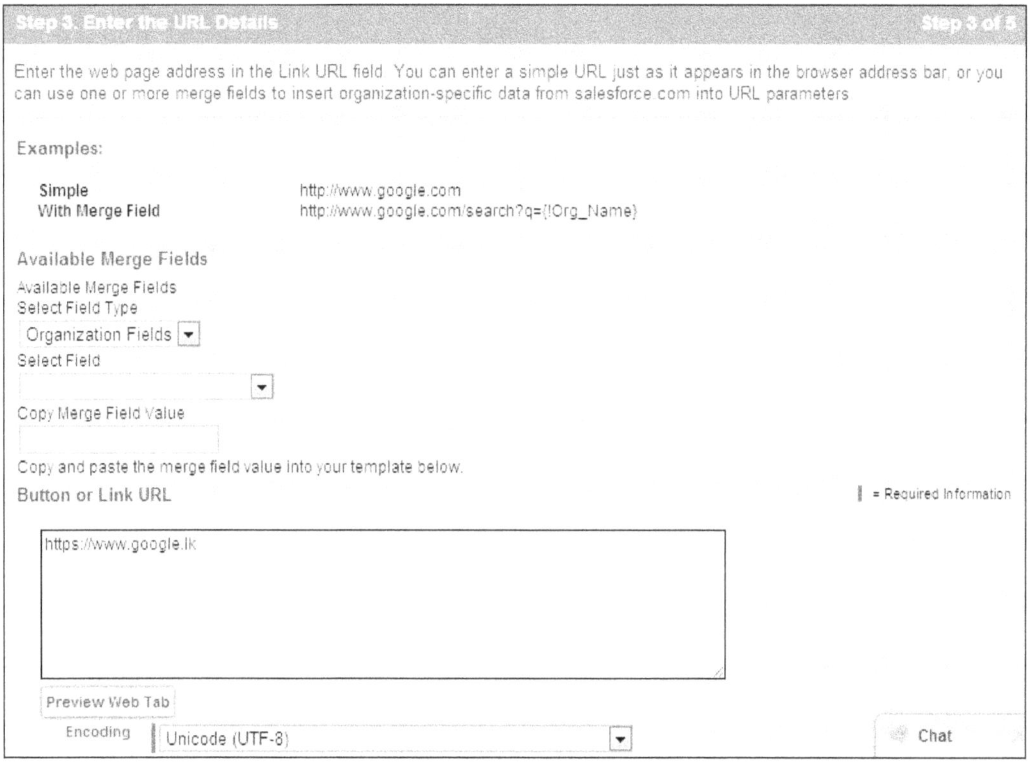

Step 3. Enter the URL Details   Step 3 of 5

Enter the web page address in the Link URL field. You can enter a simple URL just as it appears in the browser address bar, or you can use one or more merge fields to insert organization-specific data from salesforce.com into URL parameters.

Examples:

| Simple | http://www.google.com |
| With Merge Field | http://www.google.com/search?q={!Org_Name} |

Available Merge Fields

Available Merge Fields
Select Field Type

Organization Fields ▼

Select Field

▼

Copy Merge Field Value

Copy and paste the merge field value into your template below.

Button or Link URL   ‖ = Required Information

https://www.google.lk

Preview Web Tab

Encoding   ‖ Unicode (UTF-8)   ▼   Chat

Enter the URL details

6. In this step, you can enter the web page address in the **Button or link URL** field. You can enter a simple URL just as it appears in the browser address bar, or you can use one or more merge fields to insert organization-specific data from Salesforce.com into the URL parameters.

7. Click on **Next**. This step allows you to specify which application will use this tab by default. Therefore, you can choose the custom apps for which the new custom tab will be available. You can also examine or alter the visibility of tabs from the detail and edit pages of each custom app.

8. Click on **Save**. Now, you can see that the newly created web tab is listed and a new tab has been created. After clicking on **Save**, you will see an additional tab added to the UI.

Customizing page layouts

Page layout marks the view of any object. It is the view of the Model-View-Controller paradigm of Salesforce. Page layouts are needed to collect, display, and update the data of the app. Every object has a standard user interface with one or more page layouts. When you create a custom object, the Force.com platform creates standard page layouts for us. The Force.com platform allows us to modify it and create new page layouts according to the requirements. Since page layouts are customizable, you can arrange page layouts according to the requirements of the application. There is no limit on creating page layouts for an object. We can have *n* number of page layouts for any object. Multiple page layouts are supported by the security aspects of the app. Page layouts can be assigned to the profiles or record type. (For more details about profiles and record types, refer to *Chapter 4, Designing Apps for Multiple Users and Protecting Data*.) Mainly, there are two different types of layouts:

- Search layouts
- Page layouts

Search layouts

Search layouts decide the fields to be displayed in search results. These layouts are configured for each object and they affect the organization. The tab view, list view, search result, lookup dialog, lookup phone dialog, and search filter fields can be categorized under Search layouts. Search layouts are very poorly customizable. You can find the search layouts using the following steps:

1. Navigate to **Setup** | **Create** | **Objects** to display the custom object list. (For a standard object navigate to **Setup** | **Customize** | <Object Name> | **Search Layouts**).

2. Click on the object you want. In this case, click on the **Holiday Calendar** object link. It brings up the attributes of the object.

3. Go to the **Search Layouts** section of the Holiday Calendar object.

	Search Layouts			Search Layouts Help ?
Action	**Layout**	**Columns Displayed**	**Buttons Displayed**	**Modified By**
Edit	Search Results	Holiday Calendar Name, Holiday, Holiday Reason		Chamil Madusanka, 12/28/2013 2:19 AM
Edit	Lookup Dialogs	Holiday Calendar Name	N/A	Chamil Madusanka, 11/28/2013 7:06 AM
Edit	Lookup Phone Dialogs	Holiday Calendar Name	N/A	Chamil Madusanka, 11/28/2013 7:06 AM
Edit	Holiday Calendars Tab	Holiday Calendar Name, Holiday, Holiday Reason	N/A	Chamil Madusanka, 12/28/2013 2:20 AM
Edit	Holiday Calendars List View	N/A	New,Accept,Change Owner	Chamil Madusanka, 11/28/2013 7:06 AM
Edit	Search Filter Fields		N/A	Chamil Madusanka, 11/28/2013 7:06 AM

Search the Layout section of the Holiday Calendar object

When you click on a custom object tab, the Tab View will be displayed. This is a type of list view, which shows the recent items that were modified. The only customization you can make is to select the fields to include in this search layout. The following screenshot shows the tab view layout of the `Holiday Calendar` object:

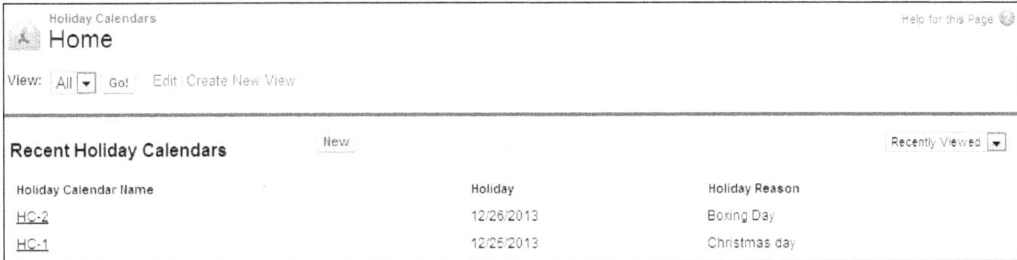

Holiday Calendars			Help for this Page
🎿 Home			
View: All ▼ Go! Edit Create New View			

Recent Holiday Calendars	New		Recently Viewed ▼
Holiday Calendar Name	Holiday	Holiday Reason	
HC-2	12/26/2013	Boxing Day	
HC-1	12/25/2013	Christmas day	

The Tab View of the Holiday Calendar

In the **Search Layout** section, you can see the customization point of the tab view as the `[Object's Plural Name]` tab. In this case, you can customize the tab view of the `Holiday Calendar` by clicking on the **Edit** link which is next to the **Holiday Calendars Tab**.

When you click on the **Go** button of the tab view (refer to the preceding tab view screenshot), you can see `List View` of that particular object. The following screenshot shows the list view layout of the `Holiday Calendar` object:

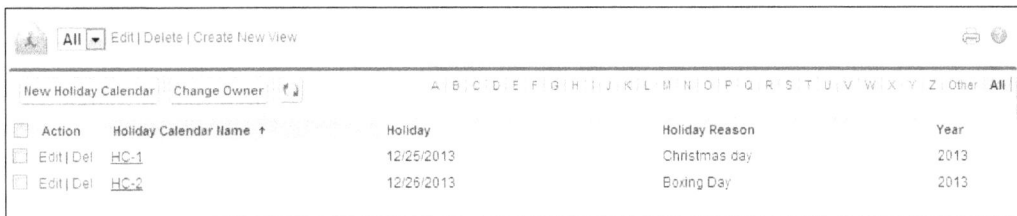

🎿 All ▼ Edit	Delete	Create New View			🖨 ❓
New Holiday Calendar Change Owner 🔲		A B C D E F G H I J K L M N O P Q R S T U V W X Y Z Other **All**	
Action Holiday Calendar Name ↑	Holiday	Holiday Reason	Year
Edit|Del HC-1	12/25/2013	Christmas day	2013
Edit|Del HC-2	12/26/2013	Boxing Day	2013

In the **Search Layout** section, you can see one customization point of the list view as `[Object's Plural Name] List View`. In this case, you can customize the tab view of the `Holiday Calendar` object by clicking on the **Edit** link, which is next to the Holiday Calendar's list view. In there, you can customize the buttons on the Holiday Calendars list view by removing any standard buttons or by adding custom buttons. The other customization point is in the list view itself. Refer to the preceding screenshot. In this screen, you can delete, edit, and create a new list view by selecting the fields that are seen on the list view. The list view can also be seen on the related list view of the object.

Search Results: Select the fields to include in this search layout.

> Note that your choices only determine the display of search results and do not affect the fields that are actually searched.

Your selections also determine the fields that are available to users when customizing their search results columns. In this customization, you can override the search result column customizations for all users and add custom buttons to this view.

Lookup Dialog: This layout is to define the search result of the lookup popup. You can select the fields to include in this lookup layout here as well.

Page layouts

A page layout controls the position, appearance, visibility, editablity, and organization of the fields and related lists. The detail view and the edit view can be categorized under the page layouts. Page layouts are very highly customizable. You can find the page layouts using the following steps:

1. Navigate to **Setup** | **Create** | **Objects** to display the custom object definition detail page.

2. Click on the object you want. In this case, click on the **Employee** object link. It brings up the attributes of the object.

3. Go to the **Page Layouts** section of the Employee object.

Page Layouts		New	Page Layout Assignment		Page Layouts Help ?
Action	Page Layout Name	Created By		Modified By	
Edit | Del	Employee Layout	Chamil Madusanka, 11/28/2013 7:27 AM		Chamil Madusanka, 12/15/2013 2:50 AM	

Page Layout section on the object definition

There is a default page (in this case, it's **Employee Layout** — refer to the preceding screenshot) layout that can be included in a section for the detail page buttons, a section for system information, a section for custom links, and a section for related lists.

Detail View: A detail view is the view page that shows the details of the record. This is a highly customizable layout.

> One page layout represents the detail page and the edit page of a particular object. But some elements such as related lists, custom links, and system information are not shown in the edit view.

We can go to the detail view by clicking on the record from the list view / tab view or by entering the record ID to the URL as follows:

```
http://SALESFORCE BASE URL/RecordID
```

> SALESFORCE BASE URL = `server instance.salesforce.com`.
> To check the different server instances go to `http://trust.salesforce.com`.

The following is the detail page of an employee record:

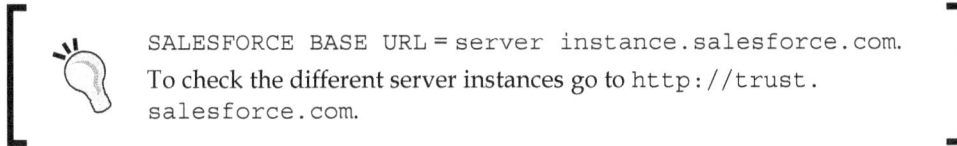

Edit View: The edit view provides the input fields of the particular object to add a new record or edit an existing record. In the edit view, you cannot see any system information fields or audit fields (such as created date, created by) and related lists. There are fields that are only present in the detail section. Both the detail view and the edit view are controlled by the same page layout. The detail page is the actual page layout, and edit page inherits properties from the detail page view. The following screenshot is of the edit view for the same employee record which is in the preceding screenshot:

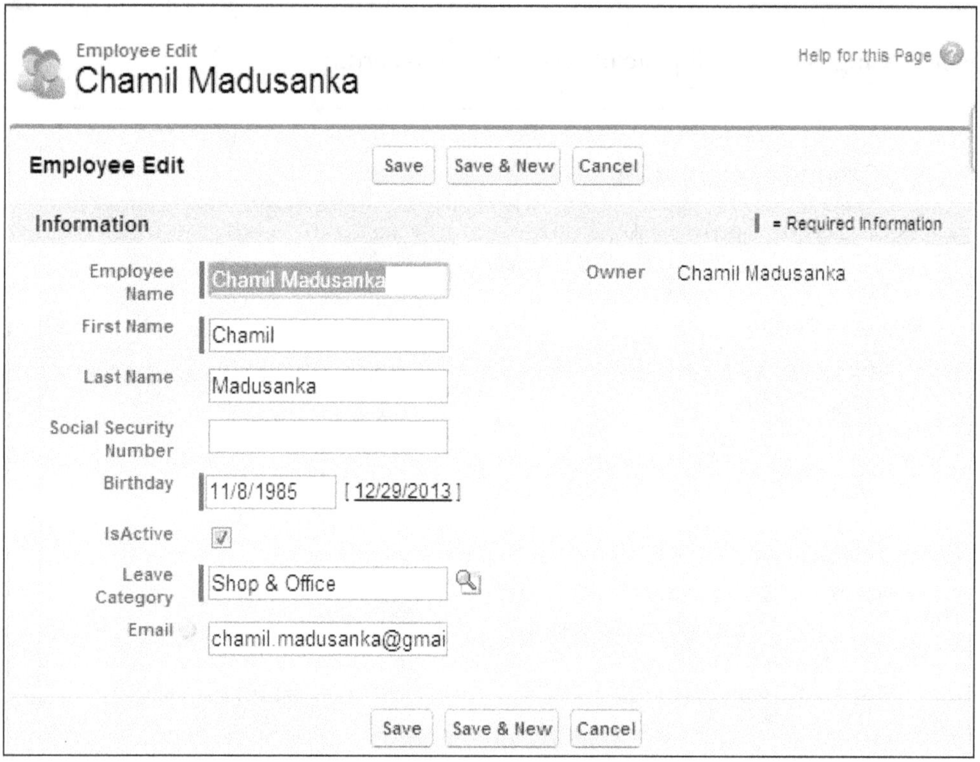

The page layout editor

The Force.com platform provides the page layout editor to organize the fields and related lists of an object on the detail view and the edit view. The page layout editor is allowed to make read-only fields, required fields, and include the Visualforce pages.

Let's try the page layout editor of the Employee object. You can find the page layouts using the following steps:

1. Navigate to **Setup** | **Create** | **Objects** to display the custom object list.

2. Click on the object you want. In this case, click on the **Employee** object link. It brings up the attributes of the object.

3. Go to the **Page Layouts** section of the Employee object and click on **Edit**, which is located next to the page layout. Then you will see the following screenshot:

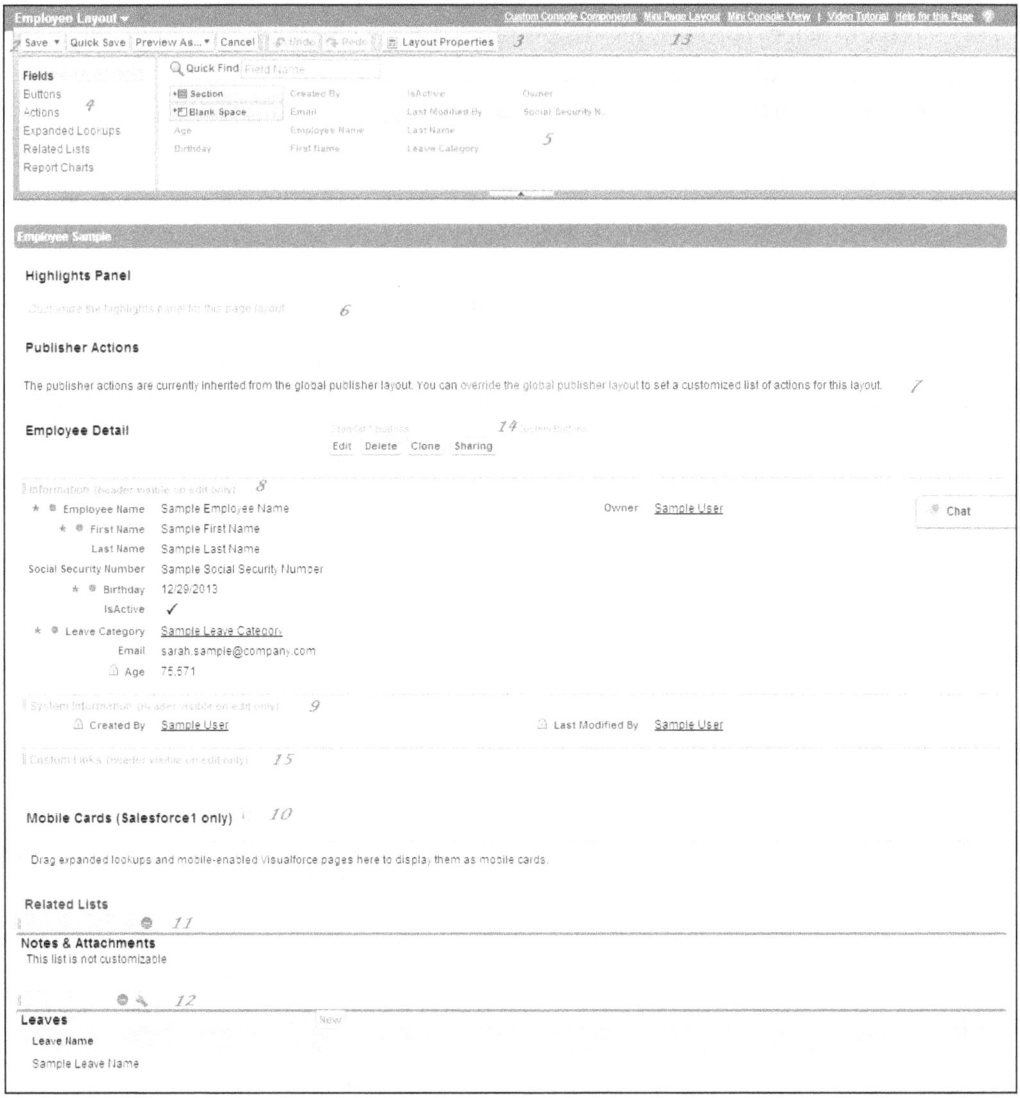

The page layout editor

The following list explains the important sections of the page layout:

1. If you have multiple page layouts for a particular object, you can select other layouts to edit quickly.

2. The modified layout can also be saved in the same layout or in a different name.

3. When you click on the layout properties button, you can change the Page Layout Name. There are two options to select: Highlights Panel and Interaction Log. Both are shown in the Console.

4. You can select between Fields, Buttons, Actions, Expanded lookups, Related Lists, and Report Charts.

5. According to the selected option that was described in the previous step, fields, buttons, and related lists are available for adding on the page. If you have already used a component, it will be disabled.

6. The highlights are used for consoles.

7. The publisher actions are currently inherited from the global publisher layout. You can override the global publisher layout to set a customized list of actions for this layout.

8. This is the detail section of the record. In here, a red star mark indicates that the field is required and a lock mark indicates that the field is locked and cannot be removed from the page layout.

9. This section contains the system information fields such as created date and created user. These fields are visible only on the detail view.

10. Expanded lookups and mobile-enabled Visualforce pages placed here display as mobile cards on a record's home page in Salesforce1. Visualforce pages in this area must be enabled for Salesforce mobile apps or they won't display in Salesforce1.

11. If the record has a lookup or master-detail relationship with the other object, then the related lists are available to the page layout.

12. You can modify and add additional properties (columns and buttons) to the related list by clicking on the option button on the related list.

13. The mini page layout of an object appears in the mini view of the Console tab, hover details and event overlays. A mini page layout can have any item that is in the associated page layout because it inherits the record type, related lists, fields, and access settings from the related page layout. Required fields on the associated page layout cannot be removed from the mini page layout. The visibility of the fields and related lists of the mini page layout can be defined in the mini page layout.

14. From the standard buttons section, you can remove certain buttons but cannot add new custom buttons. But in the custom buttons section, you can add new buttons and they are available only in the detail view.

15. New custom links can be added to the custom link sections. Custom links are optionally available in the detail view but not in the edit view.

An overview of Visualforce

You already know that we can develop Force.com applications with custom objects and standard objects in the Force.com platform. Every object has a standard user interface with one or more page layouts. However, we cannot use standard page layouts for complex requirements. Here, Visualforce comes into play. For example, if the customer needs to have drag and drop components, we cannot achieve it from the standard UI. We need to use Visualforce pages to achieve such kinds of requirements.

Visualforce is a web-based user interface (UI) framework, which can be used for building sophisticated, attractive, and dynamic custom user interfaces. Visualforce allows the developer to use standard web development technologies such as jQuery, JavaScript, CSS, and HTML5. Therefore, we can build rich UIs for any app, including mobile apps. We'll be discussing about Visualforce with standard web development technologies and Visualforce for mobile in more depth later in *Chapter 8, Building Custom Pages with Visualforce*. Similar to HTML, the Visualforce framework includes a tag-based markup language.

A Visualforce page has two major elements, called Visualforce markup and Visualforce controller. Visualforce markup consists of Visualforce tags with the prefix apex, and there can be HTML tags, JavaScript, or any other standard web development code. The Visualforce controller consists of a set of instructions to manipulate data and schema with the user interaction. It controls the interface as well. A standard controller, which is created along with the object, can be used as the Visualforce controller. A standard controller has the same logic and functionality that is used in standard pages. However, when we need to use a different logic or functionality, we can write our own Apex controller class, and we can also write extensions to standard controllers or custom controllers using the Apex language. AJAX components, expression language formula for actions, and component binding interactions are there in Visualforce.

Advantages of Visualforce

The following are the advantages of Visualforce for a developer:

- **Model-View-Controller development style**: Visualforce adheres to the MVC pattern by providing the view of the application in the Force.com platform. A view is defined by user interfaces and Visualforce markup. The Visualforce controller that can be associated with Visualforce markup takes care of the business logic. Therefore, the designer and the developer can work separately; while the designer focuses on user interface, the developer can focus on business logic. MVC architecture can be illustrated as shown in the following diagram. More details will be discussed in *Chapter 8, Building Custom Pages with Visualforce*.

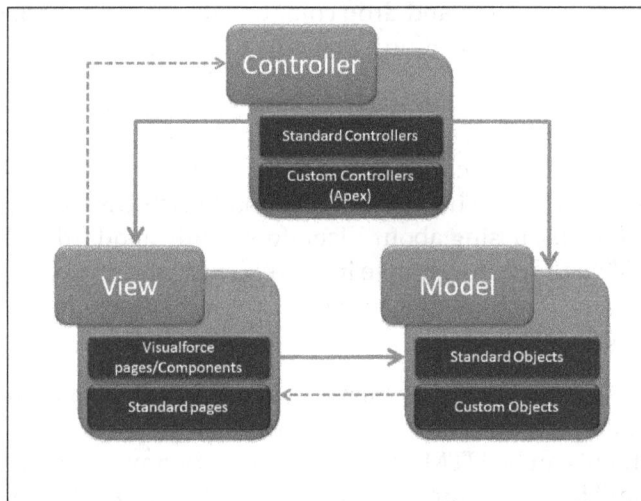

- **User-friendly development**: A developer (with an administrator profile) can have a Visualforce editor pane at the bottom of every Visualforce page. This editor pane is controlled by the development mode option of the user record. This feature allows us to edit and see the resulting page at the same time and in the same window. This Visualforce editor has the code-saving feature with autocompilation and syntax highlighting. Note that the Visualforce editor will appear only if the development mode is checked in the particular user information.

- **A broad set of ready-to-serve Visualforce components**: Visualforce has a set of standard components in several categories. There are output components, for example, `<apex:outputPanel>`, `apex:outputField>`, `<apex:outputText>`, `<apex:pageBlock>`, and so on. There are input components, for example, `<apex:inputFile>`, `<apex:inputField>`, `<apex:inputText>`, `<apex:selectList>`, and so on. These input and output components have a feature called data-driven defaults. For example, when we specify the `<apex:inputField>` component in a particular Visualforce page, the `<apex:inputField>` tag provides the edit interface for that field with data-type-related widgets (for example, the date field has the calendar, and the e-mail/phone fields have their particular validations). There are also AJAX components, for example, `<apex:actionStatus>`. AJAX components allow the user to enhance the level of interactivity for a particular interface.

- **Tightly integrated with Salesforce / Extends with custom components**: A Visualforce page can have a custom controller as well as a standard controller. A standard controller is created while creating the object and can be used for the Visualforce controller. A standard controller has the same logic and functionality that is used in standard pages. Visualforce pages adhere to these standardized methods and functionality, and we can also extend the standard components with custom components. For example, we can use an extension class for extending the standard controller of a particular Visualforce page. We can create our own Visualforce custom components instead of the in-built components of Visualforce, for example, `<apex:inputFile>`, `<apex:inputField>`, `<apex:outputField>`, and so on.

- **Flexible and customizable with web technologies**: The Visualforce markup is more flexible and more customizable through the use of web technologies, for example, JavaScript, CSS, jQuery, Flash, and so on because it is eventually rendered into HTML. A designer can use the Visualforce tags with these web technologies.

Summary

In this chapter, you learned every user interface option in the Force.com platform. You learned methods of creating custom application, custom tabs, and customizing page layouts. Now, we know that in the Force.com platform, most of the UI designing and developing can be done using point-and-click controls. However, the Force.com platform allows us to design and develop user interfaces beyond the standard UIs by using the Visualforce markup language. Finally, you have started to learn about Visualforce and further more, you will learn to build custom pages in *Chapter 8, Building Custom Pages with Visualforce*.

4
Designing Apps for Multiple Users and Protecting Data

Most of the web applications are multiuser applications that are utilized by many users. When we come to multiuser apps, the data security and permission settings become more crucial. Data is the heart of our information stack, and, most importantly, the repository of the business value of all of our applications. Therefore, we need to protect data in the application and need to design the application in a way that can be used by many users. The Force.com platform has the security foundation that protects both the data and the application. The security features of the Force.com platform provide both durability and flexibility.

In this chapter, you will learn the design considerations of a Force.com application, which accommodate multiple users and the security framework of the Force.com platform. More importantly, you will learn how the platform protects data and the application by implementing the Force.com security features.

This chapter covers the following topics:

- Design considerations
- An overview of the Force.com licenses
- The security framework of the Force.com platform

Design considerations

Before we commence with building an application on any platform, we need to architect the application first. Therefore, when you design an application on the Force.com platform, you must consider the following facts:

- You must know about the actors or users of the particular application. In a real-world scenario, an application can have many users. Therefore, your application must accommodate each and every user or actor in your application. In our leave management application, there are four types of users such as System admin, Employee, Manager, and Human Resources user (HR User). We need to add every type of user in our organization.

- You need to identify the access that every type of user will have to the data in the system. More importantly, which user can access the particular data and what will these users expect to see and do? In this case, you need to identify the data and the functionality restrictions for the particular users. In the leave management application, the HR user has complete access to the entire leave database, along with the customizations of the applications. The employee can only apply for leave, view the leave history, and view the leave balance. The approver can only view and approve the particular leave records.

- You need to address the access levels of sensitive data. In our leave management application, there is sensitive information such as social security number and leave data. The social security number can only be seen by the employee to whom it belongs. The others cannot see that in the leave management application. The leave data of a particular employee can be accessed by that particular employee and the related manger; also, the employee can create the leave record and the manager can update the record.

- You must consider how to make the user experience more streamlined and efficient.

An overview of Force.com licenses

The Force.com licenses play an important role in the security aspects of the Force.com platform. You can see all these licenses and the statistics about the usage of licenses by navigating to **Setup | Administer | Company Profile | Company Information**.

There are two types of licenses in the Force.com platform. They are as follows:

- **User Licenses**: Each user must have a user license that defines the access to applications and functionalities. Different types of user licenses allow different levels of access and define which profiles and permission sets are available to the user. There can be more than one type of user license in your organization. There are many types of user licenses. Mainly, we consider the following user licenses:

    ° **Salesforce**: This license gives you full access to the Salesforce organization. Currently, if you have not created any users, you are logged into Salesforce through this license.

    ° **Salesforce Platform**: This type of license permits only platform access to the particular user.

    ° **Work.com Only User**: This license is designed for users who need access to Work.com without having Salesforce licenses.

    ° **Chatter Free**: This license is designed for users who don't have the Salesforce license, but need access to Chatter. Users with this user license can access the standard chatter items such as profiles, groups, people, and files. However, they cannot access any Salesforce objects or data.

    ° **Chatter External**: This license is designed for users who are outside of a company's e-mail domain. We use this type of license to invite outside users to the Chatter group. They can access information and interact with users only in the groups, but they don't have any access to Salesforce objects or data.

The following screenshot shows the number of user licenses available in your organization. You can access this page by navigating to **Setup | Administer | Company Profile |Company Information**.

Name	Status	Total Licenses	Used Licenses	Remaining Licenses	Expiration Date
Salesforce Platform	Active	3	0	3	
Authenticated Website	Active	10	0	10	
High Volume Customer Portal	Active	10	0	10	
Customer Community Login	Active	10	0	10	
Work.com Only	Active	3	0	3	
Customer Portal Manager Custom	Active	5	0	5	
Identity	Active	10	0	10	
Silver Partner	Active	2	0	2	
Gold Partner	Active	3	0	3	
Customer Portal Manager Standard	Active	5	0	5	
Force.com - App Subscription	Active	2	0	2	
Partner App Subscription	Active	2	0	2	
Partner Community	Active	10	0	10	
Partner Community Login	Active	10	0	10	
Customer Community	Active	10	0	10	
Force.com - Free	Active	2	0	2	
Chatter Free	Active	5,000	0	5,000	
Chatter External	Active	500	0	500	
Salesforce	Active	2	1	1	

User Licenses — User Licenses Help (?)

The available user licenses

> User licenses are available in Enterprise, Performance, Unlimited, Developer, and Database.com editions.
>
> To view the user license types, the user needs the View Setup and Configuration user permissions.
>
> Currently, the following license types are available for purchase: Salesforce (Salesforce, Salesforce Platform, Force.com—One App, Force.com App Subscription, Knowledge Only User, Identity, Chatter Free, Chatter External, Chatter Only, Work.com Only User, Company Community), Communities, Customer Portal, Customer Portal—Enterprise Administration, Database.com User Licenses, Partner Portal, Platform Portal, Service Cloud Portal, Sites and Site.com.
>
> For more details about user licenses, refer to `https://help.salesforce.com/htviewhelpdoc?err=1&id=users_understanding_license_types.htm&siteLang=en_US`.

- **Permission Set Licenses**: There are permissions which can be assigned only to users who have a permission set license. For example, when the Use Identity Connect permission is assigned to a user, that user must have the Identity Connect permission set license. Currently, the following permission set licenses are available for purchase.

Permission Set License	Permission Included
Company Community Add-on	Allows View Knowledge
Identity Connect	Use Identity Connect
Sales Console User	Sales Console

The following screenshot shows the number of permission set licenses available in your organization. This screenshot is one section of the preceding screen. You can access this page by navigating to **Setup** | **Administer** | **Company Profile** | **Company Information**.

Permission Set Licenses				Permission Set Licenses Help ?	
Name	Status	Total Licenses	Used Licenses	Remaining Licenses	Expiration Date
Sales Console User	Active	2	0	2	

The available permission set licenses

- **Feature Licenses**: The third type of license is also assigned to a particular user to provide some additional Salesforce feature such as Marketing or Connect Offline. One user can have one or more Feature licenses.

> The feature user licenses currently available are: Chatter Answers User, Force.com Flow User, Knowledge User, Marketing User, Mobile User, Offline User, Salesforce CRM Content User, and Service Cloud User.
>
> For more details, refer to `https://help.salesforce.com/htviewhelpdoc?err=1&id=users_understanding_feature_licenses.htm&siteLang=en_US`.

The following screenshot shows the number of feature licenses available in your organization. We will not implement this through this example application and will not cover it in this book.

Feature Licenses				Feature Licenses Help ?
Feature Type	**Status**	**Total Licenses**	**Used Licenses**	**Remaining Licenses**
Marketing User	Active	2	1	1
Apex Mobile User	Active	2	1	1
Offline User	Active	2	1	1
Knowledge User	Active	2	0	2
Force.com Flow User	Active	3	0	3
Service Cloud User	Active	2	1	1
Live Agent User	Active	2	0	2
Site.com Contributor User	Active	1	0	1
Site.com Publisher User	Active	2	0	2
Chatter Answers User	Active	30	0	30
Work.com User	Active	5	0	5
Salesforce CRM Content User	Active	5	1	4

Available feature licenses

The security framework of the Force.com platform

The security framework of Force.com is a multilevel security structure that allows you to offer different level access and permissions to users within your organization. The Force.com security framework is not only about the permissions, but also ensures that the organization is protected from external access. Therefore, the Force.com security framework includes a range of security defenses that guard your data resources. Let's discuss the following different security structure levels in the Force.com security framework:

- Organization security
- User security
- Network-based security
- Session security
- Administrative security
- Component-based security
- Record-based security

All the security aspects are controlled according to data sharing among the users and access preventing the unauthorized users. It is called **Reverse Security Pyramid** in the Salesforce platform. It explains the security features that users cannot see in an application, instead of what users can see. The pyramid can be illustrated as follows:

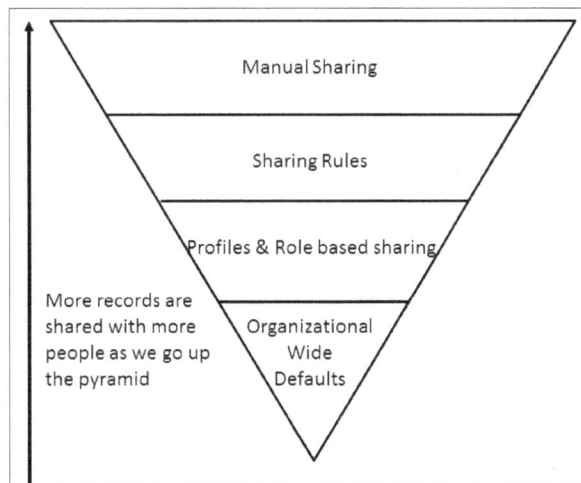

The Reverse Security Pyramid

This includes organization-wide defaults, profiles, roles, and sharing. You may get confused with these words now. All these will be discussed in the upcoming sections. As you can see in the pyramid, as it goes up, the number of users getting access increases. According to this, the bottom of the pyramid is the most restrictive and restriction decreases as we move up. Let's discuss this in detail.

Organization security

You have already seen that the Force.com platform is a multitenant platform. Because of the multi-tenancy, the same set of resources is used by many different customers. Therefore, the Force.com platform protects your organization from other customer organizations by using a unique organization identifier. And this organization security layer protects the organization from external parties. The organization security layer has security options that can be applied to your organization.

The security controls can be accessed by navigating to **Setup | Administer | Security Controls** and include the following:

1. Password policies
2. Activations
3. Login access policies
4. Certificate and key management
5. Single sign-on settings
6. Auth. providers
7. Identity provider
8. View setup audit trail
9. Expire all passwords
10. Delegated administration
11. Remote site settings
12. HTML documents and attachments settings

Password policies

To maintain the organization's security, you can set various password restrictions and login lockout policies for all users.

> Password policies are available in: Contact Manager, Group, Professional, Enterprise, Performance, Unlimited, Developer, and Database.com editions.
>
> The user password cannot exceed 16000 bytes.
>
> Logins are limited to 3600 hours per user. This limit applies to organizations created after Summer '08.

When you click on **Password Policies** that is under **Security Controls**, you will see the following screenshot. In there, you can define your password and login policies.

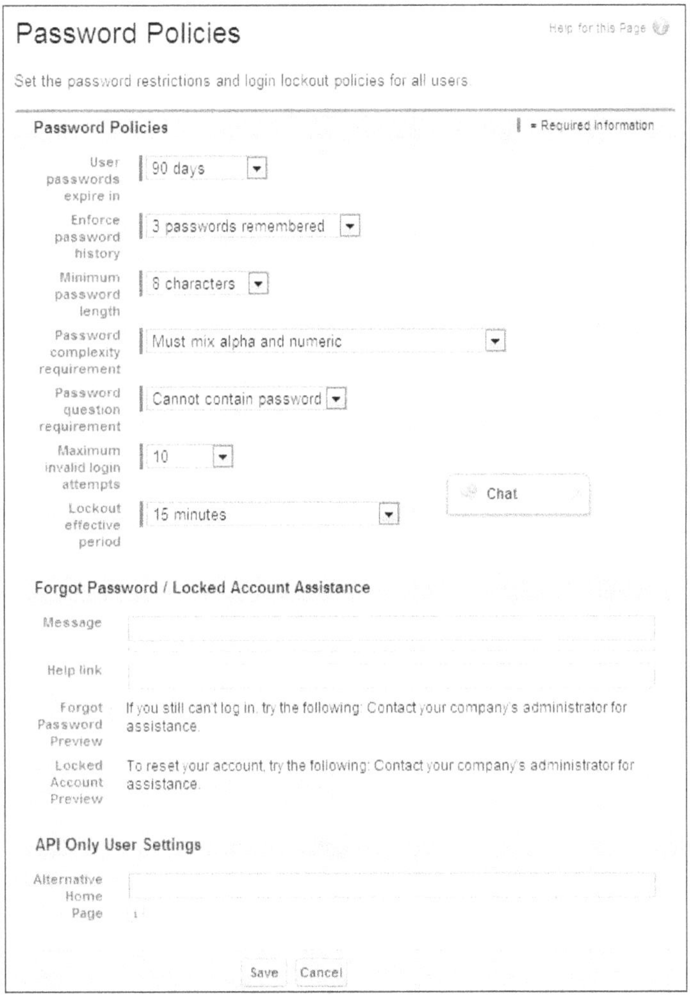

Password Policies
Help for this Page
Set the password restrictions and login lockout policies for all users
Password Policies
= Required Information
User passwords expire in
90 days
Enforce password history
3 passwords remembered
Minimum password length
8 characters
Password complexity requirement
Must mix alpha and numeric
Password question requirement
Cannot contain password
Maximum invalid login attempts
10
Chat
Lockout effective period
15 minutes
Forgot Password / Locked Account Assistance
Message
Help link
Forgot Password Preview
If you still can't log in, try the following: Contact your company's administrator for assistance.
Locked Account Preview
To reset your account, try the following: Contact your company's administrator for assistance.
API Only User Settings
Alternative Home Page
Save
Cancel

Define password policies in your organization

As shown in the preceding screenshot, the following table describes the properties of defining password policies in your organization:

Field	Description
User passwords expire in	This field defines the time duration of the password expiration. After expiration, the password users must change their password. This setting affects all the users except users with the Password Never Expires permissions.
Enforce password history	This field specifies how many previous passwords should be remembered. The default value is **3 passwords remembered**. This means, when a user is going to reset or change their password, the user cannot use one of the three previous passwords and will need to specify a new, unique password. The No password remembered option can be selected only if you have selected Never expires for the User passwords expire in field.
Minimum password length	This field specifies the minimum number of characters required for a password in your organization.
Password complexity requirement	This field specifies the complexity level of the user's password. There are three complexity levels, which are as follows: No restriction, where, any password is allowed. This is the least secure option. Must mix alpha and numeric, where at least one number and one alphabetic character is required. Must mix alpha, numeric, and special characters, where at least one number, one alphabetic character, and one special character such as ! # $ % - _ = + < > is required.
Password question requirement	When you register to a particular organization, you have to specify a security question and the answer for the selected question. This field specifies the requirements for that answer. Currently, there is only one option called Cannot contain password, which means you cannot include the password in that answer.
Maximum invalid login attempts	This field specifies the number of login failures allowed for a user before they are locked out.
Lockout effective period	This field specifies the duration of login lockout.

Field	Description
Message	This field specifies the custom message to appear in the Account Lockout email and at the bottom of the Confirm Identity screen for users resetting their passwords.
Help Link	If you define this field, this link displays with the text defined in the Message field.

Activations

The Force.com security framework has a feature to verify the identities of a user's login devices and browsers. If a user is coming from an unknown device or an unknown browser, or from a new IP address, then the Force.com security framework adds an extra security layer on top of the user authentication and single-sign-on features. In such a scenario, a user must provide an identity confirmation code, which is delivered via an e-mail, a mobile authenticator app, or SMS. If the user completes the identity confirmation challenge, the device and the client browser is marked as an active device or active browser with the activated IP.

In this activation section, you can see all the currently activated login IPs representing the device IP and browsers. The following screenshot shows the currently activated login IPs:

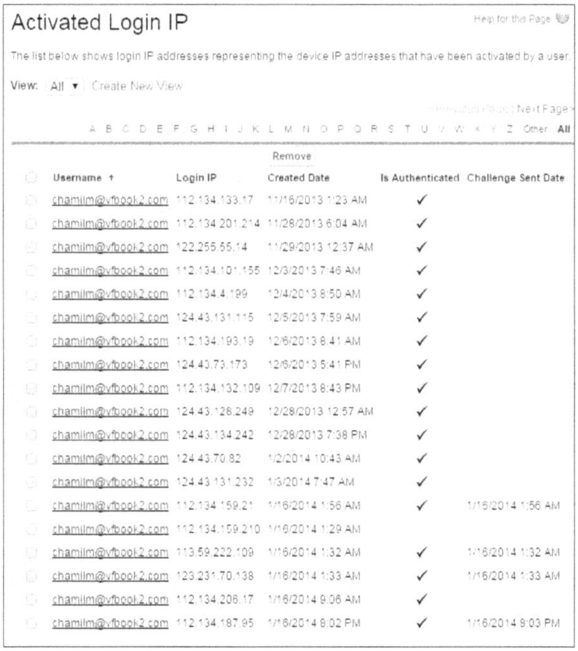

Activated login IPs

The following screenshot shows the client browsers that are currently activated:

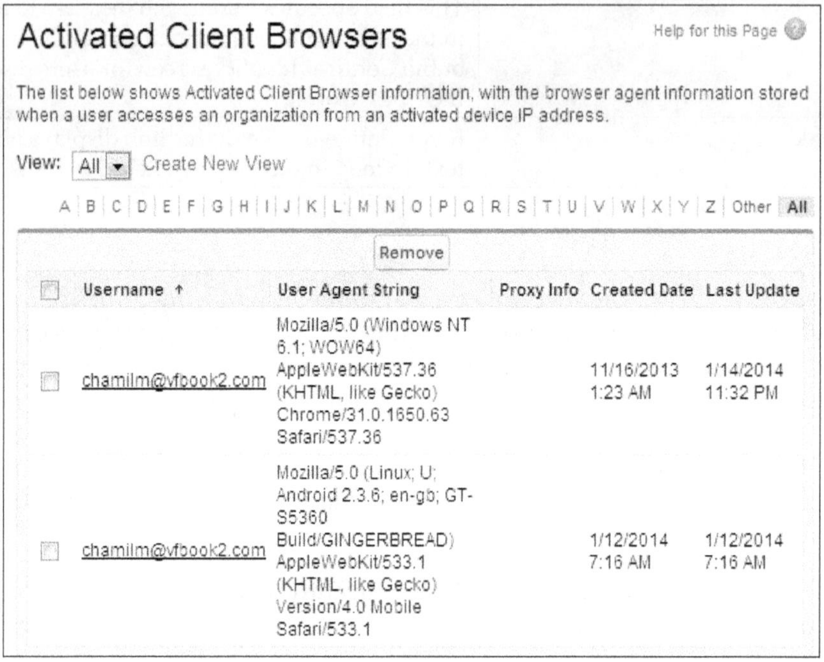

[A user can only view or revoke his/her activations.]

This activation section is available in all Salesforce editions. The administrator can revoke the activation status of any device addresses or any activated browser. After revoking the login, IP, and client browser activation, that particular user will be challenged for an identity confirmation in the next login attempt.

Login access policies

The login access policies control the support organizations to which your user can grant login access. In here, the administrator can prevent users from granting access to a publisher by selecting the **Available to Administrator Only** option. When you click on the **Login Access Policies**, you will see the following screenshot:

Login Access Policies

Help for this Page

Control which support organizations your users can grant login access to.

Manage Support Options

Save | Cancel

Support Organization	Packages	Available to Users	Available to Administrators Only
Salesforce.com Support		◉	○

Save | Cancel

Certificate and key management

Certificates are used for either authenticated single sign-on to an external website, or when using your organization as an identity provider. You only need to generate a Salesforce certificate if an external website needs verification that a request is coming from a Salesforce.com organization.

Mutual authentication certificates are applied when an HTTPS request is made to a Salesforce.com organization from a third-party service on a specified port. There are two types of certificates:

- **Self-signed**: This type of certificate is signed by Salesforce. Not all the external websites accept self-signed certificates.
- **CA-signed**: This type of certificate is signed by an external certificate authority (CA). Most of the external websites accept CA-signed certificates.

A master encryption key is used to encrypt the data contained in encrypted fields. You can archive and create keys based on your organization's security needs.

After you click on **Certificate and Key Management,** you will see the following screenshot and you can manage your certificates and master encryption keys there:

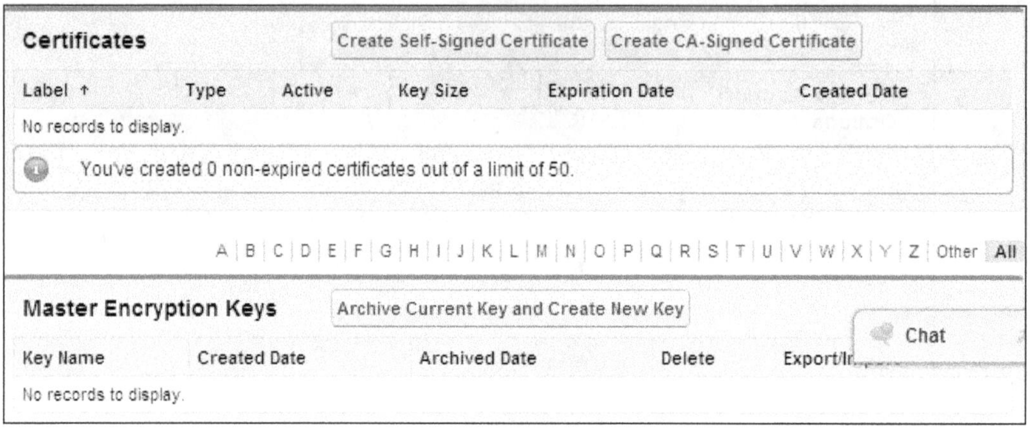

Certificates				Create Self-Signed Certificate	Create CA-Signed Certificate	
Label ↑	Type	Active	Key Size	Expiration Date		Created Date
No records to display.						

You've created 0 non-expired certificates out of a limit of 50.

A | B | C | D | E | F | G | H | I | J | K | L | M | N | O | P | Q | R | S | T | U | V | W | X | Y | Z | Other | **All**

Master Encryption Keys		Archive Current Key and Create New Key			
Key Name	Created Date		Archived Date	Delete	Export/Ir...
No records to display.					

Chat

Remote site settings

In this option, you can specify web addresses that your organization can invoke from Salesforce.com. In the Force.com platform, you can call an external site from a Visualforce page, Apex callout, and JavaScript code using XmlHttpRequest in a custom button. Those external sites must be registered in the Remote site settings page. Otherwise, you cannot call that particular external site.

> For security reasons, if Salesforce restricts the outbound ports, you can specify to one of the following ports:
>
> - **80**: This port only accepts HTTP connections
> - **443**: This port only accepts HTTPS connections
> - **1024–66535 (inclusive)**: These ports accept HTTP or HTTPS connections

To add a Web address, navigate to **Setup | Administer | Security Controls | Remote Site Setting | New Remote Site**. Then you will see the following screen:

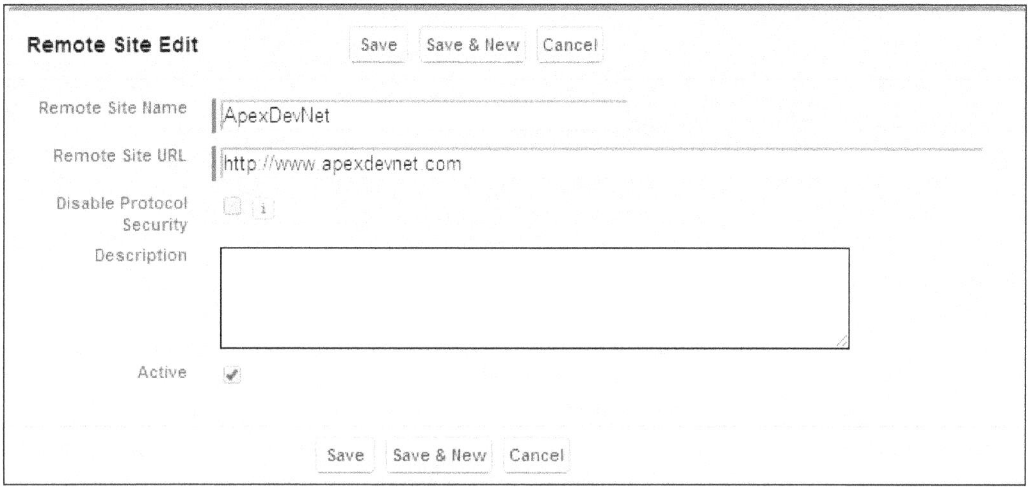

Remote site settings

The following are the properties of defining a Remote Site as shown in the preceding screenshot:

- **Remote Site Name**: This provides a descriptive term for this field.
- **Remote Site URL**: This allows you to specify the URL of the external site.
- **Disable Protocol Security**: If you select this checkbox, it allows access to the remote site regardless of the protocol. Then Salesforce can pass data from an HTTPS session to an HTTP session and vice versa.
- **Description**: Optionally, you can specify the description of the site.
- **Active**: This check box defines the status of activeness of the remote site.

All s-controls, JavaScript `OnClick` commands in custom buttons, Apex, and AJAX proxy calls can access this Web address from Salesforce.com.

Other organization security settings

There are a few other security settings that can be categorized under the Organization security, which are listed in the following table:

Security Setting	Features
Single Sign-On Settings	Configure single sign-on in order to authenticate users in salesforce.com from external environments. Federated authentication that is authentication, a single sign-on method that uses SAML assertions sent to a Salesforce endpoint, is an option available for single sign-on.
Auth. Providers	You can enable your organization users to log in to Salesforce organization using the credentials from an external service provider. Currently, there are four service providers available, namely, Facebook, Janrain, another Salesforce organization, and using an Open ID connect.
Identity Provider	Enable Salesforce.com as an identity provider so that you can use single sign-on with other websites, and define the appropriate service providers whose applications support single sign-on. You can switch to different service providers without having to log in again.
View Setup Audit Trail	The setup audit trail is used to track the recent changes that admins have made to the organization. This is a very important feature when you have multiple administrators in your organization. It shows the last 20 setup changes made to your organization. Also, you can download your organization's setup audit trail for the last six months in a CSV file format.
Expire All Passwords	This security setting is to "expire" the passwords for all the users in your organization. The next time they log in, they will be asked to set their passwords to a new value. After you "expire" passwords, users might complete the identity confirmation challenge to successfully log in to Salesforce. We discussed about this under the *Activations* section. This security setting helps you to enforce extra security for your organization. Expiring all user passwords does not affect self-service portal users, because they are not direct Salesforce users.
Delegated Administration	You can define delegated groups for your organization. You can choose to delegate user administration, custom object administration, or both for the delegated administrators of this group. Therefore, you can use delegated administration to assign limited administrative privileges to the selected non-administrator users in your organization.

Security Setting	Features
HTML Documents and Attachments Settings	This setting is to disallow users from uploading HTML files to the Document object or as an attachment. If you enable this, users cannot upload the following file extensions as a document or an attachment: htm, html, htt, htx, mhtm, mhtml, shtm, shtml, and acgi.

User security

The user security plays a very significant role in the security of the Force.com platform. In the Force.com platform, user management is easier than other cloud platforms and traditional software development.

The User is a standard object in the Force.com platform. You can see the attributes of the User object (such as **Fields**, **Page Layouts**, **Related Lookup Filters**, **Validation Rules**, **Triggers**, **Field Sets**, **Compact Layouts**, **Search Layouts**, **Limits**, **Custom Links**) by navigating to **Customize | Users**.

> You can create custom fields for the User object and add custom links to the User details page.

The administrators can view and manage the users of your organization by navigating to **Setup | Administer | Manage Users | Users**.

This user list shows all the users in your organization, partner portal, and Salesforce customer portal. Under the **Manage Users** tab, you can do following operations:

- Create a single user
- Create multiple users
- View the list of users
- View a user's details page
- Reset the password for selected users
- Edit single user records
- If Google Apps is enabled in your organization, you can export users to Google and create Google Apps accounts by clicking on **Export to Google Apps**

Let's find out how we can create a single user in your organization. Keep in mind that the maximum number of users is defined by your edition of the organization. Use the following steps to create a single user in your organization:

1. Navigate to **Setup | Administer | Manage Users | Users**.
2. Click on **New User**.
3. Then you will see the following screen:

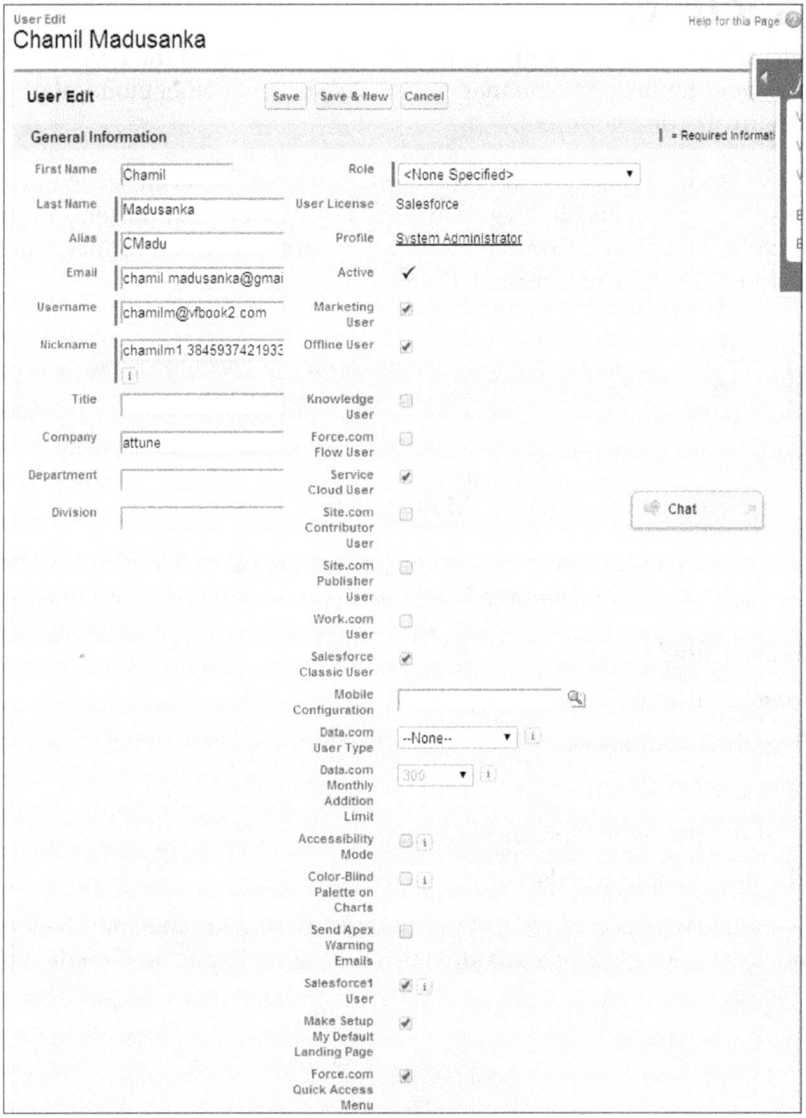

Create/Edit User record

4. Enter the user's **First Name** and **Last Name**.

5. Enter the user's **Email** and the **Username**, and **Nickname** will be populated from the **Email**. However, you can change the **Username** and the **Nickname** as you desire.

> The **Username** must be in email format. For example, chamil@eleaveforce.com.

6. Select a **Role**. Roles can define the degree of visibility that users have into the organization's data. It depends on your organization's willingness to disclose information. We will discuss more about this in the next couple of sections.

> Currently, **Role** selection is available in only Professional, Enterprise, Unlimited, Performance, and Developer editions. It is an optional field.

7. Select a **User License**.

8. Select a **Profile**. The **Profile** depends on the selected **User License**. For example, if you want to create a user with the System Administrator profile, you must select the **Salesforce** user license for that particular user.

> As with **Profile**, some options are dependent upon the selected user license. For example, the **Marketing User** and **Allow Forecasting** checkbox options are unavailable for the Force.com user license.

9. Select other options accordingly and enter the remaining user information as required.

10. If your organization has enabled the approvals, you can specify the particular user's approver settings with the manager, delegated approver, and the preference of receiving approval request emails. The **Approver Settings** of the user creation is shown in the following screenshot:

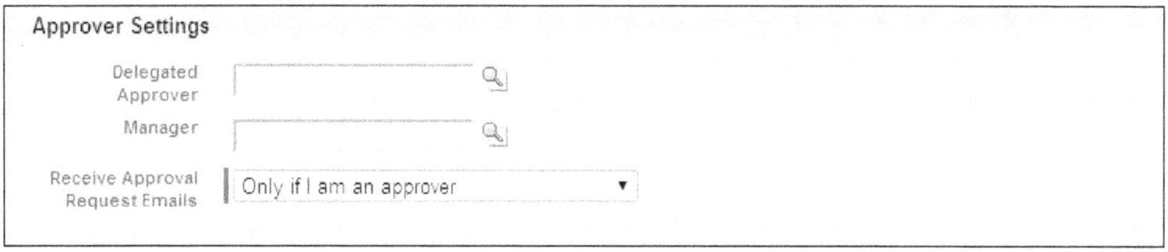

Approver setting in the user record

11. Click on **Save** to commit the created user record.

Let's find out how we can create multiple users in your organization. This feature provides a way to quickly create user records in your organization. You can create up to 10 users with this feature. However, it depends on the number of available user licenses in your organization.

Use the following steps to create multiple users in your organization:

1. Navigate to **Setup** | **Administer** | **Manage Users** | **Users**.

2. Click on **Add Multiple Users**.

3. Then you will see the following screen:

Users   Help for this Page

Add Multiple Users

Number of available Identity user licenses: 10
Number of available Chatter External user licenses: 500
Number of available Work.com Only user licenses: 3
Number of available Chatter Free user licenses: 5000
Number of available Force.com - Free user licenses: 2
Number of available Salesforce Platform user licenses: 3
Number of available Salesforce user licenses: 1
Number of available Partner App Subscription user licenses: 2
Number of available Force.com - App Subscription user licenses: 2

Add Users   Cancel

Collapse All   Expand All
attune
    CEO
        CFO
        COO
        SVP, Customer Service & Support
            Customer Support, International

User License   --None--   ▼

                    Cancel

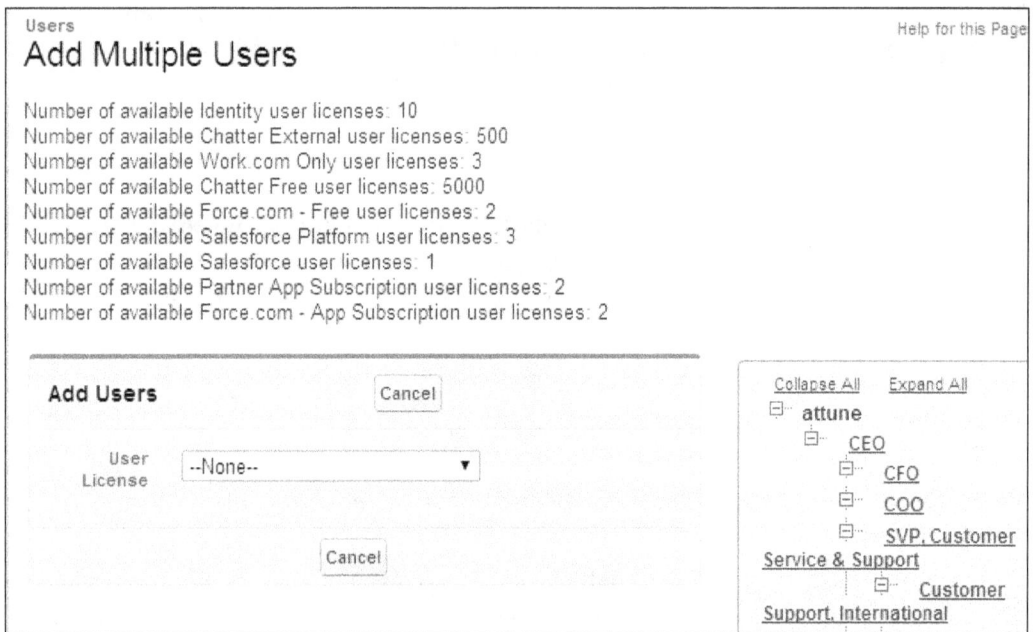

Add multiple users – Step 1

4. Choose a **User License** that you want to associate with user records which you wish to make. Then you will see the following screen. This screen will allow you to add multiple users depending on the number of available user licenses in your organization.

Add multiple users – Step 2

5. Enter the **First Name**, **Last Name**, **Email**, and **Profile** in the same way as the creation of the single user.

6. Select the **Generate passwords and notify user via email** option, if you want to generate the password and inform a particular user.

7. Click on **Save**.

Network-based security

Network-based security is one of the most interesting features in the Force.com platform. This security setting provides a level of network-based security that limits access to your organization based on the IP address of your client. You can whitelist IP addresses by defining the IP ranges that allow access to the organization. If the user's IP address is in a whitelisted IP range, that particular user can log in to the Salesforce.com organization without having to activate their computers (the logon challenge). This security setting helps to protect your organization's data from unauthorized access. You can define multiple trusted IP ranges in your organization.

You can define the whitelist for the entire organization by performing the following steps:

1. Navigate to **Setup | Security Controls | Network Access | New**.

Please specify IP range	▮ = Required Information
Start IP Address ▮ [ ]	End IP Address ▮ [ ]
Save Cancel	

Set the valid IP range

2. Enter the range of valid IP addresses (**Start IP Address** and **End IP Address**) from which user logins are trusted. Users logging in from trusted IP addresses are not asked to activate their computers and may use their user password instead of a security token to log in to the API or a desktop client such as Connect for Outlook, Connect Offline, Connect for Office, Connect for Lotus Notes, or the Data Loader.

> The start and end IP addresses in an IPv4 range must include no more than 33,554,432 addresses (225, a /7 CIDR block). Ranges such as 0.0.0.0 to 2.255.255.255 or 132.0.0.0 to 134.0.0.0 are too large.
>
> The start and end IP addresses in an IPv6 range must include no more than 79,228,162,514,264,337,593,543,950,336 addresses (296, a /32 CIDR block). Ranges such as :: to ffff:ffff:ffff:ffff:ffff:ffff:ffff:ffff or 2001:8000:: to 2001:8001:: are too large.

3. Click on **Save** to finish the creation of the IP range.

Session security

This security setting is to set the session security and session expiration timeout for your organization. This setting allows you to have a secure connection to the platform or lock a session to the originating IP address. For setting the session security in your organization, go to **Setup | Security Controls | Session Settings**.

You can customize the session settings from the following page;

Session Timeout

Timeout value   2 hours   ▼

☐ Disable session timeout warning popup
☐ Force logout on session timeout

Session Settings

☐ Lock sessions to the IP address from which they originated
☐ Lock sessions to the domain in which they were first used
✓ Require secure connections (HTTPS) i
☐ Force relogin after Login-As-User
☐ Require HttpOnly attribute
☐ Use POST requests for cross-domain sessions

Login Page Caching and Autocomplete

☑ Enable caching and autocomplete on login page

Identity Confirmation

✓ Enable SMS-based identity confirmation i
☐ Require security tokens for API logins from callouts (API version 31.0 and earlier)

Clickjack Protection

✓ Enable clickjack protection for setup pages i
✓ Enable clickjack protection for non-setup Salesforce pages i
☐ Enable clickjack protection for non-setup customer Visualforce pages with headers

Cross-Site Request Forgery (CSRF) Protection

✓ Enable CSRF protection on GET requests on non-setup pages i
✓ Enable CSRF protection on POST requests on non-setup pages i

Session Security Levels

Standard	High Assurance	
Username Password ▲	Two Factor Authentication ▲	Chat
Delegated Authentication		

Session Security page

Some of the important settings options are described in the following table:

Option	Description
Timeout value	Sets the time limit for an individual session. You can select the time value between 15 minutes and 12 hours. If a user's session is inactive for this selected time period, the user will get a warning popup. If the user still doesn't respond, the session ends. Therefore, the user has to log in again into the Force.com platform. After the end of the session, you cannot respond to the warning popup.
Disable session timeout warning popup	This setting is to define whether the warning popup we discussed in the preceding option needs to be prompted or not. This popup will be prompted 30 seconds before timeout value is specified.
Lock sessions to the IP address from which they originated	This option helps to prevent unauthorized persons from hijacking a valid session. It checks the user session for locking the IP address from the logged user.
Require secure connections (HTTPS)	This option is to determine whether HTTPS is required to log in or access Salesforce. By default, this option is enabled. The best practice is to keep it enabled.

For more details about these session security options, refer to
`https://help.salesforce.com/htviewhelpdoc?err=1&id=admin_sessions.`
`htm&siteLang=en_US`.

Administrative security

The Force.com platform has more in-built security features that can be used by the administrator to manage the permissions of each and every user of your organization. Therefore, the administrator can grant or deny access of the Force.com platform by using the following administrative security settings:

- Profiles and roles
- Administrative permissions and general user permissions
- Permission sets
- Groups
- Queues

Profiles and roles

In the Force.com platform, profiles and roles are defined as the data and other functional and administrative accessibility of users.

> The role determines what data the user can access, while the profile determines all the accessibility of the data for the particular user.
>
> A profile includes user permissions and access settings that control what users can do within the organization. Every user in the Salesforce organization must have a profile. The administrator can change the profile of any user. A user can have only one profile.

An organization has a set of standard profiles and administrators can create new custom profiles by cloning the standard profile. You can create, view, and edit profiles by navigating to **Setup** | **Manage Users** | **Profiles**. You can see the detail page of a profile by clicking on the profile name.

A profile controls following security aspects:

- System-level configuration (**Administrative permission** and **General User permission**)
- Apps that can be accessed by the user
- Tabs that can be accessed by the user
- CRUD permissions on objects
- Define the default record type and default page layout
- Define the fields that can be accessed by a user
- Define the accessible Visualforce pages and Apex classes
- Login hours and ID address range can be defined to the profile

Creating a custom profile

A custom profile can be created only by cloning a standard profile, which has limited editing facilities. Let's consider the creation of a custom profile for an employee:

1. Navigate to **Setup** | **Manage Users** | **Profiles**.
2. Click on the **New** button.
3. Select a standard profile to clone a new custom profile. Here, all the existing permissions of the selected standard profile will be copied to the newly created one. The new profile will use the same user license of the existing standard button. It's best practice to clone a read-only profile because it comes with restricted access.

4. Specify a name for the profile and click on **Save**. The new custom profile has been created and you can edit the profile according to your requirements. You can delete the custom profile but not the standard one.

5. There are a few categorized sections in the profile such as **Custom App Settings, Tab Settings, Object Permissions, Visualforce page permission, Apex class permission, Field level security permission, Administrative permission,** and **General permission. App Settings, Tab Settings, Record Type Settings, Object Permissions, Visualforce page permission, Apex class permission,** and **Field level security permission** will be discussed in the *Component-based security* section. As we discussed under the *Organization security* section, you can add the login hours and login IP ranges for the particular profile.

6. **Administrative permission** and **General User permission** will be discussed in the upcoming section (*Administrative permissions and general user permissions*).

Assigning roles

A role is like a public group that can include one or more users. The role hierarchy is like a set of interconnected public groups. Each organization has a corporate role hierarchy and roles are created according to that. The role hierarchy defines the data sharing among the users in your organization. You learned that profiles determine which objects can be accessed by the user. Roles determine which records can be accessed by the user.

To set up the role hierarchy of your organization, perform the following steps:

1. Navigate to **Setup | Manage Users | Roles**.

2. For the first timers, there will be a splash page with the **Set Up Roles** button. Click on the button to proceed.

3. You can set up the role hierarchy based on your territory, product, and company size. You can see the sample hierarchy that comes with a default organization, as shown in the following screenshot:

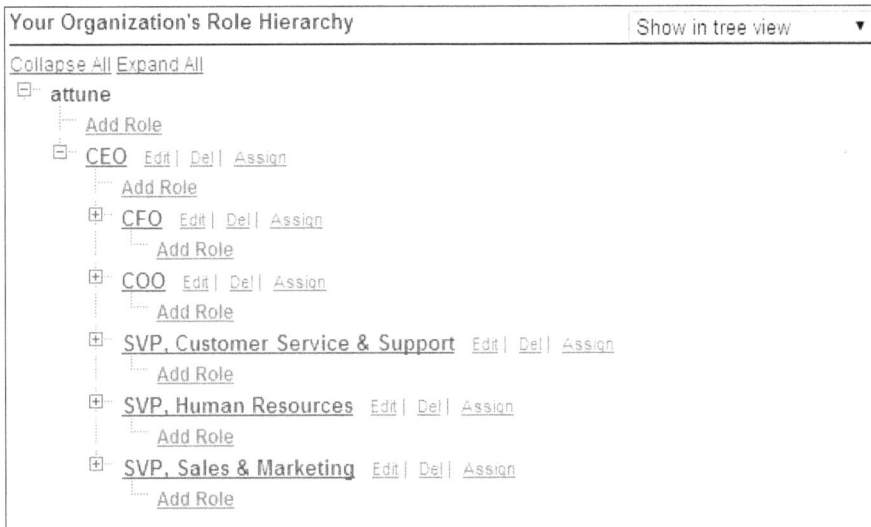

Organization's role hierarchy

This is your role hierarchy to control how your organization reports on and accesses data. All the superior roles have all the sharing permissions of roles below them in the hierarchy. Role hierarchy grants the permission in a one-way manner. For example, your manager has all the permissions you have, but you do not have all the permissions which are owned by your manager.

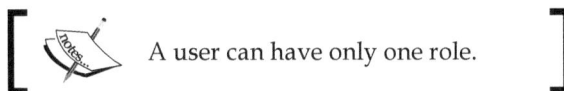

> A user can have only one role.

There are a few advantages of the role hierarchy in the Force.com platform:

- Salesforce recommends that roles aren't the actual hierarchy. The roles that we create in Salesforce just define the data access of the managers. Therefore, you don't need to build that sophisticated role hierarchy-based sharing model with an extra effort.

- In organization-wide defaults (you will learn this in the *Record-based security* section), you can define whether the role hierarchy should be used for the particular custom object or not to grant access to users whose role is superior in the hierarchy to a specified user. You can do that by selecting the **Grant Access Using Hierarchies** check box that is associated to the particular custom object.

Administrative permissions and general user permissions

There are two types of permissions in a profile: **Administrative permissions** and **General User permissions**. These permissions are used to manage system-level configuration (including security configurations) of the organization.

> The system administrator has the highest administrative permissions. Therefore, the system administrator profile has access to all the administrative permissions.

There are some special administrative permissions that are extremely powerful and important, which are as follows:

Permission	Description
Manage Users	This is the most powerful permission. A user who has this permission can create, edit, and deactivate users (including external users), by granting permissions to other users and themselves. A user with this permission is considered as a super administrator. They can manage security settings, including profiles and roles.
Customize Application	This permission allows a user to customize the organization using the **Setup** menu options such as: Edit messages and custom links, Modify standard picklist values, Create/edit/delete custom fields, Create/edit/delete page layouts, Set field-level security, Create/edit/delete custom links, Create record types, Set up business hours, Manage queues, Create/edit/delete workflow rules, tasks, field updates, outbound messages, and alerts, Create/edit/delete custom objects and custom tabs.

Permission	Description
View All Data **Modify All Data**	These permissions override any of the restrictions on the data of objects and the record-based sharing in the organization. We will discuss more about record-based sharing in the *Record-based security* section. The System Administrator has these permissions and can grant these permissions to others as well. The **Modify All Data** permission grants full object-level access (Create, Read, Update, and Delete) to the particular user. If you develop an Apex code, then you need this permission.
API Enabled	This permission grants access to any Salesforce API. It allows access to the platform from an external environment using the APIs.
View Setup and Configuration	This permission allows a user to see the organization's setup and configuration page. However, the user cannot change any information on these pages.

We just discussed important administrative permissions. The entire list of administrative and general user permissions is available at `https://help. salesforce.com/apex/HTViewHelpDoc?id=admin_userperms.htm&language=en`.

Permission sets

Similar to the profile, a permission set is a set of permission and security settings to grant access to functions and data. Although a permission set has the same settings and permissions of profiles, a permission set is used to extend the user's functional access without changing the profile. Let's consider a scenario where we can use a permission set in our organization. Let's consider that we have four users and their required permissions and settings are almost equal. However, eventually, we decide to assign two additional permissions and particular settings to one user. Here you can create a second profile and re-assign permissions to the particular user. But that is not the best way. Therefore, you can keep the profile unchanged and can create a permission set by defining the additional permissions. Then you can assign that permission set to that particular user. Therefore, the best practice is to create a profile for a common use case and additional permissions are assigned via permission sets. Then you never need to change the profile.

> While users can have only one profile, they can have multiple permission sets.

A permission set can be included in the following settings:

- **Assigned apps**: These are the settings that specify which apps are visible in the app menu
- **Assigned connected apps**: These are the settings that specify which connected apps are visible in the app menu
- **Object settings** (Tab settings, Record type settings, Object permissions, Field permissions): These are the permissions to access objects and fields, and settings such as tab availability
- **App Settings**: These are the permissions to perform app-specific actions, such as Manage Call Centers
- **Apex class access permissions**: These are the permissions to execute Apex classes
- **Visualforce page access permissions**: These are the permissions to execute Visualforce pages
- **System permissions**: These are the permissions to perform actions that apply across apps, such as Modify All Data

If your organization is enabled as an identity provider, then you can include service provider settings.

Let's consider the permission set creation process. Use the following steps to create a permission set:

1. Navigate to **Setup | Manage Users | Permission sets**.
2. Click on the **New** button. Then the following page will be displayed:

Creating a permission set

The properties of creating a permission set of the Force.com platform are described as follows:

- **Label**: This is the name to identify the permission set.

- **API Name**: This is a unique name used by the API. This name must begin with a letter and must use only alphanumeric characters and underscores. It can't include spaces, end with an underscore, or have two consecutive underscores.

- **User License**: This requires you to select a user license. The user license determines which permission sets can be assigned to a user. For example, a permission set with the Salesforce user license can only be assigned to users with the Salesforce license. If you select **--None--**, you can assign this permission set to any user as long as the enabled permissions are allowed in the user's license.

3. Click on **Save**. Then, according to your requirements, you can set the permission through the following page:

Permission set detail page

Permission setting for a permission set is similar to that of a profile. **App Settings, Tab Settings, Record Type Settings, Object Permissions, Visualforce page permission, Apex class permission**, and **Field level security permission** will be discussed in the *Component-based security* section.

Groups

A public group is a set of users. It can contain individual users, other groups as subgroups, the users in a particular role or territory, or the users in a role or territory plus all the users included in that role or territory in the hierarchy.

There are two types of groups, which are as follows:

- **Public groups**: This type of group can be created by the administrator and they can be used by everyone in the organization
- **Personal groups**: This type of group is created for personal usage by any user

Groups can be used in the following scenarios:

- When you want to set up default sharing access via a sharing rule. Sharing rules will be explained under the *Record-based security* section
- To share your records with other users
- To specify that you want to synchronize contacts owned by other users
- To add multiple users to a Salesforce CRM content library
- To assign users to specific actions in Salesforce knowledge

When you are creating a public group, you want to consider the following facts to optimize the performance of a public group:

- If you have few users who need the same access, then create a group
- If the members of the group do not change frequently, then the group is the best
- Do not create nested groups of more than five levels
- When you create a public group, select **Grant Access Using Hierarchies**; if you want to, you can share records with users in this group and these records are also shared with users higher in the role hierarchy

Queues

A queue is a special type of group that is used to manage shared workload more effectively. You can specify the set of objects that are supported by each queue, as well as the set of users that are allowed to retrieve records from the queue. The specified object records remain in the queue until a specified user accepts them for processing or they are transferred to another queue. Therefore, a queue is considered as the location where records can be routed to await processing by a group member.

Perform the following steps to create a queue in your organization:

1. Navigate to **Setup** | **Manage Users** | **Queues** | **New**.

2. In the page you get, click on the **New** button; you can specify the name of the queue and the e-mail address to use when sending notifications (for example, when a case has been put in the queue). The email address can be for an individual or a distribution list. When an object is assigned to a queue, only the queue members will be notified.

3. Select the objects you want to assign to this queue. Individual records for those objects can then be owned by this queue.

4. To add members to this queue, select a type of member, then choose the group, role, or user from the **Available Members** and move them to **Selected Members**. If the sharing model for all objects in the queue is Public Read/Write/Transfer, you do not need to assign users to the queue, as all users already have access to the records for those objects.

5. Click on **Save**. Now your queue has been created.

Component-based security

In the earlier sections, you have seen that the profiles and permission sets can be used to define permissions when you create your application and custom objects. Therefore, profiles and permission sets are used for user-based permissions. They can be used to grant profiles for different types of components, which is called component-based security. The following are the different types of component-based security settings:

- Application permissions
- Tab permissions
- Record type permissions
- Apex class and Visualforce page permissions
- Object permissions
- Field-level security permissions

Application permissions

This type of permission allows you to grant access to an application by setting the visibility of the **App Menu** in the top-right corner. If a logged in user doesn't have permission for a particular application, then that application doesn't appear in the **App Menu**. You can specify the default application for a profile and that app will be selected after the user logs in to the organization. If the user changes the selected application to another application, the user's last application is retained the next time the user logs in. There are two places where you can grant access to the particular applications: from the **Profile** and from the **Permission Sets**.

Custom App Settings				Visible	Default		= Required Information
	Visible	Default					
App Launcher	✔	○	Sales	✔	○		
Call Center	✔	○	Salesforce Chatter	✔	○		
Community	✔	○	Sample Console	☐	○		
Content	✔	○	Site.com	✔	○		
eLeaveForce	✔	●	Work.com	✔	○		
Marketing	✔	○					

Custom App Settings

The previous screenshot is from the profile we created in the *Profiles and roles* section. When you are editing the profile, you will find this portion to specify the application's permission settings.

Tab permissions

You have already learned about types of tabs and different ways of creating tabs. When you create a tab, you have the facility to specify which profiles will be allowed to access this tab as the step 2 of tab creation. You can specify the tab permission when you create or modify a profile.

Tab Settings		
☐ Overwrite users' personal tab customizations		

Standard Tab Settings

Home	Default On		Groups	Default On ▾	
Accounts	Default On ▾		Ideas	Default On ▾	
App Launcher	Default On ▾		Leads	Default On ▾	
Campaigns	Default On ▾		Libraries	Default On ▾	
Cases	Default On ▾		Opportunities	Default On ▾	
Chatter	Default On ▾		People	Default On ▾	
Coaching	Default On ▾		Performance	Default On ▾	
Console	Tab Hidden		Price Books	Default Off ▾	

Tab Settings

The preceding screenshot is a tab settings section in a profile. You can specify the tab permissions for standard tabs as well as custom tabs. There are three permission options for a tab:

- **Tab Hidden**: The user with this tab setting cannot access the particular tab in their organization.
- **Default On**: This setting adds the tab in the tab list and shows it in the tab menu.
- **Default Off**: This setting adds tab to the tab list but is not shown in the tab menu. It could be seen after clicking on the plus button in the tab section.

A particular user can customize the tabs using the following path:

Click on all tab buttons (+) at the right of the tab set and then navigate to **Customize My Tabs | Your Name | My Settings | Display & Layout | Customize My Tab**.

The user can customize their tabs by adding tabs with the **Default Off** setting; change the position of the tab within the tab menu.

Record type permissions

Record types allow you to assign different page layouts and picklist values to different profiles. Record types are defined for objects. Any object in your organization can have more than one record type. Record types use different page layouts. Therefore, you have to create another page layout for the Leave object. Let's create a record type for the Leave object. Perform the following steps:

1. Navigate to **Setup** | **Create** | **Objects** | **Leave**.

2. Click on **New** in the **Page Layout** section.

3. As an option, you may select an existing layout to clone. If you create a page layout without cloning, your page layout will not include the standard sections whose names are translated for your international users.

4. Specify a name for **Page Layout** and click on **Next**.

5. According to your requirements, you can change your page layout, which you learned about in *Chapter 3, Building the User Interface*.

You can create a record type for the Leave object by using the following steps:

1. Navigate to **Setup** | **Create** | **Object** | **Leave**.

2. Click on **New** in the **Record Type** section.

3. Leave the **Master record** type as the **Existing Record Type**.

4. Enter a name and description for the new record type. The new record type will include all the picklist values from the existing record type selected below. After saving the new record type, you will be able to customize the picklist values.

5. Select the **Enable for Profile** checkbox to make the new record type available to a profile. Users assigned to this profile will be able to create records of this record type, or assign this record type to existing records. To make the new record type the default for a profile, select the **Make Default** checkbox.

6. Click on **Next**.

7. Select the page layout that users with this profile see for records with this record type. After saving, choose the picklist values that are available with this record type.

8. Click on **Save**.

9. Then the available picklists of the object will be listed and you can edit the picklist values for the record type.

10. Select an item from the **Available Values** list and add it to the **Selected Values** list to include it as a picklist value for this record type. Note that removing an item from the picklist does not remove it from any existing records. Finally, select a default picklist value for this record type.

11. Click on **Save**.

Now you have the record type and you can use that to define multiple user interfaces for the data stored in the same object.

Apex class and Visualforce page permissions

Visualforce pages and Apex classes are used to extend the standard functionality of the Force.com platform. You can create custom pages using Visualforce pages and define the procedural functionality using Apex classes. You will learn how to define Apex classes in *Chapter 7, Custom Coding with Apex* and Visualforce pages in *Chapter 8, Building Custom Pages with Visualforce*.

Enabled Apex Class Access	Edit	Enabled Apex Class Access Help ?
No Apex Classes enabled		

Enabled Visualforce Page Access	Edit	Enabled Visualforce Page Access Help ?
Visualforce Page Name	AppExchange Package Name	
SampleVisualforceTab		

Enable access for Apex classes and Visualforce page from the Profile page

For now, you just need to know that you can prevent users from accessing Apex classes and Visualforce pages. Apex classes are running in system mode, not user mode. User permissions associated within the profile or permission set are not influenced for the execution of the classes. Therefore, you can give profile permissions to access individual Apex classes and Visualforce pages through the profiles page or permissions set page.

Object permissions

Object permissions are mainly based on the **CRUD** permission settings. CRUD stands for **Create, Read, Update, and Delete**. From the custom profiles and permission sets, you can set the CRUD permissions for standard objects and custom objects.

The following screenshot depicts the two sections to determine the object permissions from a custom profile:

	Read	Create	Edit	Delete	View All	Modify All
Accounts	✓	✓	✓	✓	✓	✓
Assets	✓	✓	✓	✓	✓	✓
Campaigns	✓	✓	✓	✓	✓	✓
Cases	✓	✓	✓	✓	✓	✓
Coaching	✓	✓	✓	✓	✓	✓
Contacts	✓	✓	✓	✓	✓	✓
Contracts	✓	✓	✓	✓	✓	✓
Documents	✓	✓	✓	✓	✓	✓
Feedback	✓	✓	✓	✓	✓	✓
Feedback Questions	✓	✓	✓	✓	✓	✓
Feedback Question Sets	✓	✓	✓	✓	✓	✓
Feedback Requests	✓	✓	✓	✓	✓	✓

	Read	Create	Edit	Delete	View All	Modify All
Goals	✓	✓	✓	✓	✓	✓
Goal Collaborators	✓	✓	✓	✓	✓	✓
Goal Links	✓	✓	✓	✓	✓	✓
Ideas	✓	✓	✓	✓		
Leads	✓	✓	✓	✓	✓	✓
Opportunities	✓	✓	✓	✓	✓	✓
Performance Cycles	✓	✓	✓	✓	✓	✓
Price Books	✓	✓	✓	✓		
Products	✓	✓	✓	✓		
Push Topics	✓	✓	✓	✓		
Solutions	✓	✓	✓	✓	✓	✓

Custom Object Permissions

	Basic Access				Data Administration	
	Read	Create	Edit	Delete	View All	Modify All
Employees	✓	✓	✓	✓	✓	✓
Holiday Calendars	✓	✓	✓	✓	✓	✓
Leaves	✓	✓	✓	✓	✓	✓

	Basic Access				Data Administration	
	Read	Create	Edit	Delete	View All	Modify All
Leave Categories	✓	✓	✓	✓	✓	✓
Leave Configurations	✓	✓	✓	✓	✓	✓
Leave Types	✓	✓	✓	✓	✓	✓

Object-level permissions

CRUD permissions can be elaborated as follows:

- **Read**: This option grants the particular user the read permission for the particular object records. This permission is required to have Create, Edit, and Delete permissions. If you remove this Read permission, Create, Edit, and Delete permissions will be automatically cleared.
- **Create**: This option grants the particular object record creation, and if you take this option, the Read permission is automatically granted.
- **Edit**: This option grants the particular object record update permission, and if you take this option, the Read permission is automatically granted.
- **Delete**: This option grants the particular object record delete permission, and if you take this option, the Read permission is automatically granted.

Object permissions control the associated object components such as tab accessibility and report. If a particular user doesn't have Read permission, that user cannot access the object associated components. You can specify the object permissions from the permission sets as well.

Field-level security permissions

In the *Object permissions* section, you learnt how to specify the object-level permissions. In the Force.com platform, you can also define permissions on individual object fields. There are two types of security options in field-level security:

- **Visible**: This option controls the visibility of the particular object field. If you remove the visible permission, the particular field cannot be marked as read-only.

- **Read Only**: This option limits a particular field to read-only access.

The field-level security permissions can be defined from either the **Profile** page or the add/edit object field wizard, or **Permission Sets** page. The following screenshot shows the section to define the field-level security from the **Profile** page:

Standard Field-Level Security			
Account	[View]	Goal Collaborator	[View]
Asset	[View]	Goal Link	[View]
Campaign	[View]	Idea	[View]
Campaign Member	[View]	Lead	[View]
Case	[View]	Opportunity	[View]
Coaching	[View]	Opportunity Product	[View]
Contact	[View]	Performance Cycle	[View]
Contract	[View]	Price Book	[View]
Event	[View]	Product	[View]
Feedback	[View]	Social Persona	[View]
Feedback Question	[View]	Solution	[View]
Feedback Question Set	[View]	Task	[View]
Feedback Request	[View]	User	[View]
Goal	[View]		
Custom Field-Level Security			
Employee	[View]	Leave Category	[View]
Holiday Calendar	[View]	Leave Configuration	[View]
Leave	[View]	Leave Type	[View]

Click on the associated **View** link of the object for which you want to define the field-level security. In the redirected field-level security for the profile page, you can specify the field-level security permissions according to your requirements.

> The field-level security affects the view and access fields through the standard interfaces (page layouts and reports) of the Force.com platform.

Record-based security

In the Force.com security framework, we covered all the security methods that protect the Force.com platform environment, functionality, and components you create. The Force.com platform has another security method that protects all the records in an object by defining different record access levels.

Record-based security affects individual rows of data in a single object. There are different sets of tools and concepts to define the record-based security in your organization:

- Record ownership
- Organization-wide defaults (OWD)
- Record sharing

The record-based permissions are not taken as independent, but are combined with the object permissions. Object permissions grant access to an object and all the records of that particular object. Therefore, access to individual records can be limited through record-based sharing, only if the particular user has the permission to access data in an object. If the user doesn't have the object permission, record-based sharing cannot grant access to the object.

Record ownership

The record ownership is the main concept behind record-based permissions. The owner has all the permissions to the record, including create, update, read, delete, transfer ownership to another user, and share the record to another user or user group.

When a user creates a record, record creator is the owner of that record. The current owner or users with **Modify All Permission** or users whose role is above the owner in the role hierarchy can change the owner of the record to another user or a queue. The ownership transfer can be done through the standard interface, data loader, as well as through Apex code. You will learn the ownership transfer through Apex in a later chapter.

The ownership transfer through the standard interface can be done by clicking on the **Change** link, which is next to the owner name in the **Record Detail** page. The following screenshot shows an **Employee Detail** page and the highlighted section contains the **Change** link that can be used to transfer the record ownership:

Employee Detail	Edit Delete Clone		
Employee Name	Chamil Madusanka	Owner	Chamil Madusanka [Change]
First Name	Chamil		
Last Name	Madusanka		

Change the owner of the record

Organization-wide defaults

The **organization-wide defaults** (OWD) sharing setting is the baseline level of access for each object and enables you to extend that level of accessing hierarchies or sharing rules. To set up OWDs, perform the following steps:

1. Navigate to **Setup | Security Controls | Sharing Settings**.

2. Click on **Edit** under **Organization-Wide Defaults**. The following screen will be displayed:

Object	Default Internal Access	Default External Access	Grant Access Using Hierarchies
Lead	Public Read/Write/Transfer	Public Read/Write/Transfer	✓
Account, Contract and Asset	Public Read/Write	Public Read/Write	✓
Contact	Controlled by Parent	Controlled by Parent	✓
Opportunity	Public Read/Write	Public Read/Write	✓
Case	Public Read/Write/Transfer	Public Read/Write/Transfer	✓
Campaign	Public Full Access	Public Full Access	✓
User	Public Read Only	Private	✓
Activity	Private	Private	✓
Calendar	Hide Details and Add Events	Hide Details and Add Events	✓
Price Book	Use	Use	✓
Employee	Public Read/Write	Public Read/Write	✓
Holiday Calendar	Public Read/Write	Public Read/Write	✓
Leave Category	Public Read/Write	Public Read/Write	✓
Leave Type	Public Read/Write	Public Read/Write	✓

User Visibility Settings

Standard Report Visibility ☐

Setting up organization-wide defaults

In this screen, you can change the **Default Internal Access** of every object except the child objects of master-detail relationships. Mainly, there are three options to select as **Default Internal Access**, which are as follows:

- **Private**: If you select this option for an object, the particular object's records can be accessed only by the owner of the record and users with **Modify All Data**, **View All Data** permissions. Users across the hierarchy cannot view their peer records.

- **Public Read Only**: This option allows all users to read all the records in an object. In this case, users across the hierarchy can view all the records of the object.

- **Public Read/Write**: If you select this option, everyone can view, edit, and delete records of the object. It depends on the user's profile permissions.

> This organization-wide default does not grant, delete, transfer, or share permissions. These are only available to owners of a record. If you select the **Grant Access Using Hierarchies** check box, it means that a particular object's records are obedient to the role hierarchies.

In your organization, you need to have a better record-based permission setup. For that, you have to follow these golden rules:

- **Set the access to all records for an object with the lowest level of permission**: In the Force.com platform, you can follow this rule by OWD. You can use the private option for objects.

- **Then grant the access to particular records for particular users**: In the Force. com platform, you can share the particular records for particular users or user groups. Record sharing will be discussed in the next section.

> Changing these defaults will cause all sharing rules to be recalculated. This could require significant system resources and time, depending on the amount of data in your organization. Setting an object to **Private** makes records visible to record owners and those above them in the role hierarchy and access can be extended using sharing rules.

Record sharing

In the preceding section, you learned to lock down the data in an object using OWD. If you lock down the records, how will the user access the records? Then we need that 2nd rule that we discussed in the OWD section, which is granting access to particular records for particular users by record sharing.

When a record is shared with the user, the particular user can access the record as you defined in the sharing model. There are three levels of sharing access: **Private**, **Read Only**, and **Read/Write**. With these access levels, you can use sharing to assign rights that are greater than the OWDs.

> You can share the records, if the records are **Only Private** or **Public Read Only** but not **Public Read/Write** in OWDs.

There are three ways that you can share a record, which are as follows:

- **Manual Sharing**: This option is available for only users who have full access to the records and that particular object has an OWD other than Public Read/Write. Only the record owner and users above the owner in the role hierarchy are granted full access to the record. You cannot grant full access to another user. If any record fulfills the above requirements, the **Sharing** button displays on the **Record Detail** page. You can share a record with a particular user or group of users.

> If a user has the **Modify All** administrative permission or **Modify All Data** administrative permission for a particular object, then that particular user can use manually shared records of that particular object.

- **Sharing Rules**: There are many scenarios that need automatic sharing within your application. In the Force.com platform, you can use sharing rules to make automatic exceptions to your organization-wide sharing settings for defined sets of users.

> You cannot grant sharing, delete, or transfer permissions that are greater than the privileges you possess for the record.

To define a sharing rule, perform the following steps:

1. Navigate to **Setup** | **Security Controls** | **Sharing Settings**.

2. The sharing rules section is in the latter part of the page as shown in the partial screenshot.

Employee Sharing Rules	New	Recalculate	Employee Sharing Rules Help (?)
No sharing rules specified.			
Holiday Calendar Sharing Rules	New	Recalculate	Holiday Calendar Sharing Rules Help (?)
No sharing rules specified.			
Leave Category Sharing Rules	New	Recalculate	Leave Category Sharing Rules Help (?)
No sharing rules specified.			
Leave Type Sharing Rules	New	Recalculate	Leave Type Sharing Rules Help (?)
No sharing rules specified.			

Sharing rules and recalculate

3. Click on the **New** button of the particular Sharing Rule section that you want to define a sharing rule for. You will see the following screenshot. You can define the sharing rule based on the owner of the record or criteria.

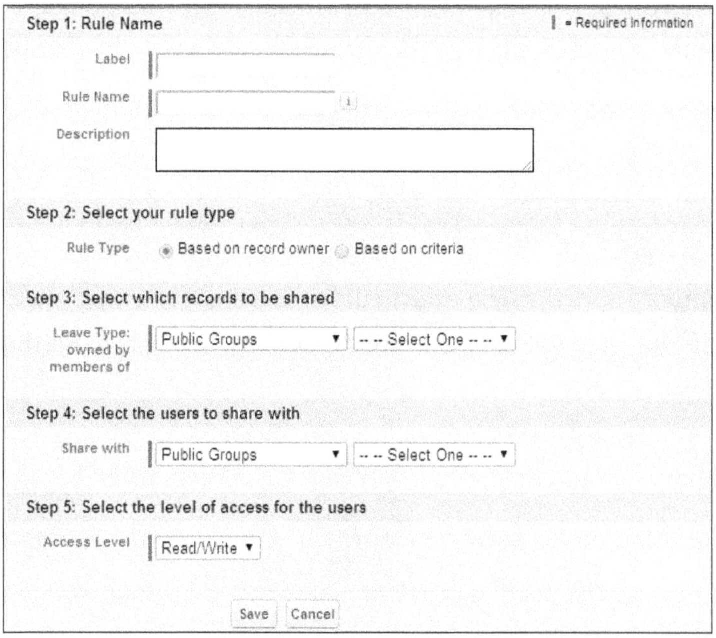

Step 1: Rule Name   I = Required Information

Label |

Rule Name | (i)

Description

Step 2: Select your rule type

Rule Type   ⦿ Based on record owner ◯ Based on criteria

Step 3: Select which records to be shared

Leave Type: | Public Groups ▾ | -- -- Select One -- -- ▾
owned by
members of

Step 4: Select the users to share with

Share with | Public Groups ▾ | -- -- Select One -- -- ▾

Step 5: Select the level of access for the users

Access Level | Read/Write ▾

Save   Cancel

Define your Sharing Rules

> Roles and subordinates include all users in a role, and the roles below that role. You can use sharing rules only to grant wider access to data, not to restrict access.

If you change the sharing rule, then you have to click on the **Recalculate** button, which is located on the **Sharing Setting** page. After you click on the particular **Recalculate** button, the sharing changes of particular object records will be affected.

- **Apex Sharing**: When we use manual sharing or sharing rules, the record owner can delete any sharing rule or manual shares. This can be a serious problem when it comes to critical functionalities. You can use Apex Sharing for such scenarios.

Apex managed sharing allows developers to programmatically share custom objects. When you use Apex managed sharing to share a custom object, only users with the **Modify All Data** permission can add or change the sharing on the custom object's record, and the sharing access is maintained across record owner changes.

You need to define sharing reasons to process Apex-based sharing for the particular object. Apex sharing reasons are used by developers when sharing a record programmatically. Using an Apex sharing reason prevents standard users from deleting the sharing and allows the developer to track why they added the sharing. To add the sharing reason, perform the following steps:

1. Navigate to **Setup** | **Create** | **Objects**.
2. Click on an object name (**Leave Category**).
3. Scroll down to the **Apex Sharing Reason** section.
4. Click on **New**.
5. Specify **Reason Label** and **Reason Name**.
6. Click on **Save**.

After you create an **Apex Reason**, you can share records through Apex code by specifying the **Sharing Reason**. The user cannot delete any share that is related to a sharing reason. You can retrieve all the shared records for a particular sharing reason using the Apex data access statement. You will learn more about the Apex sharing with the Apex code in *Chapter 7, Custom Coding with Apex*.

Summary

In this chapter, you learned the design considerations that you need to consider on Force.com applications, which accommodates multiple users and the security framework of the Force.com platform. You learned about a Force.com user license that is needed for each and every user. In the main section of the chapter, we understood about the Force.com platform security framework. Under the Force.com security framework, you learned Organization security, User security, Network-based security, Session security, Administrative security, Component-based security, and Record-based security. Now we have completed the most important chapter in this book.

In next chapter, we will cover implementing business logic in the Force.com platform.

5
Implementing Business Processes

The business process is the brain of the application. It controls the data and the functionality according to the requirement. The Force.com platform provides built-in features that help to protect the data quality using validation rules and automate the business processes using workflows and approval processes. This chapter covers the following topics:

- Preserving data quality with validation rules
- Automating the business process using workflows
- Automating the business process using approval processes

Let's implement the business logic for the Force.com application.

Preserving data quality with validation rules

Validations are common in any application. Suppose, the user has to enter a date value in a particular field. However, this date must be a future date. You have to validate the particular field. In the Force.com platform, the validation rules are there to fulfill your validation requirement.

The validation rules verify the user input data in a record against the criteria you define in the formula or the expression of the validation rule. A validation rule is associated with an object field. When a record is created or updated, the particular validation rules are executed. Define a validation rule by specifying an error condition and a corresponding error message. The error condition is written as a Boolean formula expression that returns true or false. When the formula expression returns true, the save will be aborted and the error message will be displayed. The user can correct the error and try again.

> The Force.com platform has some default validations, which are associated with field types. For example, the e-mail field type has the validation for an e-mail format, the phone field type has the related validations to input the phone number, and the number field type cannot contain any string value. With the validation rules, you can build custom validations in addition to default validations.

Validation rules are used for the following requirements in the Force.com platform:

- Enforcing conditionally required fields
- Enforcing proper data format
- Enforcing consistency
- Preventing data loss

Defining validation rules

Let's define a validation rule for the **Social Security Number** field of the Employee object. This validation rule will throw an error if the input of the **Social Security Number** field is incorrect. Use the following steps to define the validation rule for the **Social Security Number** field of the Employee object:

1. Navigate to **Setup | Create | Objects**.
2. Click on the **Employee** object.
3. Scroll down to the **Validation Rules** section.

4. Click on the **New** button of the **Validation Rules** section. The following screen will be displayed:

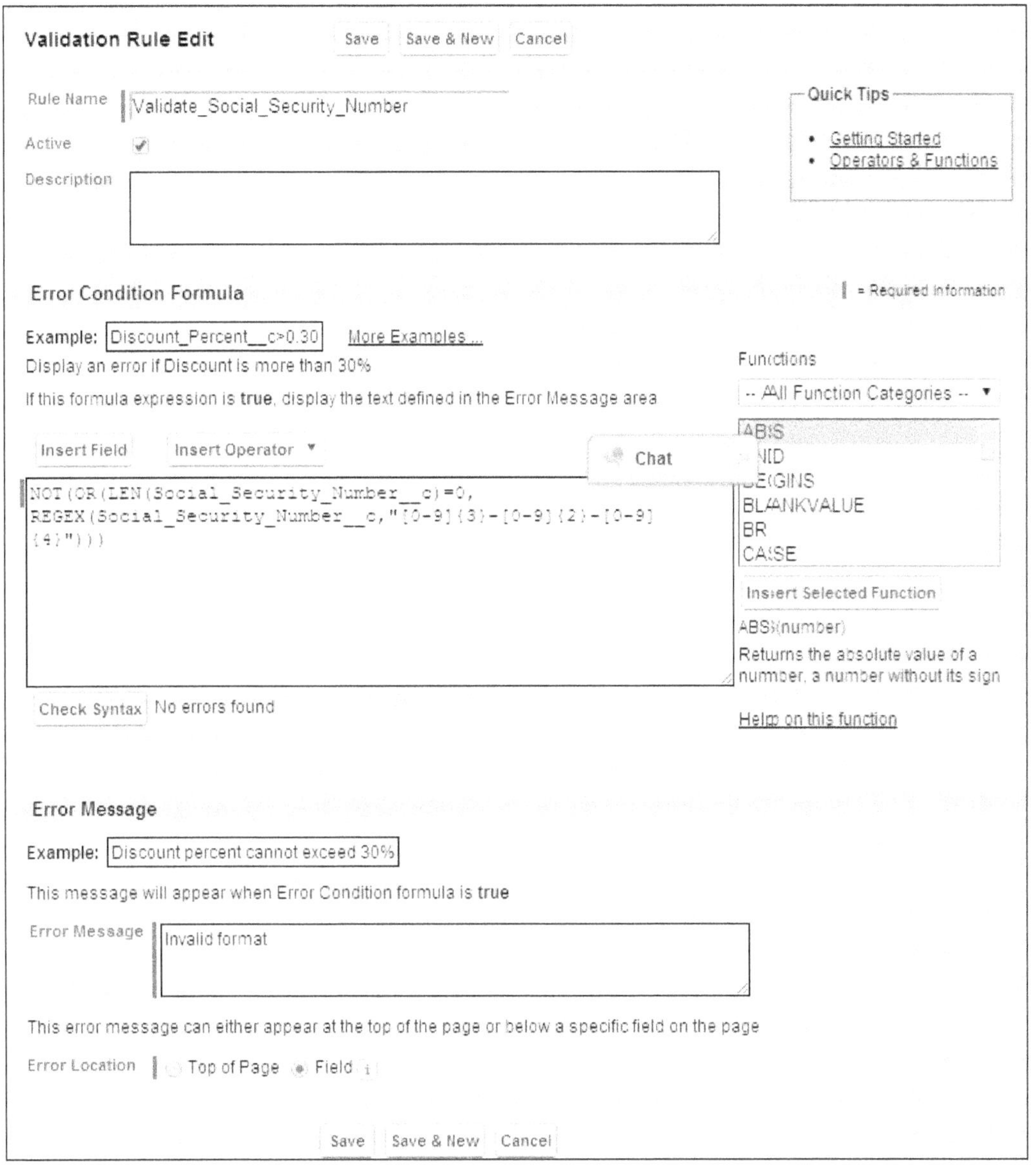

Validation Rule Edit   Save   Save & New   Cancel

Rule Name | Validate_Social_Security_Number

Active   ☑

Description

Quick Tips

- Getting Started
- Operators & Functions

Error Condition Formula | = Required Information

Example: | Discount_Percent__c>0.30 | More Examples ...

Display an error if Discount is more than 30%

If this formula expression is **true**, display the text defined in the Error Message area

Functions

-- All Function Categories -- ▼

Insert Field   Insert Operator ▼   🗨 Chat

```
NOT(OR(LEN(Social_Security_Number__c)=0,
REGEX(Social_Security_Number__c,"[0-9]{3}-[0-9]{2}-[0-9]
{4}")))
```

ABS
AND
BEGINS
BLANKVALUE
BR
CASE

Insert Selected Function

ABS(number)

Returns the absolute value of a number, a number without its sign

Check Syntax | No errors found

Help on this function

Error Message

Example: | Discount percent cannot exceed 30% |

This message will appear when Error Condition formula is **true**

Error Message | Invalid format

This error message can either appear at the top of the page or below a specific field on the page

Error Location | ○ Top of Page ● Field ℹ

Save   Save & New   Cancel

Defining validation rules in the Employee object

5. **Rule Name**: This property is a unique identifier that can contain up to 40 characters, no spaces, or special characters such as extended characters.

6. **Active**: You can use this check-box to specify whether the particular rule is enabled or disabled.

7. **Description**: A 255 character or less description that identifies the validation rule from others. This description is only used for internal purposes such as understanding the validation rule from the list of validation rules without seeing the detail page of the validation rule and it's a good practice to have the description, so it is easier to know why a validation rule was created.

8. **Error Condition Formula**: Here, you must build your expression to validate the particular field. There are a set of in-built operators and functions that can be used to build your formula expression such as **DATE, DATEVALUE, NOW, BLANKVALUE, ISBLANK, PRIORVALUE, AND,OR, IF,NOT, ISNUMBER, ROUND, CEILING, MAX, MOD, LOG, CONTAINS, TEXT, TRIM, REGEX, HTMLENCODE, URLENCODE,** and **VLOOKUP**. For the complete set of operators and functions, you can go to `https://help.salesforce.com/HTViewHelpDoc?id=customize_functions.htm&language=en_US`.

   ° If this formula expression is true, display the text defined in the **Error Message** area.

   ° We use a `Regex` to validate the social security number, which includes the proper format of a social security number. In this example, the validation message will be fired if the **Social Security Number** field is empty or not in a correct format as per the `Regex`. Here is the formula expression we used to validate the **Social Security Number**:

   ```
   NOT(OR(LEN(Social_Security_Number__c)=0, REGEX(Social_
   Security_Number__c,"[0-9]{3}-[0-9]{2}-[0-9]{4}")))
   ```

9. **Error Message**: You can specify the custom error message for your validation rule. This message will appear when **Error Condition Formula** is true. In our example, we used the error message `Invalid format`.

10. **Error Location**: The error message can either appear at the top of the page or below a specific field on the page.

11. Click on **Save**.

Considerations and tips for writing validation rules

When you define a validation rule in your organization, the following considerations must be kept in mind:

- There are five types of rules in the Force.com platform. Salesforce processes rules in the following order:

  ◦ Validation rules

  ◦ Assignment rules: Assignment rules are used to assign the owner to the records based on the condition. You can create assignment rules for lead and case objects.

  ◦ Auto-Response rules: An auto-response rule is a set of conditions for sending automatic e-mail responses to lead or case submissions based on the record's attributes. Use auto-response rules to send quick replies to customers to let them know you've received their query or issue.

  ◦ Workflow rules (with immediate actions).

  ◦ Escalation rules: Escalation rules are defined in the case object. Each rule defines a condition that determines how cases are processed.

- When you write a validation rule, you need to consider all the organization settings that can cause record validation failure (organization settings such as field update, hidden fields of page layout, assignment rules, or field level security). Whether the particular field is hidden or available, a validation rule always fires.

- Multiple validation rules can be defined on the same field; if one validation rule fails, the Force.com platform continues to check other validation rules on the same field and other fields on the same page. Then the error message is displayed at once.

- When you change the owner of the record, validation rules continue to run on individual records. However, if you use the mass transfer tool to change the ownership of multiple records, then the validation rules won't run on those records.

- When you create multiple validation rules for the same field, there could be contradicting validation rules that stop the saving of a particular record. This may happen because of poorly designed validation rules. As a best practice, you must thoroughly test your validation rules before using them.

- It's a best practice not to write a generic validation rule. Always use `RecordType.Id` so that it fires only for that record type and not for all. When you refer related fields that are from related objects, in your validation rule formula, make sure those objects are deployed.

- In the Force.com platform, there is a function called `IF` that is used to return a Boolean value by evaluating a condition. But in a validation rule formula, you don't have to begin with the `IF` function. Any Boolean error condition expression works, for example:

  - Correct: `From_Date__c < TODAY()`
  - Incorrect: `IF(From_Date__c < TODAY(), TRUE, FALSE)`

- If a validation rule formula contains the `BEGINS` or `CONTAINS` function, the blank values are considered as valid values.

- When using a validation rule to ensure that a number field contains a specific value, use the `ISBLANK` function to include fields that do not contain any value.

- When using a validation rule to ensure the picklist field contains a particular value, use the `ISPICKVAL` function to determine the particular picklist field of the record that contains the particular value.

- You can simply use check box fields in validation formulas because check box fields don't require any operator (as they return true or false values by default)

- Validation rules in combination with the `VLOOKUP` function can be used to enforce the consistency of data in Salesforce. `VLOOKUP` is only available in validation rules.

Automating the business process using workflows

Workflow is a strong feature of the Force.com platform because it is used to automate business processes. This is the business logic engine of the Force.com platform that allows us to automate ending e-mail alerts, assigning tasks, updating a field value based on the defined rules. Workflows are associated with the particular objects. When the associated object's record is inserted or updated, and meets the conditions of the workflow rule, the platform automatically executes the actions defined in the rule. This is all about the automated actions in the Force.com platform and executes them when the right time/correct statuses are coming up. The following diagram presents the steps of a workflow.

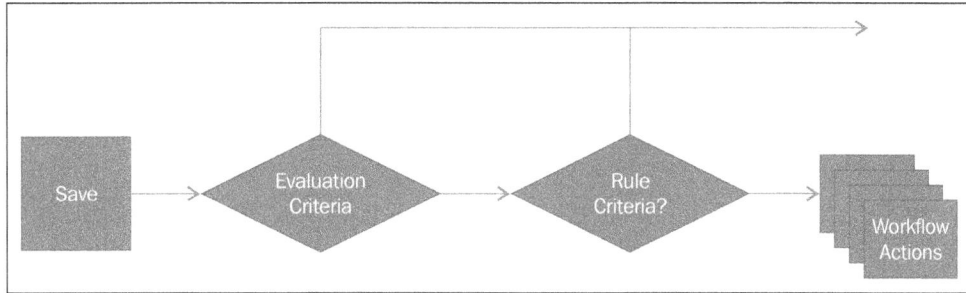

Each workflow rule consists of the following elements:

- **Criteria** that cause the workflow rules to run.

- **Immediate actions** that execute as soon as the record meets the criteria. For example, the Force.com platform can automatically send an e-mail that notifies the particular manager when a leave request is made.

- **Time-dependent actions** that execute based on elapsed time (evaluated off any date field in the Force.com platform). Time-dependent actions have a time trigger. Therefore, the action will not occur until it meets the time trigger. For example, the Force.com platform can automatically send an e-mail reminder to the particular manager if a leave request is still not processed 10 days after the record created date.

The following diagram shows the preceding elements of workflows in the Force.com platform:

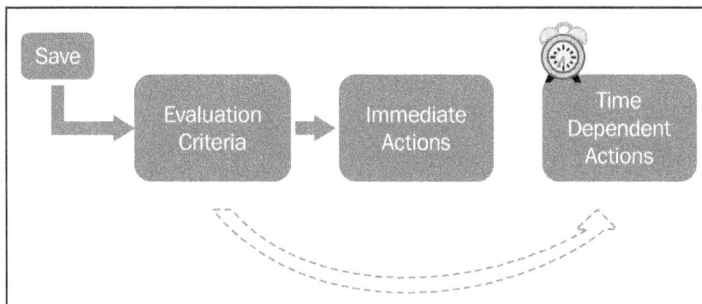

Workflow automates the following types of actions based on your organization's processes:

- **Tasks**: You can assign a new task to a user, role, or record owner through the workflow action. For example, create a task and assign to the particular manager when a leave request is made.

- **E-mail Alerts**: You can send an e-mail to one or more specified recipients. For example, send an e-mail that notifies the particular manager when a leave request is made. Attachments also can be added to the e-mail alerts.

- **Field Updates**: You can use the workflow action to update the value of a field on a record. For example, if the manager doesn't respond to the leave request 10 days after the record created date, you can define a field update to update the status field as **Delayed**.

- **Outbound Messages**: These messages send the information you specify to an endpoint you designate. The message is a secure configurable API message (in SOAP/XML format).

Creating workflow rules

The leave management application wants to create a task and assign it to the particular manager when a leave request is made with the status `Approval Pending`. Use the following steps to create this workflow in the leave management application:

1. Navigate to **Setup | Create | Workflow & Approvals | Workflow Rules**.

2. Click on **New Rule** to create a workflow rule.

3. Select the object to which this workflow rule applies. In this example, we select the **Leave** object as shown in the following screenshot:

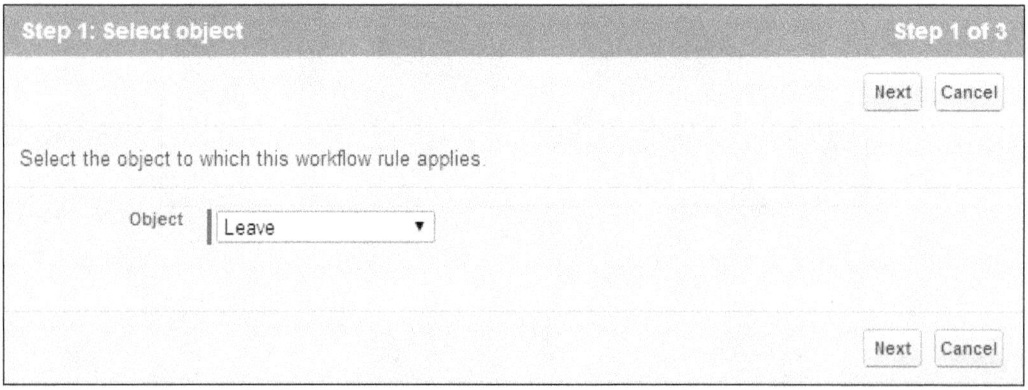

Select the object for the workflow

4. Click on **Next**. You will see the following screenshot:

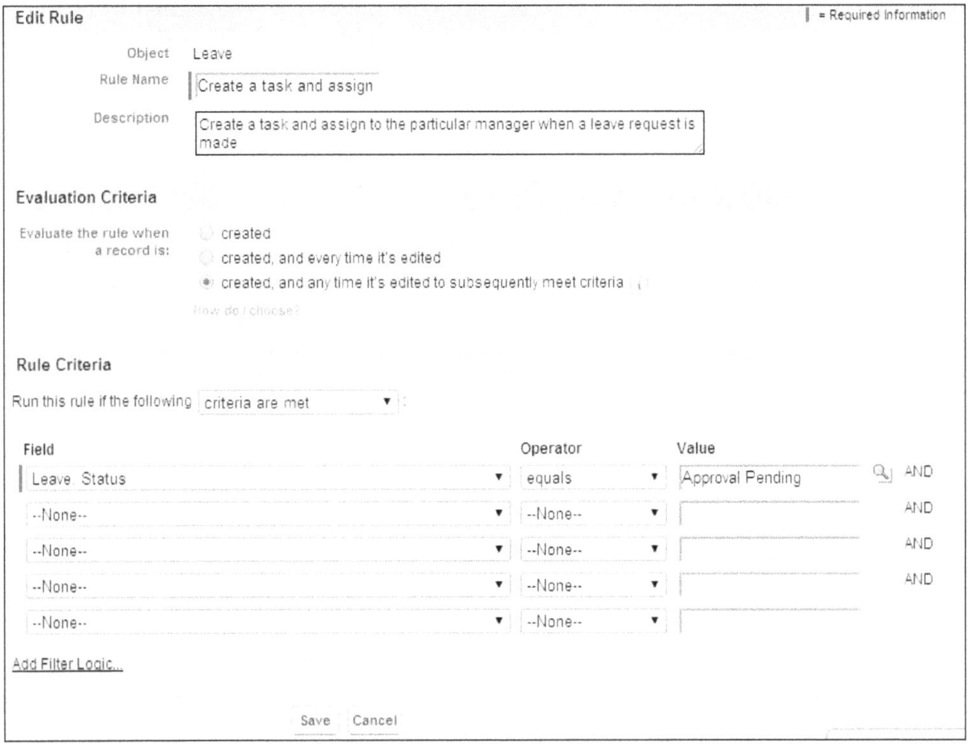

Define the Rule Name, Evaluation Criteria, and Rule Criteria

5. Enter the **Rule Name, Description**.

6. Set the **Evaluation Criteria**. There are three options for the **Evaluation Criteria** as discussed in the following table:

Evaluation criteria options	Description
Evaluate the rule when a record is *created*	If you select this option, the workflow will evaluate the rule criteria each time this particular record is created for the particular object and meets the entry criteria. A workflow rule with this option runs only one time per record.
Evaluate the rule when a record is *created, and every time it's edited*	If you select this option, the particular workflow is evaluated each time the record is created or updated. If the particular record meets the associated rule criteria and the workflow is defined with this option, the rule repeatedly runs every time the record is edited. However, if you select this option, you cannot define time-dependent actions to the rule.

Evaluation criteria options	Description
Evaluate the rule when a record is *created, and any time it's edited to subsequently meet criteria*	If you select this option, the rule is evaluated when a record is created, and when a record that doesn't meet the criteria is edited to meet the criteria.

7. Enter your **Rule Criteria** to trigger your workflow rule. There are two options to define the rule criteria:

    ° **Criteria are met**: With this selection, you can select the criteria that the record must match. If it meets the criteria, then the rule will be triggered. In this example, we used the **criteria are met** option as the status field of the leave record is equal to **New**.

    ° **Formula evaluates to true**: With this selection, you can define a formula that returns a value of true or false. If the formula returns the true value, then the rule will be triggered.

8. Click on **Save & Next**. In the next step, you can define the associated workflow actions with this workflow rule.

9. From the navigated screen, you can specify the workflow actions that will be triggered when the rule criteria are met. As we discussed earlier, there are two types of actions: **Immediate Workflow Actions** and **Time-Dependent Workflow Actions**.

Step 3: Specify Workflow Actions   Step 3 of 3

Done

Specify the workflow actions that will be triggered when the rule criteria are met See an example

Rule Criteria   Leave: Status EQUALS Approval Pending

Evaluation Criteria Evaluate the rule when a record is created, and any time it's edited to subsequently meet
                     criteria

Immediate Workflow Actions

No workflow actions have been added.

Add Workflow Action ▼

Time-Dependent Workflow Actions   See an example

No workflow actions have been added. Before adding a workflow action, you must have at least one time
trigger defined.

Add Time Trigger

---

10. From the preceding screenshot, click on **Add Workflow Action** in the **Immediate Workflow Actions** section to add an immediate workflow action to the workflow rule and click on **New Task** to create a task and assign it to the particular manager.

11. The wizard will be navigated to the **Configure Task** screen. You can configure a task by providing suitable information, as shown in the following screenshot:

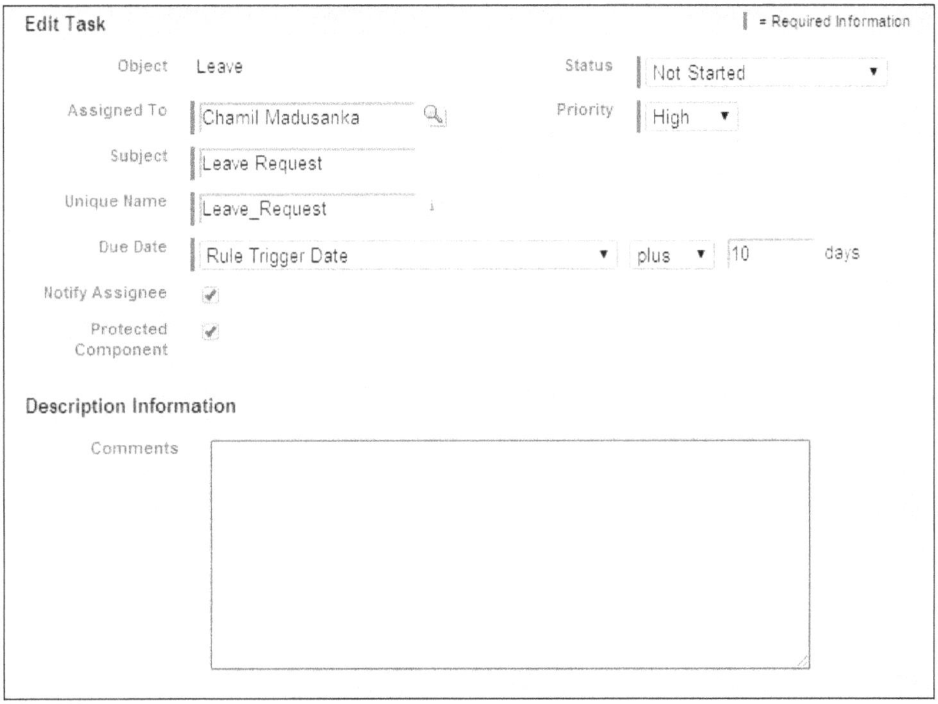

Configure a task as the workflow action

> Create a task to associate with one or more workflow rules, approval processes, or entitlement processes. When changing a task, any modifications will apply to all rules, approvals, or entitlement processes associated with it.

12. Click on **Save**. Now we have created a workflow rule and an immediate workflow action to create a task and assign it to the particular manager when a leave request is made by an employee.

Let's create **Time-Dependent Workflow Action** to the same workflow that was previously created. The `eLeaveForce` leave management application needs to send an e-mail reminder to the particular manager if a leave request is still not processed 10 days after the record created date. Use the following steps to create **Time-Dependent Workflow Action**:

1. Navigate to **Setup | Create | Workflow & Approvals | Workflow Rules** to access the workflow rules list page.

2. Click on the name of the rule with the workflow actions you want to edit. In our example, the workflow name is **Create a task and assign to the manager** as you can see the following screenshot:

Workflow **Rule Detail**	Edit	Delete	Clone	Activate		

Workflow Rule Detail   Edit Delete Clone Activate

Rule Name	Create a task and assign to the manager	Object	Leave
Active	☐	Evaluation Criteria	Evaluate the rule when a record is created, and any time it's edited to subsequently meet criteria
Description	Create a task and assign to the particular manager when a leave request is made		
Rule Criteria	Leave: Status EQUALS Approval Pending		
Created By	Chamil Madusanka, 2/15/2014 2:03 AM	Modified By	Chamil Madusanka, 2/15/2014 2:59 AM

Workflow Actions   Edit

Immediate Workflow Actions

Type	Description
Task	Leave Request

Time-Dependent Workflow Actions   See an example

🛈 No workflow actions have been added. Before adding a workflow action, you must have at least one time trigger defined.

Edit

Workflow rule detail page

3. Click on **Edit** in the **Workflow Actions** section. The wizard will be redirected to the next page, which is shown in the following screenshot:

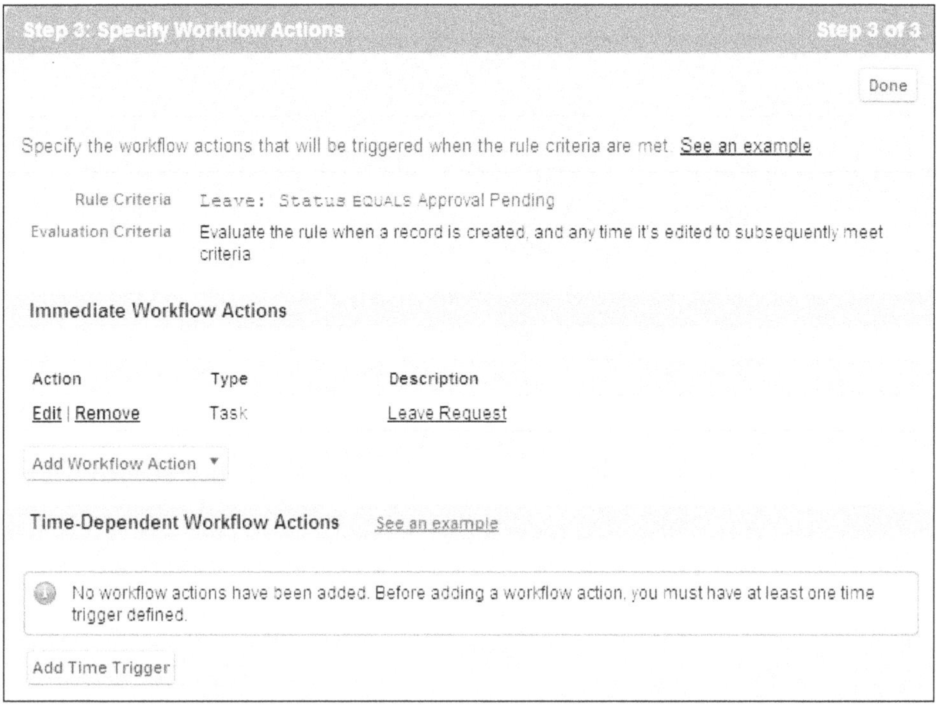

Add Time Trigger

4. Before adding a workflow action, you must have at least one time trigger defined. To define the time trigger, click on **Add Time Trigger**. You can define the time trigger from the following screen:

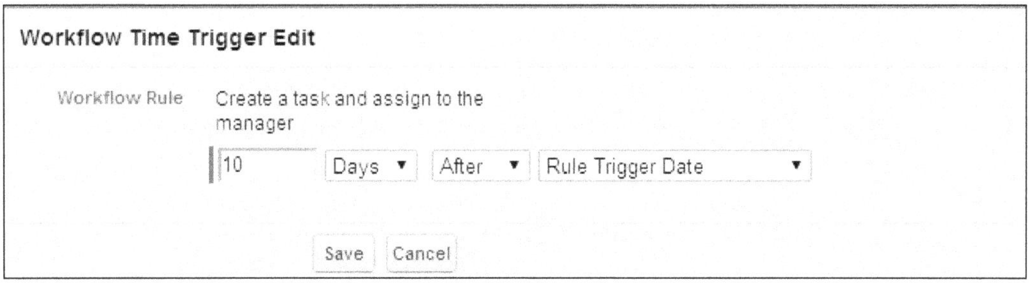

5. According to the preceding screenshot, we defined the time trigger to trigger after 10 days of the rule triggered date. Click on **Save**. Now we have created the time trigger.

6. To create the workflow action to the created time trigger, navigate to **Add Workflow Action | New Email Alert**. Then you can define your time-dependent workflow action as shown in the following screenshot:

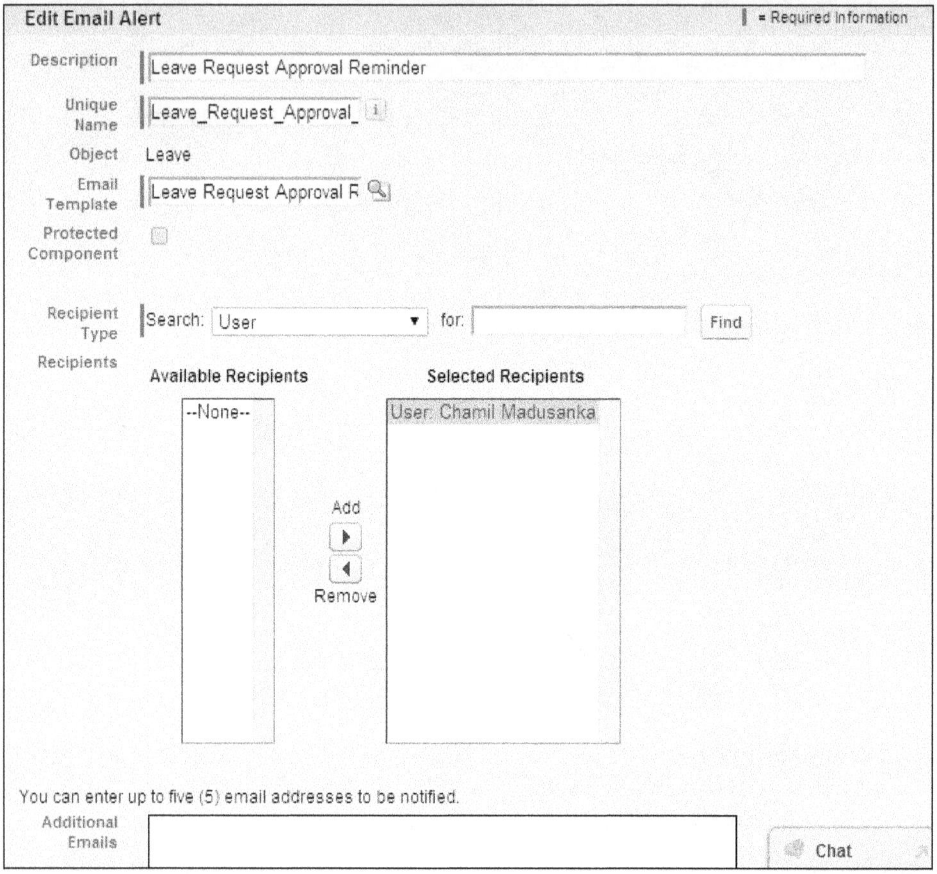

Edit Email Alert		▌ = Required Information
Description	Leave Request Approval Reminder	
Unique Name	Leave_Request_Approval_ [i]	
Object	Leave	
Email Template	Leave Request Approval R 🔍	
Protected Component	☐	

| Recipient Type | Search: | User ▼ | for: | | Find |

Recipients

Available Recipients		Selected Recipients
--None--		User: Chamil Madusanka
	Add ▶	
	◀ Remove	

You can enter up to five (5) email addresses to be notified.

| Additional Emails | | | 💬 Chat |

Define the e-mail alert for the workflow action

7. You can send an e-mail alert to five non-Salesforce users by adding their e-mail addresses in approval e-mail text box, separated by commas.

> In this scenario, we have created a new e-mail alert to trigger the action. Before you define this, you have to have an active e-mail template. We will learn more about e-mail templates in *Chapter 10, E-mail Services with the Force.com Platform*.

8. Click on **Save**.

Now you have created the immediate and time-dependent action to the same workflow rule. After you create the workflow, it will not be activated automatically as shown in the following screenshot. The workflows with the status as inactive will not be executed on the Force.com platform.

Activate your workflow

You have to activate it by clicking on the **Activate** button in the workflow detail page or activate link in the workflow list page. If your organization has time-based actions in workflow rules, the default workflow user must be set before activating the workflow. Use the following steps to set the default workflow user in your organization:

1. From the Setup page, navigate to **Create | Workflow & Approvals | Settings**. You will see the following page:

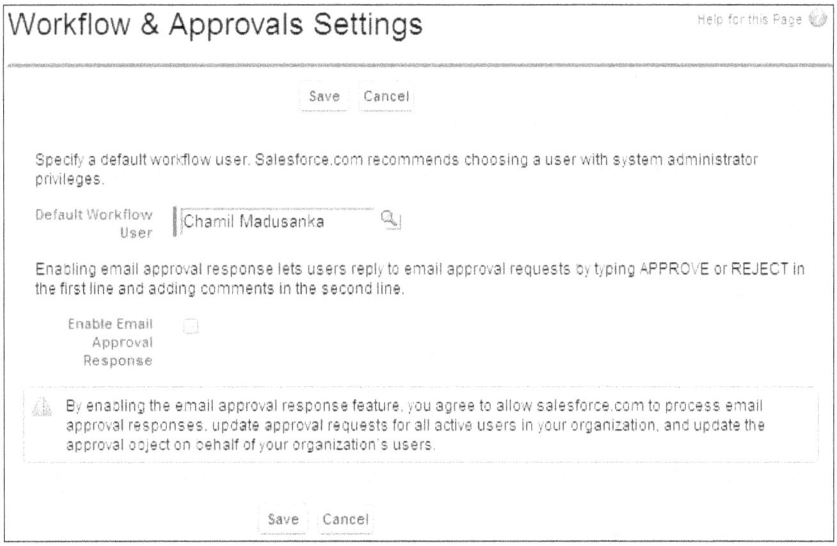

Workflow & Approval Settings

2. Specify a default workflow user. Salesforce.com recommends choosing a user with system administrator privileges.

3. Enabling an e-mail approval response lets the users reply to e-mail approval requests by typing APPROVE or REJECT in the first line and adding comments in the second line.

> By enabling the e-mail approval response feature, you agree to allow Salesforce.com to process e-mail approval responses, update approval requests for all active users in your organization, and update the approval object on behalf of your organization's users.

4. Click on **Save**. Now you can activate the workflow rule.

Time-dependent actions and time trigger considerations

When creating time-dependent actions and time triggers for workflow rules, consider the following:

- When defining a time trigger, the Force.com platform allows us to use standard and custom date and date/time fields defined for the selected object.
- You can add actions to existing time triggers.
- Time-dependent workflows are evaluated on your organization's time zone.
- Time-based actions are executed as a batch, not independently.
- The Force.com platform doesn't execute time triggers in the order they list on the item page. Time triggers with the before field execute first. Time triggers with the after field execute second.
- If you set a time trigger to an earlier time, the Force.com platform queues the associated time-based action to start executing within one hour.
- Time-based actions remain in the workflow queue as long as the workflow rule criteria are valid.
- Time-dependent workflow cannot be used when a rule is set to be evaluated every time a record is created or updated.
- The Force.com platform ignores time triggers that refer to null fields.
- When a new workflow rule is created, it does not affect the existing records.
- Developers can monitor and remove pending actions by viewing the time-dependent workflow queue.

If a record has a pending action against it at the time-based workflow queue and it has been modified, then the action will be updated in the queue.

[In one workflow you can add 40 actions, 10 field updates, and 10 e-mail alerts.]

Automating the business process using approval processes

Think about the real-world scenario of a leave approval process. The employee wants to request a leave for a particular day or date range and requests it from the manager. After the manager has approved, the HR will approve the leave. These multilevel approvals are needed to be implemented in real-world applications.

The Force.com platform provides another in-built business logic tool called **Approval Processes**, which gives us the ability to implement a chain of actions to create a single business process. An approval process can be built with single or multiple step processes that require one or more designated approvers to approve or reject the record. An approval process contains the following features:

- It tracks the progress of the approval automatically
- You can define multiple steps for the approval process
- You can define the approval and rejection actions for each step of the process
- You can define the approvers for each approval step
- Flexible routing paths allow you to implement an incredibly wide range of processes

An approval process has six primary elements that determine the particular process definition. Refer to the following diagram that shows the primary elements of the approval process:

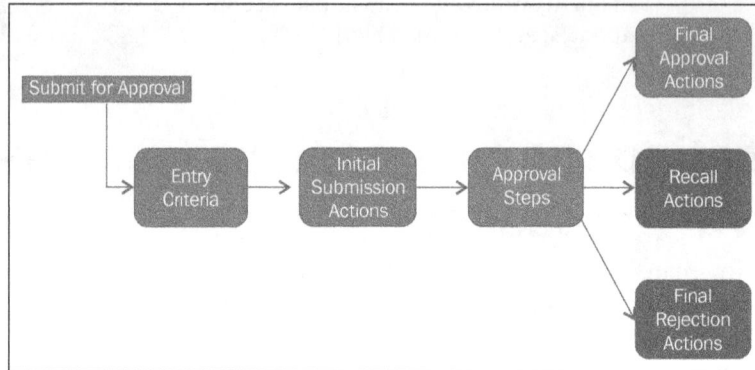

When a record is submitted for an approval, it looks for suitable approval processes that match the entry criteria with the attributes of the record. If there are any matched approval processes, the record enters into the particular approval process and performs the initial submission actions. There is a default initial submission action that locks the record. Then the predefined approval steps will take care of the record. Each step allows one or more approvers to accept or reject the record. Same as workflow rules, you can define actions (sending an e-mail alert, updating a field value, and assigning a task) for an approval process that should be performed whenever a record is submitted for approval, approved, rejected, or recalled. The following diagram shows the whole definition of an approval process:

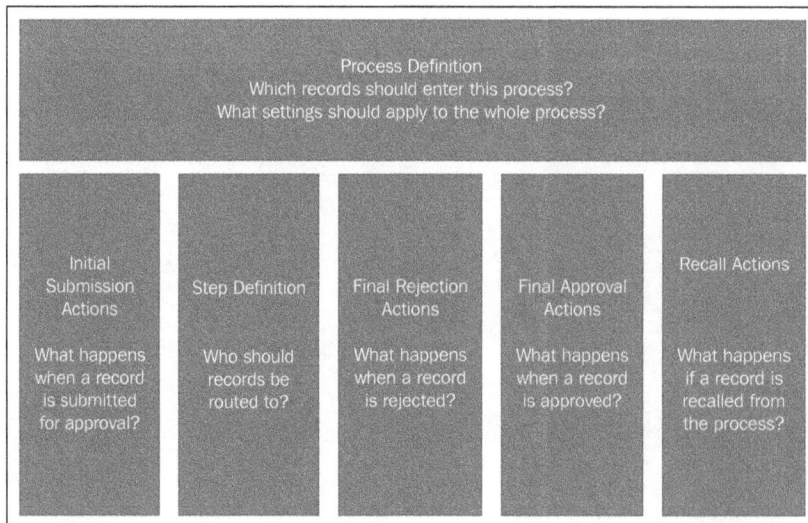

Creating a multistep approval process

The leave management application wants an approval process to approve or reject a leave request made by an employee. According to the requirement, there are two steps for this approval process.

- Approval by direct manager
- Approval by HR executive

The direct manager can approve or reject the leave request. If the direct manager approves the record, the HR executive must approve or reject the leave request. The following diagram shows the leave request approval process structure:

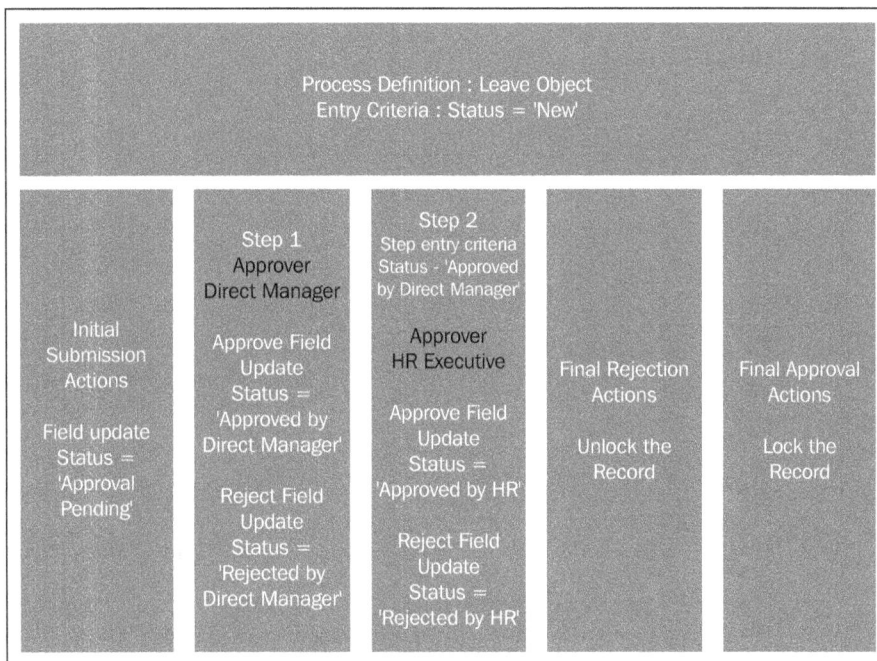

Let's create this approval process for the Leave object. Use the following steps to create the approval process:

1. From the Setup page, navigate to **Create | Workflow & Approvals | Approval Processes**.

2. Select an object from the drop-down list. After selecting the **Leave** object, if there are existing active and inactive approval processes for Leaves, they will be displayed.

3. To create a new approval process, click on **Create New Approval Process**, then you can select **Use Jump Start Wizard** to set up your approval process in a few short steps or, select **Use Standard Setup Wizard** to configure all the approval options. We will continue this example using **Use Standard Setup Wizard**.

| Manage Approval Processes For: | Leave ▼ |

A listing of both active and inactive approval processes for **Leaves** is displayed below. To create a new approval process, click Create New Approval Process then select Use Jump Start Wizard to set up your approval process in a few short steps. Or, select Use Standard Wizard to configure all approval options.

Create New Approval Process ▼

Use Jump Start Wizard

Use Standard Setup Wizard

~~Active Approval Processes~~   Reorder

No approval processes available

Inactive Approval Processes

No approval processes available

Create the approval process

4. Enter the name and description for your new approval process. For this example, we used `Leave Request Approval` as the name of the approval process. Click on **Next**.

5. If only certain types of records should enter this approval process, specify the entry criteria. In this example, we want only the record with the status field equal to **New** to enter this approval process.

> The entry criteria are similar to the entry criteria of the workflow. However, the entry criteria in an approval process is optional. We can use that according to requirements.

6. Click on **Next**. Step 3 is to specify the **Approver Field** and **Record Editability Properties**.

7. Select the field for **Automated Approval Routing**. When you define approval steps, you can assign approval requests to different users. One of your options is to use a user field to automatically route these requests. We will keep the field blank and will set the approvers to each step when creating the steps because this approval process contains multiple steps and every step has different approvers.

8. Select the **Record Editability Properties** field. When a record is in the approval process, it will always be locked, and only an administrator will be able to edit it. However, you may choose to also allow the currently assigned approver to edit the record. Keep the default value as **Administrators Only** so that administrators can edit records during the approval process.

9. Click on **Next**.

10. In step 4, you can select the e-mail template that will be used to notify approvers that an approval request has been assigned to them. Note that this template will be used for all steps for this process. If you wish to use the default e-mail template, keep the field with a blank value.

> The approver can approve or reject the approval request via e-mail by replying to the e-mail with `approve`, `approved`, `yes`, `reject`, `rejected`, or `no` on the first line of the e-mail body and adding comments in the second line. The approver must have the API enabled system permission to approve or reject via e-mail reply.

11. Click on **Next**.

12. In step 5, you can select fields to display on approval page layout. The approval page is where an approver will actually approve or reject a request. After selecting the fields, click on **Next**. You have the option to display approval history information in addition to the fields selected.

13. You can choose the security settings on the approval page. There are two options, which are as follows:

    ° Allow approvers to access the approval page only from within the application: With this option, users must log in to Salesforce to view the approval page.

    ° Allow approvers to access the approval page only from within the application, or externally from a wireless-enabled mobile device: With this option, users can access the approval page (external version) from any browser, including a mobile device.

14. In step 6, you can specify which users are allowed to submit the initial request for approval. For example, the leave request should normally be submitted for approval only by their owners (which means the employee here). You can allow submitters to recall approval requests by selecting the **Allow submitters to recall approval requests** option in this step.

15. Click on **Save**.

16. You have just created an approval process. However, you cannot activate this process until you define at least one approval step. You will see a decision box to continue creating the approval process. Select **Yes, I'd like to create an approval step now** and click on **Go** to create the steps for this approval process.

17. Enter a **Name**, **Description** (optionally), and **Step Number** for your new approval step as shown in the following screenshot:

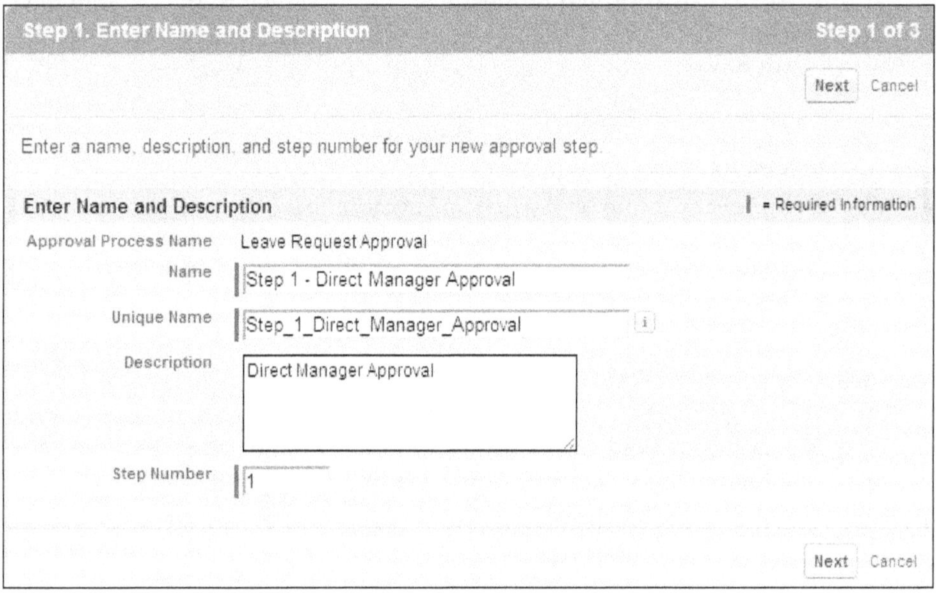

Step 1. Enter Name and Description		Step 1 of 3

Enter a name, description, and step number for your new approval step.

Enter Name and Description | = Required Information

Approval Process Name	Leave Request Approval
Name	Step 1 - Direct Manager Approval
Unique Name	Step_1_Direct_Manager_Approval
Description	Direct Manager Approval
Step Number	1

Define the approval step

18. Click on **Next**.

19. In the next stage of creating an approval step, you can specify whether a record must meet certain criteria before entering this approval step. If these criteria are not met, the approval process can skip to the next step, if one exists. In this example, all records should enter this step. Therefore, select the **All records should enter this step** option and click on **Next**.

20. Step 3 of creating an approval step is to select assigned approvers. You can specify the user who should approve records that enter this step. Optionally, you can choose whether the approver's delegate is also allowed to approve these requests. The delegate is the person listed in the **Delegated Approver** field on the assigned approver's user record.

21. There are three options to select the approver of the step, which are as follows:

    ° **Let the submitter choose the approver manually**: If you select this option, the user will get a popup to manually select the next approver.

    ° **Automatically assign to queue**: If you select this option, you can select a queue to assign approval requests. We have discussed the queue in *Chapter 4, Designing Apps for Multiple Users and Protecting Data*.

    ° **Automatically assign to approver(s)**: If you select this option, you can assign the approval request to one or more of the following approvers types:

    User: This option is to assign any user from your organization.

    Queue: This option is to select a queue to assign the approval request.

    Related User: This option is to select a user lookup field on the submitted record such as the **Created By**, **Last Modified By** field or additionally created user lookup fields. You can add related user fields up to 25 approvers. This is called parallel approvers. When multiple approvers are selected, you have two options to consider:

Approve or reject based on the FIRST response	Require UNANIMOUS approval from all selected approvers
The approval process will take the first response to the approval request, which determines whether the record is approved or rejected. The approval process will continue. It will not wait for the other approver's response.	This option waits for all the approvers' responses to continue the approval process. If any of the approvers reject the request, the approval step is considered as a rejected step.

22. In this example, we let the approval submitter select his/her direct manager as the next approver. Therefore, select the first option called **Let the submitter choose the approver manually**. Click on **Save**.

23. Select **No, I'll do this later. Take me to the approval process detail page to review what I've just created** option and click on **Go**.

24. Now you see the detail page of the leave request approval process.

25. Create step 2 of the approval process in the same way as step 1. Use the following attributes to define step 2:

    ◦ **Step name**: Step 2 - HR Executive Approval

    ◦ **Description**: HR Executive Approval

    ◦ **Step entry criteria**: Status field equals to Approved by Direct Manager

    ◦ **Approvers of the step**: Select **Automatically assign to queue** and **select a queue**. You must create the queue before defining this approval step.

26. Let's create the initial submission, approval, and rejection actions for each step. In this example, we have the following approval actions:

    ◦ **Initial Submission Action**: At this point, the Force.com platform locks the record by default. Additionally, you can add more actions as per your requirements. Initial submission actions take place when a record is initially submitted for approval. In this example, we use a **Field Update** as an initial submission action.

      Field – Status

      Old Value – New

      New Value – Approval Pending

    ◦ **Step 1 Approval Action**: In this example, we use a **Field Update** as the approval action of step 1.

      Field – Status

      Old Value – Approval Pending

      New Value – Approved by Direct Manager

    ◦ **Step 1 Rejection Action**: In this example, we use a **Field Update** as the rejection action of step 1.

      Field – Status

      Old Value – Approval Pending

      New Value – Rejected by Direct Manager

- ○ **Step 2 Approval Action**: In this example, we use a **Field Update** as the approval action of step 2.

  Field – Status

  Old Value – Approved by Direct Manager

  New Value – Approved by HR

- ○ **Step 2 Rejection Action**: In this example, we use a **Field Update** as the rejection action of step 2.

  Field – Status

  Old Value – Approved by Direct Manager

  New Value – Rejected by HR

- ○ **Final Approval Action**: This takes place after a record has received all the necessary approvals. In this example, we don't use any additional action and only the default action is used, that is, **Lock the record from being edited**.

- ○ **Final Rejection Action**: This takes place when a record has been completely rejected from the approval process. In this example, we don't use any additional action and only the default action is used, that is, **Unlock the record for editing**.

- ○ **Recall Action**: This takes place when a submitted approval request is recalled. In this example, we use **Field Update** as the recall action.

  Field – Status

  Old Value – Any other value

  New Value – New

27. To create the approval action of step 1, go to the particular detail page of the approval process.

28. Under the **Approval Steps** section, click on **Show Actions**.

29. In the **Approval Actions** section, navigate to **Add New | Field Update**.

30. To define the field update, provide **Name**, **Description** (optionally), and select the field to update. In this example, we select the **Status** field. Then we need to specify the new field value of the field as shown in the following screenshot:

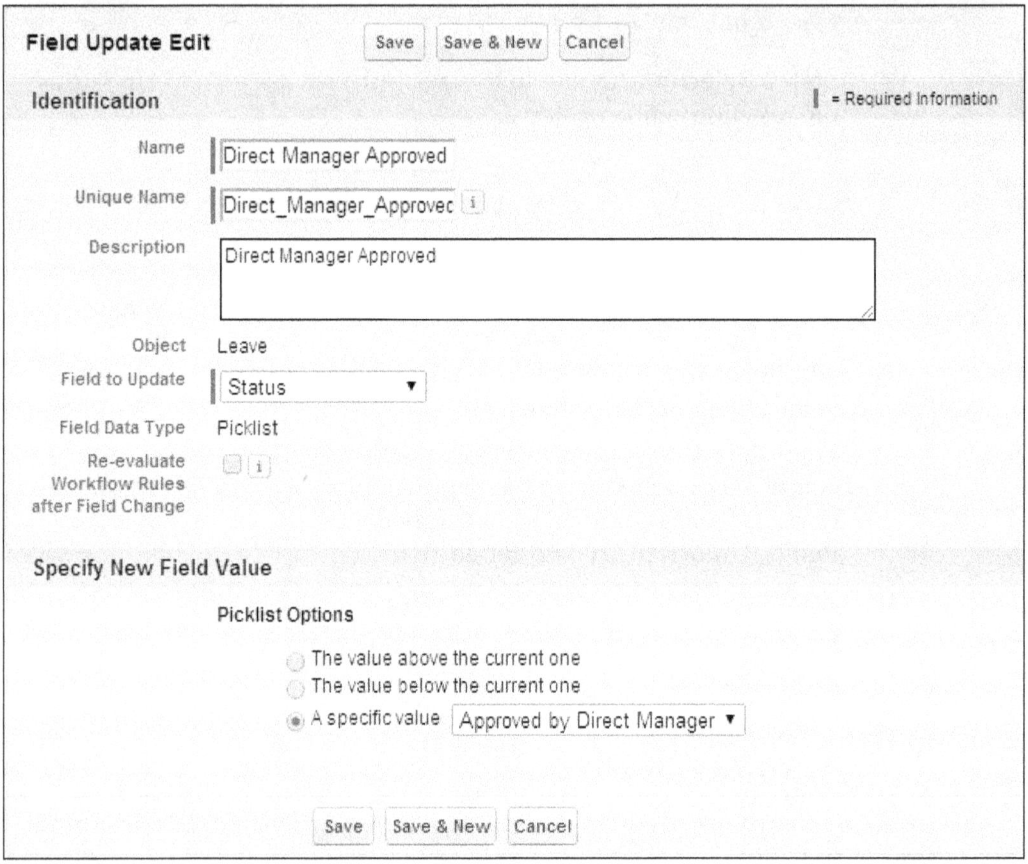

Define the approval action

31. Select the **Re-evaluate Workflow Rules after Field Change** checkbox if you want workflow rules on this object to be re-evaluated after the field value is updated. After the update, if it matches with the entry criteria of any workflow, then that workflow will fire.

32. Click on **Save**.

33. Likewise, create all the approval and rejection actions as we defined in the preceding section. After completing the leave request approval process, the form will appear as shown in the following screenshot:

Initial Submission Actions		
Action	**Type**	**Description**
	Record Lock	Lock the record from being edited
Edit | Remove	Field Update	Approval Pending

Approval Steps New Approval Step

Action	Step Number	Name	Description	Criteria	Assigned Approver	Reject Behavior
Show Actions | Edit | Del	1	Step 1 - Direct Manager Approval	Direct Manager Approval		Manually Chosen	Final Rejection
Show Actions | Edit | Del	2	Step 1 - HR Executive Approval	HR Executive Approval	Leave: Status EQUALS Approved by Direct Manager	Queue:HR Executives	Final Rejection

Final Approval Actions Add Existing Add New ▼

Action	Type	Description
Edit	Record Lock	Lock the record from being edited

Final Rejection Actions Add Existing Add New ▼

Action	Type	Description
Edit	Record Lock	Unlock the record for editing

Recall Actions Add Existing Add New ▼

Action	Type	Description
	Record Lock	Unlock the record for editing

The detail page of the approval process

Once you have finished creating the approval process with the approval actions, you can visualize the read-only diagram on the process visualizer. To view the process visualizer, click on the **View Diagram** button, which is located on the detail view of the approval process. The following screenshot shows the process visualizer of the leave request approval:

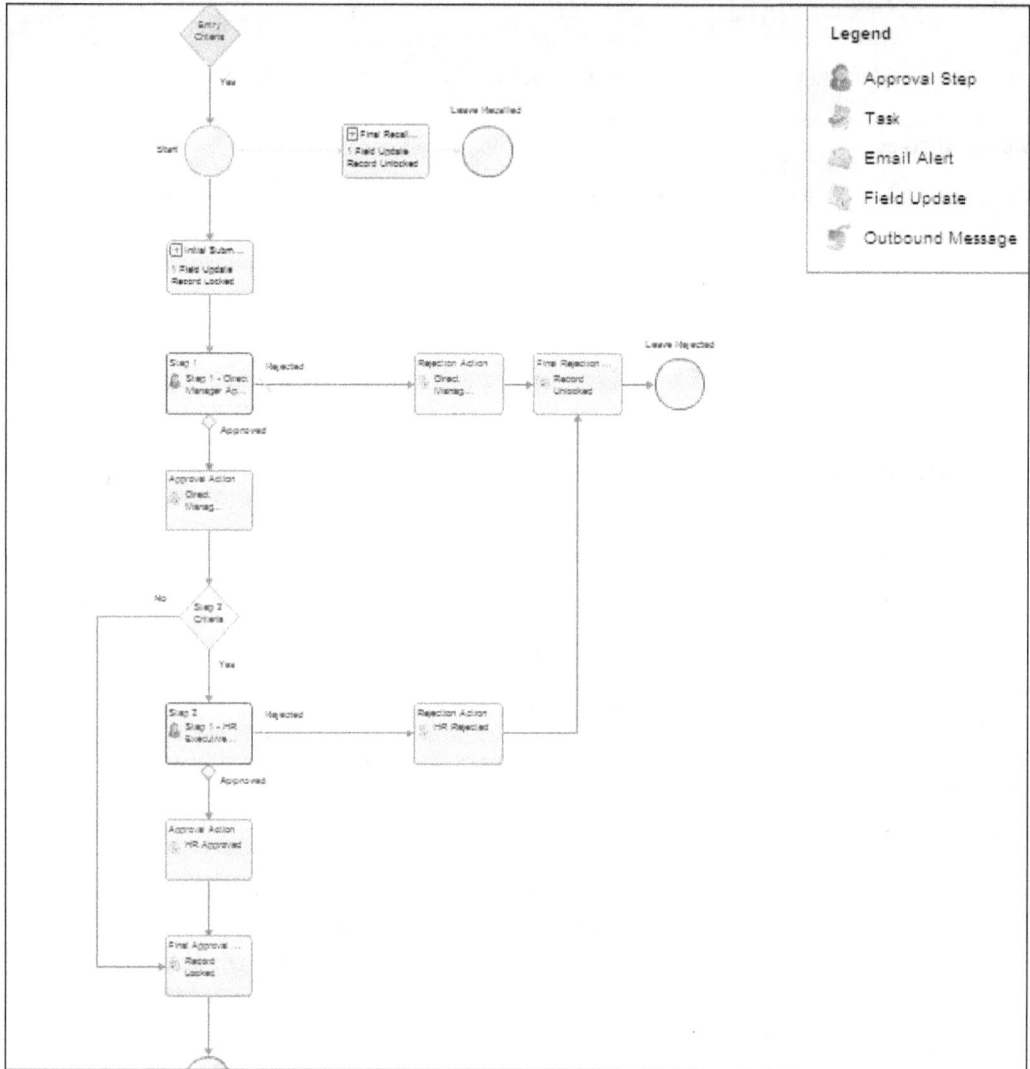

The flow diagram of the Leave approval process

Without activating the approval process, you cannot use the particular approval process.

Approval process considerations

When you implement an approval process in your organization, you must consider the following facts:

- Before you use the approval process, you have to activate the particular approval process. You cannot delete any activated approval processes. Therefore, you have to make sure that the particular approval process is inactive and there are no records that have been submitted for approval. If there are any submitted records, you have to delete them and remove them from the Recycle Bin as well.

- When you create an approval process for a detail object of a master-detail relationship, the owner field is unavailable for the approval page layout and you cannot select the detail object's owner field as an initial submitter.

- End users must have an idea about all the approval processes in their organization because when they click on the Submit for Approval, they don't know which approval process is actually running. If you have multiple approval processes for the same object, the administrator can reorder the approval processes according to the functional requirement.

- If you define the approval process by allowing the user to select an approver manually, you should also allow the user submitting a request to select themselves as the approver.

- The field update action can be defined with the option which the workflow rule on the particular object to be re-evaluated after the field value is updated. However, if the re-evaluated workflow has a cross-object field update, it will be ignored.

- The approver can approve or reject the approval request via e-mail by replying to the e-mail with `approve`, `approved`, `yes`, `reject`, `rejected`, or `no` on the first line of the e-mail body and adding comments in the second line. The approver must have the API-enabled system permission to approve or reject via e-mail reply. Also, for e-mail approval, we need to explicitly go and check the **Enable Email Approvals** checkbox in the **Settings** tab and we need to make sure that **Email Templates** should explain **How to respond via Email**.

- If the approval process has a field update that fails the standard validation rules for the particular field, then an error message is displayed for the submitter of the approval process. However, the field updates don't evaluate custom validation rules on the particular field.

- The approval steps can be assigned to a particular queue as the assigned approvers. You can assign queues available only for objects that are supported queues.

- The e-mail approval response feature is not available for approval processes for which the assigned approver is a queue.

- If you assigned a queue as the assigned approver, any member of the queue can approve or reject the approval request.

- If you assigned a queue as the assigned approver, each queue member's delegated approver also receives the approval request e-mail notification.

- You are not allowed to assign a group or queue as a delegated approver.

- Up to 25 approvers can be assigned to an approval step.

- Up to 30 steps can be defined to an approval.

- You cannot create an outbound message as an approval or rejection action on a junction object.

Comparing workflow and approval processes

You have learned about the workflow rules and the approval processes that are both used to automate the business processes by implementing the logic as a service of the Force.com platform. The following table shows you a comparison between workflow rules and approval processes:

Workflow Rules	Approval Processes
The workflows are triggered upon save	The approval processes are triggered only when a user clicks on **Submit for Approval** or automates this by using the apex trigger
This consists of one set of criteria and actions	This consists of multiple steps
This can be modified or deleted	They have entry criteria, step criteria, and step actions
	They have initial submission actions, approval and rejection actions, and actions for each step
	They have some attributes that can't be modified (processes must be deactivated before they can be deleted)
This is completely automated	This requires manual involvement for every step

Summary

In this chapter, we learned how to implement the business processes in the Force.com application. In the first section of this chapter, we understood how to protect data quality with validation rules. Finally, we learned to automate the business processes using workflow rules and approval processes. In the next chapter, we will discuss data management on the Force.com platform.

6

Data Management on the Force.com Platform

In the previous chapter, we have seen the implementation of efficient business logic, which is essential in a Force.com application. As in any efficient business logic, the correct data in an organization is a priority for a Force.com platform. The Force.com platform provides some operations and tools to manipulate data in an organization. In this chapter, we will cover the typical data management operations and data management tools. There will be a section to explain about record IDs and considerations of object relationships in data management. This chapter covers the following topics:

- Data management operations
- Force.com record IDs
- Data management tools

Data management operations

You already know that the MVC model of the Force.com platform detaches the business logic from the presentation layer and the data. Therefore, the Force.com platform provides various data management operations as follows:

- **Exporting Data**: The Force.com platform provides data exporting operations to download all the data of the organization and makes periodic backups of certain objects. This operation can be used to get reference IDs of particular records to perform the insert or update operation of those records.
- **Inserting Data**: You can insert new records to standard or custom objects of your organization. For example, you can insert the user's list and load the existing employee records.

- **Updating Data**: Updating data is useful in the Force.com platform to perform a de-duplication of existing data that removes duplicate records.

- **Upserting Data**: The Upsert operation is a combination of the Update and Insert operations. It is used to keep the Salesforce organization in sync with another system and to migrate the new and existing records from a legacy system.

- **Deleting Data**: The delete operation is practiced to free up space used by too much legacy data and fix data mistakes in the system.

The operations mentioned earlier are used in the data loader tool and through the command-line interface. More details about the Data Loader tools are presented in the *Data Management tools* section.

The CRUD commands

CRUD stands for **Create, Read, Update,** and **Delete**. Among the preceding data management operations, the Force.com platform provides four operations using the API. Therefore, records can be created, edited, retrieved, and deleted from the server instance. The insert operation needs data without the Force.com record ID because the record ID is generated by the Force.com platform. However, the update and read operations need the Force.com ID or an external ID. (More details are mentioned in the *External IDs* section.) The delete operation only needs the Force.com record ID to perform its functions.

The Upsert command

In addition to the general CRUD commands, there is a special command called upsert. It is an API-based function and is a combination of the insert and update functions. Therefore, the upsert function needs to determine whether the particular record is about to insert or update. It uses the Force.com ID or an external ID to figure it out. There are three scenarios in the upsert function:

- If the ID doesn't match with an existing record ID, a new record will be created

- If the ID matches once with an existing record ID, the existing record will be updated

- If the ID matches with multiple records, an error will be reported

When importing data, you can prevent the creation of duplicate records using the upsert function.

Force.com record IDs

In the Force.com platform, the Record ID is an important thing to understand before learning about data management operations. The Record ID is the unique identifier of a record. It is analogous to a primary or foreign key field in a database table. The record IDs can be obtained in the following ways:

- URL of the record detail view
- Running reports
- Web services API
- Formulas
- Data loader (API Access)

The Force.com platform generates the record ID when a new record is created. There are two forms of a record ID:

- **15-digit case-sensitive form**: This form is used in the URL and report. The reports framework does not expose IDs for all objects.
- **18-digit case-insensitive form**: This form is used in Data Loader. When you migrate data from legacy systems or from a comma-separated values (CSV) file or export data to a CSV file, you have to use an 18-digit format. An API always returns the record IDs in an 18-digit format, but APIs will accept either the 15-digit or 18-digit format.

Characteristics of record IDs

The record IDs of the Force.com platform has following characteristics:

- The record ID is generated by the Force.com platform. For example, this is a generated record ID of an employee record `a049000000ALLif`.
- The 15-digit record ID is case sensitive, which means `a049000000ALLif` and `a049000000ALLIF` are two different record IDs.
- An organization cannot have two different records with the same record ID.
- A record ID is not just a random number. It has important information to identify the record. The record ID can be split into two parts: object identifier and record identifier:
    - Object identifier: These are the first three digits of the record ID. It helps to identify the object type of the record. Every object has the object identifier as the prefix to the record ID.

○ Record identifier: These are the remaining digits of the record ID. The following screenshot shows the two parts of the record ID.

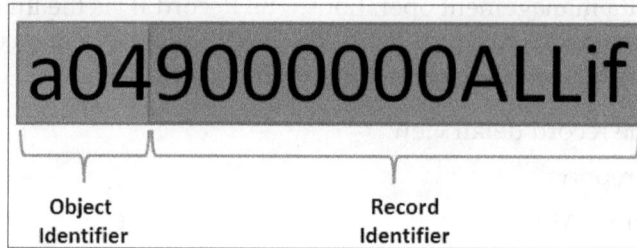

Information from the record ID

- Standard objects have standard prefixes, which are the same across every Salesforce organization.

Prefix	Object Name
001	Account
003	Contact
005	User
006	Opportunity
00e	Profiles
00Q	Leads
00T	Tasks
00U	Event
015	Document
01t	Product
500	Case
701	Campaign
800	Contract

Inserting system fields

In the Force.com platform, the **Created Date**, **Created By**, **Last Modified Date**, and **Last Modified By** fields are considered as the system fields or standard fields in a Salesforce object. Normally, we cannot insert or update those fields with our desired values. The Force.com platform generates values for system fields. However, there are scenarios such as uploading the initial data set from a legacy system and we need to fill those system fields with the values that are there in the legacy system. Therefore, the Force.com platform provides the facility to set the **Created Date**, **Created By**, **Last Modified Date**, and **Last Modified By** fields on the initial creation of records. The following are the features of modifiable system fields:

- They are only accessible through APIs, which means via the data loader.

- This modification is backwards compatible with all SOAP-based APIs.

- You can insert system fields for any custom object, but for restricted standard objects such as **Account**, **Opportunity**, **Contact**, **Lead**, **Case**, **Task**, and **Event**, you have to contact Salesforce.com customer support to enable this feature in your organization.

- The fields can be modified only once in the lifetime of the initial insert.

- Normally, these fields are read-only for existing records.

> You can insert values for system fields only at initial data migration.

External IDs

The External ID is a flag that can be added to the custom field to indicate that it should be indexed and treated as an ID. A `Text`, `Number`, `Email`, or `Auto Number` custom field can be marked as an External ID. We covered that in *Chapter 2*, *Building the Data Model*. The External ID is useful when you are migrating data from other systems. The External ID acts as the foreign key that links the data of the two systems. The External IDs are searchable and appear for the queries. An object can have three External IDs.

The External ID is important because it increases report and API SOQL performance, and it is used with upsert operation to easily integrate apps with other systems. Using upsert and External IDs helps in auditing the flow of information across systems.

For example, consider that we are going to migrate `Leave Types` from a legacy system and we need to maintain those leave types between two systems. Therefore, we have to create a new **Number** field called `Leave Type Number` in the `Leave Type` object and mark it as an External ID. We have learned to create External IDs in *Chapter 2, Building the Data Model*. The following table shows sample records of `Leave Type` from the legacy system:

Leave Type Number	Leave Type Name	Active
1	Medical Leave	true
2	Annual Leave	true
3	Casual Leave	true

When we are migrating data from a legacy system, we have to map the preceding table with the Salesforce object. `Leave Type Number` from the legacy system is mapped with `Leave Type Number` (External ID) of the Salesforce object.

Leave Type Number (External ID)	Leave Type Name	Active
1	Medical Leave	true
2	Annual Leave	true
3	Casual Leave	true

Therefore, we can upsert data using the External ID field and we won't have to use Force.com record IDs to load data. When you are using External IDs, you can prevent duplication of the loaded data.

When you are loading data into related objects, you can use the External ID and the upsert operation. However, you don't need to use Force.com record IDs. If you are using the External ID to load related object records, you can do that only with the upsert operation.

Data management tools

The Force.com platform provides two types of data management tools:

- Cloud-based tools
- API-based tools

We can use these types of tools to import data or export data or to transfer ownerships.

Cloud-based tools

Cloud-based tools are offered in the Force.com platform itself and we don't have to download the particular tool to our local computer. These types of tools are easy to use and we can perform the particular operations quickly. The following tools can be categorized under the cloud-based data management tools:

- Import Wizard
- **Data Export**
- **Mass Transfer Records**
- **Mass Delete Records**
- **Analytic Snapshot**
- **Data Loader** (which will be discussed in *Appendix A, Force.com Tools*)

The data import wizard

The import wizard is a major cloud-based tool on the Force.com platform. It is used to import data into the organization quickly. The import wizard tool supports loading `Account`, `Contact`, `Leads`, `Campaign Members`, `Solutions`, or any custom objects. Using the import wizard, we can import up to 50,000 records at a time.

> The import wizard is only accessible to system administrators or users with administrative permissions.

To use the import wizard, perform the following steps:

1. Navigate to **Setup | Administer | Data Management**.

2. You will see the following:

Select the import wizard

3. All the highlighted links are used to import data. Therefore, you can select the particular link to start the import wizard for importing particular data. We will continue this example with **Import Custom Objects**.

4. Before you begin, create the custom object and any custom fields on the object, including master-detail and lookup relationship fields.

5. Import any records that relate to your custom object records. For example, if your custom object has a lookup relationship with accounts, import those accounts before importing your custom object. Import the parent first because to relate child records with the parent requires the parent record ID.

6. To create your import file, export a custom object report (for this example, use Leave Type) from Salesforce.com or a simple CSV file. We will introduce the reports in *Chapter 9, Analytics as a Service with the Force.com Platform*. Therefore, use a CSV file with three or four columns, including the `OwnerId` column. If your column labels match the field labels in Salesforce.com, the columns will be automatically mapped for you in the import operation.

7. If your custom object has owners, make sure your import file includes an owner column. Populate that column with the names of the record owners. Alternatively, populate the column with the Salesforce.com IDs or External IDs of those users.

8. Review your data for accuracy, and make sure that your file has 50,000 or fewer records.

> Salesforce.com recommends that you import a small test file of five records before importing all of your data to ensure that you have correctly prepared your import file.

9. Click on **Start the Import Wizard!**

10. From the list in the popup menu, choose the type of record that you are importing, as shown in the following screenshot:

Step 1. Choose Record			Step 1 of 3
			Next

Welcome to the custom object import wizard.

From the list below, choose the type of record that you are importing.

Label	Master Object	Description
Leave Type		
Leave Category		
Holiday Calendar		
Employee		
Leave	Employee	This is the main object that store leave info of all employees

Next

Choose object type

11. For this example, select the **Leave Type** object and click on the **Next** button.

12. The next step is to prevent duplication of selected object type (**Leave Type**) records from being created as a result of this import. Select **Yes** to prevent duplicate records from being created, as shown in the following screenshot:

Step 2. Prevent Duplicates	Step 2 of 7

Previous   Next

To prevent duplicate Leave Type records from being created as a result of this import, choose Yes below.

Do you want to prevent duplicates from being created?

○ No - insert all records in my import file.

◉ Yes - prevent duplicate records from being created. Note: You must select this option if you want to update existing records.

Which field on Leave Type do you want to use for matching? [i]

◉ Leave Type Name

○ Salesforce.com ID [i]

External ID [i]

If existing records are found, what do you want to do? [i]

◉ Do not update existing records and only insert new records

○ Update existing records and do not insert any new records

○ Update existing records and insert new records

Previous   Next

13. As shown in the preceding screenshot, you can indicate the field you will be matching against to prevent duplicates. Your selection determines the values that your import file should provide. Basically, you have three options: the **Name**, **Salesforce.com ID**, and **External ID** field. To match records by **Salesforce.com ID**, you must include a column in your import file that contains the Salesforce.com ID of each `Leave Type` record. You can only update the existing records when they match with the Salesforce.com ID. The External ID is the field that contains record IDs from a system outside of Salesforce.com. Similar to Salesforce.com IDs, you can match against this field as you import or integrate. Select **Leave Type Name** for this example.

14. You can decide, as shown in the preceding screenshot, what behavior you would like for records that match the existing records and for those that do not match the existing records. To update the matching records with the data in your file, you must change the default option. We will keep the default option to continue this example.

15. Click on **Next**.

16. Records are owned by users. If there is a record owner column in your file, you can specify below the user field that represents the next step. If you do not include a record owner column in your file, you will be saved as the owner of all the created records.

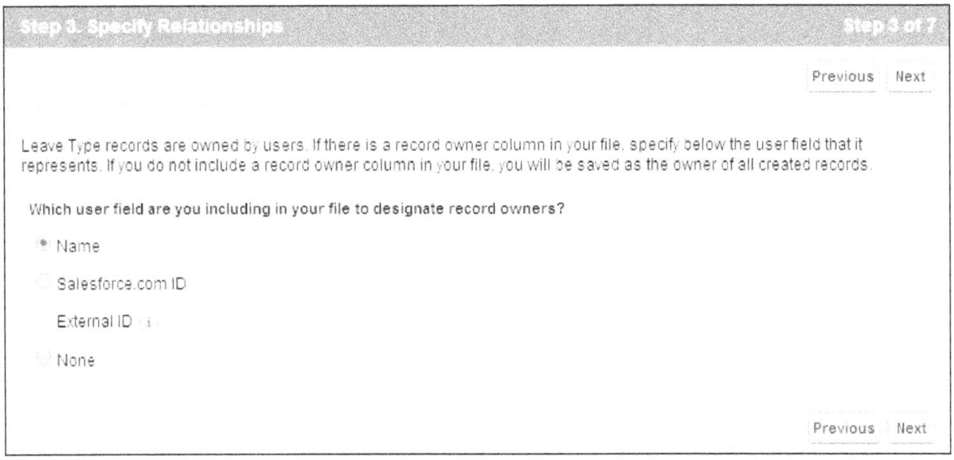

17. Click on **Next**. In the next step, you can upload the CSV file that contains the particular data to be imported. Additionally, you can specify the character encoding of your CSV file (in most cases, you can accept the default value provided) and specify whether the workflow rules for new and updated records will be triggered or not. This is an advantage of the import wizard where you have the option to not trigger the workflow rule. Step 4 is shown in the following screenshot:

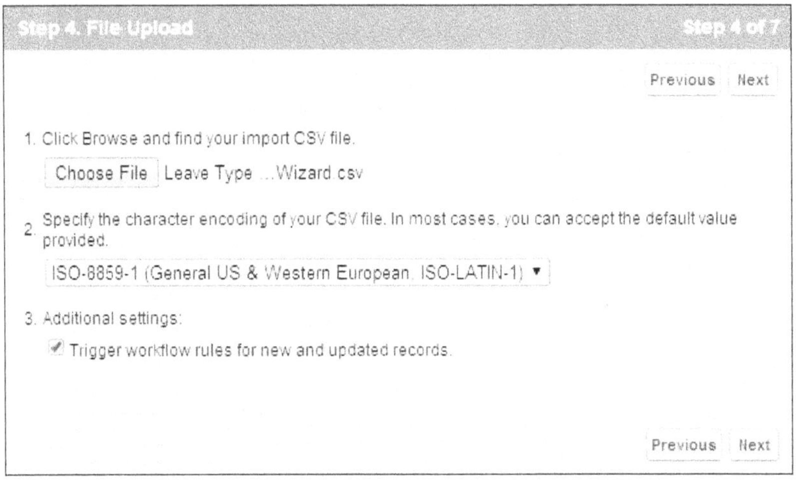

18. Click on **Next**. In the next step, you can use the drop-down lists, as shown in the following screenshot, to specify the Salesforce.com fields that correspond to the columns in your import file. For your convenience, identically matching labels will be automatically selected.

Step 5. Field Mapping	Step 5 of 7

Previous   Next

Use the drop-down lists below to specify the salesforce.com fields that correspond to the columns in your import file. For your convenience, identically matching labels will be automatically selected.

Import Field	Salesforce.com Field
Name (col 0)	Leave Type Name ▾
IsActive (col 1)	IsActive ▾

Previous   Next

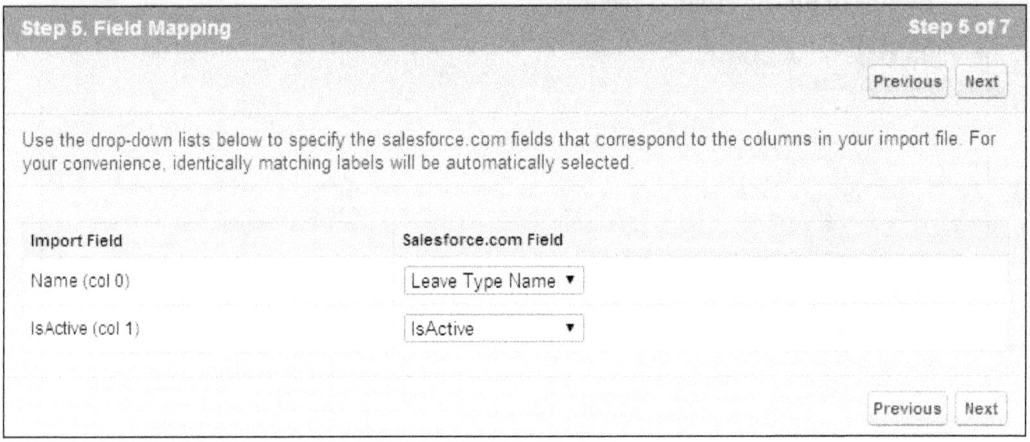

19. Click on **Next**. As shown in the following screenshot, we haven't included an owner field in our import file:

	A	B
1	Name	IsActive
2	Annual Leave	TRUE
3	Casual Leave	TRUE
4	Medical Leave	TRUE
5	No Pay Leave	TRUE
6	Deployment Leave	TRUE
7	Maternity Leave	TRUE
8	Special Leave	TRUE

Content of the CSV file

20. Therefore, you will get the following step to verify the import settings before importing the data. In this case, all the records will be inserted with you as the record owner.

21. Click on **Import Now!**

22. Now, Salesforce.com will start importing your file. You will be notified via e-mail when your import is completed.

> You can check on the status of your import by viewing **Import Queue**.

23. Click on **Finish**.

After receiving the notification, you can check the particular object tab and you will see the records that we imported.

Data export

Data export lets you prepare a copy of all your data in Salesforce.com. From this page, you can start the export process manually or schedule it to run automatically. When an export is ready for download, you will receive an e-mail containing a link that allows you to download the CSV files. The export files are also available at the following path for 48 hours, after which they are deleted.

1. Go to **Setup** | **Administer** | **Data Management** | **Data Export**.

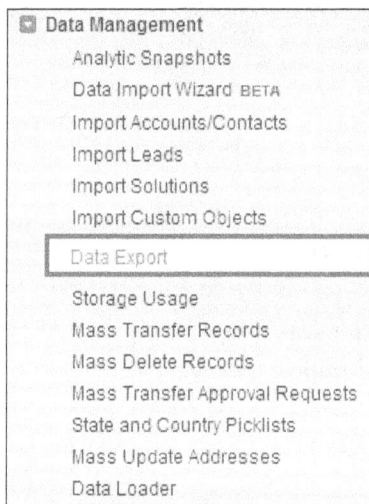

> Data Management
> Analytic Snapshots
> Data Import Wizard BETA
> Import Accounts/Contacts
> Import Leads
> Import Solutions
> Import Custom Objects
> Data Export
> Storage Usage
> Mass Transfer Records
> Mass Delete Records
> Mass Transfer Approval Requests
> State and Country Picklists
> Mass Update Addresses
> Data Loader

2. The backup files can be generated once every six days for weekly export or once every 28 days for monthly export. Click on **Export Now** or **Schedule Export**. The properties are as follows:

    ° **Export Now**: Immediate data export can be executed with this option, which is only available if adequate time has elapsed since your final export.

    ° **Schedule Export**: Schedulable data export can be executed with this option. The data can be exported weekly or monthly.

3. Select the encoding type for your export file.

4. Select **Include images, documents, and attachments** and **Include Chatter files and Salesforce CRM Content document versions** to include those items in your export data. If you select these options, it will take additional time to export.

5. Select **Replace carriage returns with spaces** to replace the carriage returns or line breaks in your export file with spaces. This is useful when you plan to use your export files for importing or other integrations.

6. Under **Exported Data**, select what type of information you would like to include in the export. The data types listed below use the Apex API names. If you are not familiar with these names, select **Include all data** for your export.

> Formula and roll-up summary fields are always excluded from exports.

7. Click on **Start Export** or **Save**.

Your export will be queued. You will receive an e-mail notification when it is completed.

Mass transfer records

A Salesforce.com object record has an owner and there are some scenarios to transfer the ownership from one user to another. For example, people are frequently changing their job. Therefore, we need to transfer their records to another user. You can use the mass transfer tool for this functionality. It supports for account, leads, service contracts, a queue of users, and any custom object records. If you are going to transfer any records that you don't own, you must have the following required user permissions as well as read sharing access to the records:

Operation	Permission needed
To mass transfer accounts and service contracts:	Transfer Record AND Edit on the object type AND Transfer Leads
To mass transfer leads:	Transfer Leads OR Transfer Record AND Edit on leads
To mass transfer custom objects:	Transfer Record AND Edit on the object type

Use the following steps to mass transfer Leave Type records:

1. Go to **Setup | Administer | Data Management | Mass Transfer Records**.

2. Click on the link for the type of record to transfer. For this example, it is Leave Type.

3. Optionally, you can select the user of the existing record owner in the **Transfer from** field.

4. Select the user of the new record owner in the field.

5. Optionally, you can filter by additional fields.

6. You can use filters by entering multiple items in the third column, separated by commas.

7. For date fields, enter the value in the format 3/6/2014.

8. For date/time fields, enter the value in the format 3/6/2014 1:31 PM.

9. Click on **Find** to get the filtered records.

10. Click on **Transfer** to complete the operation.

Mass delete records

Using this tool, you can delete multiple records of Account, Contact, Products, Solutions, Leads or Activities at one time.

Before running a mass delete, it is recommended to run a report to archive data and set up to receive a weekly export of your data. The weekly export service is included with Enterprise Edition, and is available for an additional cost with Professional Edition. Use the following steps to mass delete contact records:

1. Go to **Setup | Administer | Data Management | Mass Delete Records**.

2. Click on the link for the type of record to delete.

3. Review what will happen when you mass delete your contact records. Once data is deleted, it will be moved to the Recycle Bin. If you want to delete records permanently, select the **Permanently delete the selected records** option.

> When this option is selected, you cannot restore deleted records from the Recycle Bin. Please be careful when selecting this option.

4. Specify the criteria to find contacts to mass delete.

5. Click on **Search**.

6. Click on **Delete**.

API-based tools

The Force.com platform provides the Apex Data Loader, which is an API-based, downloadable program that helps you perform data management operations in your organization. There are many decent Extract Transform Load (ETL) Tools available on AppExchange, such as Dataloader.io and many more, which can be utilized.

Apex Data Loader

The Force.com platform provides the Apex Data Loader, which is an API-based ETL Tool. The Apex Data Loader is a client application for the bulk import or export of data. Use it to insert, update, delete, undelete, or extract Salesforce.com records.

The Apex Data Loader can move data into or out of any type of Salesforce.com record, including standard objects and custom objects. This tool can be used for mass data delete of objects as well. Unlike the import wizard, the Data Loader can load more than 50,000 records. You can schedule regular data loads (such as nightly feeds) using the Data Loader. When importing data, it reads, extracts, and loads data from CSV files. When exporting data, it outputs CSV files. Additionally, you can do data loading or exporting using **Java Database Connectivity (JDBC)**.

There are two versions of the Data Loader:

*   **User Interface version**: This is an interactive version of the Data Loader. You can specify configuration parameters, CSV files that are used for the import and export, field mapping in between the CSV file and the Salesforce object through the GUI version.

*   **Command-line version**: This version has less interactivity but more speed than the GUI version. You can specify the configuration, mapping, CSV files and action in files through the command-line version too. Especially, this version allows you to set up the Data Loader for automated processing.

This is not a cloud-based tool. Therefore, you have to download the desktop application built for Windows. To download the Data Loader, use the following steps:

1. Go to **Setup** | **Administer** | **Data Management**.
2. Click on **Data Loader**.
3. Download the Data Loader.
4. Launch the installing wizard and follow the instructions.

Exporting data using Data Loader

After you install the Data Loader, double-click on the Data Loader icon. As per the following screenshot, you can export, insert, update, and upsert your data in the organization.

Starting the Apex Data Loader

Use the following steps to export data through the Data Loader. Let's export some data from the Leave type object:

1. Click on the **Export** button in the Apex Data Loader.

> The difference between **Export** and **Export All** in Apex Data Loader is as follows:
>
> - **Export**: It is used to export the Salesforce Data, excluding the Recycle Bin's data, into your local system.
> - **Export All**: It is used to export the Salesforce Data, including the Recycle Bin's data, into your local system.

2. If you are not logged into the Data Loader, you have to log in now by providing the user credentials of your organization. Keep in mind to append the security token to the password.

> If you forgot or don't know your security token, you can reset your security token from the following path:
> **Your Name** | **My Settings** | **Personal** | **Reset My Security Token**
> The Security Token is reset each time the password changes for a specific user.

3. The following screenshot shows the login of the Data Loader:

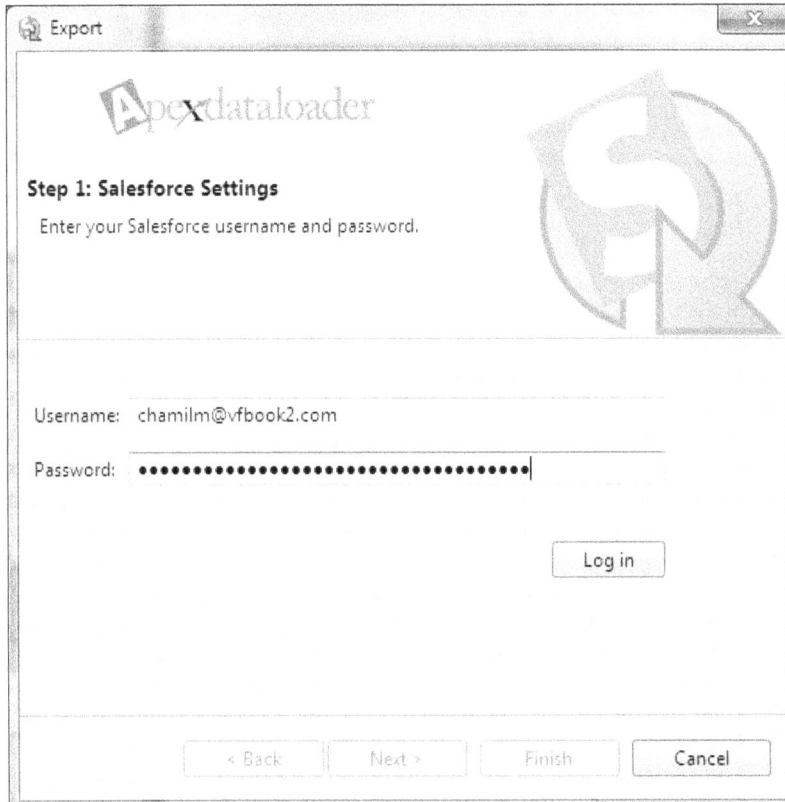

4. After successful log in, click on **Next** to proceed.

5. In the next step, you can select the object that you are going to export and choose the target destination for extraction. Specify the filename with the .csv extension. Click on **Next**.

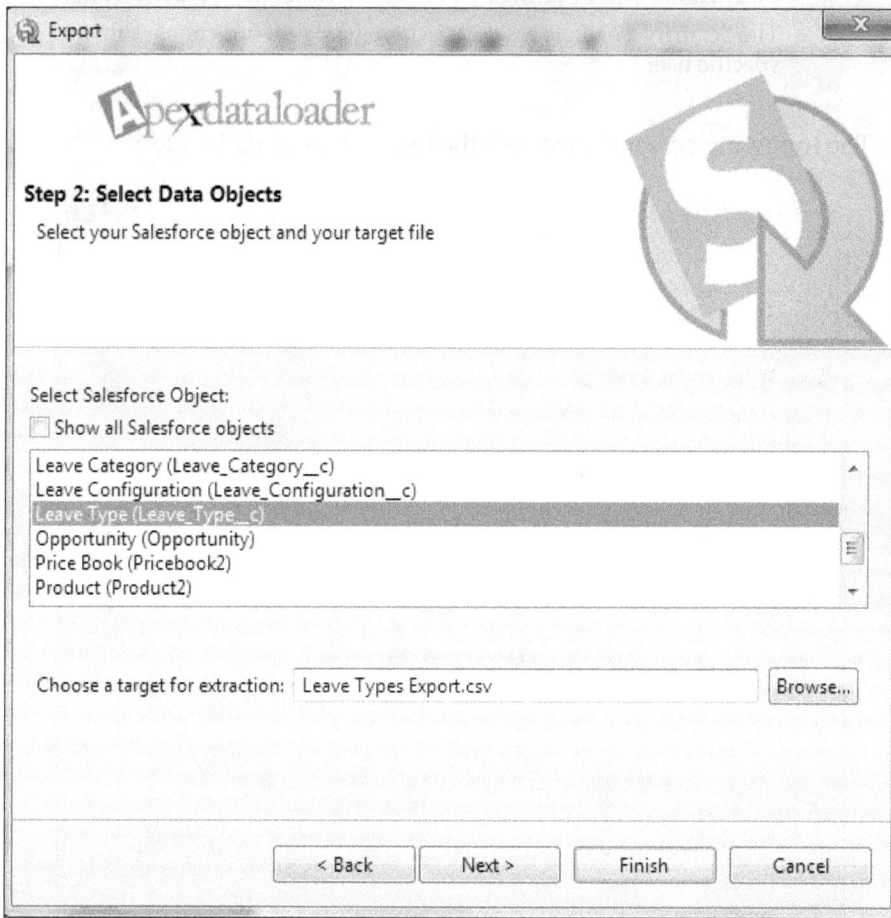

6. In the next step, you can define the query to export data. Here, you can add conditions to the query and the final query will be prepared automatically with the selected fields and conditions.

7. Click on **Finish** to start the data extraction.

8. There are two files called success.csv and error.csv in the final report. If there are any errors in the extraction the error.csv file will contain the reason for the error.

The exported records will be contained in the file you specified.

Upserting data using Data Loader

You have learned about the upsert operation in the *Data Management operations* section. Let's try out the upsert operation with the Apex Data Loader. For this example, we are going to use the `Employee` object, which has an External ID called `Social Security Number`:

1. Click on the **Upsert** button, which is located on the main screen of the Data Loader.

2. Select the object you are going to upsert. For this example, we are using the `Employee` object.

3. Choose the target destination for extraction. Specify the file name with the `.csv` extension. Click on **Next**.

4. In the next step, you need to select the field on your Salesforce object to use for matching. If you have External IDs for the particular object, they will appear on the pick list. The matching ID is very important because it is used to prevent duplicates on your records. In this example, we will select the **Social Security Number** as the matching ID.

5. Click on **Next**. In the next step, you can define the mapping, which maps the object field with the CSV file. Click on the **Create or Edit a Map** button in this step as shown in the following screenshot:

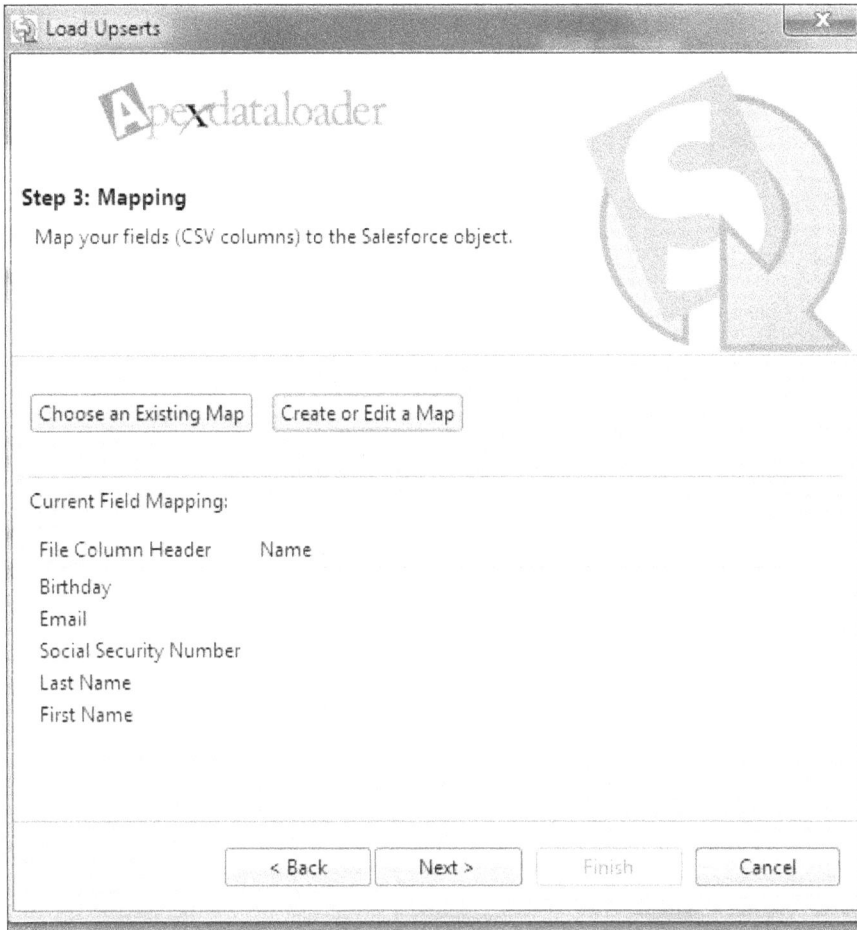

6. You will get the following screenshot and you can map the Salesforce object fields and the fields of the CSV file. You can drag the Salesforce object field down to the CSV field. If the Salesforce object field name and the CSV field names are the same, you can click on the **Auto-match fields to columns** button. Then the Data Loader will take care of the field mapping.

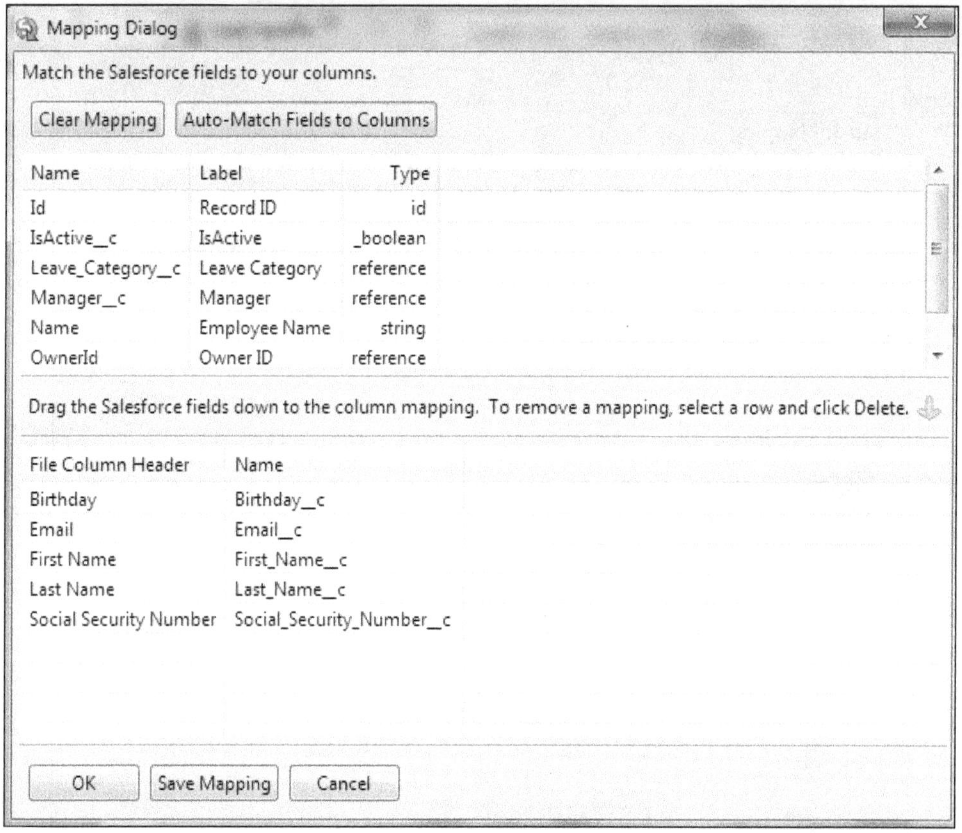

Match the Salesforce fields to CSV columns

7. You can save your mapping file as an external file for future use. Click on **OK** to finish the mapping. The mapping gets saved on your desktop as an `.SDL` extension file.

8. Click on **Next**. Select the directory where your success and error files will be saved.

9. Click on **Finish**.

Now we have tried out the export and the upsert operations through the Data Loader. The insert and update operations are very similar to upsert operation. The only difference between upsert and insert/update is that insert/update don't use External IDs to match the record. Therefore, you can try them on your own.

Further details about the Data Loader can be found at `http://na12.salesforce.com/help/pdfs/en/salesforce_data_loader.pdf`.

Summary

In this chapter, we have learnt about the data management operations in the Force.com platform, including the CRUD commands and upsert command. We learned about the behavior and importance of the Force.com IDs and the External IDs. Finally, we covered the data management tools in the Force.com platform, including cloud-based tools and API-based tools. In the next chapter, you are going to learn about Apex, which is used for custom coding in the Force.com platform.

7
Custom Coding with Apex

Up to this point, you have learned to develop the Force.com application using the declarative methods (point and click developments). We have used many declarative methods such as creating the object's structure, relationships, workflow rules, and approval process to develop the Force.com application. The declarative development method doesn't require any coding skill and specific Integrated Development Environment (IDE).

This chapter will show you how to extend the declarative capabilities using custom coding of the Force.com platform. Apex controllers and Apex triggers will be explained with examples of the sample application. The Force.com platform query language and data manipulation language will be described with syntaxes and examples. At the end of the chapter, there will be a section to describe bulk data handling methods in Apex.

This chapter covers the following topics:

- Introducing Apex
- Working with Apex
- Writing Apex code
- Triggers
- Force.com platform query languages
- Data manipulation on the Force.com platform
- Bulk data handling with Apex

Introducing Apex

Apex is the world's first on-demand programming language that allows developers to implement and execute business flows, business logic, and transactions on the Force.com platform. As you learned in *Chapter 1, Getting Started with Force.com*, there are two types of Force.com application development methods: declarative developments and programmatic developments. Apex is categorized under the programmatic development method. Since Apex is a strongly-typed, object-based language, it is connected with data in the Force.com platform and data manipulation using the query language and the search language.

The Apex language has the following features:

- Apex provides a lot of built-in support for the Force.com platform features such as:
  - Data Manipulation Language (DML) with the built-in exception handling (DmlException) to manipulate the data during the execution of the business logic.
  - Salesforce Object Query Language (SOQL) and Salesforce Object Search Language (SOSL) to query and retrieve the list of sObjects records.
  - Bulk data processing on multiple records at a time.
  - Apex allows handling errors and warning using an in-built error-handling mechanism.
  - Apex has its own record-locking mechanism to prevent conflicts of record updates.
  - Apex allows building custom public Force.com APIs from stored Apex methods.
- Apex runs in a multitenant environment. The Force.com platform has multitenant architecture. Therefore, the Apex runtime engine obeys the multitenant environment. It prevents monopolizing of shared resources using the guard with limits. If any particular Apex code violates the limits, error messages will be displayed.
- Apex is hosted in the Force.com platform. Therefore, the Force.com platform interprets, executes, and controls Apex.

- Automatically upgradable and versioned:

  - Apex codes are stored as metadata in the platform. Therefore, they are automatically upgraded with the platform. You don't need to rewrite your code when the platform gets updated. Each code is saved with the current upgrade version. You can manually change the version. It is easy to maintain the Apex code with the versioned mechanism.

- Apex can be used easily. Apex is similar to Java syntax and variables. The syntaxes and semantics of Apex are easy to understand and write codes.

- Apex is a data-focused programming language. Apex is designed for multithreaded query and DML statements in a single execution context on the Force.com servers. Many developers can use database stored procedures to run multiple transaction statements on the database server. Apex is different from other databases when it comes to stored procedures; it doesn't attempt to provide general support for rendering elements in the user interface.

> The execution context is one of the key concepts in Apex programming. It influences every aspect of software development on the Force.com platform.

- Apex is a strongly-typed language that directly refers to schema objects and object fields. If there is any error, it fails the compilation. All the objects, fields, classes, and pages are stored in metadata after successful compilation.

- Easy to perform unit testing. Apex provides a built-in feature for unit testing and test execution with the code coverage.

Apex allows developers to write the logic in two ways:

- **As an Apex class**: The developer can write classes in the Force.com platform using Apex code. An Apex class includes action methods which related to the logic implementation. An Apex class can be called from a trigger. A class can be associated with a Visualforce page (Visualforce Controllers/Extensions) or can act as a supporting class (WebService, Email-to-Apex service/Helper classes, Batch Apex, and Schedules). Therefore, Apex classes are explicitly called from different places on the Force.com platform.

- **As a database trigger**: A trigger is executed related to a particular database interaction of a Force.com object. For example, you can create a trigger on the Leave Type object that fires whenever the Leave Type record is inserted. Therefore, triggers are implicitly called from a database action.

Apex is included in the Unlimited Edition, Developer Edition, Enterprise Edition, Database.com, and Performance Edition. The developer can write Apex classes or Apex triggers in a developer organization or a sandbox of a production organization. After you finish the development of the Apex code, you can deploy the particular Apex code to the production organization. Before you deploy the Apex code, you have to write test methods to cover the implemented Apex code. Further details about the deployment will be described in *Chapter 12, Deploying the Force.com Application.*

Apex code in the runtime environment

You already know that Apex code is stored and executed on the Force.com platform. Apex code also has a compile time and a runtime. When you attempt to save an Apex code, it checks for errors, and if there are no errors, it saves with the compilation. The code is compiled into a set of instructions that are about to execute at runtime.

Apex always adheres to built-in governor limits of the Force.com platform. These governor limits protect the multitenant environment from runaway processes.

Apex code and unit testing

Unit testing is important because it checks the code and executes the particular method or trigger for failures and exceptions during test execution. It provides a structured development environment. We gain two good requirements for this unit testing, namely, best practice for development and best practice for maintaining the Apex code. The Force.com platform forces you to cover the Apex code you implemented. Therefore, the Force.com platform ensures that you follow the best practices on the platform.

Apex governors and limits

Apex codes are executed on the Force.com multitenant infrastructure and the shared resources are used across all customers, partners, and developers. When we are writing custom code using Apex, it is important that the Apex code uses the shared resources efficiently. Apex governors are responsible for enforcing runtime limits set by Salesforce. It discontinues the misbehaviors of the particular Apex code. If the code exceeds a limit, a runtime exception is thrown that cannot be handled. This error will be seen by the end user. Limit warnings can be sent via e-mail, but they also appear in the logs.

Governor limits are specific to a namespace, so AppExchange certified managed applications have their own set of limits, independent of the other applications running in the same organization. Therefore, the governor limits have their own scope. The limit scope will start from the beginning of the code execution. It will be run through the subsequent blocks of code until the particular code terminates.

Apex code and security

As you learned in *Chapter 4, Designing Apps for Multiple Users and Protecting Data*, the Force.com platform has a component-based security, record-based security and rich security framework, including profiles, record ownership, and sharing. Normally, Apex codes are executed as a system mode (not as a user mode), which means the Apex code has access to all data and components. However, you can make the Apex class run in user mode by defining the Apex class with the sharing keyword. The with sharing/without sharing keywords are employed to designate that the sharing rules for the running user are considered for the particular Apex class.

Use the with sharing keyword when declaring a class to enforce the sharing rules that apply to the current user.

Use the without sharing keyword when declaring a class to ensure that the sharing rules for the current user are not enforced. For example, you may want to explicitly turn off sharing rule enforcement when a class acquires sharing rules after it is called from another class that is declared using with sharing.

> The profile also can maintain the permission for developing Apex code and accessing Apex classes. The author's Apex permission is required to develop Apex codes and we can limit the access of Apex classes through the profile by adding or removing the granted Apex classes.

Although triggers are built using Apex code, the execution of triggers cannot be controlled by the user. They depend on the particular operation, and if the user has permission for the particular operation, then the trigger will be fired.

Apex code and web services

Like other programming languages, Apex supports communication with the outside world through web services. Apex methods can be exposed as a web service. Therefore, an external system can invoke the Apex web service to execute the particular logic. When you write a web service method, you must use the `webservice` keyword at the beginning of the method declaration. The variables can also be exposed with the `webservice` keyword. After you create the `webservice` method, you can generate the **Web Service Definition Language (WSDL)**, which can be consumed by an external application. Apex supports both **Simple Object Access Protocol (SOAP)** and **Representational State Transfer (REST)** web services.

Apex and metadata

Because Apex is a proprietary language, it is strongly typed to Salesforce metadata. The same sObject and fields that are created through the declarative setup menu can be referred to through Apex. Like other Force.com features, the system will provide an error if you try to delete an object or field that is used within Apex. Apex is not technically autoupgraded with each new Salesforce release, as it is saved with a specific version of the API. Therefore, Apex, like other Force.com features, will automatically work with future versions of Salesforce applications. Force.com application development tools use the metadata. More details about Force.com development tools can be found in the *Appendix, Force.com Tools*.

Working with Apex

Before you start coding with Apex, you need to learn a few basic things.

Apex basics

Apex has come up with a syntactical framework. Similar to Java, Apex is strongly typed and is an object-based language. If you have some experience with Java, it will be easy to understand Apex. The following table explains the similarities and differences between Apex and Java.

Similarities	Differences
Both languages have classes, inheritance, polymorphism, and other common object oriented programming features	Apex runs in a multitenant environment and is very controlled in its invocations and governor limits
Both languages have extremely similar syntax and notations	Apex is case sensitive

Similarities	Differences
Both languages are compiled, strongly-typed, and transactional	Apex is on-demand and is compiled and executed in the cloud
	Apex is not a general purpose programming language, but is instead a proprietary language used for specific business logic functions
	Apex requires unit testing for deployment into a production environment

This section will not discuss everything that is included in the Apex documentation from Salesforce, but it will cover topics that are essential for understanding concepts discussed in this book. With this basic knowledge of Apex, you can create Apex code in the Force.com platform.

Apex data types

In Apex classes and triggers, we use variables that contain data values. Variables must be bound to a data type and that particular variable can hold the values with the same data type.

All variables and expressions have one of the following data types:

- Primitives
- Enums
- sObjects
- Collections
- An object created from the user or system-defined classes
- Null (for the null constant)

Primitive data types

Apex uses the same primitive data types as the web services API, most of which are similar to their Java counterparts. It may seem that Apex primitive variables are passed by value, but they actually use immutable references, similar to Java string behavior. The following are the primitive data types of Apex:

- `Boolean`: A value that can only be assigned true, false, or null.
- `Date`, `Datetime`, and `Time`: A Date value indicates particular day and not contains any information about time. A Datetime value indicates a particular day and time. A Time value indicates a particular time. Date, Datetime and Time values must always be created with a system static method.

- ID: 18 or 15 digits version.

- Integer, Long, Double, and Decimal: Integer is a 32-bit number that does not include decimal points. Integers have a minimum value of -2,147,483,648 and a maximum value of 2,147,483,647. Long is a 64-bit number that does not include a decimal point. Use this datatype when you need a range of values wider than those provided by Integer. Double is a 64-bit number that includes a decimal point. Both Long and Doubles have a minimum value of -263 and a maximum value of 263-1. Decimal is a number that includes a decimal point. Decimal is an arbitrary precision number.

- String: String is any set of characters surrounded by single quotes. Strings have no limit on the number of characters that can be included. But the heap size limit is used to ensure to the particular Apex program do not grow too large.

- Blob: Blob is a collection of binary data stored as a single object. Blog can be accepted as Web service argument, stored in a document or sent as attachments.

- Object: This can be used as the base type for any other data type. Objects are supported for casting.

Enum data types

Enum (or enumerated list) is an abstract data type that stores one value of a finite set of specified identifiers. To define an Enum, use the enum keyword in the variable declaration and then define the list of values. You can define and use enum in the following way:

```
Public enum Status {NEW, APPROVED, REJECTED, CANCELLED}
```

The preceding enum has four values: NEW, APPROVED, REJECTED, CANCELLED. By creating this enum, you have created a new data type called Status that can be used as any other data type for variables, return types, and method arguments.

```
Status leaveStatus = Status. NEW;
```

Apex provides Enums for built-in concepts such as API error (System.StatusCode). System-defined enums cannot be used in web service methods.

sObject data types

sObjects (short for Salesforce Object) are standard or custom objects that store record data in the Force.com database. There is also an sObject data type in Apex that is the programmatic representation of these sObjects and their data in code. Developers refer to sObjects and their fields by their API names, which can be found in the schema browser.

sObject and field references within Apex are validated against actual object and field names when code is written. Force.com tracks the objects and fields used within Apex to prevent users from making the following changes:

- Changing a field or object name
- Converting from one data type to another
- Deleting a field or object
- Organization-wide changes such as record sharing

It is possible to declare variables of the generic sObject data type. The new operator still requires a concrete sObject type, so the instances are all specific sObjects. The following is a code example:

```
sObject s = new Employee__c();
```

Casting will be applied as expected as each row knows its runtime type and can be cast back to that type. The following casting works fine:

```
Employee__c e = (Employee__c)s;
```

However, the following casting will generate a runtime exception for data type collision:

```
Leave__c leave = (Leave__c)s;
```

> sObject super class only has the ID variable. So we can only access the ID via the sObject class.

This method can also be used with collections and DML operations, although only concrete types can be instantiated. Collection will be described in the upcoming section and DML operations will be discussed in the *Data manipulation* section on the Force.com platform. Let's have a look at the following code:

```
sObject[] sList = new Employee__c[0];
List<Employee__c> = (List<Employee__c>)sList;
Database.insert(sList);
```

Collection data types

Collection data types store groups of elements of other primitive, composite, or collection data types. There are three different types of collections in Apex:

1. **List**: A list is an ordered collection of primitives or composite data types distinguished by its index. Each element in a list contains two pieces of information; an index (this is an integer) and a value (the data). The index of the first element is zero. You can define an Apex list in the following way:

   ```
   List<DataType> listName = new List<DataType>();
   List<String> sList = new List< String >();
   ```

2. There are built-in methods that can be used with lists adding/removing elements from the end of the list, getting/setting values at a particular index, and sizing the list by obtaining the number of elements. A full set of list methods are listed at http://www.salesforce.com/us/developer/docs/ dbcom_apex250/Content/apex_methods_system_list.htm. The Apex list is defined in the following way:

   ```
   List<String> sList = new List< String >();
   sList.add('string1');
   sList.add('string2');
   sList.add('string3');
   sList.add('string4');
   Integer sListSize = sList.size(); // this will return the
     value as 4
   sList.get(3); //This method will return the value as
     "string4"
   ```

   Apex allows developers familiar with the standard array syntax to use that interchangeably with the list syntax. The main difference is the use of square brackets, which is shown in the following code:

   ```
   String[] sList = new String[4];
   sList [0] = 'string1';
   sList [1] = 'string2';
   sList [2] = 'string3';
   sList [3] = 'string4';
   Integer sListSize = sList.size(); // this will return the
     value as 4
   ```

   Lists, as well as maps, can be nested up to five levels deep. Therefore, you can create a list of lists in the following way.

   ```
   List<List<String>> nestedList = new List<List<String>> ();
   ```

3. **Set**: A set is an unordered collection of data of one primitive data type or sObjects that must have unique values. The Set methods are listed at `http://www.salesforce.com/us/developer/docs/dbcom_apex230/Content/apex_methods_system_set.htm`.

   Similar to the declaration of List, you can define a Set in the following way:

   ```
   Set<DataType> setName = new Set<DataType>();
   Set<String> setName = new Set<String>();
   ```

   There are built-in methods for sets, including add/remove elements to/from the set, check whether the set contains certain elements, and the size of the set.

4. **Map**: A map is an unordered collection of unique keys of one primitive data type and their corresponding values. The Map methods are listed in the following link at `http://www.salesforce.com/us/developer/docs/dbcom_apex250/Content/apex_methods_system_map.htm`.

   You can define a Map in the following way:

   ```
   Map<PrimitiveKeyDataType, DataType> = mapName = new
     Map<PrimitiveKeyDataType, DataType>();
   Map<Integer, String> mapName = new Map<Integer, String>();
   Map<Integer, List<String>> sMap = new Map<Integer,
     List<String>>();
   ```

   Maps are often used to map IDs to sObjects. There are built-in methods that you can use with maps, including adding/removing elements on the map, getting values for a particular key, and checking whether the map contains certain keys. You can use these methods as follows:

   ```
   Map<Integer, String> sMap = new Map<Integer, String>();
   sMap.put(1, 'string1'); // put key and values pair
   sMap.put(2, 'string2');
   sMap.put(3, 'string3');
   sMap.put(4, 'string4');
   sMap.get(2); // retrieve the value of key 2
   ```

Apex logics and loops

Like all programming languages, Apex language has the syntax to implement conditional logics (IF-THEN-ELSE) and loops (for, Do-while, while). The following table will explain the conditional logic and loops in Apex:

IF	<ul><li>Conditional IF statements in Apex are similar to Java.</li><li>The IF-THEN statement is the most basic of all the control flow statements. It tells your program to execute a certain section of code only if a particular test evaluates to true.</li><li>The IF-THEN-ELSE statement provides a secondary path of execution when an IF clause evaluates to false.</li></ul>
	```if (Boolean_expression){```
	```statement;```
	```statement;```
	```statement;```
	```statement;}```
	```else {```
	```statement;```
	```statement;}```

For	<ul><li>There are three variations of the FOR loop in Apex, which are as follows:</li></ul>
	```FOR(initialization;Boolean_exit_condition;increment)```
	```{```
	``` statement;```
	```}```
	
	```FOR(variable : list_or_set)```
	```{```
	``` statement;```
	```}```
	
	```FOR(variable : [inline_soql_query])```
	```{```
	``` statement;```
	```}```
	<ul><li>All loops allow for the following commands:<ul><li>**break**: This is used to exit the loop</li><li>**continue**: This is used to skip to the next iteration of the loop</li></ul></li></ul>

While	• The `while` loop is similar, but the condition is checked before the first loop, as shown in the following code:
	
	``
	while (Boolean_condition) {
	code_block;
	};
	``

Do-While	• The do-while loop repeatedly executes as long as a particular Boolean condition remains true.
	
	• The condition is not checked until after the first pass is executed, as shown in the following code:
	
	``
	do {
	//code_block;
	}
	while (Boolean_condition);
	``

Writing Apex code – object-oriented programming in Apex

As in most OOP languages, classes are templates through which objects are instantiated that contain attributes and methods. Class methods or attributes can be invoked by other Apex scripts within the same organization except methods that have the `webservice` keyword. The `webservice` methods are available externally to the organization. Classes are stored with the version of the API used to compile them. Classes have an `isValid` flag that is true if dependent metadata has not changed since compilation. Classes may contain one level of inner classes. Inner class is a way of organizing the classes (same as the package in Java).

Creating Apex code

Apex classes can be created and edited through the **Setup** menu of the organization and Force.com IDE and Developer Console. You can interact with Apex classes via the setup page by navigating to **Setup | Develop | Apex Classes**. You will see the following screenshot:

Apex Classes

Help for this Page

Force.com Apex Code is an object oriented programming language that allows developers to develop on-demand business applications on the Force.com platform.

> **Percent of Apex Used: 0%**
> You are currently using 33 characters of Apex Code (excluding comments and @isTest annotated classes) in your organization, out of an allowed limit of 3,000,000 characters. Note that the amount in use includes both Apex Classes and Triggers defined in your organization.

Estimate your organization's code coverage i
Compile all classes i
View: All ▼   Create New View

A | B | C | D | E | F | G | H | I | J | K | L | M | N | O | P | Q | R | S | T | U | V | W | X | Y | Z | Other | **All**

	Developer Console	New	Generate from WSDL	Run All Tests	Schedule Apex		
Action	Name ↑	Namespace Prefix	Api Version	Status	Size Without Comments	Last Modified By	Override Log Filters
Edit | Del | Security	LeaveController		29.0	Active	33	Chamil Madusanka, 4/18/2014 11:08 PM	

Landing page of Apex classes

You can find the currently available classes in the preceding screenshot. This page allows you to create new classes, edit the existing classes, delete the existing classes, and assign security for the existing classes.

> The **New**, **Edit**, and **Delete** options for Apex classes are not available in the production organization.

You can create, edit, and view a class through the Developer Console via **Your Name | Developer Console**. You will see the popup as shown in the following screenshot:

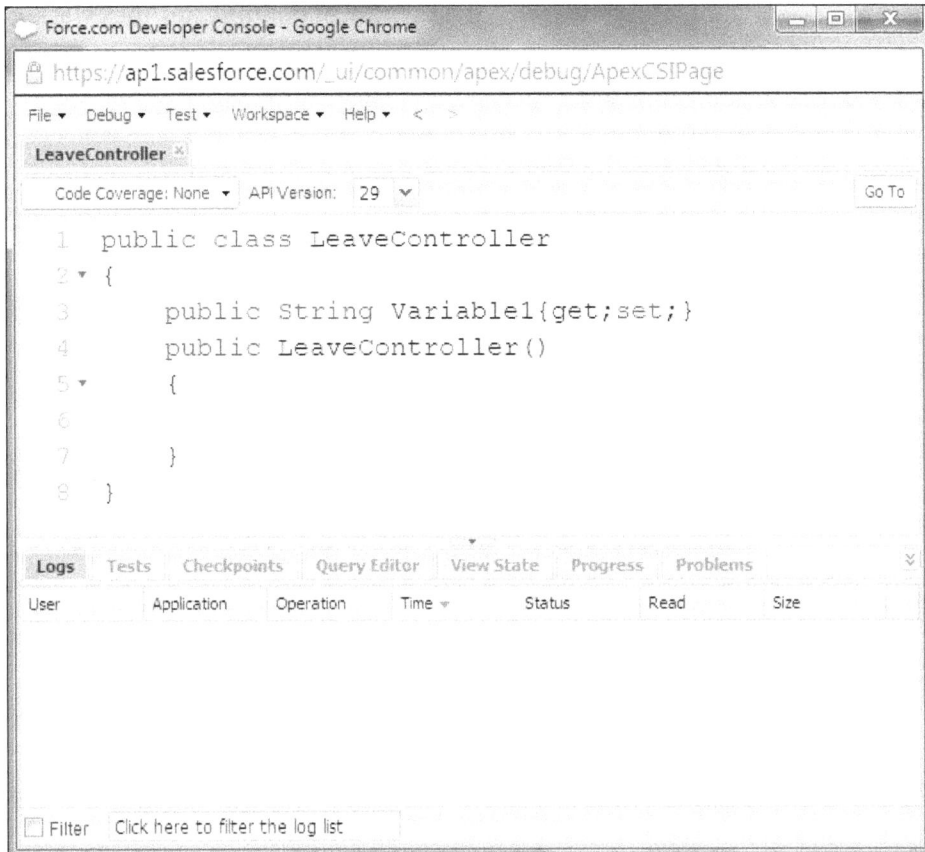

Create/edit Apex classes via the Developer Console

The same as with Apex classes, you can develop triggers from the Setup page, the Force.com IDE, and the Developer Console. When you are using the Setup page, you must navigate to **Setup | Develop | Apex Triggers**. More details about triggers are available in the *Triggers* section.

The Force.com IDE is a plug-in for the standard eclipse framework and it is a highly productive development environment for Apex developments and testing. More details about Force.com IDE are available in the *Appendix, Force.com Tools*.

Syntax to define classes

When you are writing an Apex class, you must be aware about the class syntax. The following code template shows the whole syntax of defining an Apex class.

```
Private|public|global
[virtual|abstract|with sharing|without sharing|(none)]
Class ClassName [implements InterfaceNameList | (none)] [extends
  ClassOrInterfaceName | (none)]{
//The body of the class here
}
```

There are three types of class syntax that must be adopted by the developer:

- **Access Modifiers**: Classes have different access levels depending on the keywords used in the class definition. The following table shows the types of class access modifiers in Apex:

Modifier	Description
Global	The class is accessible by all Apex everywhere including web services and e-mail services. All methods/attributes with the `webservice` keyword or dealing with e-mail services must be global. All methods, attributes, and inner classes that are global must be within a global class to be accessible.
Public	This class is visible across your application or namespace. You must use global or public access modifier for the outer classes.
Private	This class is an inner class and is only accessible to the outer class or a test class. The default access modifier of an inner class is private.

- **Inheritance**: Inheritance syntaxes are optional in the declaration of a class. There are three types of inheritance syntaxes in Apex as follows:

Keyword	Description
Virtual	This modifier declares that this class allows extensions and overrides and can be used as a superclass.
Abstract	This modifier declares that this class contains abstract methods.
Extends	This keyword is used to identify this as a subclass. The `super` keyword can be used to invoke constructors and methods from the parent class.

- **Sharing**: You already know that, by default, most Apex runs as system (except for anonymous blocks). Use the `with sharing` and `without sharing` keywords to change if the current user's sharing rules should be applied to the executing logic. If neither is used in declaring a class, the sharing rules of the calling class remain in effect.

Syntax to define interfaces

Like in Java, Apex has a concept called interface, which only includes method signatures and not the actual implementation code for the method. Another class must be created that supplies the implementation. Apex supports both top-level and inner interfaces.

The following is an example of an interface that defines the `Manager` behavior. It has the `isSeniorExecutive` method signature with the `Boolean` return type, as shown in the following code:

```
public interface Manager{
  //An interface that defines what a manager looks like in general
  Boolean isSeniorExecutive();
}
```

The following class is the other class that implements the preceding interface. The `isSeniorExecutive` method has actually implemented it in this class:

```
Public class OperationalManager implements Manager{
  Public Boolean isSeniorExecutive(){
    Return true;
  }
}
```

Syntax for attributes and methods

When we discuss the attributes and methods, we must be aware of Apex statements and their syntaxes. In the Apex language, there are some standard syntax conventions for Apex statements as follows:

1. **Semi-colon (;)**: This is used to end an individual statement.

2. **Braces, or curly brackets ({})**: This is used to indicate a code block.

3. **Parentheses()**: This is used to group values such as variables for a method call, define argument of a method, evaluated expression in a conditional statement.

4. **Two forward slashes (//)**: This is used to comment a single line.

5. **Forward slash with asterisk (/* */)**: This is used to comment multiline code.

Access modifiers

Attributes (variables) are frequently used in Apex code to hold data values. Until you declare the variable, you cannot refer the variable. If you try to refer before the declaration, you will receive a compile-time error. Variables are case insensitive within your code. A variable must have a data type, which we will discuss in the *Apex data type* section.

You can declare a variable within a class and within a method with the following syntax:

1. Type ([]) variable_name (= initialization).

2. If you are going to declare an array, you must use the square brackets ([]).

3. The declared variable can be initialized using the equal (=) sign and a particular value. If you do not initialize a value to the particular variable, the variable has a value of null.

4. Like classes, attributes and methods have different access levels depending on the keyword used in the declaration. There are four types of access modifiers to define the visibility of attributes and methods:

    ° **private**: If you use this access modifier, then the particular method/variable is accessible only within the class where it is defined.

    ° **protected**: This method/variable is also available to any inner classes or subclasses. It can be used by instance methods and member attributes.

    ° **public**: This method/variable can be used by any Apex code in this application namespace.

    ° **global**: This method/variable is accessible by all Apex code everywhere.

> The default access modifier for attributes and methods is private.

The following code snippet shows the attribute declaration:

```
modifiers dataType variableName initialization;
private Integer I,j,k, myInt;
String myString = 'Hello World';
```

The following code snippet shows the method declaration:

```
modifiers returnDataType methodName(inputParameterList){
//method code
}
Public Integer getInt(){
  Return myInt;
}
```

As in Java, methods can be overloaded with more than one method for a class having the same name but different signatures. The following two methods have the same name but different number of input parameters.

```
Public Integer getInt(){
  return myInt;
}
Public Integer getInt(Integer subInt){
  return myInt+ subInt;
}
```

This code explains method overloading in Apex.

The static keyword

Static methods are accessed through the class itself and not through an object of the class. Static methods are generally utility methods that do not depend on an instance. You can use static attributes to store data that is shared within the class. All instances of the same class share a single copy of static attributes within the same context. This can be a technique used for setting flags to prevent recursive code. Therefore, the static variables are re-initialized for every transaction. You must use the static keyword to create the static methods and variables as follows:

```
Public class MyClass{
  Public static Integer myStaticVar = 7;
  Public static void myStaticMethod(){
    //code here
  }
}
```

You can call the static method without creating an instance as follows:

```
MyClass. myStaticMethod();
```

The final keyword

In Apex, you can create constants, which means the variable can be assigned a value once (with a static initialization method, the constant is defined in a class or at the declaration itself). You can declare a constant using the static and final keywords as follows:

```
Public class myCls{
   static final Integer PRIVATE_CONST1;
   static final Integer PRIVATE_CONST2 = 100;
   public static Integer calculate(){
      return 10+20;
   }
   // initializer method
Static {
   PRIVATE_CONST1 = calculate();
}
}
```

As defined in the preceding class, you can declare the constants with the initialization at the declaration itself and through a static initialization method. The static initialization code is a code block that starts with the static keyword. This type of code block is initialized on the initiatory usage of the class.

> If you do not use the static keyword in such a code block, then it will become the instance initialization code as follows:
>
> ```
> {
> //code body
> }
> ```

Every time you create an object instance of a class, the instance initialization code block is executed before the constructor. This type of code block is used when you don't want to use your own constructor in a class. You can use this code block to initialize variables.

Any number of static or instance initialization code blocks can be specified in a class. They can be specified anywhere within the class and will be executed in the order they appear in the code file.

Class constructors

Like in Java, Apex also has the constructor concept, which is a code block that is executed when an object instance is created from a class. A constructor for a class is not a required matter. We can write classes without user-defined constructors. On such an occasion, implicitly a no-argument constructor will be used.

You can define a constructor same as the method declaration. However, there are a few differentiations between method and constructor declarations.

- A constructor doesn't have an explicit return type
- A constructor uses the same name of the class
- The constructor is not inherited by the object created from it

As shown in the following code snippet, you can instantiate an object instance using the new keyword:

```
ClassName objectName = new ClassName();
MyFirstClass myObject1 = new MyFirstClass();
MyFirstClass myObject2 = new MyFirstClass();
```

Once you have instantiated an object, you can refer to methods and attributes using dot notation.

```
myObject1.myMethod1();
myObject2.myVariable = 'TestValue';
```

In an Apex class, you can create overloaded constructors that have a different number of arguments.

```
public class ConstructorExample{
  private static final Integer SIZE = 10;
  Integer NewSize;
  //constructor with no arguments
  public ConstructorExample(){
    this(SIZE); //using this keyword, calling the one argument
      constructor
  }
  public ConstructorExample(Integer mySize){
    NewSize = mySize;
  }
}
```

The usage of a constructor is as follows:

```
ConstructorExample myObj1 = new ConstructorExample(25);
ConstructorExample myObj2 = new ConstructorExample();
```

> There are two different ways of using this keyword
>
> You can use this keyword in dot notation to represent the current instance of the class to access instance attributes and methods.
>
> ```
> public class this keyword(){
>     String s;
>     this.s = 'TestString';
> }
> ```
>
> Alternatively, you can use it in the constructor to call another constructor to do constructor chaining. It must be the first statement in the constructor.

After learning these basic details of Apex coding, you can write your own Apex class. The whole example of an Apex code will be discussed with Visualforce page developer in the next chapter.

Triggers

As you learned in the previous section, Apex code can be used to write classes or triggers. A trigger is an Apex script that executes when a **data manipulation language (DML)** event occurs on a specific sObject. Therefore, triggers are directly bound with the records of a particular sObject. If the particular record is affected, then the related trigger will be executed:

- The record is accessed via the standard page or Visualforce page
- The record is accessed via a web services API

Triggers can be created on any custom or top-level standard object. There are four types of DML events that affect a trigger of a particular object:

1. Insert
2. Update
3. Delete
4. Undelete

The preceding DML events can be executed either before or after the event. You can specify that in the trigger defining:

- **before**: Before triggers can update variable values before they are saved to the database.

- **after**: After triggers can access field values that are set automatically (such as ID or last updated fields) or to affect changes in other records (such as auditing or queued events).

Trigger syntax

As you learned, a trigger can be executed before or after the event as you specified. Then, you can specify the trigger events by combining DML events with the before or after triggers. Those trigger events (trigger options) are defined in the trigger declaration as follows:

```
trigger <trigger_name> on <object_name> (<trigger_events>) {
code_block;
}
```

The possible values for `<trigger events>` are:

- `before insert`
- `before update`
- `before delete`
- `after insert`
- `after update`
- `after delete`
- `after undelete`

You can specify the multiple triggers for a single object or single trigger with multiple trigger events for a single object. The following code snippet shows you how to define a trigger with multiple triggers for a single object:

```
trigger beforeWrite on Leave (before insert, before update) {
code_block;
}
```

If you use the preceding way to define a trigger, you can designate the separate execution code for each trigger event or some of the trigger events or you can allow the trigger to run all the code segments for all the trigger events.

Trigger context variables

When you need to separate the code segments of the particular trigger event, you can use the following trigger context variables. Every trigger can have a set of trigger context variables that can be used in the current execution context of the trigger. There are three types of trigger context variables, which are as follows:

1. **Execution context variables**: This type of variables are used to identify the current execution context of the trigger. It represents a Boolean value. You can check the current execution using one or a combination of these variables; isInsert, isUpdate, isDelete, isUndelete, isAfter, and isBefore. For example, you can specify the execution context variable within the trigger as given in the following code segment.

    ```
    if(Trgger.isBefore){
      if(Trgger.isInsert){
        code_block;
      }
    }
    ```

    The code block will be executed only before insert.

2. **Record context variables**: This type of variable allows you to access records that are affected by the trigger. There are four types of record context variables: new, old, newMap, and oldMap. The new and old variables are array type variables that allow for bulk data manipulation within the trigger. The newMap and oldMap variables represent the maps with the key as record ID and value as the record itself. You cannot access these variables in every trigger execution context. The availability of record context variables is distributed as shown in the following table:

Action	Timing	New	Old
Insert	Before	Can be modified (newMap not available)	Not available
	After	Can be read	Not available
Update	Before	Can be read	Can be read
	After	Can be read	Can be read
Delete	Before	Not available	Can be read
	After	Not available	Can be read

For example, you can specify the record context variable within the trigger as follows. Suppose that the trigger is defined for the Leave object and this code segment will be executed in a before trigger.

```
for( Leave__c tempLeave : Trigger.new){
}
```

3. **Other trigger context variables**: The size variable can be accessed in all triggers and it represents the number of records in the trigger invocation.

> Apex triggers execute no matter how the triggering data is being saved. Apex triggers execute regardless of whether the action originates in the user interface, through the AJAX Toolkit, or from the web services API. If you only want the code to execute through the UI, consider making a Visualforce page and controller.

Triggers and the order of execution

Once a record is saved, logical operations are executed in an order within the Force. com platform. When you learn about triggers, it is better to understand the position of the order in which the triggers are taking place. This is listed as follows:

1. Load the original record from the database or initialize to insert.

2. Override the old values from loading new record field values.

3. System validation rules execute to verify the required fields.

4. All the before triggers are executed.

5. Runs most system validation steps again and checks user validation rules.

6. The record is saved to the database, but not yet committed.

7. The record is reloaded from the database.

8. All after triggers are executed.

9. The assignment rules are executed.

10. The autoresponse rules are executed.

11. The workflow rules are executed. If there are any field updates in workflows, then the record updates again and executes the before and after triggers again.

12. The escalation rules are executed.

13. The parent rollup summary formula fields are updated.

14. All DML operations are committed to the database.

15. Post-commit logics, such as sending an e-mail, are executed.

> Assignment rules, escalation rules, and autoresponse rules are created as a part of an extension to the Salesforce application.

Exceptions in triggers

Triggers are not only used for data manipulations and data processing, but also for stopping particular data operations. Within the current record, you can add a database exception to the current record or a field using the `addError()` method. This implementation can be done in a `before` trigger. When you are using the `addError()` method in a before trigger and it causes to not proceed with the current, the operations will not be completed and the `addError()` method returns `DmlException`. Therefore, all the DML operations will be rolled back. You can add your own error message via the `addError()` method.

You can use the following template to define the `addError()` method to the record. If applied at the sObject level, the error message appears at the top of the page.

```
ObjectInstance.addError('Your error message');
```

You can use the following template to define the `addError()` method to the particular object field. If applied at the field level, the error message appears next to the field.

```
ObjectInstance.ObjectField.addError('Your error message');
```

This functionality becomes extremely useful for adding custom validation rules when data is saved. You will better understand about this in the *Creating triggers* section.

Creating triggers

Triggers can be created through the UI under or through a Force.com IDE project:

- Via the Force.com IDE, right click on the `src` folder and navigate to **New | Apex Trigger**

- Via the UI (setup page), it depends if the triggering object is a standard or custom object

    ○ For standard objects, navigate to **Setup | Customize | Object | Triggers**

    ○ For custom objects, navigate to **Setup | Create | Objects | Object | Triggers**

- You can also view all triggers in the organization by navigating to **Setup | Develop | Apex Triggers**

In order to be executed, triggers must have the **Is Active** checkbox selected.

Let's create a trigger for our `Leave management` application. Consider the scenario when an employee applies for leave, a leave request record will be inserted to the `Leave` object. In the `Leave` object, there are two fields called `From_Date__c` and `To_Date__c`, which are used to capture the leave starting date and leave end date respectively. And we have the field called `Number_of_Days__c` to capture the number of leave days in between the leave starting date and end date. Now, we need two validations:

- Check whether `From_Date__c` is lower than `To_Date__c`
- If `From_Date__c` is lower than `To_Date__c`, then check whether `Number_of_Days__c` is less than or equal to days between `From_Date__c` and `To_Date__c`

If any of the preceding validations fail, then all the operations will be stopped returning a suitable error message using the `addError()` method.

Let's create the trigger now. Perform the following steps for creating a trigger:

1. Define the trigger name and trigger events as follows. In this scenario, we use the before insert and before update trigger events.

```
trigger LeaveTrigger on Leave__c (before insert, before update) {
//code here
}
```

2. Define the trigger execution context variables.

```
trigger LeaveTrigger on Leave__c (before insert, before update) {
  if(Trigger.isBefore){
    //Trigger Execution context: before
      if(Trigger.isInsert || Trigger.isUpdate){
        //Trigger Execution context: insert/update
          }
    }
}
```

3. The next step is to add the `for` loop to iterate through the array of new records:

```
trigger LeaveTrigger on Leave__c (before insert, before
  update) {
    if(Trigger.isBefore){ //Trigger Execution context:
    before
    if(Trigger.isInsert || Trigger.isUpdate){//Trigger
      Execution context: insert/update
        for(Leave__c tempLeave : Trigger.new){//Use new
          record context variable
```

```
            }
        }
    }
}
```

4. Finally, define the `addError()` exception to the particular logical context. Here is the complete trigger of the preceding scenario:

```
trigger LeaveTrigger on Leave__c (before insert, before
    update) {

    if(Trigger.isBefore){ //Trigger Execution context: before
        if(Trigger.isInsert || Trigger.isUpdate){//Trigger
            Execution context: insert/update
            for(Leave__c tempLeave : Trigger.new){//Use new
                record context variable
                if(tempLeave.From_Date__c
                    > tempLeave.To_Date__c){
                    //Validation 1
                    tempLeave.From_Date__c.addError('To
                        date must be greater than From
                            Date.');
//use adderror method
                    tempLeave.To_Date__c.addError('To
                        date must be greater than From
                            Date.');
                }
                else if(tempLeave.From_Date__c
                    < tempLeave.To_Date__c &&
                        tempLeave.From_Date__c.
daysBetween(tempLeave.To_Date__c)
                    < tempLeave.Number_of_Days__c){ //Validation 2
                    tempLeave.Number_of_Days__c.addError('Cannot
exceed the
                    number of days than the days between
                        from & to dates');
                }
            }
        }
    }
}
```

Now, you can check how the trigger is working by adding a leave request record. You will see the following error message:

Validate the record insert using a trigger

Trigger considerations

When you are creating a trigger, you have to consider the following facts:

* You cannot use `Trigger.new` and `Trigger.old` in Apex DML operations.

* `Trigger.old` is always read only.

* You cannot delete `Trigger.new`.

* In before triggers, you can change the object field value using `Trigger.new`, but in after triggers, you cannot save `Trigger.new`, which results in an exception.

* If you use `Trigger.new[0]`, you must be careful because it only refers to the first record in the multirecord batch. Your manipulation will be affected to only the first record.

* Within triggers, the other records of the same sObjects type or records for other sObjects can be modified. Keep in mind, however, that this can cause further triggers to execute. Further triggers are considered to be part of the same execution context.

* Upsert events cause insert and update triggers.

* Merge events fire delete triggers for the losing records and then update triggers for the winner.

- The after undelete trigger only works with recovered records. Undelete events only run on top-level objects, although related records are also undeleted.

- Field history is not recorded until the end of a trigger event.

- All triggers are considered to be bulk triggers and should be able to process multiple records at a time. Remember that triggers execute via API access as well, which can submit multiple records for each DML verb.

- All triggers run as system by default. This means that triggers may have access to objects and fields that the current user does not. You can override this using the sharing keywords on a class called by the trigger.

- Trigger code cannot contain a static keyword.

- Triggers can only contain keywords applicable to an inner class because, eventually, triggers get converted into an inner class.

- Triggers are only invoked for DML operations handled by the Salesforce application server, so some system bulk operations do not fire triggers, for example, cascade deletion, mass campaign status updates, renaming picklists, managing price books, and so on.

- Certain fields are set during the system save operation and cannot be modified by triggers, for example, `IDs`, `Task.isClosed`, `Opportunity.isWon`, `createdDate`, `lastUpdated`, `Case.isClosed`, and so on.

- Triggers can prevent DML operations from occurring by calling the `addError()` method.

- The maximum trigger size is 200 records. If more than 200 records are submitted, then the system generates chunks of 200 records and executes the trigger multiple times.

Now that you understand the basics of triggers, you can move on to learning about the languages used to access data in your Force.com platform application.

Force.com platform query languages

The query languages are used to access data for data manipulation. There are two query languages in the Force.com platform:

1. **Salesforce.com Object Query Language (SOQL)**
2. **Salesforce.com Object Search Language (SOSL)**

Both of these languages are used to retrieve a set of data from the Force.com platform.

Salesforce.com Object Query Language (SOQL)

We assume that you are already familiar with query language such as SQL, which is the universal standard for interacting with relational databases. In the Force.com platform, we considered the data repository of the Force.com platform as the relational database. Therefore, we use SOQL instead of SQL for data-retrieving purposes. There are similarities as well as differences in SOQL and SQL.

Similarities	Differences
Most of the syntax	SOQL can only retrieve data (query-only language) while SQL can both read and write data.
Some overlapping functionalities	SOQL uses relationships but not Joins, while SQL implements relationships between tables using the JOIN syntax. SOQL has the ability to identify relationship fields to find the connection between objects.
	SOQL does not support all the SQL keywords. For example, DISTINCT is not supported in SOQL.

SOQL basic syntax

The high-level SOQL syntax uses the following pattern:

```
SELECT <fieldname(s)> FROM sObject [WHERE <conditions>] [ORDER BY
    <field names>] [LIMIT <integer>]
```

The preceding pattern is elaborated in the following table:

Area of the SOQL statement	Description
fieldnames	It defines the list of object fields to be returned from the SOQL query, or count() expression that returns the number of records retrieved by the query.
	The ID field is returned by all the SOQL statements.
	The * qualifier that is used to query all the fields in the SELECT clause is not supported in SOQL.
	If you try to use a field without selecting the query, then an exception will be thrown at run time.

Area of the SOQL statement	Description
`Object`	In this area, you must use an sObject name that you are going to retrieve data for. You can define an alias for the object after the object name, as follows: ```SELECT l.Id, l.Name FROM Leave__c l```

`WHERE <conditions>`	This clause can have multiple conditions, which limit the records to be returned from the query.
	
	A condition is a combination of a field of a target object and a value for the particular field.
	
	The field and the value are linked by a comparison operator such as =, !=, <, >, <=, and >=, as well as LIKE, IN, and NOT IN.
	
	Multiple conditions can be combined using AND and OR keywords. It is recommended to use parentheses to ensure the clarity of the multiple conditions.
	
	For example,
	
	```where (p.Name like 'abc') OR (p.Name like 'abc%' and p.Status__c = 'Approved')```
	
	If you use a variable in a SOQL WHERE clause, you must use the colon (:) as follows:
	
	```String[] Status = new string[] ('New', 'Approved', 'Pending'); select Name from Leave__c l where l.Status__c IN :Status;```

`order by <field>`	This is an optional clause that specifies the order of the records returned from the SOQL query.
`limit integer`	The optional LIMIT clause places a limit on the number of records returned from an SOQL query.

There are three return types of an SOQL query, which are as follows:

List of sObjects: `List<Leave__c> leaves = [SELECT Id, Name, Employee__c, Status__c FROM Leave__c WHERE Status__c = 'Approved'];`

Single sObject: `List<Leave__c> leaves = [SELECT Id, Name, Employee__c, Status__c FROM Leave__c WHERE Id = 'a049000000ALLif'];`

Integer: `Integer I = [SELECT COUNT(Id)FROM Leave__c WHERE Status__c = 'Pending'];`

Although there is no direct limit on the number of records returned, there is a 3 MB heap size limit for synchronous Apex.

If exactly one record is not returned, then a QueryException will be thrown.

SOQL keywords

You have learned a few keywords in the preceding section while you were learning the syntax of an SOQL query. There are some more keywords that can be used in SOQL queries as shown in the following table:

Keyword	Description

AND/OR	This is used for combining multiple conditions in the WHERE clause. The following query returns the leave records that are in approved status and an employee is attached to the record:
	
	`List<Leave__c> leaves = [SELECT Id, Name, Employee__c,`
	`Status__c FROM Leave__c WHERE Employee__c != null AND`
	`Status__c = 'Approved'];`

IN	This is used for bulk queries and arguments, which can be a set or a list of IDs or string values.
	
	A colon (:) is used to bind a variable, which is as follows:
	
	`Set<Id> Ids = new Set<Id>{'`
	`   a049000000ALLif','`
	`     a049000000ALeif'};`
	`List<Leave__c> leaves = [SELECT`
	`   Id, Name, Employee__c,`
	`     Status__c FROM Leave__c`
	`       WHERE Id IN: Ids];`

LIKE	This is used for selecting records using wildcards. The values for the LIKE operator frequently use the wildcards '_' (to indicate a single character) or '%' (to indicate any number of characters, including no characters at all). This is shown in the following code:
	
	`List<Employee__c> emp = [SELECT Id, Name FROM`
	`   Employee__c WHERE Name LIKE 'Cha%'];`

Keyword	Description

NOT	This is used for negative conditions as shown in the following code:
	
	``
	List<Leave__c> leaves = [SELECT
	    Id, Name, Employee__c,
	      Status__c FROM Leave__c
	        WHERE Id NOT IN: empIds];
	``

ORDER BY	This keyword is used for sorting results or for returning top results.

GROUP BY	This is used for sorting results based in aggregate functions. You can use GROUP BY ROLLUP to calculate subtotals. It returns an aggregate result, which is explained in the following code:
	
	``
	List<AggregateResult> agr =
	    [SELECT COUNT(Name),
	      Employee__c FROM Leave__c
	        GROUP BY Employee__c];
	``

LIMIT	This keyword is used for placing a ceiling on records returned. When used with ORDER BY, it returns the top records. You can use LIMIT ensure that fewer rows are returned.

FOR UPDATE	This locks the returned record from being updated by another request, which is shown in the following code:
	
	``
	List<Leave__c> leaves = [SELECT
	    Id, Name, Employee__c,
	      Status__c FROM Leave__c
	        WHERE Status__c = 'New'
	          FOR UPDATE];
	``

ALL ROWS	This returns both active records and records in the recycle bin. You cannot use the ALL ROWS keyword with the FOR UPDATE keyword, which is shown in the following code:
	
	``
	List<Leave__c> leaves = [SELECT
	    Id, Name, Employee__c,
	      Status__c FROM Leave__c
	        WHERE Status__c = 'New'
	          ALL ROWS];
	``

> Only the fields that are selected are populated in SOQL. However, the ID field is implicitly returned. If there is any unpopulated field, then the null value will be returned.

SOQL functions

SOQL functions are used in queries to perform some specific functionality in an SOQL query. There are two types of SOQL functions:

1. **Aggregate functions**: These types of functions are used to roll up and summarize your data for analysis. These functions can be used in a SOQL query without using the GROUP BY clause. The currently available aggregate functions are AVG(), COUNT(), COUNT_DISTINCT(), MIN(), MAX(), and SUM(). Let's have a look at the following code:

```
SELECT COUNT(Id)FROM Leave__c WHERE Status__c = 'Pending'
```

2. **Date functions**: These types of functions are used to group or filter records by date periods. For example, if you want to query leave records with the count of the leave records for each calendar year, you can use the CALENDAR_YEAR() function. There are a few date functions in SOQL: CALENDAR_MONTH(), CALENDAR_QUARTER(), CALENDAR_YEAR(), DAY_IN_MONTH(), DAY_IN_WEEK(), DAY_IN_YEAR(), DAY_ONLY(), FISCAL_MONTH(), FISCAL_QUARTER(), FISCAL_YEAR(), HOUR_IN_DAY(), WEEK_IN_MONTH(), and WEEK_IN_YEAR(), which is explained in the following code:

```
SELECT CALENDAR_YEAR(CreatedDate), COUNT(Id)FROM Leave__c
  GROUP BY CALENDAR_YEAR(CreatedDate)
```

> Queries including aggregate functions do not support queryMore. A runtime exception occurs with a query containing an aggregate function that returns more than 2000 rows in a for loop.

SOQL relationship queries

You have learned SOQL to query records from a single sObject. SOQL does not only support single objects to perform data retrieving but also supports related objects for relationship queries. Relationship names can be chained together to access grandparents, and so on. For example, Employee__r.Leave_Category__r.Name.

Therefore, you can access:

- **A parent object from a child object**: Here you can access a parent object from the child object using the dot notation and __r syntax (instead of __c syntax) as in the following SOQL query, which is shown in the following code:

```
SELECT Employee__r.Name, Id, Name FROM Leave__c
```

Therefore, you can traverse the object relationship up to five levels.

- **Retrieve data from child objects of a particular target object**: You can use SOQL to retire data from child objects of the target object as follows:

```
Select e.Name, e.Leave_Category__c, e.Id, e.Age__c, (Select
    Id, Employee__c, Leave_Type__c, From_Date__c, To_Date__c,
    Number_of_Days__c, Status__c From Leaves__r) From
    Employee__c e
```

In this query, `Employee__c` is the target object and it retrieves the leave records of that particular employee using a subquery in the main query. You can use only one level of child query for an SOQL query.

In SOQL, there is no JOIN keyword in action. But SOQL facilitates the JOIN behavior via relationship queries. The following table shows the JOIN behavior of SOQL. Here, we use Leave and Employee object relationship to explain the JOIN behavior of SOQL. Use the following two tables and records to understand the SOQL JOIN behavior. The following screenshot illustrates the Employee table:

Employee__c	
Id	Name
a049000000ALLif	Chamil Madusanka
a049000000BLPif	Panthaka Senarathna
a049000000CLUif	Ruwantha Lankathilaka
a049000000DLYif	Pethum Weerasinghe
a049000000ELHif	Tharanga Perera

Employee records

The following screenshot illustrates the Leave table:

Leave__c		
Name	Employee__c	Status__c
L-1	a049000000ALLif	New
L-2	a049000000BLPif	Approved
L-3	a049000000CLUif	New
L-4	a049000000DLYif	Rejected
L-5	a049000000ELHif	Approved

Leave records

The following table explains the SOQL JOIN behavior:

JOIN	Examples
| Right outer join<br> | For this join behavior, we need to query all the leave records with the associated employee data. The query is as follows:<br><br>```
SELECT Name, Employee__r.Name FROM
    Leave__c
```<br><br>The following screenshot is the result of the preceding code:<br><br>List&lt;Leave__c&gt;<table><tr><th>Name</th><th>Employee__r.Name</th></tr><tr><td>L-1</td><td>Chamil Madusanka</td></tr><tr><td>L-2</td><td>Panthaka Senarathna</td></tr><tr><td>L-3</td><td>Ruwantha Lankathilaka</td></tr><tr><td>L-4</td><td>Pethum Weerasinghe</td></tr><tr><td>L-5</td><td>Tharanga Perera</td></tr></table> |
| Left outer join<br> | Get employees and the related leave data.<br><br>```
SELECT Name,  (SELECT Name, Status__c
    FROM Leaves__c) FROM Employee__c
```<br><br>The following screenshot is the result of the preceding code:<br><br>List&lt;Employee__c&gt;<table><tr><th>Name</th><th>Leave__r</th></tr><tr><td>Chamil Madusanka</td><td>(Related List)</td></tr><tr><td>Panthaka Senarathna</td><td>(Related List)</td></tr><tr><td>Ruwantha Lankathilaka</td><td>(Related List)</td></tr><tr><td>Pethum Weerasinghe</td><td>(Related List)</td></tr><tr><td>Tharanga Perera</td><td>(Related List)</td></tr></table><br>Name: L-1, Status__c: New<br>Name: L-5, Status__c: Approved |

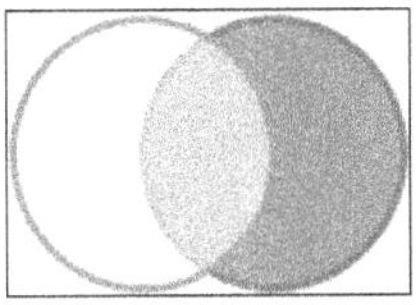

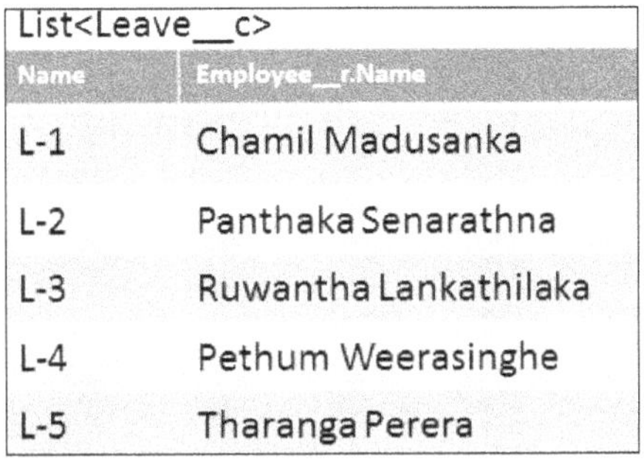

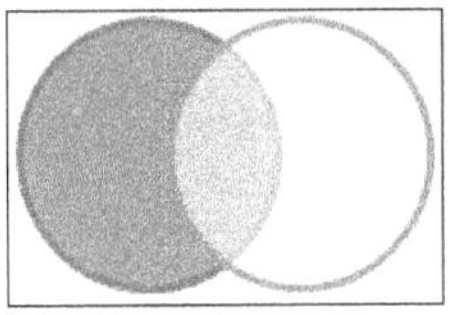

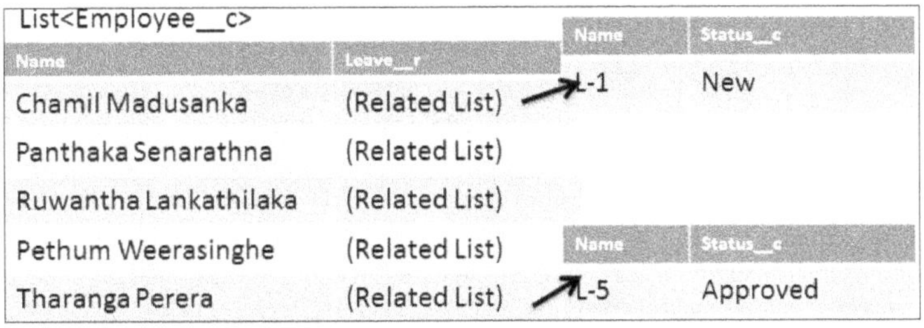

JOIN	Examples
Semi-join (left inner join) 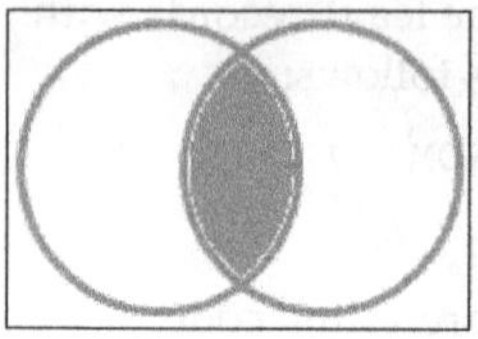 	This will only get employees with related leaves. ``` SELECT Name FROM Employee__c WHERE Id IN (SELECT Employee__c FROM Leave__c) ``` The following screenshot is the result of the preceding code: **List<Employee__c>** | Name
---
Chamil Madusanka
Panthaka Senarathna
Ruwantha Lankathilaka
Pethum Weerasinghe
Tharanga Perera	

Right inner join
 	
	This will only get ;leave records with related employees.
	
	``
	SELECT Name, Status__c,
	    Employee__r.Name FROM Leave__c WHERE
	    Employee__c != null
	``
	
	The following screenshot is the result of the preceding code:
	
	List<Leave__c>
	
	| Name
		Status__c	Employee__r.Name

---	---	---
L-1	New	Chamil Madusanka
L-2	Approved	Panthaka Senarathna
L-3	New	Ruwantha Lankathilaka
L-4	Rejected	Pethum Weerasinghe
L-5	Approved	Tharanga Perera	

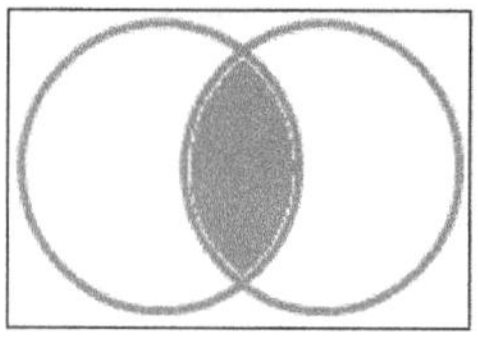

JOIN	Examples
Right anti-join	This will only get leaves without related employees. ```SELECT Name, Status__c FROM Leave__c WHERE Employee__c = null``` We don't get any record in this scenario because in this data set, all the leave records have a related employee.
Left anti-join	This will only get employees without related leaves. Here is the following code; ```SELECT Name FROM Employee__c WHERE Id NOT IN (SELECT Employee__c FROM Leave__c)``` We don't get any record in this scenario because in this data set, all the leave records have a related employee.

Salesforce.com Object Search Language (SOSL)

While SOQL queries retrieve data based around a single sObject, SOSL enables searches across multiple sObjects. SOSL is supported in both square-bracket and method-based searches. SOSL cannot be called from a trigger. A SOSL statement returns a list or lists of sObjects and searches in text, e-mail, and phone fields.

The syntax of SOSL is as follows:

```
FIND <search_term> IN <search_group> RETURNS <field_spec>
```

The following table explains the basic syntax of SOSL:

Syntax	Description

FIND	• String to search for, surrounded by single quotes
	
	• Wildcard supportive
	
	   • *: This matches one or more characters in the middle or at the end of the search string
	
	   • ?: This matches one character in the middle or at the end of the search string
	
	```List<List<sObject>> results = [FIND 'cha*'];```

Syntax	Description

`IN`	• This is an optional clause to limit fields searched
	• Four options
	   • `ALL FIELDS` (this is the default one)
	   • `PHONE FIELDS`
	   • `NAME FIELDS`
	   • `EMAIL FIELDS`
	
	```List<List<sObject>> results = [FIND 'cha*' IN NAME FIELDS];```

`RETURNING`	• This is an optional clause to limit the results to specified object types
	
	```List<List<sObject>> results = [FIND 'cha*' IN NAME FIELDS RETURNING Employee__c, Contact];```
	```List< Employee__c > emp = (List<Employee__c>)results[0];```
	```List< Contact > contacts = (List< Contact >)results[1];```
	Also returns fields values for specific fields per sObject type.
	
	```List<List<sObject>> results = [FIND 'cha*' IN NAME FIELDS RETURNING Employee__c(Name, Age), Contact(FirstName, LastName)];```
	```List< Employee__c > emp = (List<Employee__c>)results[0];```
	```List< Contact > contacts = (List< Contact >)results[1];```

`WHERE`	• This is an optional and additional keyword that used to filter on specific field values ```List<List<sObject>> results = [FIND 'cha*' IN NAME FIELDS RETURNING Employee__c(Name, Age WHERE CreatedDate = THIS_FISCAL_QUARTER)];```

Dynamic SOQL and SOSL

You have learned the fixed SOQL and SOSL queries, which means returning fields and conditions are fixed in the query. But there are situations to build queries that depend on the application context, that's called dynamic SOQL and SOSL. The dynamic SOQL and SOSL are created at runtime with Apex code. It allows you to build more flexible apps. The best example for such a scenario is that the search functionality is based on the user's input.

You can use the `query()` method to execute the query string within the Apex code. This method returns either a single sObject or a list of sObjects. This query method can be used anywhere an inline SOQL query can be used, such as in a `for` loop.

```
Set<Id> empIds = new Set<Id>();
empIds.add('a049000000ALLif');
empIds.add('a049000000AELif');
String QueryString= 'SELECT Id, Name FROM Leave__c  ';
If(empIds.size() > 0){
  QueryString +=' WHERE Employee__c IN: empIds ';
}
List<sObject> dynamicList = Database.query(QueryString);
```

> We have used the hardcoded IDs in the preceding code. It is only to explain the code. Avoid the use of hardcoded IDs in actual Apex classes.

As mentioned in the preceding code sample, you can bind variables in the dynamic query string. It allows us to make more flexible queries for particular applications. However, variable fields cannot be bound in the query string as above binding. It must append to the query string.

Like SQL, dynamic SOQL can cause your database methods to execute accidentally. That vulnerability is called SOQL injection. If your application depends on the user's input to build a dynamic SOQL statement, then you need to handle the input properly and carefully. You can prevent the SOQL injection by using the `escapeSingleQuotes` method. You must pass the user input to this method and it adds the escape character to all single quotations to the method parameter.

You learned SOQL and SOSL query languages in the Force.com platform. Now, we will move to the data manipulation language in the Force.com platform.

Data manipulation on the Force.com platform

DML statements allow users to retrieve, insert, delete, and update sObject data in the Force.com database. Apex has a set of DML commands, as follows, which can take a single sObject or a list of sObjects:

- `insert`: This command is used to add records to the particular Force.com database object. The ID is automatically generated for a record while executing this command.

- `update`: This command is used to update fields of an existing record in the Force.com database object. The update is based on the ID of the particular record.

- `upsert`; Based on the ID field, this command can either insert or update the particular records. If the record has a value for the ID field, then the record will be updated, and if the record doesn't have a value for the ID field, the record will be inserted.

- `delete`: This command is used to delete records from the Force.com database based on the ID of the record. If any record is adhered to cascade deleting (such as a master-detail relationship), this command also allows cascading delete.

- `merge`: This command is used to merge the same sObject type into one record. The merge operation is limited up to three records.

- `undelete`: This command is used to retrieve deleted records from the Recycle Bin and restore in the original Force.com object. However, the Recycle Bin keeps data only for 15 days after the delete operation is performed. For this command, you should use the `ALL ROWS` keyword in the query to be able to retrieve the deleted record.

There are two versions of DML in Apex such that DML standalone statements and DML database methods. These two forms behave differently when acting on multiple records.

Standalone statements

There are special keyword commands for DML operations: `insert`, `update`, `upsert`, and `delete`. If an error is encountered with any one record, then all of the records fail (all or nothing). In the following example, we are inserting a `leaveType` record with the standalone DML statement:

```
Leave_Type__c leaveType = new Leave_Type__c(Name='Annual
    Leave',IsActive__c=true);
insert leaveType;
```

Database methods

These database methods are performing the same data manipulation actions. These are static methods available from the `Database` class, which is as follows:

```
Leave_Type__c leaveType = new Leave_Type__c(Name='Annual
Leave',IsActive__c=true);
Database.insert(leaveType);
```

With database methods, you can define the behavior after occur an error while executing this method. If you use the preceding method, it means that if an error is encountered with any one record, then all of the records fail (all or nothing). The other way is that you can specify the `allOrNone` Boolean parameter. The default value is true. As shown in the following code, you can specify the parameter as `false`:

```
Database.insert(leaveType, false);
```

If it is false, record errors are handled on a case-by-case basis and the process continues despite having an error in a record. The database class methods also return a `SaveResult` object that is used to understand what happened during the save.

The set of database methods are listed at `https://www.salesforce.com/us/developer/docs/apexcode/Content/apex_methods_system_database.htm`.

SaveResult

A `SaveResult` object is returned with a `Database.insert()` or `Database.update()` method. There are similar result classes for the other operations as well, such as `DeleteResult`. If a single record was submitted, then a `Database.SaveResult` object is returned.

```
Database.SaveResult mySaveResult = Database.insert(leaveType);
```

If a list of records was submitted, then a List<Database.SaveResult> list object is returned. Each record in the list corresponds to a record in the submitted list. If the result is only a single record, you can use single SaveResult instead of a list:

```
List<Database.SaveResult> mySaveResult =
   Database.insert(leaveType);
```

A SaveResult object has three methods available:

- getId(): The return type is ID data type
- getErrors(): The return type is List<Database.Error>
- isSuccess(): The return type is Boolean

The following code snippet shows the usage of the preceding methods:

```
Leave_Type__c leaveType1 = new Leave_Type__c(Name='Annual
   Leave',IsActive__c=true);
Leave_Type__c leaveType2 = new Leave_Type__c(Name='Annual
   Leave',IsActive__c=true);
List< Leave_Type__c > LTList = new List< Leave_Type__c >{
   leaveType1, leaveType2 }
List<Database.SaveResult> mySaveResult =
   Database.insert(LTList,false);
for(Database.SaveResult sr : mySaveResult){
   if(!sr.isSuccess()){
     Database.Error err = sr.getErrors()[0];
   }
}
```

Database.DMLOptions

The Database.DMLOptions object provides the ability to add extra information during a transaction. There are a few properties that can be used to play with Database.DMLOptions:

- allowFieldTruncation: This specifies the truncation behavior.
- localeOptions: This specifies the locale options.
- assignmentRuleHeader: This triggers the assignment rules. It is used only for account, case, or lead records.
- emailHeader: This triggers e-mail notification based on certain events such as creation of a new case or task, creation of a case comment, conversion of a case e-mail to a contact, new user e-mail notification, and password reset.

DML and Loops

When we use DML with loops, there are three types of patterns, which need your consideration:

- **Single sObject loop**: This pattern will execute a DML statement for each sObject record. If it is exceeding the limit of DML statements, then the execution will be stopped and exception will be thrown:

```
for(Leave__c leave : [SELECT Id FROM Leave__c]){
  Databse.update(leave);
}
```

- **Single sObject loop variation**: This pattern allows you to process more DML than the sObject list loop method, but heap size will be a limitation:

```
List<Leave__c> leaveList = new List<Leave__c>();
for(Leave__c leave : [SELECT Id FROM Leave__c]){
leaveList.add(leave);
}
Database.update(leaveList);
```

- **sObject list loop**: This pattern will enable you to process a maximum of 10,000 records with only 50 DML statements without worrying about heap size limitations, which is shown in the following code:

```
for(List<Leave__c> leaveList: [SELECT Id FROM Leave__c]){
for(Leave__c leave : leaveList){
//code block
}
Database.update(leaveList);
}
```

Apex SOQL and DML governor limits

The execution limits are in place to help ensure that developers write the most efficient code possible. Most of the time when these limits are reached, there are easy solutions available. If you get the following statements, you have to fix them with the following solutions:

- If the total number of allowed SOQL queries exceed, then move SOQL queries outside loops
- If the total number of allowed executed script statements exceed, then reduce the number of loops or recursion.

- If the number of allowed DML statements exceed, then perform the Insert, update, or delete records in bulk

- If the total number of allowed records retrieved by SOQL queries exceed, then create selective queries that filter on indexed fields, such as primary keys, foreign keys, names, audit dates, or external ID fields.

> If you are hitting governor limits, consider mass-updating records to using asynchronous batch Apex instead.

Data integrity and transactions

Since data integrity is one of the major requirements in an IT system, you have to make sure that each scenario is using the correct data values within your application. The Force.com platform has some inbuilt features to protect the data integrity. But there are possibilities to have any data integrity issues due to conflicting user actions. When we talk about data integrity, the atom of the data integrity is the transaction, which is considered as all or no unit of work. The transaction level is controlled differently depending on the type of DML statement used. If the standalone commands are used, the transaction is always all or nothing. If any record fails, all records fail. If the database methods from statements are used, the transaction level can be set via the `opt_allOrNone` parameter. If it is set to `false`, records can succeed or fail individually. All transactions are controlled by the trigger, web service, or anonymous block that executes the Apex script. If the Apex script completes successfully, all the changes are committed to the database. If the Apex script does not complete successfully, all database changes are rolled back.

Sometimes during the processing of records, your business rules require that partial work be rolled back so that the processing can continue in another direction. Apex gives you the ability to generate a savepoint, that is, a point in the transaction that specifies the state of the database at the time. Any DML statement that occurs after the savepoint can be discarded, and the database can be restored to the same condition it was in at the time you generated the savepoint.

> Assert methods are used to check the equality of particular values in a particular time. Three types of assert methods are `assert`, `assertEquals`, and `assertNotEquals`.

The following example shows you the way of using savepoint and rollback
database methods:

```
Leave_Type__c leave = new Leave_Type__c{Name="Annual Leave",
  Is_Active__c=true};
Insert leave;
System.assertEquals(true, [SELECT Is_Active__c FROM Leave_Type__c
  WHERE Id = leave.Id]. Is_Active__c);
//Create ta savepoint while Is_Active__c is true
Savepoint sp = Database.setSavepoint();
/Change the Is_Active__c
Leave. Is_Active__c = false;
Update leave;
System.assertEquals(false, [SELECT Is_Active__c FROM Leave_Type__c
  WHERE Id = leave.Id]. Is_Active__c);
//Rollback to the previous true value
Database.rollback(sp);
System.assertEquals(true, [SELECT Is_Active__c FROM Leave_Type__c
  WHERE Id = leave.Id]. Is_Active__c);
```

In the preceding code snippet, we have used the `setSavepoint()` and `rollback()`
methods. Before setting the savepoint, inserted Leave_Type is an active leave type.
But after we set the savepoint, we updated the record as `Is_Active__c = false`.
Then we rolled back the transaction and the `Is_Active` value of the particular record
was updated to `true` again.

Summary

In this chapter, you have learned to develop custom coding in the Force.com
platform, including the Apex classes and triggers. You learned two query
languages in the Force.com platform: SOQL and SOSL. Finally, we covered
the data manipulation language and data integrity.

In the next chapter, you will learn about developing custom pages using Visualforce.
You will also have the opportunity to use the knowledge of Apex coding that you
learned in this chapter.

8
Building Custom Pages with Visualforce

In the previous chapter, you learned custom coding using Apex. When we want to build custom pages in the Force.com platform, we want to learn about Visualforce, and Apex will be associated when building custom pages. This chapter will introduce Visualforce (which provides a different kind of user interface than standard pages), its architecture, its advantages, and its usage. There will be sections to describe Visualforce pages and Visualforce controllers with examples of sample applications. Finally, there will be an explanation section on Visualforce custom components.

This chapter covers the following topics:

- Introducing Visualforce
- The concepts of Visualforce
- The architecture of Visualforce
- Visualforce pages
- Visualforce controllers
- The order of execution of a Visualforce page
- Visualforce custom components
- Advantages of Visualforce

Introducing Visualforce

In the Force.com platform, you can build powerful applications using only declarative methods. But there are situations where declarative methods aren't enough to build the application. In the Force.com platform, every standard object and custom object have their own standard user interface. We can customize the standard UI by creating multiple page layouts. But when we work on a sophisticated UI requirement with different UI styles and custom components, the standard UI will have its own limitations. This is where the Visualforce markup language comes into play.

We all know that HTML is a markup language. Similar to HTML, Visualforce is a framework that includes a tag-based markup language that allows us to build sophisticated, attractive, and dynamic custom user interfaces. Almost all the standard web technologies (such as CSS, JavaScript, jQuery, HTML5, and so on) can be used along with Visualforce. Therefore, we can build rich UIs for any app, including mobile apps. Visualforce can fulfill user interface requirements outside the standard look and feel.

Because of the uniquely identified page names, Visualforce pages can be created by entering page names in the browser address bar. To have this facility, the user has to enable **Development Mode** in the particular user record.

There is another way to create a Visualforce page through the setup area. Go to **Setup** | **Develop** | **Pages** | **New**.

You will be redirected to a blank Visualforce page and you can specify the name of the page there.

The concepts of Visualforce

The Force.com platform uses the Model View Controller (MVC) architectural pattern to develop an application. Visualforce is an implementation of the MVC architecture. The MVC architecture can be illustrated as follows:

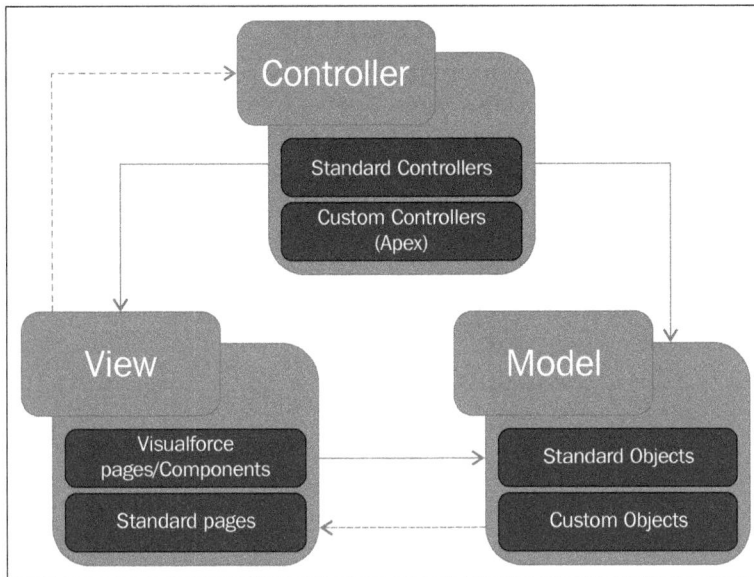

The MVC structure is explained as follows:

- **Model**: The model specifies the structure of the data. The data model of the Force.com platform is defined by objects. The platform is designed to map every entity to an object.

- **View**: The data is represented through the view. The page layouts and Visualforce pages are considered as the view of the MVC architecture.

- **Controller**: In the Force.com platform, the business logic (rules and actions) that manipulates the data is considered the controller. Apex classes, triggers, workflows, validation rules, and approval processes are considered the controllers of the Force.com platform.

The Visualforce architecture

When you are developing a Visualforce page, you have to know how the Visualforce page is working. Visualforce has its own set of components that are similar to other markup languages. These components allow us to build complicated components with a single Visualforce tag. Eventually, all Visualforce components are rendered as HTML components. When we request the page by entering the page URL in the address bar, those components are processed and rendered on the server and then sent to the client. This methodology has higher performance and enhanced functionality than client-only methods. The following diagram shows how the Visualforce page runs on the Force.com platform:

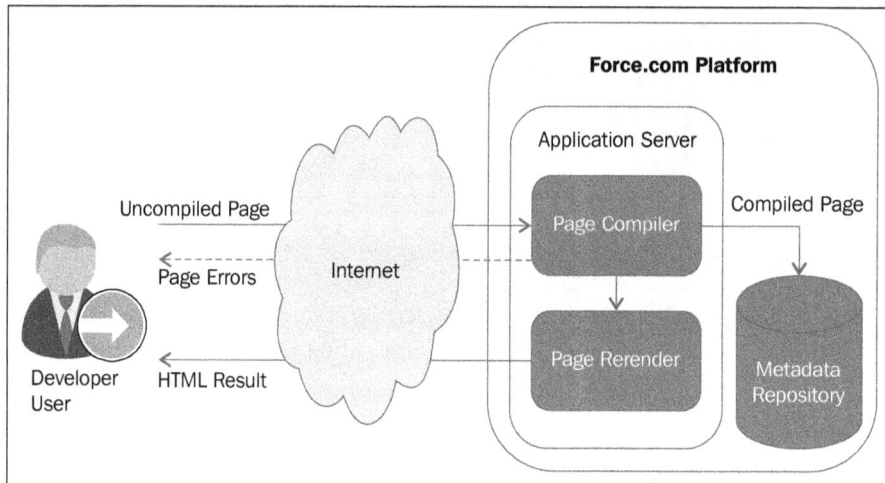

Execution flow while saving a Visualforce page on a server

In the preceding diagram, the developer saves a Visualforce page in the Force. com platform. The compilation of the markup language and the related controller happens while the save operation is under way. On successful compilation, the Visualforce markup is converted into the abstract set of instructions. Those instructions can be understood by the Visualforce renderer. The set of instructions is saved to the metadata repository and sent to the Visualforce renderer. The Visualforce renderer converts the instructions to HTML (HTML can be understood by the browser). Then the page is refreshed. On unsuccessful compilation, the save operation stops and returns the errors to the developer.

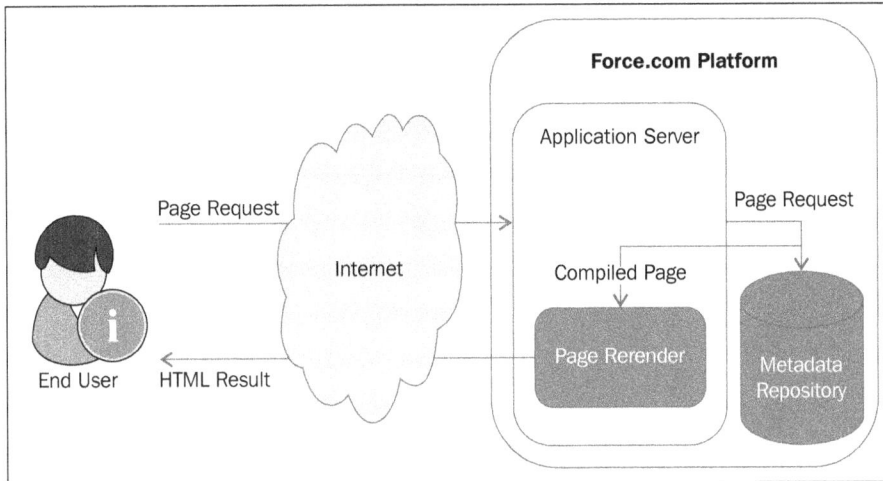

Execution flow of a Visualforce page

In the preceding diagram, an end user requests a Visualforce page and then the application server fetches the page from the metadata repository. Then the page is passed to the Visualforce renderer to perform the HTML translation. When a non-developer end user requests a page, there is no compilation phase. This is because the page is already compiled and stored in the metadata repository.

Visualforce pages

The custom user interface of the Force.com platform has two major elements: Visualforce markup and Visualforce controller. Visualforce represents the view aspect of the Model-View-Controller architecture. Visualforce markup consists of Visualforce components with the `apex:` prefix; standard HTML; and Standard web development code such as JavaScript, jQuery, CSS, and other JavaScript frameworks.

AJAX components, expression language formula for actions, and component binding interactions are present in Visualforce. Visualforce components cover two areas of page functionality. One set of components are used to create user interface objects that automatically interact with sObjects or with functions that are implemented in the Force.com platform. The other set of components are used to handle the interactions between the page and the Force.com platform. The second set doesn't need to refresh the whole page, which is similar to how **Asynchronous JavaScript and XML (AJAX)** works.

There are different situations to integrate a Visualforce page in the Force.com platform. You can create a custom tab for a Visualforce page. You can override a standard tab and standard or custom buttons/links with a Visualforce page. And you can even embed a Visualforce page in a particular detail of the page layout.

The following code shows you a basic example of a Visualforce page:

```
<apex:page title="myPage">
  <!--This is Comment
  //This is not a comment. This is just a text.
  <h1> </h1>
  <p/>
  This is your new page: myNewPage
</apex:page>
```

There are few tag basics of a Visualforce page:

- Visualforce standard components begin with the `<apex:` prefix
- Visualforce pages must be enclosed within the `<apex:page> </apex:page>` tag
- The attributes of a Visualforce tag has values to further define the tag
- The attribute values are typed to be strings, collections, IDs, and so on
- There are full list of standard tags and attributes

There are three types of ready-to-use standard Visualforce components in the Force. com platform:

- **Output components**: For example, `<apex:outputPanel>`, `<apex:outputField>`, `<apex:outputText>`, `<apex:pageBlock>`, and so on.
- **Input components**: For example, `<apex:inputFile>`, `<apex:inputField>`, `<apex:inputText>`, `<apex:selectList>`, and so on.
- **AJAX components**: For example, `<apex:actionStatus>`. Used to improve a user's interaction with a page (such as partial page refresh).

The full set of Visualforce standard components can be accessed through `http://www.salesforce.com/docs/developer/pages/Content/pages_compref.htm`.

> Data-driven defaults are included in the input and output components. For example, suppose you have to use date type field. You use the `<apex:inputField>` component in a page and bind that date field. Then the edit interface will show the widgets related to date (calendar).

Expression syntax and data binding

Visualforce uses the expression syntax (also found in merge fields, formulas) to bind components with Salesforce data and the actions of the controller of the page. All content within the {!} symbol will be evaluated as an expression. For example, {!$User.Email} shows the e-mail of the currently logged in user.

- You can insert a dynamic object using the {!ObjectName.PropertyName} syntax.
- You can insert global data with the $ syntax, for example:
  - {!$User.FieldName}
  - {!$Page.otherVisualforcePage}
  - {!$Component.otherVisuallforceComponent}

> The custom labels and translations can be added using $Label.
> Local variables can be made to stand in for these formulations as they can become long and unmanageable using the <apex:variable> tag.

Visualforce components are connected with controllers or other components through data binding. There are three types of data binding:

- **Data bindings**: Used to pull data from the data set of the controller
- **Action bindings**: Used to call action methods in the controller
- **Component bindings**: Used to interact with other components via the ID attribute of the component

> The data context is provided to controllers by the ID parameter, just like standard pages. For more information, refer to https://c.ap1.visual.force.com/apex/SampleVisua lforceTab?id=a019000000AVh1A.

The following code sample demonstrates data binding in a Visualforce page. Here, we have implemented dynamic object binding and global data binding. This particular page is built to view a particular employee's record.

```
<apex:page standardController="Employee__c">
  <apex:pageBlock title="Hello {!$User.FirstName}">
  <apex:outputLabel value="You are viewing the employee record of
    {!Employee__c.Name}"></apex:outputLabel>
      <apex:pageBlockSection >
```

```
            <apex:outputField value="{!Employee__c.First_Name__c}"/>
            <apex:outputField value="{!Employee__c.Last_Name__c}"/>
            <apex:outputField value="{!Employee__c.Email__c}"/>
            <apex:outputField
              value="{!Employee__c.Leave_Category__c}"/>
            <apex:outputField value="{!Employee__c.Manager__c}"/>
          <apex:outputField value="{!Employee__c.IsActive__c}"/>
          </apex:pageBlockSection>
      </apex:pageBlock>
      <apex:pageBlock title="Leaves">
        <apex:pageBlockTable value="{!Employee__c.Leaves__r}"
          var="leave">
          <apex:column value="{!leave.From_Date__c}"/>
          <apex:column value="{!leave.To_Date__c}"/>
          <apex:column value="{!leave.Leave_Type__c}"/>
          <apex:column value="{!leave.Number_of_Days__c}"/>
          <apex:column value="{!leave.Status__c}"/>
        </apex:pageBlockTable>
      </apex:pageBlock>
  </apex:page>
```

This is the output of the preceding code. It represents the particular employee record and his/her leave requests:

Hello Chamil				
You are viewing the employee record of Chamil Madusanka				
First Name	Chamil		Last Name	Madusanka
Email	chamil.madusanka@gmail.com		Leave Category	Shop & Office
Manager			IsActive	✓

Leaves				
From Date	To Date	Leave Type	Number of Days	Status
7/7/2014	7/7/2014	Casual Leave	1.0	New

Data binding example

Visualforce and standard web development technologies

Visualforce is not an isolated markup language. All the standard web technologies can be used with the native Visualforce page to build rich UI for the Force.com platform. However, HTML rendering of Visualforce is complicated and there are many ways to change Visualforce's generated default HTML by using additional resources such as CSS or JavaScript.

Styling Visualforce pages

Visualforce is designed to accomplish both simple user interface requirements and sophisticated user interface requirements. There's no way to meet sophisticated UI requirements by using the standard styles of Salesforce. Therefore, using your own style, you can change the look and feel of a Visualforce page and introduce sufficient sophistication.

Most of the standard Visualforce components use the `style` and/or the `styleClass` attribute. You can use those attributes to make your Visualforce page different from standard pages. There are two types of styles: Salesforce styles and custom styles.

Salesforce styles

All the standard pages use the Salesforce standard styles. You can use standard styles in Visualforce pages as well. For example, if you use the `<apex:inputField>`, `<apex:pageBlock>`, `<apex:pageBlockTable>`, and `<apex:detail>` components in a Visualforce page, they will come with the default Salesforce standard styles. The default color scheme of Visualforce pages depends on the tab style you specify in the `tabStyle` attribute of the `<apex:page>` or `<apex:apgeBlock>` component. When we use a standard controller in a Visualforce page, all the Visualforce page components inherit the styles of the associated objects.

When we use a custom controller, we can use the styles of any of the standard tabs of Salesforce by using the `tabStyle` attribute on the `<apex:page>` tag.

Custom styles

The standard styles can be overridden by using the custom styles. The style and/or `styleClass` attributes are used to apply custom styles. If you want to add an inline custom style, then you have to use the style attribute. If you want to add a custom inline via a CSS class name that is specified in a CSS class, then you have to use the `styleClass` attribute.

In the following example, the sample Visualforce page has custom styles that have been added via the `style` and `styleClass` attributes:

```
<apex:page >
    <style>
        .sample {font-weight: bold;}
    </style>

    <apex:outputText value="This text is styled via style attribute"
style="font-weight: bold;"/> <br/>

    <apex:outputText value="This text is styled via styleClass
attribute" styleClass="sample"/>
</apex:page>
```

In the preceding example, the Visualforce page is implemented with CSS, which writes on the page itself. But there are situations when we need to use the same style in multiple pages. Then we can store the CSS file as a static resource. This is another way to bind custom styles to the Visualforce markup.

Static resources are uploaded to the Force.com platform via the setup screen. The Force.com platform allows us to upload images, stylesheets, JavaScript, and archives (`.zip` and `.jar` files). The following is the stylesheet (CSS filename: `main.css`) we have used above the Visualforce page:

```
.sample {font-weight: bold;}
```

Let's see how we can upload this stylesheet into the static resources. The resource name is `CustomMainStyle` (this has to be unique). The resource can be created by navigating to **Setup** | **Develop** | **Static Resources** | **New**.

Using static resources to store CSS file

The `CustomMainStyle` static resource can be utilized in a Visualforce page as follows. The `<apex:stylesheet>` tag is used to include a stylesheet.

```
<apex:page >
<apex:stylesheet value="{!$Resource.CustomMainStyle}"/>
<apex:outputText value="This text is styled via styleClass attribute
via static resources" styleClass="sample"/>
</apex:page>
```

> You can entirely remove standard styles from a Visualforce page by specifying the `standardStylesheets`, `showHeader`, and `sidebar` attributes as false. If you stop loading standard Salesforce stylesheets, you can reduce the size of your Visualforce page.
>
> ```
> <apex:page sidebar="false" showHeader="false"
> standardStylesheets="false">
> </apex:page>
> ```

You can specify static resources by uploading archive files such as ZIP and JAR files. This ZIP file can contain any resources such as images, CSS files, and JavaScript files. The URLFOR function is used to refer to individual resources of archive files in the Visualforce page. URLFOR is a two-parameter function: name of the static resource and the path to the particular file within the ZIP file. The following example shows the usage of a ZIP file of a static resource (`main.css` file in the `CustomStyleZipFolder` directory):

```
<apex:page >
<apex:stylesheet
  value="{!URLFOR($Resource.CustomStyleZip,'/CustomStyleZipFolder
    /main.css')}"/>
<apex:outputText value="This text is styled via styleClass
  attribute via static resources" styleClass="sample"/> <br/>
<apex:outputText value="Following image is loaded via css class"/>
<br/>
<apex:outputPanel styleClass="imageCls">
</apex:outputPanel>
<apex:outputText value="Following image is loaded directly from
  static resource"/> <br/>
<apex:image
  value="{!URLFOR($Resource.CustomStyleZip,'/CustomStyleZipFolder
    /images/sfLogo.jpg')}" width="120" height="100"/>
</apex:page>
```

There is a special scenario with the static resources where you can use relative paths of files in the static resource. With this method, you can relatively refer the contents of the archive. For example, the `main.css` file has the following style:

```
.sample {font-weight: bold;}
.imageCls {background:url(images/sfLogo.jpg) no-repeat top left;
     width: 100px;
          height: 100px;
          display: block;
     }
```

In the preceding CSS code, we are using a relative path of an image (`sfLogo.jpg`). We create the `CustomStyleZipFolder` directory, which contains the image folder and the `main.css` file. Then we can include the `main.css` file without worrying about the related images that are specified in the CSS file.

> The maximum size of a single static resource is 5 MB. The maximum size of a static resource that we can have in an organization is 250 MB.

Using JavaScript in Visualforce pages

JavaScript is one of the key technologies of Visualforce development. JavaScript offers the framework for passing between other HTML elements, the Visualforce controller, and JavaScript objects. We can use JavaScript libraries as well as some Visualforce components (such as `<apex:actionFunction>`, `<apex:actionSupport>`, `<apex:commandButton>`, and `<apex:commandLink>`) with Visualforce pages. JavaScript code can be written in a Visualforce page itself or included in a separate JavaScript file from a static resource. We can use the `<apex:includeScript>` component to include a JavaScript library from static resources. For example, `<apex:includeScript value="{!$Resource.MyJSFile}"/>`.

Accessing Visualforce components with JavaScript

In JavaScript code, you can refer to Visualforce components through the ID of the Visualforce component. The values of the `id` attribute are unique and the `id` attribute is a part of the DOM ID of a particular component.

The binding of two components using the `id` attribute is demonstrated in the following code sample:

```
<apex:outputLable value="Label Name" for="leave"/>
<apex:inputField id=" leave " value="{!Leave__c.Name}">
```

The way to handle simple JavaScript in a Visualforce page is shown in the following code sample. In the example, the pick list value is to be changed by selecting the checkbox. The JavaScript file is included within the `<script>` tag.

The JavaScript function has two arguments. The first argument is the element that triggered the event (input) and the second one is the DOM ID (id) of the target pick list field. The `{!$Component.inputStatus}` expression obtains the DOM ID of the HTML element generated by the `<apex:inputField id="inputStatus" value="{!leave.Status__c}"/>` component.

```
<apex:page controller="LeaveStatusUpdateController" id="pageId">
  <script type="text/javascript">
    function updateStatus(input,id) {
      if(input.checked){
        document.getElementById(id).value="Approved by Direct
          Manager";
            }else{
              document.getElementById(id).value="New";
                }
          }
  </script>
    <apex:form id="formId">
    <apex:pageBlock id="pageBId">
    <apex:pageBlockTable id="tableId" value="{!Leaves}"
      var="leave">
      <apex:column value="{!leave.Employee__r.Name}"/>
      <apex:column value="{!leave.From_Date__c}"/>
      <apex:column value="{!leave.To_Date__c}"/>
      <apex:column value="{!leave.Leave_Type__c}"/>
      <apex:column value="{!leave.Number_of_Days__c}"/>
      <apex:column id="checkId" headerValue="Status">
      <apex:inputField id="inputStatus" value="{!leave.Status__c}"
        />
        </apex:column>
        <apex:column headerValue="Approval" >
        <apex:selectCheckboxes
          onclick="updateStatus(this,
            '{!$Component.inputStatus}');" >
            </apex:selectCheckboxes>
            </apex:column>
          </apex:pageBlockTable>
      </apex:pageBlock>
      </apex:form>
  </apex:page>
```

The following code is associated with the controller class for the preceding Visualforce page. It retrieves the pending leaves (leaves in the new status) that are assigned to the logged in user for his/her approval as follows:

```
public with sharing class LeaveStatusUpdateController {
   public List<Leave__c> Leaves{get;set;}
   public LeaveStatusUpdateController(){
     Leaves = new List<Leave__c>();
     Employee__c loggedEmp = new Employee__c();
     loggedEmp = [SELECT Id, Name FROM Employee__c WHERE User__c =:
       UserInfo.getUserId()];
     Leaves = [Select Id,
       Name,From_Date__c,To_Date__c,Leave_Type__c,Number_of_Days__c,
         Status__c, Employee__r.Name FROM Leave__c WHERE
           Employee__r.Manager__c =: loggedEmp.id AND Status__c
             ='New'];
   }
}
```

JavaScript remoting for Apex controllers

Javascript remoting is the process that provides support for some methods in APEX controllers that are to be called via JavaScript. This feature allows us to implement complex and dynamic behaviors that cannot be accomplished using standard Visualforce AJAX components. JavaScript remoting was released as a Developer Preview in Spring 2011. Since the Summer 2011 release, JavaScript remoting provides support for additional return data types. Also, the references to the same objects are no longer duplicated in the response. JavaScript remoting has three main parts:

- The JavaScript code that is used to invoke a remote method
- The remote method in the Apex controller
- The callback function (written in JavaScript) in a Visualforce page

To use JavaScript remoting, your request must take the following form:

```
[<namespace>.]<controller>.<method>([params...,]
<callbackFunction>(result, event)
{
// callback function logic
}, {escape:true});
```

The description of the preceding code is as follows:

- namespace: This is your organization's namespace. This is only required if the class comes from an installed package.
- controller: This is the name of your Apex controller.

- `method`: This is the name of the Apex method you're calling.
- `params`: This is a comma-separated list of parameters that your method takes.
- `callbackFunction`: This is the name of the function that handles the response from the controller. It returns the status of the call and the method result.
- `escape`: This specifies whether your response should be escaped (by default, true) or not (false).

The remote method must begin with the `@RemoteAction` annotation as follows:

```
@RemoteAction
global static String getLeaveId(String objectName) { ... }
```

The remote method can have the following data types as arguments:

- Apex primitives (string, integer, and so on)
- Collections (set, list, and map)
- sObject (standard objects and custom objects)
- User-defined Apex classes and interfaces

The remote method can return the following data types:

- Apex primitives (string, integer, and so on)
- sObjects (standard objects and custom objects)
- Collections (set, list, and map)
- User-defined Apex classes and enums
- SelectOption
- PageReference
- SaveResult
- UpsertResult
- DeleteResult

> The remote method must be uniquely identified by the name and number of parameters. For example, we cannot write a remote method with the same method name and an equal number of arguments and different types of arguments.

The following example shows how to use JavaScript remoting in a Visualforce page:

```
<apex:page controller="JavaScriptRemotingController" id="pageId">
  <script type="text/javascript">
function updateStatus(input,id) {
var inputStatus=id;
JavaScriptRemotingController.processLeave(inputStatus,function(result
,event){
},{escape:true});
}</script>
 <apex:form id="formId">
    <apex:pageBlock id="pageBId">

        <apex:pageBlockTable id="tableId" value="{!Leaves}"
var="leave">
            <apex:column value="{!leave.From_Date__c}"/>
             <apex:column value="{!leave.To_Date__c}"/>
             <apex:column value="{!leave.Leave_Type__c}"/>
             <apex:column value="{!leave.Number_of_Days__c}"/>
             <apex:column value="{!leave.Status__c}"/>
          <apex:column id="checkId" headerValue="Status">
               <apex:inputField id="inputStatus" value="{!leave.
Status__c}" />
          </apex:column>
          <apex:column headerValue="Approve Leave" >
              <apex:selectCheckboxes onclick="updateStatus(this,'{!
leave.Id}');">
               </apex:selectCheckboxes>
          </apex:column>

        </apex:pageBlockTable>
    </apex:pageBlock>
    </apex:form>
</apex:page>
```

This is the associated Apex controller:

```
global with sharing class JavaScriptRemotingController {

    public List<Leave__c> Leaves{
        get{
         Leaves = new List<Leave__c>();
         Leaves = [Select Id, Name,From_Date__c,To_Date__c,Leave_
Type__c,Number_of_Days__c,Status__c FROM Leave__c LIMIT 1000];
         return Leaves;
        }
```

```
        set;
    }

    public JavaScriptRemotingController(){

    }

@RemoteAction
global static Leave__c processLeave(String para){
    Leave__c updateLeave;
    try{
        updateLeave=[Select Id, Name,From_Date__c,To_Date__c,Leave_
Type__c,Number_of_Days__c,Status__c FROM Leave__c WHERE Id =: para];
        updateLeave.Status__c = 'Approved by Direct Manager';
            update updateLeave;
          //return updateLeave;
    }catch(DMLException e){
          ApexPages.addMessages(e);
          return null;
    }
return null;
}
}
```

Using jQuery in Visualforce pages

jQuery is an open source JavaScript library that allows us to implement client-side scripting of HTML. jQuery has been designed to be capable of extending the main libraries with new plugins for introducing a wide variety of new features. And also it allows us to navigate a document, select a DOM element, create animations, handle events, and develop Ajax applications.

When we develop Visualforce pages, jQuery can be used to simplify the UI developments. For example, jQuery is used to simplify the DOM manipulations and give access to the library of UI elements and simplify the Ajax techniques and technologies of mobile devices.

The following example shows the jQuery version of our previous example. This is used to explain the jQuery code in Visualforce. This example uses the Leave__c standard controller.

```
<apex:includeScript
value="https://ajax.googleapis.com/ajax/libs/jquery
/1.7.2/jquery.min.js"/>
```

The page in the following example code needs the ID parameter with a leave record ID. The URL appears as follows: `https://c.ap1.visual.force.com/apex/JQuery Example?id=a059000000BVClN`.

This page renders the leave detail page. We are using jQuery to fulfill our requirement. Therefore, the Visualforce page needs to include the jQuery library for jQuery implementations. In the preceding example, we use an online reference of the main jQuery library.

You can also use static resources to include the jQuery library. The usage is the same as in the JavaScript and CSS examples.

> There are other JavaScript libraries with the same default global variable name ($). If we also use the same global variable name, there will be a conflict at the client side. Our jQuery functions will not work. To eliminate that conflict, we can use `jQuery.noConflict()` and assign it to another global variable and use that new global variable in our jQuery code.

```
<apex:page StandardController="Leave__c" id="pageId">
   <apex:includeScript value="https://ajax.googleapis.com/ajax/libs/
jquery/1.7.2/jquery.min.js" />

   <script type="text/javascript">
       j$ = jQuery.noConflict();
       j$(document).ready(function() {
           j$('.checkBox').click(function () {
               j$('.inputStatus').val('Approved by Direct Manager');
           });

       });
   </script>
   <apex:form id="formId">
   <apex:pageBlock id="pageBId">
       <apex:pageBlockSection id="pBlockSection">
           <apex:outputField value="{!Leave__c.From_Date__c}"/>
           <apex:outputField value="{!Leave__c.To_Date__c}"/>
           <apex:inputField styleClass="inputStatus"
   value="{!Leave__c.Status__c}" />
           <apex:pageBlockSectionItem id="pbSectionItem">
               <apex:outputLabel value="Mark as Approved"></
   apex:outputLabel>
               <apex:selectCheckboxes styleClass="checkBox" >
                   </apex:selectCheckboxes>
               </apex:pageBlockSectionItem>
```

```
                </apex:pageBlockSection>
            </apex:pageBlock>
            </apex:form>
        </apex:page>
```

> If we don't use an id attribute for a particular component, Visualforce uses a dynamically generated id, for example, j_id0, j_id0:j_id1. Consider an example: we have specified the id attribute for `<apex:inputField id="inputOne"/>`, but we haven't specified any id attribute for the parent components of inputOne. We can select such a component using jQuery. They are called partial selectors. Here's an example:
>
>   j$('[id*= inputOne]')

There are many things that can be done with the combination of Visualforce and jQuery. But this book will not be covering all the things related to that topic.

HTML5 and Visualforce pages

HTML5 is the new standard of HTML. The previous version of HTML was HTML 4.01. HTML5 has new features such as new elements, new attributes, video and audio support, 2D/3D graphic support, full CSS3 support, local storage, local SQL database support, and featured web applications. With these features, we can reduce the use of external plugins. There are also more markups to replace scripting. HTML5 has better a error-handling mechanism too.

When it comes to Force.com developments, we can use HTML5 for Visualforce page developments and develop mobile web applications. In the Force.com platform, HTML5 plays a major role in developing web-based mobile applications. For example, recently, Salesforce has released Salesforce touch, which uses HTML5.

By default, Visualforce pages function with docType of HTML 4.01 transitional. Since the Winter 2012 version, Visualforce pages are supported to change the docType attribute in the `<apex:page>` tag. In a pure HTML5 page, the `<!DOCTYPE html>` tag must be specified at the top of the page. The docType attribute of `<apex:page>` achieves that requirement.

The following is the example usage for the docType Visualforce attribute on the `<apex:page>` component:

```
<apex:page docType="html-5.0"><!-- HTML5 --></apex:page>
<apex:page docType="html-4.0.1-transitional"><!-- HTML 4.0.1
Transitional -->
</apex:page>
<apex:page docType="xhtml-5.0.1-strict"><!-- XHTML 5.0.1 Strict-->
</apex:page>
```

The following example is a Visualforce page with a drag-and-drop functionality that has been coded using HTML5. Here, we have a rectangle and an image that is referring static resources. We can drag the image into the rectangle.

```
<apex:page docType="html-5.0" sidebar="false" showHeader="false"
standardStylesheets="false" cache="true" >

<html>
<head>
<style type="text/css">
#div1 {width:400px;height:400px;padding:10px;border:1px solid
#aaaaaa;}
</style>
<script>
function allowDrop(ev)
{
ev.preventDefault();
}
function drag(ev)
{
ev.dataTransfer.setData("Text",ev.target.id);
}
function drop(ev)
{
ev.preventDefault();
var data=ev.dataTransfer.getData("Text");
ev.target.appendChild(document.getElementById(data));
}
</script>
</head>
<body>
<p>Drag the Salesforce logo into the rectangle:</p>
<div id="div1" ondrop="drop(event)" ondragover="allowDrop(event)"></
div>
<br/>
<img id="drag1" src="{!URLFOR($Resource.CustomStyleZip,'/
CustomStyleZipFolder/images/sfLogo.jpg')}" draggable="true"
ondragstart="drag(event)" width="400" height="400"/>
</body>
</html>
</apex:page>
```

There are many things that can be done with the combination of Visualforce and HTML5. But this book will not be covering all the things related to that topic. You will find more details on HTML5 and Visualforce at `http://www.developerforce.com/guides/Visualforce_in_Practice.pdf`.

Visualforce controllers

Visualforce controllers are Apex classes that specify the data available and the behavior when a user interacts with components on a page. Controllers typically define different types of methods:

- Data methods to display data
  - Getter methods to retrieve data from the controller
  - Setter methods to pass data from the page to the controller

- Action methods to perform logic
  - Specialized action methods for specific behaviors
  - Navigation action methods to take the user somewhere else (redirect pages)

There are four main types of Visualforce controllers:

- Standard controllers
- Standard list controllers
- Custom controllers
- Controller extensions

Standard controllers

Standard controllers are provided for all standard and custom objects that are available via the API. This type of controller provides the same common data, functionality, and logic used for standard Salesforce pages. All standard and custom objects that can be queried using the API have an associated standard controller to provide access to standard Salesforce data and behavior. Therefore, we can use standard controllers with Visualforce pages as follows:

```
<apex:page standardController="objectAPIName">
```

For example, if we use the `Contact` standard controller for a Visualforce page, we can implement the standard `Save` method for `Contact` without writing any additional Apex code. This behavior is the same as implementing the `Save` method on the standard `Contact` edit page.

[✎ You cannot use the controller attribute with the
standardController attribute in the page tag.]

Standard controller – data bindings

Standard controllers include a getter or setter method specified by the ID in the query string parameter (on the URL). This is what allows the page to access data using the {!sObject} merge field syntax. This also allows developers to test using URL parameters with known IDs. For example:

```
https://c.ap1.visual.force.com/apex/SampleVisualforceTab?id=a01900000
0AVh1A
```

Obviously, the object type of the ID specified must match the standard controller specified for the page.

Standard controller – traversing data

As the API queries, you can see the expression syntax to retrieve data from objects related to the current object. There are two ways to traverse from the current object:

- You can traverse up five levels of child-to-parent relationships. Here's an example: {!contact.Account.Owner.FirstName}.

- You can traverse down one level of parent-to-child relationships to return an array of all child rows of that parent. Here's an example: {!account.Contacts}.

Standard controller – data validation messages

When using a standard controller, all of the same validation rules apply as those when using the object's associated page layout. If the validation rule error location is on a field that is displayed on the page using the <apex:inputField> component, the error will be displayed next to the field. If not, the <apex:messages> component can be used to display the message on the top of the page. A page that is associated with a standard controller automatically inherits the tab style for the associated object.

Standard controller – actions

Action methods perform logic or navigation when a page event occurs. Action methods are invoked using the {!actionmethod} syntax. For example, if your action method's name is MyFirstMethod, then you can use the {!MyFirstMethod} notation to call the action method from the page markup. Action methods in controllers are bound to the action attribute available on the following components:

- <apex:commandButton>: This component creates a button that calls an action
- <apex:commandLink>: This component creates a link that calls an action
- <apex:actionPoller>: This component periodically calls an action
- <apex:actionSupport>: This component creates an event (such as onclick, onmouseover, and so on) on another named component and calls an action
- <apex:actionFunction>: This component defines a new JavaScript function that calls an action
- <apex:page>: This component calls an action when the page is loaded

> This action method can be defined in a standard controller or a custom controller or a controller extension.

A standard controller defines the following standard action methods:

- save: This method inserts/updates a record. Upon successful completion, it will be redirected to the standard detail page or a custom Visualforce page.
- quicksave: This method inserts/updates a record. There are no redirections to a detail page or custom Visualforce page.
- edit: This method navigates the user to the edit page for the current record. Upon successful completion, it will be returned to the page that invoked the action.
- delete: This method deletes the current record. It redirects the user to the list view page by selecting the most recently viewed list filter.
- cancel: This method cancels an edit operation. Upon successful completion, it will be returned to the page that invoked the edit action.
- list: This method redirects to the list view page by selecting the most recently viewed list filter.
- view: This method returns the standard detail page.

For example, the following page allows us to insert a new employee or update an existing employee record. If we are going to use this page to update an employee record, then the URL must be specified with the ID of the particular record as the parameter. Every standard controller has a `getter` method that returns the record specified by the ID query string parameter in the page URL. When we click on **Save**, the `save` action is triggered on the standard controller and the details of the employee are updated. If we are going to use this page to insert an employee record, then the ID must not be specified as a parameter in the URL. In this scenario, when we click on **Save**, the `save` action is triggered on the standard controller and a new employee record is inserted.

The following code explains the usage of object accessibility. According to the example, you can see the **Save** button only if the particular user has security permission to access the customer record.

```
<apex:page standardController="Employee__c">
<apex:form >
  <apex:pageBlock title="Create new employee">
    <apex:pageBlockButtons >
      <apex:commandButton value="Save" action="{!save}"
        rendered="{!$ObjectType.Employee__c.accessible}"/>
      <apex:commandButton value="Cancel" action="{!cancel}"/>
    </apex:pageBlockButtons>
    <apex:pageBlockSection >
      <apex:inputField value="{!Employee__c.First_Name__c}"/>
      <apex:inputField value="{!Employee__c.Last_Name__c}"/>
      <apex:inputField value="{!Employee__c.Email__c}"/>
      <apex:inputField
        value="{!Employee__c.Leave_Category__c}"/>
      <apex:inputField value="{!Employee__c.Manager__c}"/>
    <apex:inputField value="{!Employee__c.IsActive__c}"/>
    </apex:pageBlockSection>
  </apex:pageBlock>
</apex:form>
</apex:page>
```

The Visualforce page generated by the preceding code is as follows:

Create new employee	Save Cancel		
First Name		Last Name	
Email		Leave Category	🔍
Manager	🔍	IsActive	✔
	Save Cancel		

Creating a new employee page using the standard controller

The following page allows us to view an employee record. In this page too, the URL must be specified in the ID query string parameter. The `getter` method of the `Employee__c` standard controller returns the record specified by the ID query string parameter in the page URL.

```
<apex:page standardController="Employee__c">
<apex:form >
  <apex:pageBlock title="Create new employee">
     <apex:pageBlockButtons >
         <apex:commandButton value="Save" action="{!save}"
rendered="{!$ObjectType.Employee__c.accessible}"/>
     </apex:pageBlockButtons>

     <apex:pageBlockSection >
         <apex:outputField value="{!Employee__c.First_Name__c}"/>
         <apex:outputField value="{!Employee__c.Last_Name__c}"/>
         <apex:outputField value="{!Employee__c.Email__c}"/>
         <apex:outputField value="{!Employee__c.Leave_Category__c}"/>
         <apex:outputField value="{!Employee__c.Manager__c}"/>
      <apex:outputField value="{!Employee__c.IsActive__c}"/>
     </apex:pageBlockSection>
  </apex:pageBlock>
</apex:form>
</apex:page>
```

This is the output of the code. Here, the URL must be specified with the ID of the particular record as the parameter:

Create new employee		Edit	Cancel		
First Name	Chamil			Last Name	Madusanka
Email	chamil.madusanka@gmail.com			Leave Category	Shop & Office
Manager				IsActive	✓
		Edit	Cancel		

Viewing an employee record using the standard controller

To check the accessibility of a particular object for the logged in user, you can use the {!$ObjectType.objectname.accessible} notation. This expression returns a Boolean value. As an example, if you want to check the accessibility of the Customer object, you can use {!$ObjectType.Employee__c.accessible}.

Standard list controllers

For almost every standard controller, there exists a standard list controller that allows you to create pages that display and act on a set of records, such as list pages, related lists, and mass action pages. It allows us to filter records on a particular page. We can use standard list controllers for Account, Asset, Campaign, Case, Contact, Contract, Idea, Lead, Opportunity, Product2, Solution, and User objects and all custom objects.

You can select the standard list controller instead of the regular standard controller by specifying the recordSetVar attribute in the page tag, which is as follows:

```
<apex:page standardController="Employee__c"
  recordSetVar="employees">
```

The standardController attribute specifies the type of records that we want to access. The recordSetVar attribute indicates that the page uses a list controller and the variable name (used to access data) of the record collection.

The following markup explains how the page can access a list of records when the page is associated with a list controller. In the following example, you can refer to a list of customer records:

```
<apex:page standardController="Employee__c"
  recordSetVar="employees" sidebar="false">
  <apex:pageBlock >
    <apex:pageBlockTable value="{!employees}" var="a">
```

```
        <apex:column value="{!a.name}"/>
      </apex:pageBlockTable>
    </apex:pageBlock>
  </apex:page>
```

The following screenshot illustrates the result of the preceding code:

Employee Name

Chamil Madusanka

Ruwantha Lankathilaka

The result page of the employee list example

Standard list controller – actions

Just as the standard controller actions, standard list controller actions can be used in all the standard Visualforce components that have the action attribute. The following action methods are supported by all standard list controllers:

- `save`: This action method inserts/updates a record. Upon successful completion, it will be redirected to the standard detail page or custom Visualforce page.
- `quicksave`: This method inserts/updates a record. There are no redirections to a detail page or a custom Visualforce page.
- `List`: This method redirects to the list view page by selecting the most recently viewed list filter when the filter ID is not specified by the user.
- `cancel`: This method cancels an edit operation. Upon successful completion, it will be returned to the page that invoked the edit action.
- `first`: This method displays the first page of records in the set.
- `last`: This method displays the last page of records in the set.
- `next`: This method displays the next page of records in the set.
- `previous`: This method displays the previous page of records in the set.

List views in Salesforce standard pages can be used to filter records that are displayed on the page. For example, on the customer home page, you can select start with c view from the list view dropdown and view the customers whose name starts with the letter c. You can implement this functionality on a page associated with a list controller.

Pagination can be added to a page associated with a list controller. The pagination feature allows you to implement the next and previous actions. For example, to create a simple list of customers with a list view and pagination, create a page with the following markup:

```
<apex:page standardController="Employee__c"
  recordSetvar="employees">
  <apex:form id="theForm">
    <apex:pageBlock title="Viewing employees">
      <apex:pageBlockSection >
        <apex:selectList value="{!filterid}" size="1">
         <apex:selectOptions value="{!listviewoptions}"/>
           <apex:actionSupport event="onchange"
             rerender="list"/>
        </apex:selectList>
      </apex:pageBlockSection>
      <apex:pageBlockSection id="list">
        <apex:dataList var="a" value="{!employees}" type="1">
         {!a.name}
           </apex:dataList>
      </apex:pageBlockSection>
      <apex:panelGrid columns="2">
        <apex:commandLink action="{!previous}"
           rerender="list">Previous</apex:commandlink>
        <apex:commandLink action="{!next}"
           rerender="list">Next</apex:commandlink>
      </apex:panelGrid>
    </apex:pageBlock>
  </apex:form>
</apex:page>
```

> By default, a list controller returns 20 records per page. To control the number of records displayed on each page, use a controller extension to set the pageSize attribute.

The result of the preceding code is shown in the following screenshot:

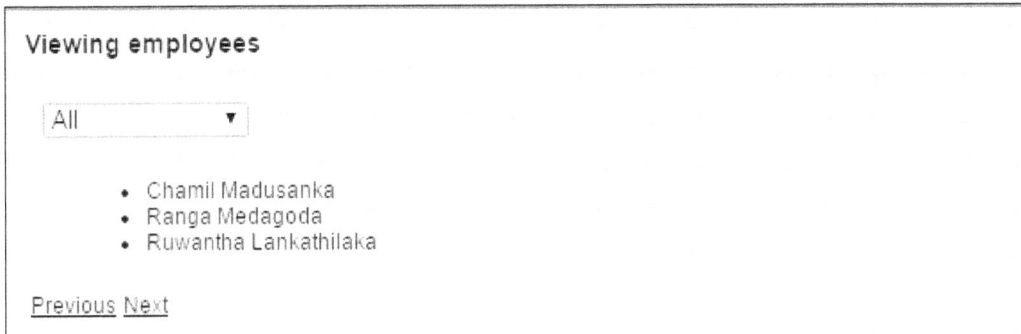

Viewing employees

| All ▼ |

- Chamil Madusanka
- Ranga Medagoda
- Ruwantha Lankathilaka

Previous Next

The result page of the employee list example

Custom controllers

Standard controllers can often provide all of the functionality and data that you need for your Visualforce page. But there are some scenarios where we cannot proceed with the standard controller. Therefore, we have to use custom controllers that are used to implement the logic and functionality without using a standard controller. The following are some scenarios where we might have to employ a custom controller:

- Implement a completely different functionality without relying on the standard controller's behavior
- Override the existing functionality
- Make new actions available to the page
- Customize the navigation
- Use HTTP callouts or web services
- Use a wizard
- Have greater control over information that can be accessed on a page
- Run your page without applying permissions

> Only one custom controller can be used on a particular page.

Custom controllers are invoked by using the following markup syntax:

```
<apex:page controller="ControllerClassName" >
```

Custom controllers are written using Apex and we discussed the basic phases (such as creating an Apex class, defining it, defining the interface, and so on) of the Apex class. Therefore, you are familiar with building an Apex class now.

Controller methods

When we build a custom controller or a controller extension, we have to implement the attributes and methods within the controller class. Those attributes and methods are the core of the controllers. Both custom controllers and controller extensions typically define three types of methods:

- Getter methods
- Setter methods
- Action methods

Getter methods

Getter methods are used to retrieve data from the controller to the Visualforce page. Every value calculated by a controller and displayed in a page must have a corresponding `getter` method. There are two ways to define a getter method:

- Typically, getter methods are named using the syntax `<getVariable>`, where `<variable>` is the name of the attribute that is returned by the `getter` method.

```
public class GetterSetterExample{
    String GetterVariable;

    public String getGetterVariable() {
        return GetterVariable;
    }
}
```

- A getter method can define an attribute by using the default `getter` and `setter` methods:

```
public class GetterSetterExample{
    public String GetterVariableDefault{get;set;}
}
```

The variable can be accessed on the Visualforce page using the `{!GetterVariableDefault}` expression. All standard controllers come with a `getObject()` method to allow access to the object's data via the `{!object.field}` syntax.

Setter methods

Setter methods are used to pass user-defined values to the Apex controller. Setter methods are defined in the same way as getter methods. Setter methods take the syntax `<setDataName()>`. The following example uses the default `getter` and `setter` methods to search for an employee who is already in the database:

```
public with sharing class SearchEmployeeController {
    public List<Employee__c> ExistingEmployees { get; set; }
    public String Keyword { get; set; }
    public SearchEmployeeController(){
        ExistingEmployees = new List<Employee__c>();
    }
    public void SearchEmployees() {
        ExistingEmployees = [SELECT Id, Name, First_Name__c, Email__c
          FROM Employee__c WHERE Name LIKE: ('%'+Keyword+'%')];
    }
}
```

The following code is the Visualforce page that uses the preceding controller. The `Keyword` attribute has the default `getter` and `setter` methods for the `<apex:inputText>` component, which is used to acquire the user's input. The `ExistingEmployees` list attribute also has the default `getter` and `setter` methods to search and display the search result of employees. When the user enters a keyword to search for and clicks on the **Search** button, the `SearchEmployees()` action method will be executed and this will acquire the keyword search text and run the query to search for the employees. Before the action method executes, the keyword setter method will be executed. Then the query result will be collected in the `ExistingEmployees` list attribute, the `ExistingEmployees` getter method will be executed, and the page will display the search result, which is as follows:

```
<apex:page controller="SearchEmployeeController">
  <apex:form >
    <apex:pageBlock >
       <apex:pageBlockSection >
          <apex:pageBlockSectionItem >
             <apex:outputLabel value="Employee Name Or
keyword"></apex:outputLabel>
                <apex:inputText value="{!Keyword}"/>
          </apex:pageBlockSectionItem>
           <apex:commandButton value="Search" action="{!SearchEmp
loyees}"/>
         </apex:pageBlockSection>
      </apex:pageBlock>

    <apex:pageBlock title="Search Result" id="searchResult">
```

```
        <apex:pageBlockTable value="{!ExistingEmployees}"
var="oneItem" rendered="{!ExistingEmployees.size > 0}">
            <apex:column value="{!oneItem.Name}"/>
            <apex:column value="{!oneItem.Email__c}"/>
        </apex:pageBlockTable>
        <apex:outputText value="No records to display"
rendered="{!ExistingEmployees.size == 0}"></apex:outputText>
      </apex:pageBlock>
   </apex:form>
</apex:page>
```

> Any setter methods are automatically executed before any action methods.

Action methods

Action methods are used to implement the custom or extended logic and functionality in a custom controller or controller extension. Action methods in controllers are bound to the action attribute available on the following tags:

- `<apex:commandButton>`
- `<apex:commandLink>`
- `<apex:actionPoller>`
- `<apex:actionSupport>`
- `<apex:actionFunction>`
- `<apex:page>`

Action methods can be triggered by a button click or JavaScript event. The preceding employee search example has an action method called `SearchEmployees`. `SearchEmployees` is used to query employee records according to the user input given for employee search.

Navigation methods

Action methods may also include navigation controls. If you write a method in a controller or an extension with the return type `PageReference`, it will act as a navigation method. The Apex `PageReference` object represents a UI page. It consists of a URL and a set of query parameter name/value pairs. A `PageReference` object is used to accomplish the following things:

- View or set URL query string parameter name/value pairs for a page
- Navigate the user to a different page as a result of an action method

There are four different ways to instantiate pages depending on the type of page:

- For the current page:

```
PageReference pageRef = ApexPages.currentPage();
```

- For a Visualforce page:

```
PageReference pageRef = Page.visualforcepagename
```

> Note that this method requires a Visualforce page to exist in order to compile the controller.

- For a Salesforce (possibly non-Visualforce) page:

```
PageReference pageRef = new PageReference('partialURL');
```

> partialURL refers to everything after https://salesforceserver.salesforce.com, such as /, +, and recordID to refer to the detail page for a specific record.

- For a non-Salesforce website:

```
PageReference pageRef = new PageReference('FullURL');
```

You can navigate to the new page by using the following:

```
pageRef.setRedirect(true);
return pageRef;
```

The setRedirect method only applies to URLs within the Salesforce.com domain. URLs outside of the Salesforce.com domain are always redirected despite the value of setRedirect. If you use the setRedirect(true) statement within a navigation method, you cannot maintain the view state of the particular page.

> The view state is where the information necessary to maintain the state of the database between requests is saved.

The following example shows you how to implement a navigation method in a custom controller and trigger the navigation method from the Visualforce page. Navigation methods can be implemented in a controller extension in the same manner as the following example:

```
public with sharing class NavigationController {
    Employee__c newEmployee;
    public Employee__c getNewEmployee(){
    if(newEmployee == null)newEmployee = new Employee__c();
```

```
      return newEmployee;
    }
    public PageReference cancel() {
      return null;
    }
    public PageReference save() {
      try{
        insert newEmployee;
        PageReference empPage = new
          PageReference('/'+newEmployee.Id);
        empPage.setRedirect(true);
        return empPage;
        }
      catch(Exception ex) {
        return null;
      }
    }
  }
```

The following Visualforce page uses the preceding controller to implement the navigation method. In this page, the **Save** button triggers the save navigation method and after the employee record is inserted, it redirects to the detail page of the inserted record:

```
<apex:page controller="NavigationController">
<apex:form >
  <apex:pageBlock title="Create new employee">
    <apex:pageBlockButtons >
      <apex:commandButton value="Save" action="{!save}"
        rendered="{!$ObjectType.Employee__c.accessible}"/>
      <apex:commandButton value="Cancel" action="{!cancel}"/>
    </apex:pageBlockButtons>
      <apex:pageBlockSection >
        <apex:inputField value="{!NewEmployee.First_Name__c}"/>
        <apex:inputField value="{!NewEmployee.Last_Name__c}"/>
        <apex:inputField value="{!NewEmployee.Email__c}"/>
        <apex:inputField value="{!NewEmployee.Birthday__c}"/>
        <apex:inputField
          value="{!NewEmployee.Leave_Category__c}"/>
        <apex:inputField value="{!NewEmployee.Manager__c}"/>
        <apex:inputField value="{!NewEmployee.IsActive__c}"/>
      </apex:pageBlockSection>
  </apex:pageBlock>
</apex:form>
</apex:page>
```

> A custom controller uses a non-parameterized constructor.
> You cannot create a constructor that includes parameters for
> a custom controller.

Controller extensions

Controller extensions are used to add custom behavior or additional data to the standard controller or custom controller. With a controller extension, the logic and functionality of a standard or custom controller can be extended. Therefore, a controller extension cannot be used without standard controller or custom controller. It needs a standard or custom controller. Controller extensions are also written using Apex. The following are some scenarios where we might have to employ a controller extension:

- Keeping the majority of functionality of a standard or custom controller as it is and adding more functionality
- Building a Visualforce page that should run according to the user's permissions

Controller extensions are invoked using the following markup syntax:

```
<apex:page standardController="Employee__c" extensions="MyClass1,
  MyClass2" >
```

The following class is a simple example of a controller extension. This controller extension is used to extend the logic and the functionality of the `Employee__c` custom object's standard controller. In this extension, we have a one-parameterized constructor to fetch the leave record from the standard controller. The `getRecord()` method fetches records from the standard controller. The `fetchLeaves()` method is a custom method that is implemented to query the leave records of a particular employee.

```
public with sharing class EmployeeWithLeaveExtension {
  public Employee__c Employee{get;set;}
  public List<Leave__c> Leaves{get;set;}
  public EmployeeWithLeaveExtension(ApexPages.StandardController
controller) {
    Employee = new Employee__c();
    Employee = (Employee__c)controller.getRecord();
    fetchLeaves();
  }
  public void fetchLeaves(){
    Leaves = new List<Leave__c>([Select Id,
      Name,From_Date__c,To_Date__c,Leave_Type__c,Number_of_Days__c,
        Status__c FROM Leave__c WHERE Employee__c =: Employee.Id
          ]);
  }
}
```

The following Visualforce page uses the preceding controller extension. On this page, we have two page blocks: the first block shows us the employee details and the second block shows the leaves of the particular employee.

```
<apex:page standardController="Employee__c"
  extensions="EmployeeWithLeaveExtension">
  <apex:pageBlock title="Hello {!$User.FirstName}">
  <apex:outputLabel value="You are viewing the employee record of
    {!Employee__c.Name}"></apex:outputLabel>
      <apex:pageBlockSection >
        <apex:outputField value="{!Employee__c.First_Name__c}"/>
        <apex:outputField value="{!Employee__c.Last_Name__c}"/>
        <apex:outputField value="{!Employee__c.Email__c}"/>
        <apex:outputField
          value="{!Employee__c.Leave_Category__c}"/>
        <apex:outputField value="{!Employee__c.Manager__c}"/>
      <apex:outputField value="{!Employee__c.IsActive__c}"/>
      </apex:pageBlockSection>
  </apex:pageBlock>
  <apex:pageBlock title="Leaves">
    <apex:pageBlockTable value="{!Leaves}" var="leave">
    <apex:column value="{!leave.From_Date__c}"/>
    <apex:column value="{!leave.To_Date__c}"/>
    <apex:column value="{!leave.Leave_Type__c}"/>
    <apex:column value="{!leave.Number_of_Days__c}"/>
    <apex:column value="{!leave.Status__c}"/>
    </apex:pageBlockTable>
  </apex:pageBlock>
</apex:page>
```

Considerations to create custom controllers and controller extensions

When you are creating custom controllers and controller extensions, keep the following consideration in mind:

- The most important thing to keep in your mind is Apex governor limits (Apex runs in a multitenant environment, therefore the Apex runtime engine strictly enforces a number of limits to ensure that runaway Apex doesn't monopolize shared resources. That's called Apex governor limits).

- Apex classes can be run in the system mode and user mode by using `without sharing` and `with sharing` respectively. Sensitive data can be exposed without sharing controllers.

- The `webservice` method must be defined as global. All other methods are public.

- Try to access the database in less time by using sets, maps, or lists. This will increase the efficiency of your code.

- Apex methods and variables are not instantiated in a guaranteed order.

- You cannot implement the Data Manipulation Language (DML) constructor method of a controller.

- You cannot define the `@future` annotation for any `getter` method, or constructor method of a controller.

- Primitive data types (string, integer, and so on) are passed by value and non-primitive Apex data types (list, maps, set, sObject, and so on) are passed by referring to a component's controller.

The order of execution of a Visualforce page

Every Visualforce page is executed according to a life cycle. This life cycle is determined from the creation of the page and its destruction during the user session. There are two types of Visualforce page request that define the life cycle of a particular page:

- Get request
- Postback request

Get requests of a Visualforce page

The get request is created after you request a new page by entering a URL or clicking on a button/link. The following diagram shows the behavior of the get request and how the Visualforce page interacts with the controller during the get request:

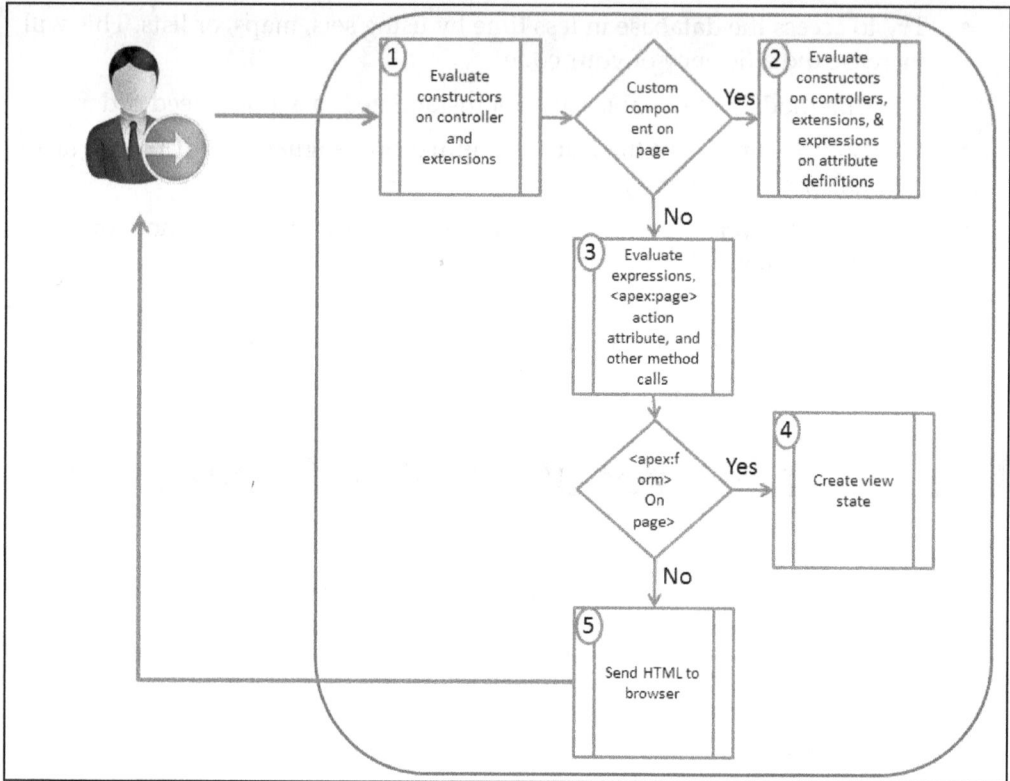

Order of execution for get requests of a Visualforce page

The order of execution is as follows:

1. First, it initiates the controller objects by calling the constructor method.

2. If there are any custom components, they are created and constructor methods are called on their associated class. If any attribute is specified in a component using an expression, those expressions are also evaluated.

3. Any `assignTo` attributes and expressions are evaluated. After that, the action attribute on the `<apex:page>` component is evaluated and all the `getter` or `setter` methods are called.

4. If the page contains an `<apex:form>` tag, then all of the information representing the state of the database is encrypted and saved in the view state between page requests. Whenever the page is updated, that view state is also updated.

5. Finally, the resultant HTML is sent to the browser. If there are any client-side technologies (such as JavaScript and CSS), the browser executes them.

Postback requests of a Visualforce page

Page updates are performed by postback requests. The following diagram shows the behavior of the postback request and how the Visualforce page interacts with the controller during the postback request:

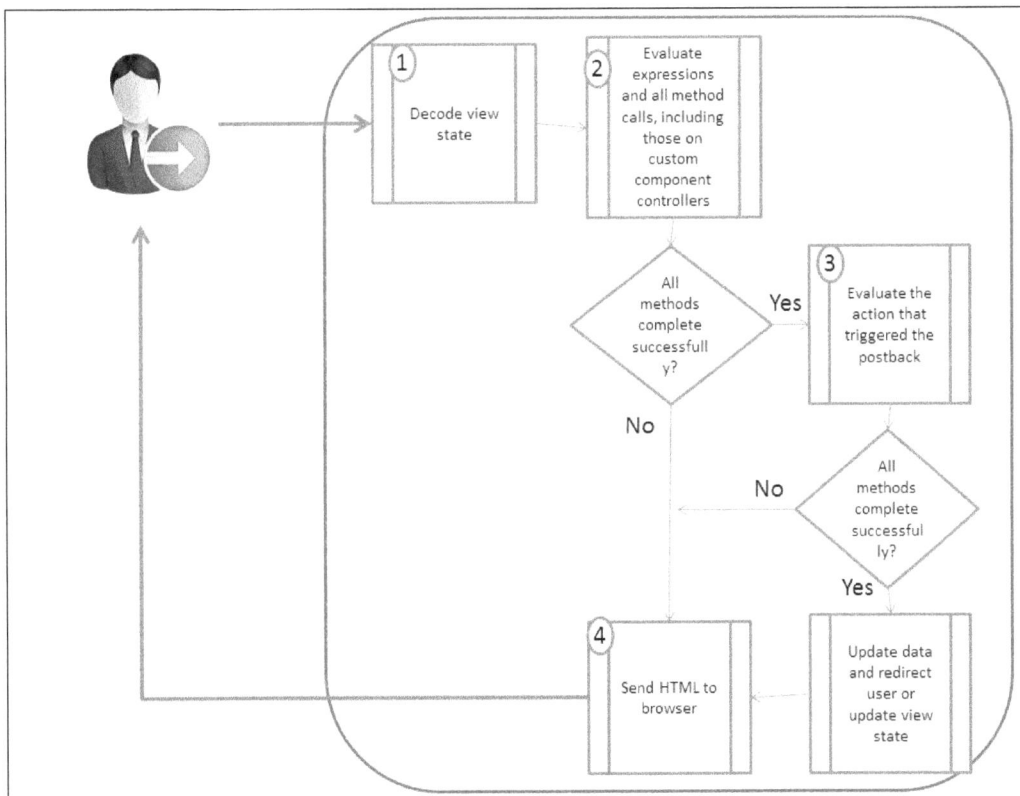

Order of execution for a postback request of a Visualforce page

The order is as follows:

1. Decodes the view state and it uses as the basis for updating the values on the page during a postback request.

2. Expressions are evaluated and setters are executed.

3. The action is executed. On its successful completion, the data is updated. If the postback request redirects the user to the same page, the view state is updated.

4. The results are sent to the browser.

> If we want to execute an action without performing validations on the input or data changes on the page, we can use an immediate attribute with the true value for a particular component.

The postback request can end with a page redirect and sometimes the custom controller or the controller extension may be shared on both the originating page and the redirected page. If the postback request contains an `<apex:form>` component, only the ID query parameter is returned.

> The action attribute of the `<apex:page>` component is evaluated only during a get request. Once the user is redirected to another page, the view state and controller objects are deleted.

Visualforce custom components

There are lots of standard Visualforce components (such as `<apex:detail>`, `<apex:pageBlock>`, `<apex:pageBlockTable>`, and `<apex:relatedList>`) that can be reused in Visualforce pages. A standard Visualforce component is a prebuilt, encapsulated code segment. These standard Visualforce components are built according to common usage. They are ready to be used in Visualforce pages. The Force.com platform allows us to build our own Visualforce components. Just as functions work in a programming language, custom Visualforce components allow us to encapsulate the common design patterns and reuse those patterns in one or more Visualforce pages.

The Force.com platform allows us to develop custom Visualforce components that can be reused within a particular application. Custom components can be developed using both Apex and Visualforce. For example, suppose we want to create an employee summary with his/her recent leaves and we need to use this functionality in different locations in our leave management app.

We also need to specify the number of recent leaves. According to the specified number, the number of recent leaves displayed in the employee's summary will be changed. The use of Visualforce custom components becomes the best choice to implement such a specific requirement.

A Visualforce custom component can have zero or more attributes to pass as parameters into the component. A custom component with attributes is like a parameterized Apex method. We can change the value of an attribute during the final usage level (in a Visualforce page).

Creating and using a custom component

We can create a Visualforce component to use in a Visualforce page. Navigate to **Setup** | **Develop** | **Components** | **New** to create a new Visualforce component. We need to specify the following properties while creating a custom component:

- **Label**: This custom component will be identified in the setup tools by using the label.
- **Name**: Using this name, the particular custom component will be identified in the Visualforce markup. This must be unique within the organization.
- **Description**: This gives the description of the custom component.
- **Body**: The **Visualforce Markup** code must be placed within the body section.

The following screenshot displays the aforementioned custom components:

Creating new Visualforce components

> The name of the custom component should begin with a letter and it should not end with an underscore. Furthermore, spaces or two consecutive underscores should not be included in the name.
>
> The maximum amount of data that a custom component can contain is 1 MB, or approximately 100,000 characters.
>
> We can specify the version of Visualforce and the API used with the particular component by using the version setting.

The body of a custom component can be defined as follows:

```
<apex:component>
  <!—Desire markup here-->
</apex:component>
```

The component markup is same as other Visualforce pages. It can be a combination of Visualforce and HTML tags. We can also add customized CSS and JavaScript.

All the markup should be defined within the `<apex:component>` tag. Our custom component example is an employee's leaves summary with recent leaves. Suppose our custom component name is `EmployeeSummary`; we can use this component in multiple Visualforce pages. The usage is as follows:

```
<apex:page>
  <c: EmployeeSummary />
</apex:page>
```

Custom attributes and custom controllers

When we are creating complex custom components, we need to use some other features to build custom components. Mainly, we have to use custom attributes and custom controllers for custom components. The attributes can be defined within the `<apex:component>` tags for passing values from the Visualforce page (the page that used the component) to the custom component or to the controller of the component.

We have implemented the example (`EmployeeSummary`) explained from the beginning of this section. The following is the component markup and it contains the definition of attributes and the definition of components. We have two attributes to be passed, which are employee ID and the number of recent leaves that we want to show in the page. These two parameters are used to pass the values to the component's controller.

```
<apex:component controller="EmployeeSummaryComponenetController">
  <!-- Attribute Definitions -->
```

```
<apex:attribute name="employeeId" Type="String" required="true"
  description="employee id" assignTo="{!EmpID}"/>
<apex:attribute name="noOfRecentLeaves" Type="Integer"
  required="true" description="Number of recent leaves"
    assignTo="{!RecentNo}"/>
<!-- Attribute Definitions : End -->
<!-- Component Definition -->
<apex:componentBody >
  <apex:pageBlock >
    <apex:pageBlockSection title="Employee Details">
      <apex:outputField value="{!CurrentEmployee.Name}"/>
      <apex:outputField
        value="{!CurrentEmployee.Leave_Category__c}"/>
      <apex:outputField value="{!CurrentEmployee.Email__c}"/>
      <apex:outputField value="{!CurrentEmployee.Manager__c}"/>
    </apex:pageBlockSection>
      <apex:pageBlockSection title="Recent Leave Details">
      <apex:pageBlockTable value="{!RecentLeaveList}"
        var="leave">
        <apex:column value="{!leave.From_Date__c}"/>
        <apex:column value="{!leave.To_Date__c}"/>
        <apex:column value="{!leave.Number_of_Days__c}"/>
        <apex:column value="{!leave.Leave_Type__c}"/>
        <apex:column value="{!leave.Status__c}"/>
      </apex:pageBlockTable>
    </apex:pageBlockSection>
  </apex:pageBlock>
</apex:componentBody>
<!-- Component Definition : End -->
</apex:component>
```

The following code snippet shows the custom controller that is associated with the
EmployeeSummary custom component. This controller is used to manipulate the values
of the attributes. In this example, we have queried the employee record and the recent
leave details of the particular employee. The query results of CurrentEmployee and
RecentLeaveList depend on the EmpID and RecentNo values.

```
public class EmployeeSummaryComponenetController{
  public String EmpID{get;set;}
  public Integer RecentNo{get;set;}
  public Employee__c CurrentEmployee{
  get{
    CurrentEmployee = new Employee__c();
    CurrentEmployee = [SELECT Id,
                      Name,
```

```
                            Leave_Category__c,
                            Email__c,
                            Manager__c
                            FROM Employee__c
                            WHERE Id =: EmpID];
            return CurrentEmployee;
        }
        set;
    }

    public List<Leave__c> RecentLeaveList{
        get{
            RecentLeaveList = new List<Leave__c>();
            RecentLeaveList = [Select Id,
                Name,From_Date__c,To_Date__c,Leave_Type__c,
                    Number_of_Days__c,Status__c FROM Leave__c WHERE
                        Employee__c =: EmpID ORDER BY CreatedDate DESC
                            LIMIT :RecentNo];
            return RecentLeaveList;
            }
            set;
        }
    }
}
```

This is how custom components are to be used. Here, we have passed the employee ID and the number of recent leave values that we want to see:

```
<apex:page standardController="Employee__c">
  <c:EmployeeSummary employeeId="{!Employee__c.Id}"
noOfRecentLeaves="2"></c:EmployeeSummary>
</apex:page>
```

The following screenshot shows the result of the `EmployeeSummary` custom component.

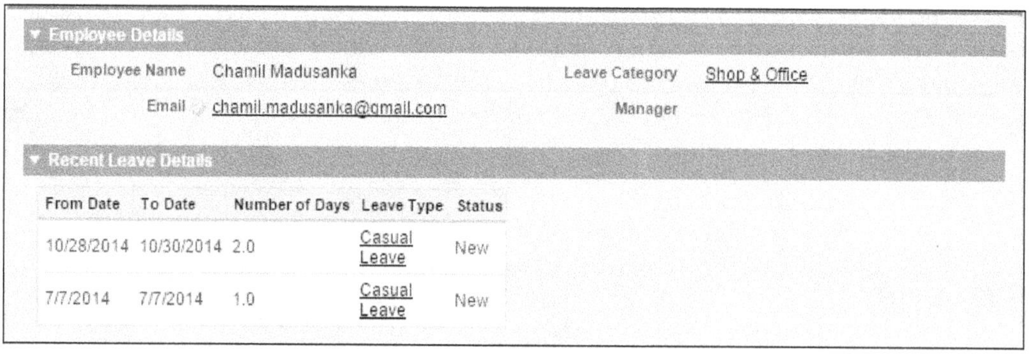

Result of the custom Visualforce component

Advantages of Visualforce

The following are the advantages of Visualforce for a developer:

- **Model-View-Controller development style**: Visualforce adheres to the MVC pattern by providing the view of the application in the Force.com platform. A view is defined by user interfaces and Visualforce markup. The Visualforce controller, which can be associated with Visualforce markup, takes care of the business logic. Therefore, the designer and the developer can work separately. While the designer focuses on the user interface, the developer focuses on business logic.

- **User-friendly development**: A developer (with an administrator profile) user can have a Visualforce editor pane at the bottom of every Visualforce page. This editor pane is controlled by the **Development Mode** option of the user record. This feature allows us to edit and see the resulting page at the same time and in the same window. This Visualforce editor has the code-saving features of autocompilation and syntax highlighting.

- **A broad set of ready-to-serve Visualforce components**: Visualforce has a set of standard components in several categories. There are output components, for example, `<apex:outputPanel>`, `<apex:outputField>`, `<apex:outputText>`, and `<apex:pageBlock>`. There are input components, for example, `<apex:inputFile>`, `<apex:inputField>`, `<apex:inputText>`, and `<apex:selectList>`. These input and output components have a feature called data-driven defaults. For an example, when we specify the `<apex:inputField>` component in a particular Visualforce page, the `<apex:inputField>` tag provides the edit interface for that field with data-type-related widgets (for example, the Date field has the calendar, and the e-mail/phone fields have their particular validations). There are also AJAX components, for example, `<apex:actionStatus>`. AJAX components allow the user to enhance the level of interactivity for a particular interface.

- **Tightly integrated with Salesforce / extends with custom components**: A Visualforce page can have a custom controller as well as a standard controller. A standard controller is created while creating the object and can be used for the Visualforce controller. A standard controller has the same logic and functionality that is used in standard pages. Visualforce pages adhere to these standardized methods and functionality. And we can also extend the standard components with custom components. For example, we can use an extension class for extending the standard controller of a particular Visualforce page. We can create our own Visualforce custom components instead of Visualforce in-built components, for example, `<apex:inputFile>`, `<apex:inputField>`, and `<apex:outputField>`. In the next two chapters, we will discuss more about Visualforce controllers and Visualforce custom components.

- **Flexible and customizable with web technologies**: The Visualforce markup is more flexible and more customizable through the use of web technologies, for example, JavaScript, CSS, jQuery, and Flash because it is eventually rendered as HTML. A designer can use the Visualforce tags with these web technologies.

Summary

In this chapter, we have learned about developing custom pages using Visualforce and we have used the knowledge of Apex coding, which we learned in *Chapter 7, Custom Coding with Apex,* by implementing the custom controllers and controller extensions. We have covered not only Apex controllers, but also standard controllers and standard list controllers. The other main section was building custom Visualforce component which was used as an encapsulated and reusable component in Visualforce. The next chapter will cover building reports and dashboards in the Force.com platform.

9
Analytics as a Service with the Force.com Platform

We have come a long way with our `Leave Management` application. We built our data model according to the business requirements, created pages to capture data, and implemented and automated the business processes. Basically, we built the functional application on the Force.com platform. Now, we have the ability to store our data related to the `Leave Management` application. Analytics plays a vital role in any company's development. We can define a company or a product successfully only if it has gone above in the metrics. These metrics or the tracking of metrics are perfectly engineered in the Force.com platform. Salesforce has advanced into analytics on a larger scale, posting a challenge for all giants in analytics. The investment of Salesforce confirms the importance of analytics in our organization. We can make things better only when we know the pros and cons of a situation from a centralized point of view.

Now, it's time to pay attention to a different side, analytics. In the application, there are roles for HR executives who need to keep track of the application records in different ways. Therefore, we are going to introduce the reports and dashboard of the Force.com platform and analytical features of the Force.com platform.

This chapter covers the following topics:

- Reports
- Custom report types
- Dashboards
- Reporting snapshots

Reports

The reports provide a way to combine and analyze data in the Force.com platform. We can use reports to leverage the data onto the application that has accumulated over time. Reports are a good way to examine your data in many combinations, and display it in an easy-to-understand format. A report returns a set of records according to the particular criteria, and displays them in an organized way. The filtering, grouping, sorting, and graphical charting can be added to a report. Therefore, users can monitor and analyze the data that's being generated in the organization by building reports.

Reports can include standard objects and/or custom objects and show only the data and fields that are visible to the user running the report. When new objects and fields are added to Salesforce and once we check the checkbox of **Allow Reports** in the particular object creation, they are immediately available for reporting. Reports can be saved. Running a saved report shows the data in real-time based on the parameters that have been saved. Ultimately, reports are always running in real-time. Report security is determined by the folder in which a report is stored.

Report formats

There are four different report formats in the Force.com platform. Each report format differs from the other by the complexity and the functionality of the report:

- Tabular reports
- Summary reports
- Matrix reports
- Joined reports

Tabular reports

This is the most simplest and the fastest way to examine your data in the organization. It provides a list of data without the subtotal. However, you can't apply the grouping and charting in this report format. Nonetheless, you can create a dashboard from the tabular report when the row limit is set to a number between 1 and 99. Therefore, you can use this report format when you want a simple data list with a grand total. Tabular reports, as the name suggests, are table-based reports in which we can see data with grand totals in one place. They are the simplest form of reports.

For example, the following tabular report shows the list of employees in the organization. It has only the grand total and list of records with added columns, which is similar to a spreadsheet:

Summary reports

The summary report format is similar to the tabular format but, additionally, this format allows you to do the following:

- Group your data by row
- Sort them
- View subtotals
- Create charts
- Unlike tabular reports, this can be used in the dashboard (more about dashboard will be discussed in the upcoming section)

For example, the following report is a summary report, which retrieves the leave records of employees and is grouped by the **Leave Type** column. It shows the subtotal for each group and the graphical chart to understand the data set easily:

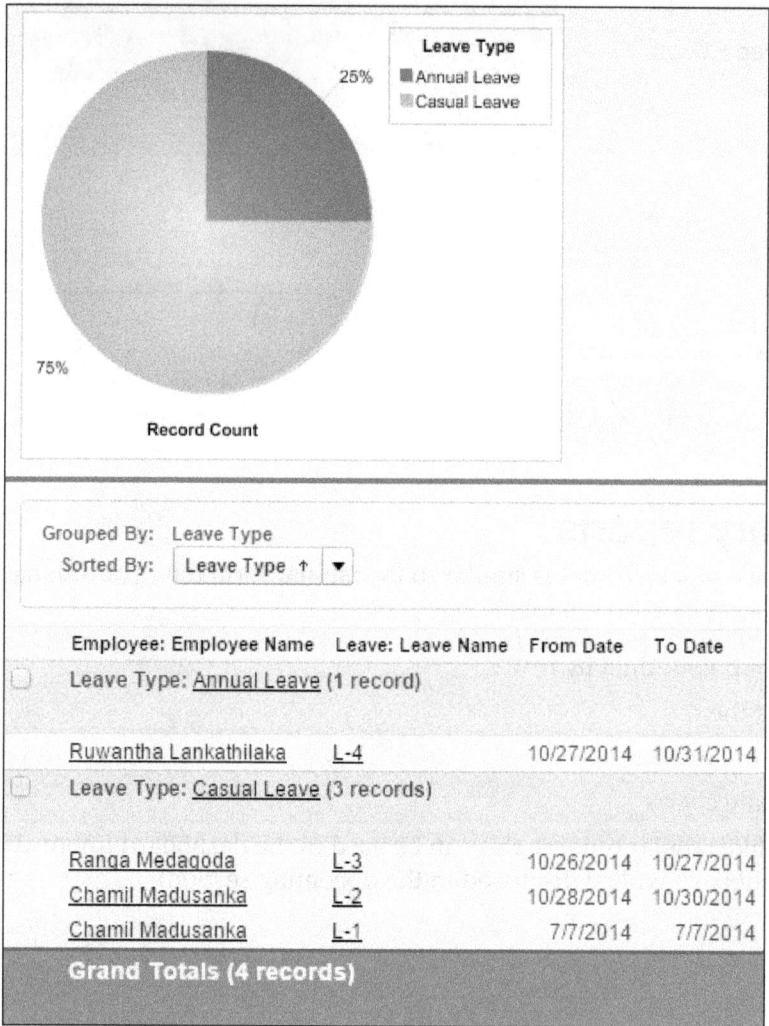

The summary reports are time consuming in the setup phase, but are more flexible and give more options to manipulate and organize data to analyze. This is the most trending format in the Force.com reporting tool.

Matrix reports

This type of format allows you to group data both by row and by column. Therefore, you can summarize the data in a grid view. Use this type for comparing related totals by two different dimensions. For example, the following matrix report is grouped by **Employee** (row) and **Leave Type** (column). Therefore, it returns the matrix view of employees who apply leave in numbers. The matrix reports also can have graphical charts and it can be used in dashboards. The following figure provides an overview of what we have discussed:

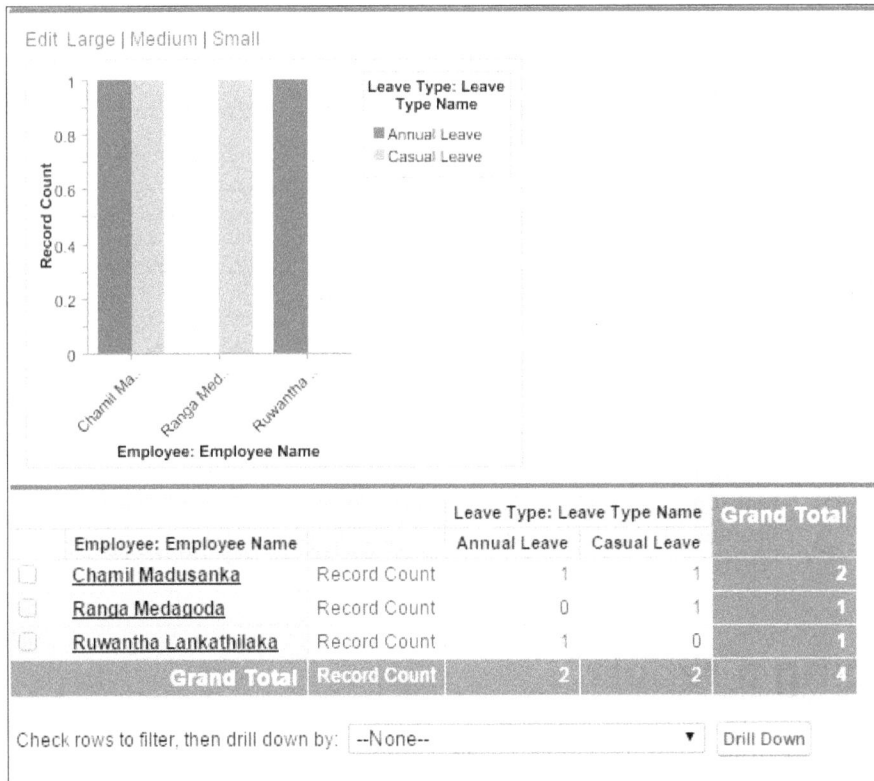

Joined reports

A joined report is a combination of multiple report types and it allows you to create different views. Because of these multiple report types, data of a joined report are organized in blocks and each block acts as a subreport with its own columns, sorting, and filtering. The following joined report consists of the employee records in one block and the leave records in the other block. The report pulls data from two report types, which are as follows:

> Tabular or summary reports must be used as the source report for reporting snapshots. Tabular reports cannot be used with custom summary formulas, charts, and conditional highlighting. A tabular report does not have charts but the matrix and summary reports do.

Building a report

Building a report in the Force.com platform is much easier because of the report builder, which allows you to drag and drop columns quickly and comprehensively. Before we create the report, identify the report builder tool in the Force.com platform. It consists of three main panes, which are as follows:

- **Fields pane**: Fields from the selected report type are displayed in this pane. The custom summary formulas and bucket fields can be create/edit/view/ delete in this pane.

- **Filters pane**: You can add custom filters, time frames, and set the view for the selected dataset of the report.

- **Preview pane**: This pane provides a dynamic preview of the report. All the customization, such as adding column/summary fields/formulas, removing, column/summary fields/formulas, reordering and grouping can be viewed at the same time as you change them. The limited number of records will show in the preview. You must run the report to see all the records. These filters are shown in the following screenshot:

The report builder

To create a new report, perform the following steps:

1. Click on the **Report** tab in the tab menu. If it is not available in the tab menu, click on the plus button located in the right side of the tab menu. Then there will be the **Reports** link. Refer to the following screenshot:

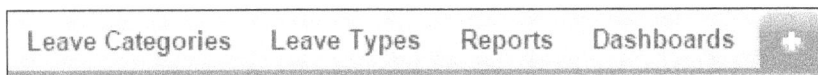

2. After clicking on the **Reports** tab, you will get the following screen, where you need to click on the **New Report** button:

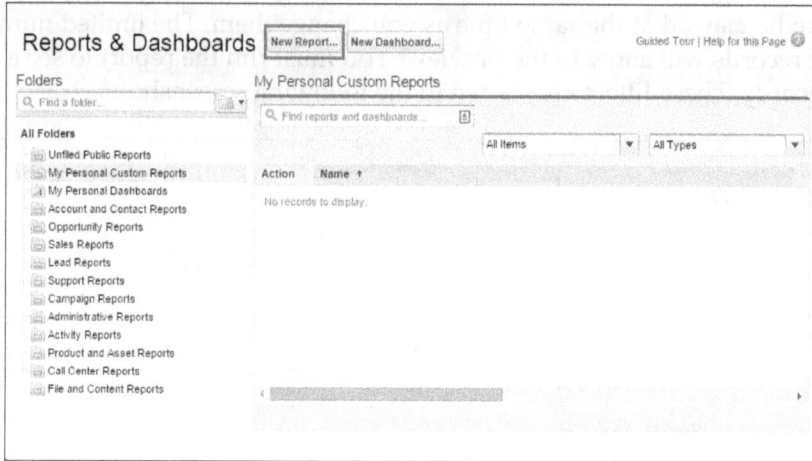

3. Select the report type and click on the **Create** button. The report type is a set of rules that determine which records and fields appear in the report. There are two types of report types: Standard report types and Custom report types. Now you can choose a standard report type from the following screen. The custom report type will be discussed in a next section. For this example, we choose **Employees with Leaves and Leave Type report type**. Report type is an important point, which will be explained later. If we do not provide this information, then topics will not be communicated to the user properly. The following screenshot gives us an idea about creating a new report:

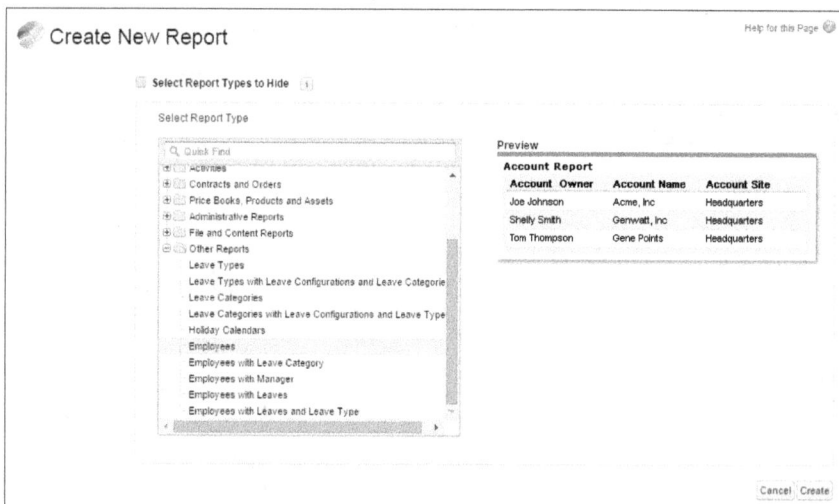

4. The following screen will be displayed.

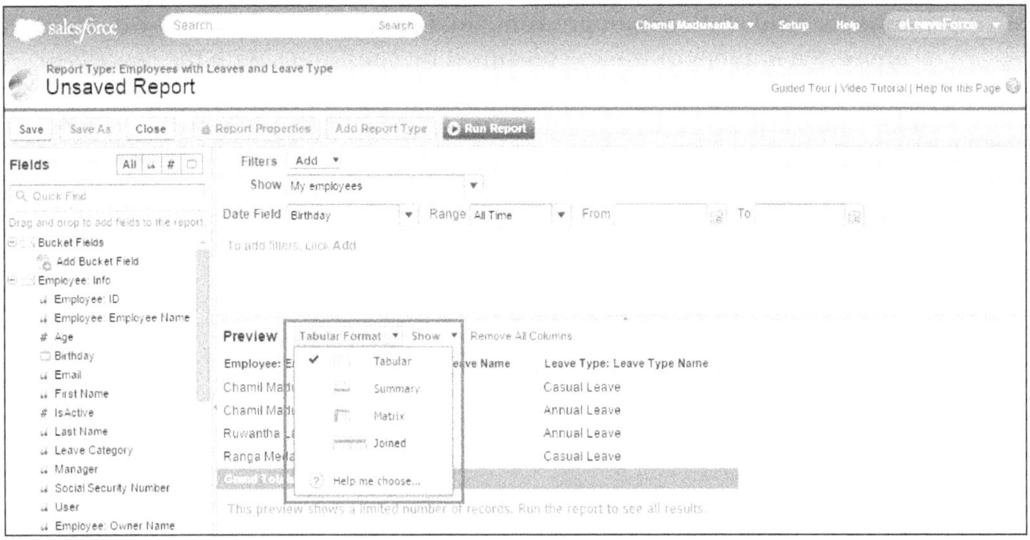

5. Choose a report format type of **Tabular**, **Summary**, **Matrix**, or **Joined** format. You have to select the format that is complex enough to fulfill your analysis requirements. We discussed about these report formats in the preceding subsection. Here we will proceed with the **Matrix** format. The **Joined** format is only available for Enterprise, Unlimited, and Developer Editions.

6. Customize your report according to your requirements. In this example, we want to create a matrix report with two groupings; row grouping by **Employee** field and column grouping by **Leave Type** field. Then we can examine the number of leaves consumed by employees with the leave type categorization. You can add the group by dragging and dropping particular fields into the drop zone. The following screenshot shows the editing mode of the report.

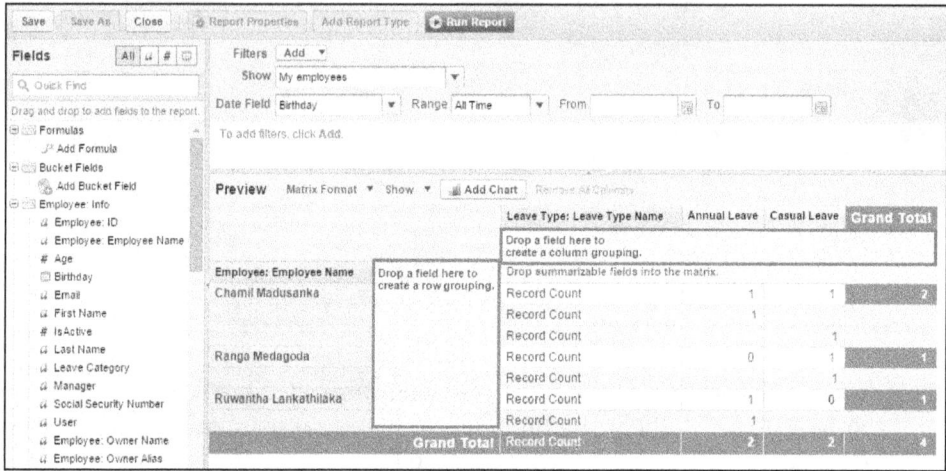

Drop zone for grouping

7. If you want to add a chart to this report, click on **Add Chart** in the report builder, which is shown in the following screenshot:

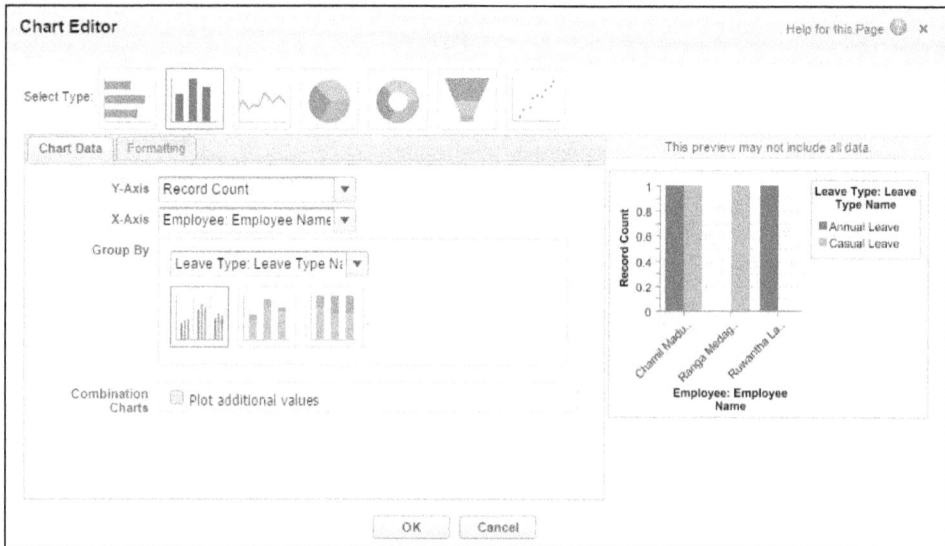

8. In the preceding screen, select a chart type. There are seven types of chart: Horizontal bar charts, Vertical bar charts, Line charts, Pie charts, Donut charts, Funnel charts, and Scatter charts.

9. Enter the appropriate settings on the **Chart Data** tab for the chart type you selected and the appropriate settings on the **Formatting** tab. Click on **OK**.

10. Specify the filter criteria for the report, if needed.

11. Click on **Save** to save the changes of the built report. Specify the report name, optional description, and the report folder to save the report. Each user, user group, or role can have their own level of permission to the report folder. If you do not wish to share the report, you can save it in the **My Personal Custom Reports** folder, and if you want to share the report to all users, then save it in the **Unfiled Public Reports** folder, is shown in the following screenshot:

The following permissions are there in a report folder.

- Viewer: only see the data
- Editor: determine what data is shown
    - Manager: control access

12. Click on **Save and Run Report**. Now, your report is ready.

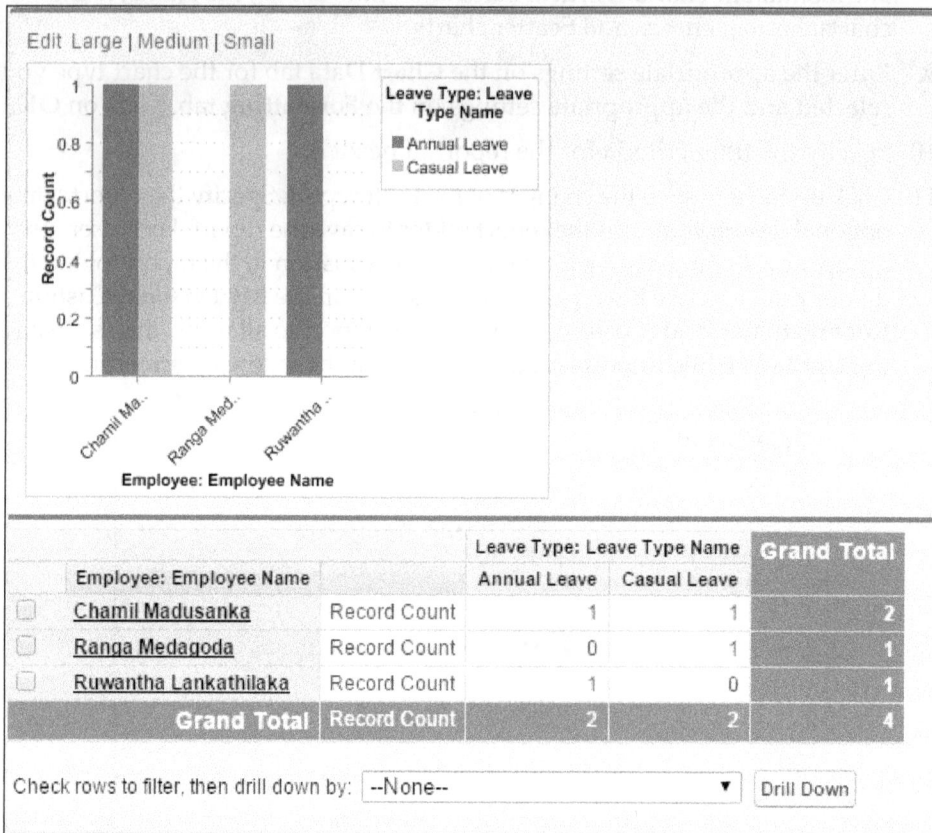

Employee: Employee Name		Leave Type: Leave Type Name		Grand Total
		Annual Leave	Casual Leave	
Chamil Madusanka	Record Count	1	1	2
Ranga Medagoda	Record Count	0	1	1
Ruwantha Lankathilaka	Record Count	1	0	1
Grand Total	Record Count	2	2	4

Check rows to filter, then drill down by: --None-- ▼ Drill Down

Custom report types

In the Force.com platform, the Report type is a set of rules that determine which records and fields appear in the report. The Report types are categorized into two;

- Standard report types
- Custom report types

Custom report types allow you to build a skeleton in the report wizard from which users can create and customize reports. With custom report types, you can enable users to create reports from the predefined objects, object relationships, and fields that you specify. You build custom report types of the relationships (master-detail and lookup) between objects so that you can:

- Choose which standard and custom objects to display to users creating and customizing reports
- Define the relationships between objects displayed to users creating and customizing reports
- Select which objects' fields can be used as columns in reports

> The visibility of custom report types in the report wizard is controlled by the user's access to the objects in the report type.

To create a custom report type, perform the following steps:

1. Go to **Setup | Build | Create | Report Types**.
2. Click on **New Custom Report Type**.
3. In the following screen, select **Primary Object** for your custom report type to define the custom report type. Specify what type of records (rows) will be the focus of reports generated by this report type. For example, if reporting on `Employees with Leave with Leave Type`, select **Employee** as the primary object.
4. Enter the **Report Type Label** name and then **Report Type Name** will be populated. The label can be up to 255 characters long. The name is used by any API. For this example, we used `Employees with Leave - Custom` as the name of the custom report type.
5. Enter a description for your custom report type, up to 1000 characters long. This description will be visible to users who create reports.
6. Select the category to store the custom report type in. For this example, we choose **Other Reports**.

7. Select a **Deployment Status, Deployed**, or **In Development**. A report type with deployed status is available for use in the report wizard. While in development, report types are visible only to authorized administrators and their delegates.

Step 1. Define the Custom Report Type	Step 1 of 2

> Next   Cancel

Report Type Focus   **|** = Required Information

Specify what type of records (rows) will be the focus of reports generated by this report type.

Example: If reporting on "Contacts with Opportunities with Partners," select "Contacts" as the primary object.

Primary Object | Employees   ▼ |

Identification

Report Type Label | Employees with Leave - Custom |

Report Type Name | Employees_with_Leave_Cus i |

Note: Description will be visible to users who create reports.

Description | Employees with Leave - Custom |

Store in Category | Other Reports   ▼ |

Deployment

A report type with deployed status is available for use in the report wizard. While in development, report types are visible only to authorized administrators and their delegates.

Deployment Status   ○ In Development

                           ● Deployed

> Next   Cancel

8. Click on **Next**.

9. The next step is to define the report records set. This report type will generate reports about the primary object (in the example, it is the `Employee` object). You can define the related objects of the primary object here. Click on the **Click to relate another object** area and select the particular related objects that are returned in the report results by choosing a relationship to another object. In this example, we choose the **Leaves** object as our secondary object, which is shown in the following screenshot:

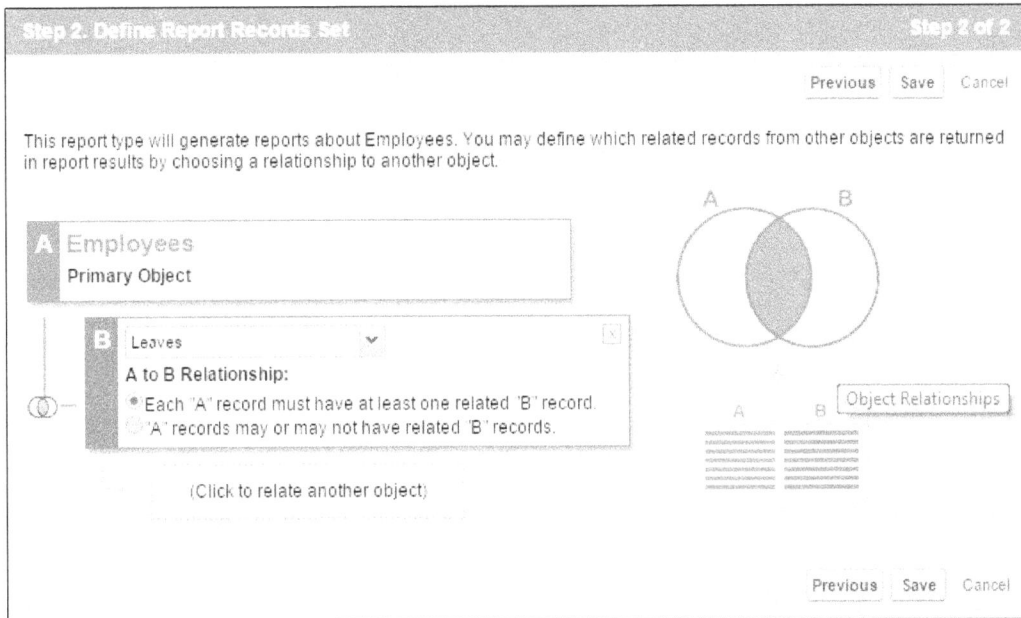

10. You can select one of the following criteria for each child object selected from the preceding screenshot:

   ○ **Each "A" record must have at least one related "B" record**: Only parent records with child records are shown in the report (for our example we select this option)

   ○ **"A" records may or may not have related "B" records**: Parent records are shown, whether or not they have child records

11. Click on **Save**. Now you have to create the custom report type and be ready to use it in the report creation, as we discussed in the *Introducing Reports* section. You can click on the buttons on this page to preview or update information for the custom report type. The custom report is shown in the following screenshot:

Custom Report Type
Employees with Leave - Custom
« Back to List: Custom Report Types

Help for this Page

Below is the information for this custom report type. You can click the buttons on this page to preview or update information for the custom report type.

Custom Report Type Definition   Edit | Delete | Clone

Report Type Label	Employees with Leave - Custom	Report Type Category	Other Reports
Report Type Name	Employees_with_Leave_Custom	Deployment Status	Deployed
Description	Employees with Leave - Custom		
Created By	Chamil Madusanka, 10/27/2014 3:50 PM	Modified By	Chamil Madusanka, 10/27/2014 3:50 PM

Object Relationships   Edit

Object Relationships Help (?)

Employees (A)
⌊.... with at least one related record from Leaves (B)

Fields Available for Reports   Edit Layout | Preview Layout

Fields Available for Reports Help (?)

Source	Selected Fields
Employees	17
Leaves	13

Created custom report type

Dashboards

Dashboards are the graphical representation of report data. Dashboards are shown on the home page of your organization. You can have up to 20 dashboard components on the home page. The advantage of the dashboard is that you can visualize the data of multiple reports on a single page and schedule the dashboard for e-mail distribution. This is the easiest way to see the entire organization in a single view. The dashboard shows data as of the last time the dashboard was refreshed.

Building a dashboard

Building a dashboard in the Force.com platform is much easier because of the dashboard builder, which allows you to drag and drop components and data sources quickly and comprehensively. Before we create the dashboard, identify the dashboard builder tool in the Force.com platform. It mainly consists of three panes:

- **Components**: There are five types of dashboard components: charts, tables, gauges, metrics, or Visualforce page/components. You can drag and drop the particular components in the dashboard area.

- **Data Sources**: This is the place from where we get the data source for the dashboard. You can drag and drop either a report or Visualforce as a data source in the particular dashboard area or onto the dashboard component. It will automatically prepare the dashboard for you.

- **Dashboard Area**: Dashboards are located in the dashboard area. We can drag and drop components and data sources to the dashboard area. There are three columns in the dashboard area, as shown in the following screenshot:

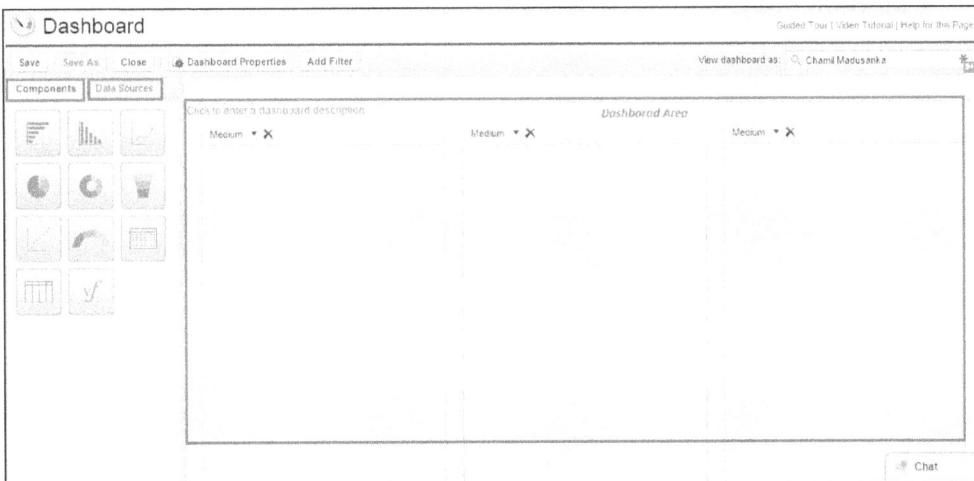

The dashboard builder

Perform the following steps to create a dashboard:

1.   Click on the **Dashboard** tab in the tab menu.

2.   Then you will see the recently viewed dashboard. Then click on **Go to Dashboard**.

3.   Click on **New Dashboard**.

4.   You will be redirected to the dashboard builder which we discussed earlier.

5.   Drag and drop the particular component and data source to the component. For this example, we use the vertical bar chart and **Employee with leave report**.

6.   You can specify your own title for the particular dashboard component by clicking on the title area.

7.   Click on **Dashboard Properties**

8.   Enter HR Manager Dashboard for the title and accept the autogenerated unique name.

9.   Choose the **My Personal Dashboards** folder for now. Like the report folder, you can create a dashboard folder and the dashboard folder controls who has access to a dashboard. You can specify who has access to a folder and what level of access each user has (read only or read/write)

10. On the right-hand side, you can specify the **Dashboard Running User** name. Show all users the same data in the dashboard by choosing a specific running user, or show data according to each viewer's access level by choosing **Run as the logged-in user**. For example, support the team working on customer cases and the whole team wants to see all open cases. Therefore the running user will be of their manager. The following screenshot displays **Dashboard Running User**:

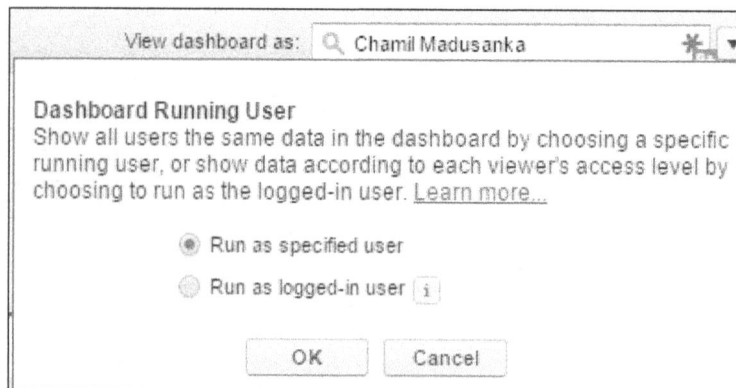

Define the dashboard running user

11. Click on **Save**.

12. Click on **Save & Close** to close the dashboard.

> Dashboards can be scheduled for automatic refresh and can be e-mailed out to selected users. Dashboard push alerts allow users to follow dashboard components in chatter.

The HR manager dashboard is displayed in the following screenshot:

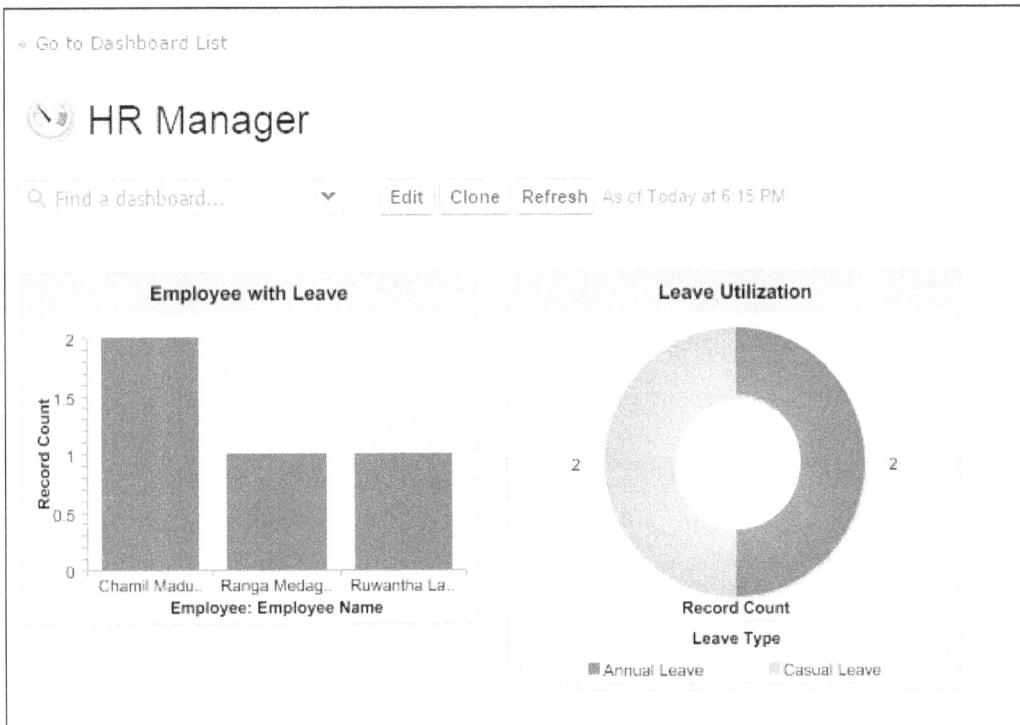

To add your dashboard to the home page, use these steps:

1. Navigate to **Setup | Customize | Home | Home Page Layouts**.

2. This page allows you to create different tab layouts for the **Home** Tab.

3. Click on **Edit** on the home page layout which is assigned to you.

4. In here, you can choose the components to include on your home page layout. Select the **Dashboard Snapshot**.

5. Click on **Next**.

6. Click on **Save**. Now your dashboard is located in your home page.

7. By clicking on the refresh button, you can refresh your dashboard with the most recent data.

> Clicking on a dashboard component that is created from a report will take the user to the underlying report. When viewing the report, a user will see only those records that the security model allows them to use.

Reporting snapshot

Reporting snapshots allow you to create a tabular or summary report, and then take a snapshot of the data on that report by mapping the fields on the report to fields on a custom object. In other words, this is called a report on historical data. You can establish a schedule for capturing the snapshot. You can report on the data in the custom object to view historical data and analyze trends.

For example, HR managers can set up a reporting snapshot that reports on the leave utilization by employees. This can be scheduled to run everyday at 6.00 p.m. and store the data in a custom object. The HR manager can then spot the trend in the leave utilization.

Setting up a reporting snapshots

Before setting up the reporting snapshot, you need to be aware of the following reporting snapshot terminology:

- **Source report**: This is the custom report scheduled to run and load data as records into a custom object

- **Target object**: This is the custom object that receives the results of the source report as records

- **Running user**: This is the user whose security settings determine the source report's level of access to data

Use the following steps to set up a reporting snapshot:

1. Create a source report using the report builder.

2. Create a target object (a custom object with fields to store the data from the report).

3. Go to **Setup | Administer | Data Management | Reporting Snapshots**.

4. Click on **New Reporting Snapshot**.

5. Enter **Reporting Snapshot Name, Description** (optionally) for the reporting snapshot.

6. Specify the **Running User** name. The data this user can view and report on will be loaded as records into the target object.

7. A reporting snapshot runs a **Source Report**, and then loads the report data as records into a **Target Object** field. Select a **Source Report** and **Target Object** from the dropdown list.

8. Click on **Save** to save the definition of your reporting snapshot, or click on **Save & Edit Field Mappings** to save your reporting snapshot and map its fields.

9. After you create the reporting snapshot, you can map the fields on your source report to the fields on your target object. It will automatically load information from the report to the target object.

10. After creating the reporting snapshot and the field mapping, you can schedule it to run daily, weekly, or monthly.

The following are the benefits of using reporting snapshots:

- Running faster reports by reporting on data that is already summarized
- Creating dashboards that refresh quickly by associating them with presummarized data
- Sorting and filtering specific data summaries via list views
- Viewing trends in data via custom object records

Summary

In this chapter, we became familiar with the analytical aspects of the Force.com platform by including the reports and dashboards. You have learned the custom report types, which allow us to build flexible reports on the Force.com platform. We also discussed the reporting snapshots that allow us to analyze using historical data in the Force.com application.

In the next chapter, we focus on the e-mail feature of the Force.com platform that allows extending the application out into the broader population of users through the use of e-mail.

10

E-mail Services with the Force.com Platform

In all the previous chapters, we focused on building a solution for users on the Force.com platform. In this chapter, we will focus on the e-mail feature of the Force.com platform that helps in extending the application to the broader population of users through e-mails.

The following list of topics will be covered in this chapter:

- Handling inbound e-mails
- Sending e-mails
- Visualforce e-mail templates

Handling inbound e-mails

In the digital world, e-mail is the most commonly used method of communication since 1993. It has become a significant part of the business world. Therefore, the Force.com platform provides a forceful, secure, and authenticate e-mail service as a part of the application. The Force.com platform handles almost all the messaging tasks for you, and you have to only focus on the business logic. Once you configure the e-mail functionality for executing a particular Apex code logic, your incoming e-mails will use the e-mail service according to the logic that you have implemented. Then the service will send out e-mails accordingly.

The e-mail services of the Force.com platform accept standard e-mails from any e-mail client. This simple e-mail can invoke one or more actions from the e-mail service. The Force.com e-mail feature allows us to apply some additional security controls because this simple e-mail can have an affect on the business functions of the application.

The E-mail senders who have specific addresses or domains can be limited. By doing this, the e-mails from the other addresses would be automatically rejected.

Enable advanced security to avoid e-mail spoofing by supporting one or more Domain Keys, protocol SPFs, and Sender IDs.

In order to handle the incoming e-mails, you have to complete the following tasks:

- Create an Apex class that acts as an inbound e-mail handler. This Apex class must be implemented by the `Messaging.InboundEmailHandler` interface.
- Set up the e-mail service and bind the e-mail handler Apex class through the declarative method.

Implementing the InboundEmailHandler interface

Like Java, the Apex interface specifies a set of methods by declaring the method name, the parameters, and the return type. Therefore, interfaces are included only with their method signatures, and not with their actual code. For implementing the interface, you have to write the actual code in the Apex class. The Force.com platform provides some interfaces for assisting in further developments. The `Messaging.InboundEmailHandler` is one of those developments. It enables the platform to call your code when an inbound message arrives.

Like creating the other normal Apex classes, you can create the Apex class by navigating to **Setup | Develop | Apex Classes | New**.

The following code sample shows the basic implementation of the `Messaging.InboundEmailHandler` interface.

```
global class ProcessApplicants implements
  Messaging.InboundEmailHandler
{
global Messaging.InboundEmailResult
  handleInboundEmail(Messaging.InboundEmail email,
    Messaging.InboundEnvelope env)
```

```
{
Messaging.InboundEmailResult result = new
   Messaging.InboundEmailresult();
return result;
}
}
```

In the preceding code, the interface defines a single method called
`handleInboundEmail`. This method adds two parameters to your code by the
Salesforce.com platform.

```
global Messaging.InboundEmailResult
   handleInboundEmail(Messaging.InboundEmail email,
     Messaging.InboundEnvelope env)
```

The parameters contain the information gathered from the inbound message.
The first parameter (`Messaging.InboundEmail`) contains the content of the e-mail
received, and the second parameter (`Messaging.InboundEnvelope`) contains
the to, and from e-mail addresses. The `handleInboundEmail` method returns
the `InboundEmailResult` object and the result can be used to handle errors.

In the following example, we are going to apply and process a leave through an
e-mail. There are also a few assumptions that we need to make before implementing
the logic, and these are:

1. The subject of the incoming e-mail must contain the leave type (Annual
    Leave, Casual Leave, Medical Leave, and so on). For example, the subject
    must be in the following format:

    Annual Leave

    Sender's e-mail will match with that employee's record (to identify the
    person who has sent a request for the leave) and it will create a leave record
    for that employee.

    The e-mail body must contain two date values, which define the "from" date
    and "to" date.

    In this e-mail service, we will not accept any attachments.

    After processing, a leave record will be created and then it will be sent
    for approval.

2. The preceding logic has been implemented in the following Apex class,
    which is used as the Apex handler.

    ```
    global class ProcessLeave implements
       Messaging.InboundEmailHandler
    {
    ```

```
global Messaging.InboundEmailResult
  handleInboundEmail(Messaging.InboundEmail email,
    Messaging.InboundEnvelope env)
{
    Messaging.InboundEmailResult result = new
      Messaging.InboundEmailresult();
    Employee__c emp = new Employee__c();
    Leave__c newLeave = new Leave__c();
    List<Leave_Type__c> leaveType = new
      List<Leave_Type__c>();
    String[] emailBody;
    try {
//read the email and split lines
        emailBody = email.plainTextBody.split('\n', 0);
        Date fromDate =date.parse(emailBody[0]);
        Date toDate = date.parse(emailBody[1]);
        Integer noOfDays =
          Integer.valueOf(emailBody[2]);
        //fetch the employee
        emp = [SELECT Id, Name FROM Employee__c WHERE
          Email__c =: email.fromAddress];
//fetch the leave type
        leaveType = [SELECT Id, Name FROM Leave_Type__c
          WHERE Name =: email.subject.trim()];

        if(leaveType.size() > 0){
//create new leave record
            newLeave.Employee__c = emp.Id;
            newLeave.Leave_Type__c = leaveType[0].Id;
            newLeave.From_Date__c= fromDate;
            newLeave.To_Date__c = toDate;
            newLeave.Number_of_Days__c = noOfDays;
            insert newLeave;

            //start approval process
            Approval.ProcessSubmitRequest req = new
              Approval.ProcessSubmitRequest();
            req.setComments('Submitted for approval.
              Please approve.');
```

```
            req.setObjectId(newLeave.Id);
             //submit the approval request for
               processing
            Approval.ProcessResult approvalResult =
              Approval.process(req);


        }
        else
        {
            //Not matched leave email
            result.success = false;
            result.message = ' Failed :The Leave type
             does not matched. ';
        }

    }
    catch(Exception e){
        result.success = false;
        result.message = 'Failed';
    }

    return result;
    }
}
```

Setting up the e-mail service

We have created the Apex class that can handle incoming e-mails. Now, we need to configure the e-mail service on your Force.com platform instance. To setup the e-mail service, follow these steps:

1. Navigate to **Setup** | **Develop** | **Email Services**.

2. Click on the **New Email Service option**. Specify the configurations as shown here:

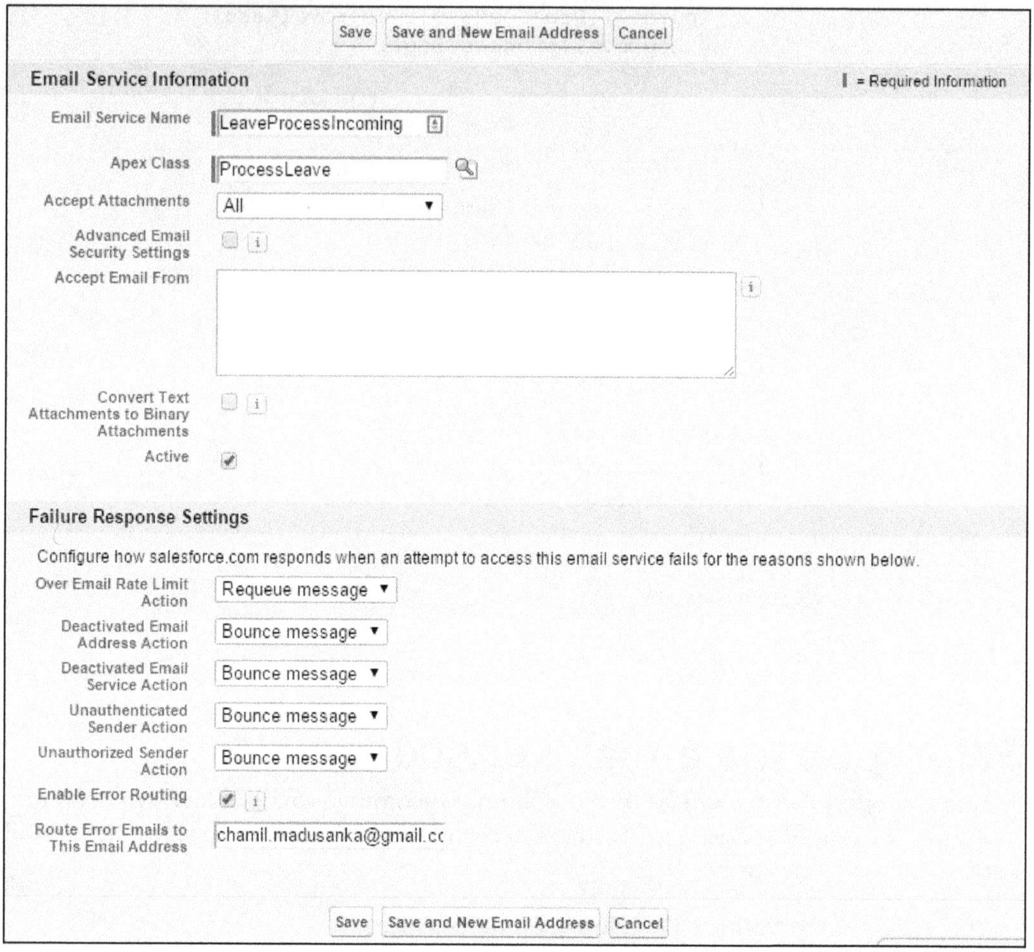

Setting up the E-mail service

3. The **E-mail Service Name**: This is the name of the e-mail service

4. The **Apex Class**: Select the Apex class (which is implemented by the `Messaging.InboundE-mailHandler` interface) that you want to use for processing the incoming e-mail. In this example, we have used the Apex class called `ProcessLeave`.

5. **Accept Attachments**: Specify whether your e-mail service accepts attachments. There are four options for this.

    ° **None**: If you select this option, then the e-mail service will accept all the incoming messages, but it will discard any attachments.

    ° **Text Attachments Only**: If you select this option, then the e-mail service will accept all the incoming messages but it will only accept the attachments that are **Multipurpose Internet Mail Extension (MIME)** type of text, MIME type of application/octet-stream, or files with either .vcf or .vcs extensions. Other attachments will be discarded.

    ° **Binary Attachments Only**: If you select this option, then the e-mail service will accept all the incoming messages, but it will only accept the binary attachments (limited to 5 MB per attachment), such as video, audio, images. Non binary attachments will be discarded.

    ° **All**: If you select this option, then the e-mail service will accept all the incoming messages and attachments.

6. **Advanced E-mail Security Settings**: Optionally, you can select this to configure the e-mail service to validate the sending server before processing the incoming message. Before enabling this option, make sure that your users' e-mail domains support at least one of the following protocols: SPFs, Sender IDs, or DomainKeys. When this option is enabled, Salesforce.com will use these protocols to verify the legitimacy of the e-mail sender's server. If the server passes at least one protocol and does not fail any, then Salesforce.com will process the e-mail. If the server fails a protocol or does not support any of the protocols, then Salesforce.com does not process the e-mail.

7. **Accept E-mail From**: List the e-mail addresses and domains of the senders whose e-mails you want this e-mail service to accept. Separate multiple entries by commas, for example, chamil@mycompany.com, yahoo.com, gmail.com. Leave this field blank if you want the e-mail service to receive e-mails from any e-mail address or domain.

8. **Convert Text Attachments to Binary Attachments**: Optionally, converts text attachments to binary attachments.

9. Active – Select the Active option if you want the e-mail service to be activated when you click on Save.

10. Failure Response Settings – You can configure the failure responses for a particular e-mail service due to the following reasons:

    ° Over E-mail Rate Limit Action

    ° Deactivated E-mail Address Action

    ° Deactivated E-mail Service Action

> ° Unauthenticated Sender Action
>
> ° Unauthorized Sender Action
>
> You can select the following failure response options: Bounce Message, Discard Message, or Re-queue Message (this option is available only for the Over E-mail Rate Limit Action failure response). You can send the notification error e-mail to a specified e-mail address instead of the sender's e-mail address. This prevents the sender from being notified when the e-mail services cannot process an incoming e-mail.

11. Click either on the **Save** option to save your changes, or on the Save and New E-mail Address option to create new e-mail addresses for this e-mail service.

12. To specify an e-mail address for this e-mail service click on the New E-mail Address option. The e-mail service will process the messages sent to this address. One e-mail service can have multiple e-mail addresses.

    ° **E-mail Address**: Specify the local part of the e-mail address. Salesforce.com assigns the domain name part of the address.

    ° **Active**: Select the Active option if you want the e-mail service address to be activated when you click on Save.

    ° **Context User**: Choose the Context User. The e-mail service assumes the permissions of the context user when processing the messages this address receives. For example, if the e-mail service is configured to modify the contact records upon receiving the updated contact information, then the e-mail service only modifies a record if the context user has the permission to edit the records.

    ° **Accept E-mail From**: You can either enter the e-mail addresses or the domain names that are authorized for sending the e-mails to the service. Separate the multiple entries by commas, for example, `george@mycompany.com`, `yahoo.com`, `gmail.com`. Leave this field blank if you want the e-mail service to receive e-mails from any e-mail address.

13. Click on the **Save** option to save the e-mail address of the created e-mail service.

14. The e-mail address will get populated.

Now we have implemented the inbound Apex handler, and setup the e-mail service to capture the incoming e-mails. You can test your e-mail service by sending an e-mail to the populated e-mail address in the e-mail service as follows:

Annual Leave   _ ⤢ ✕

leaveprocessincoming@1id34tuw86ch8qzq3qe8ufhbcml3ly5ust7h98e7vt0m5l6upk.9-q4uheai...

Annual Leave

11/20/2014
11/22/2014
2

--
Chamil Madusanka Weerasena Aratchi
Senior Software Engineer (Salesforce.com/Force.com)
Author of Visualforce Developer's Guide (ISBN: 9781782179818)
Organizer of Sri Lanka Salesforce Platform Developer User Group
About me: http://about.me/chamilmadusanka
Read my articles on LinkedIn

Send   A   🖉   ▲   🖼   ⊖   ☺   Saved   🗑   ▾

Example of inbound e-mail format

The e-mail will be received by the e-mail service, and then it will be processed through the Apex handler. On a successful read, a new leave record will be created and submitted for approval. The following screenshot illustrates the created record:

```
         Leave
 🚩     L-12

                                                       Customize Page | Edit Layout | Printabl
« Back to List: Leaves

              Open Activities [0]  |  Approval History [2]  |  Activity History [0]  |  Notes & Attachments [0]

 Leave Detail                            🔒  Unlock Record   Edit   Delete   Clone

         Leave Name    L-12
           Employee    Chamil Madusanka
         Leave Type    Annual Leave
          From Date    11/20/2014
            To Date    11/22/2014
     Number of Days    2.0
             Status    Approval Pending
         Created By    Chamil Madusanka, 11/16/2014 8:48 PM        Last Modified By    Chamil Madusanka,

                                         🔒  Unlock Record   Edit   Delete   Clone
```

Sending e-mails

In the previous section, we learned to handle inbound e-mails. Now, it's time to learn about outbound e-mails, which can either be basic text based messages or rich HTML based messages (with or without attachments), and sending them through Apex. The Force.com platform allows us to send e-mails by using a broad set of built-in classes and methods. The outbound e-mails can be sent by a trigger, Visualforce controller, e-mail services or by any other platform.

There are two types of e-mails that can be sent by the Force.com platform.

- **Single e-mails**: These are e-mails with the same e-mail body and they are sent to one or more e-mail addresses.

- **Mass e-mails**: These are the e-mails with the personalized message bodies that may be sent to a large number of addresses. However, currently, this feature has an upper limit, and the different versions of this platform have different limits, such as Professional Edition(250), Enterprise Edition(500), and Unlimited and Performance Edition (1000).

The following table shows the key differences between single e-mail and mass e-mails:

	Single E-mail	Mass E-mail
Multiple recipients	Yes	Yes
Personalized body	Yes (single body only)	Yes
Special permission needed	No	Yes, has to be enabled
Merge fields	Yes	Yes
Personalized merge fields	Yes (only one record at a time)	Yes
Templates	Yes	Yes
Template possibilities	Text/HTML/Visualforce/ Custom Templates	Text/HTML/Custom Template

The governor limits are applied to e-mails that are sent through Apex. Therefore, you have to consider the limits while architecting the outbound e-mails of your organization. There are two sets of limits for the outbound e-mails:

- The organization is restricted to sending a certain number of e-mails per 24 hours
- The organization is limited to 10 e-mail invocations (using the `Messaging.sendEmail()` method) per transaction

To explain the single e-mail and the mass e-mail mechanisms, we will use two triggers that notify the employee and the manager about the approval of a specific leave. The first e-mail will send a single e-mail through a Visualforce template. The second e-mail will send a mass e-mail through a text template.

Sending a single e-mail

The first e-mail sends a single e-mail by using a Visualforce template. It will be received by the employee responsible for that leave record. For this instance, the logic is implemented by the trigger, which is associated with the `Leave` object. But, you can implement your logic anywhere that you choose to execute Apex.

The following code segment is from the Leave trigger. Note that this code segment runs in the after update context of the trigger. The code block shown here will first fetch the e-mail template (Visualforce templates will be discussed in next section) through which the e-mail message will be conveyed, then it will fetch the leave records, which would have been updated to **Approved by Manager** or **Rejected by Manager**, and then a Messaging.SingleEmailMessage instance will be created for each iteration. After setting the required data into the e-mail message, it will add it to the list of Messaging.SingleEmailMessage. Finally, it will call the sendEmail method outside the loop.

```
if(Trigger.isAfter)
  {
    if(Trigger.isUpdate)
      {
        final String template = 'E-mailDemoSendSingleTemplate';
        Id templateId;
        try
          {
//Fetch the particular e-mail template
            templateId = [select id from E-mailTemplate where
            Name = :template].id;
            List<Messaging.SingleE-mailMessage> messages = new
              List<Messaging.SingleE-mailMessage>();
Messaging.SingleE-mailMessage message

            for (Leave__c tempLeave : [select Employee__c,
              Status__c, Employee__r.E-mail__c from Leave__c where
                Id in :Trigger.new and Status__c IN ('Approved by
                  Direct Manager','Rejected by Direct Manager')])
              {
                message = new Messaging.SingleE-mailMessage();
                message.setTemplateId(templateId);
                message.setWhatId(tempLeave.Id);
                message.setToAddresses(new String[]
                  {tempLeave.Employee__r.E-mail__c});
                messages.add(message);
              }
            Messaging.sendE-mail(messages);
          }
        catch(QueryException e)
          {
            system.debug('e:::::::::::::::::::::::'+e);
          }
      }
  }
```

You are not required to use the e-mail templates. But, the templates are suitable for building the messages. Without using a template, you can directly set the message body by using the `setHtmlBody()` or `setPlainTextBody()` function.

If you are using a template, then setting `setTargetObjectId()` is required for sending the e-mail messages. This is a single argument method with ID which can be an ID of the contact, lead, or user to which the e-mail will be sent. The ID you specify sets the context and ensures that the merge fields in the template contain the correct data. Otherwise it is optional. You can also call `setBccAddresses(String[])`, `setCcAddresses(String[])`, `setCharset(String)`, `setDocumentAttachments(ID[])`, `setFileAttachments(E-mailFileAttachment[])`, `setHtmlBody(String)`, `setInReplyTo(String)`, `setPlainTextBody(String)`, `setOrgWideE-mailAddressId(ID)`, `setReferences(String)`, `setSubject(String)`, `setTargetObjectId(ID)`, `setToAddresses(String[])`, and `setWhatId(ID)` for the same. If your template consists of merged fields, then `setTargetObjectId()` and `setWhatId()` can be used for building corresponding messages for corresponding recipients.

Now, if the manager updates the leave record to **Approved by Manager** or to **Rejected by Manager**, then the leave trigger will send personalized e-mails to the corresponding recipients by notifying them regarding the leave approval result.

Sending mass e-mails

The second e-mail option, that is, the mass e-mail option differs from the single e-mail option. The two options use merged fields and addresses differently. The mass e-mail messages can be sent to a list of contacts, leads, accounts, or users. When a new leave type is inserted into the application, all the employees get a notification regarding it. Unlike the trigger in the *Sending single e-mail* section, the succeeding code will send the e-mail to all the contacts that are related to the employees. The code is started with the instantiation of the `MassE-mailMessage`. Like in the single e-mail service, you can proceed with the mass e-mail service by either creating an e-mail template or by creating the message body using the `setHtmlBody()` or `setPlainTextBody()`. If you have to merge the fields, then using a template would be a better option. The following code shows the implementation of the mass e-mail feature:

```
trigger leaveType on Leave_Type__c (after insert) {
    Id[] targetObjectIds = new Id[] {};
    Id[] whatIds = new Id[] {};
    final String template = 'E-mailDemoSendMassTemplate';
    Messaging.MassE-mailMessage message = new Messaging.MassEmailMessage();
```

```
message.setTemplateId([select Id from E-mailTemplate where
  Name = :template].Id);
Map<Id,Employee__c> allEmployees = new
  Map<Id,Employee__c>([SELECT Id FROM Employee__c LIMIT
    50000]);
Contact[] contacts = [select Id from Contact where Employee__c
  IN:allEmployees.keyset()];
for (Contact c : contacts) {
  targetObjectIds.add(c.Id);
}

message.setTargetObjectIds(targetObjectIds);
Messaging.sendE-mail(new Messaging.E-mail[] {message});
}
```

The main difference between the mass e-mail service and the single e-mail service
is that the single e-mail service uses the `TargetObjectId` method, which can send
a message to only one target object ID, while the mass e-mail service uses the
`setTargetObjectIds()method`, which can send a message to a list of target object
IDs. The `setTargetObjectIds()` method accepts contacts, leads, and users, which
specify the context and ensure that merge fields in the template. For example in this
trigger, if you specify the contacts as `TargetObjectIds`, then you can specify the
corresponding `WhatIds` that map the merged fields of the template. The `WhatIds()`
method accepts the contract, case, opportunity, and product object IDs.

[
If you specify `whatIds`, specify one for each `targetObjectId`.
Otherwise, you will receive an `INVALID_ID_FIELD` error.
]

Sending e-mails with attachments

We learned about sending single and mass e-mails through the Force.com platform.
The e-mail attachments which are Blob types. The Force.com platform allows us to
send e-mails with attachments by using the `ApexMessaging.EmailFileAttachment`
class. In the `Messaging.SingleEmailMessage`, there are two options for generating
the attachments for e-mail messages:

- The `setDocumentAttachments` method: This method allows us to create
  attachments with the help of the standard document of the Force.com
  platform. Multiple documents can be specified in an e-mail message,
  but the total size of all the attachments must not exceed 10 MB.

- The `setFileAttachments` method: This method allows us to create a list of the file names of the binary and the text files that you want to attach to the e-mail. Multiple documents can be specified in an e-mail message, but the total size of all the attachments must not exceed 10 MB and the maximum size must not exceed 5 MB per file.

To add an attachment, you need to add a couple of lines to your previous code. You can send an attachment with your e-mail by using the `setDocumentAttachments` method:

```
public static void sendWithDocumentAttachment()
  {
   try{
    Messaging.SingleE-mailMessage mail = new
      Messaging.SingleEmailMessage();
      mail.setToAddresses( new String[] {
       'chamil.madusanka@gmail.com'});
      mail.setSubject('Message from Apex!');
      mail.setPlainTextBody('This is the message body');
      mail.setDocumentAttachments(new Id[] {[select Id from
       Document where Name = 'eLeaveForce logo'][0].Id });
      Messaging.sendE-mail(new Messaging.SingleE-mailMessage[] {
        mail });
       }
       catch(Exception e){
        ApexPages.addMessages(e);
        Messaging.SingleE-mailMessage mail=new
         Messaging.SingleEmailMessage();
        String[] toAddresses = new String[]
         {'chamil.madusanka@gmail.com'};
        mail.setToAddresses(toAddresses);
        mail.setReplyTo('chamil.madusanka@gmail.com');
        mail.setSenderDisplayName('Apex error message');
        mail.setSubject('Error from Org : ' +
         UserInfo.getOrganizationName());
        mail.setPlainTextBody(e.getMessage());
        Messaging.sendE-mail(new Messaging.SingleE-mailMessage[]
          { mail });
       }
    }
```

Similar to the single e-mail sending, you must instantiate the `Messaging.SingleEmailMessage` object and specify the other settings, such as `toAddress`, by using a template or setting the e-mail message body within the code. Then, fetch the desired document from the standard Documents by using the query and the file name. The `mail.setDocumentAttachments` method adds the attachment for you.

The following code shows the setFileAttachments method for adding an attachment to your e-mail. This option provides more flexibility than the setDocumentAttachments option. It dynamically generates the attachment file and attaches it to the e-mail.

```
public static void sendWithDynamicAttachment()
  {
    try{
      Messaging.SingleE-mailMessage mail = new
        Messaging.SingleE-mailMessage();
          mail.setToAddresses( new String[] {
            'chamil.madusanka@gmail.com' });
          mail.setSubject('Message from Apex!');
          mail.setPlainTextBody('This is the message body');
          Messaging.E-mailFileAttachment mailAttachment;
          mailAttachment = new Messaging.E-mailFileAttachment();
          mailAttachment.setFileName('readme.txt');
          mailAttachment.setBody(Blob.valueOf('This is an Apex-
            generated attachment'));
          mail.setFileAttachments(new
            Messaging.EmailFileAttachment[]{mailAttachment});
          Messaging.sendE-mail(new
            Messaging.SingleEmailMessage[] { mail });
      }
    catch(Exception e){
      ApexPages.addMessages(e);
      Messaging.SingleE-mailMessage mail=new
        Messaging.SingleEmailMessage();
      String[] toAddresses = new String[]
        {'chamil.madusanka@gmail.com'};
      mail.setToAddresses(toAddresses);
      mail.setReplyTo('chamil.madusanka@gmail.com');
      mail.setSenderDisplayName('Apex error message');
      mail.setSubject('Error from Org : ' +
        UserInfo.getOrganizationName());
      mail.setPlainTextBody(e.getMessage());
      Messaging.sendE-mail(new Messaging.SingleE-mailMessage[] {
        mail });
      }
  }
```

The difference between these two codes is that in the preceding code, we generated the attachment within the code by using the Messaging.EmailFileAttachment method.

Visualforce e-mail templates

The Force.com platform provides the ability for creating and using e-mail templates, which includes merging fields and personalizing content. There are four different types of e-mail templates.

- Text
- HTML (using Letterhead)
- Custom (without using Letterhead)
- Visualforce

You can use all these e-mail templates while sending a single e-mail. But for mass e-mails, you can only use Text, HTML, and Custom templates. In this section, we are going to discuss the Visualforce template. The Visualforce e-mail template reduces a considerable amount of code which is needed for sending an e-mail.

At the beginning of the chapter, you heard about merging fields and personalizing content. How can this be done? You can use merge fields to personalize your e-mail content. You can add a substitute text to any merge field. The substitute text is displayed only if the merge record does not contain the data for that field. Enter the substitute text after a comma in the merge field, for example, `{!Contact.FirstName}`. When you save the template, the merge field will appear in the e-mail body of the template, and it will have the following syntax: `{!NullValue(Contact.FirstName)}`.

Use the steps shown here for creating a Visualforce template:

1. Navigate to **Setup | Communication Templates | Email Templates**.
2. Click on the **New Template option**.
3. Choose **Visualforce** as the type of e-mail template you want to use. Click on **Next**.
4. Then, select the **Folder** in which you want to store the template.
5. Select the **Available For Use** option. If you do not select this option, then the template will not be used for sending the e-mails.
6. Enter an **E-mail Template Name**. Here, we will use `EmailDemoSendSingleTemplate`.
7. The **Template Unique Name** is used by API and the managed packages. The name must begin with a letter and use only alphanumeric characters and underscores. The name cannot end with an underscore or have two consecutive underscores.
8. For the **Encoding** option, specify the character set for the template.

9. In the **Description** option, you can add a description. Both the template name and the description are only for your internal use.

10. In the **E-mail Subject**, specify the subject line of your template.

11. The **Recipient Type** option will select the type of recipient that will receive the e-mail template. There are three options for this: **Contact**, **Lead**, and **User**.

12. **Related To Type**: The Salesforce.com object type that the template is retrieving data from the particular merge fields. This can be any object that has a standard controller, including the custom objects, which are supported by Visualforce.

Step 2. Visualforce Email Template: New Template	Step 2 of 2

Previous | Save | Cancel

Email Template Information   ▌ = Required Information

Folder   Unfiled Public Email Templates ▾

Available For Use ☑

Email Template Name   EmailDemoSendSingleTempl

Template Unique Name   EmailDemoSendSingleTempl [i]

Encoding   General US & Western Europe (ISO-8859-1, ISO-LATIN-1) ▾

Description   [   ]

Visualforce Template Attributes   ▌ = Required Information

These values will be inserted into your component. You may edit these values later from the template editor.

```
<messaging:emailTemplate subject="Sample: Follow up email from phone call"
recipientType="Contact" relatedToType="Account">
<messaging:htmlEmailBody>
    <!-- Begin Default Content REMOVE THIS -->
```

Email Subject   Leave Approval Notification

Recipient Type   Contact ▾ [i]

Related To Type   Leave__c   ▾ [i]

Previous | Save | Cancel

Create Visualforce template

13. Click on **Save**.

14. Click on the **Edit Template** option to specify the template.

15. Enter the markup for your Visualforce template and then **Save**.

You can test your template by clicking on **Send Test and Verify Merge Fields**.

Summary

In this chapter, we learned how to extend the Force.com application by using e-mail communication. We became familiar with handling inbound e-mail messages through the e-mail service in the Force.com platform and sending single and mass e-mails. Finally, we learned about the Visualforce templates, which are used to make flexible e-mail communications. In the next chapter, we will learn how to build public websites using Force.com platforms.

11
Building Public Websites with Force.com Sites

There is valuable information related to application data in a Force.com organization. It can be user, contact, and other business data. However, if you wish to extend your Force.com application outside your organization with limited access permission, you have to use a web application and integrate your Force.com instance with that web application. In the past, the web application could be written in PHP, JSP, or ASP.NET and it needed a web server too. Now, extending the Force.com application to the outside organization is easier with the Force.com sites. In this chapter, we focus on Force.com sites that allow extending the application out into the broader population of users through the use of public websites.

This chapter covers the following topics:

- Force.com sites
- Creating and customizing your first Force.com site
- Best practices while using the Force.com site

Force.com sites

Force.com sites provide the facility to build and deploy public websites and web applications using the Force.com platform. These websites and web applications can be directly integrated with the particular Salesforce organization without using a username and password of a particular user. Using the Force.com sites, you can build your site, which matches the look and feel of your company's brand, and through the Force.com site's page, you can publicly expose information relating to your organization.

There are no data integration issues in between Force.com sites and your Salesforce instance because sites are hosted in the Force.com sites. When you collect data from a Force.com site's page, data validations are executed automatically because pages are built using Visualforce pages. Users can access the site through a unique Force.com custom domain and the URL or registered own branded domain or subdomain that redirects to the particular site.

You can create multiple sites for different audiences, which satisfy different business needs. The following are some scenarios that you can use for building Force.com sites:

- A public community site to gather customer feedback
- A Salesforce CRM ideas site
- A public support FAQ
- A recruitment portal for the company
- A web form for capturing leads
- A product catalog

Force.com sites are directly connected with the Salesforce organization. Therefore, the availability of the Force.com sites depends on the availability of the Salesforce organization. When major releases are proceeding, your organization will be unavailable with a prior notice. At the same time, your branded Force.com site will be unavailable. You can view specific maintenance windows, listed by instance, at `https://trust.salesforce.com/trust/status`.

Creating and customizing your first Force.com site

To create a Force.com site, you need to perform the following main steps:

1. Register a domain name.
2. Create a Force.com site using the domain name.
3. Assign the Visualforce pages to the site.
4. Set up the security access permissions.

Registering a domain name

To get started, first register the Force.com domain of your organization. Your Force.com domain must be unique and must consist of only alphanumeric characters. Salesforce.com recommends using your company's name or a variation of your company's name, such as `eleaveportal`. Perform the following steps to register a domain:

1. Navigate to **Setup | Develop | Sites**. You'll see the domain setup screen:

2. Enter a unique name as the domain prefix and click on **Check Availability**. The domain prefix can contain only underscores and alphanumeric characters and it must begin with a letter. It cannot contain spaces.

3. Read and accept the Force.com sites terms of use by selecting the checkbox.

4. Click on **Register My Force.com Domain**. Once you register, you will not be able to modify your Force.com domain name. By registering a custom web address through a domain name registrar and associating it with your site, you can create a completely branded experience for your users. With the sites, login page and Visualforce pages, you can customize the look and feel, the branding, and the public security settings for each of your sites.

On different editions, domain URLs appear in different formats. Consider the domain prefix as `eleaveportal`. For different editions the URL would be as follows:

- Developer Edition `https://eleaveportal-developer-edition.na1.force.com`
- Sandbox `https://eleaveportal.mysandbox.cs1.force.com`
- Production `https://eleaveportal.secure.force.com`

Creating a Force.com site using the domain name

Now, you are ready to create your Force.com site with the reference of a created domain. Perform the following steps to create a Force.com site:

1. Navigate to **Setup | Develop | Sites | New**.

2. Specify the values for **Site Label**, which is the name of the site as it appears in the user interface and **Site Name**, which is the name used when referencing the site in the Force.com API.

3. Optionally, you can provide a description to the site under **Site Description** as follows:

   ° **Site Contact**: This is the name of the user responsible for receiving site-related communication from site visitors and Salesforce.com.

   ° **Default Web Address**: You can specify a unique Force.com URL for this site. Salesforce.com provides the first part of the URL; you need to create the suffix using only alphanumeric characters.

   ° **Active**: This activates the site as soon as you click on **Save**.

   ° **Active Site Home Page**: You need to specify the landing page that is redirected when the site is active. Here, you can select the Visualforce page that you developed for the home page of the site.

   ° **Inactive Site Home Page**: Optionally, you can select a landing page, which is redirected when the site is inactive. In this example, we select a page that displays whether the site is down for maintenance.

4. Optionally, you can select **Site Template** that provides the page layout and style sheet for your site.

5. You can specify the **Site Robots.txt** file that determines which parts of your public site web spiders and other web robots can access.

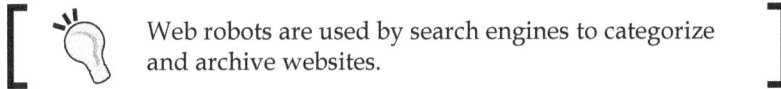

> Web robots are used by search engines to categorize and archive websites.

Define the following parameters:

- **Site Favorite Icon**: Optionally, you can select an icon that appears in the address field of the browser when you visit a particular site. If you specify the favorite icon here, you will not have to specify it on every page. Due to caching, it will take one day to reflect on the site.

- **Analytics Tracking Code**: Use this field to associate an analytics tracking code with your site. To track your site using Google Analytics, paste the Web Property ID — also known as the UA number — into this field.

- **URL Rewriter Class**: You can create and select an Apex class used for URL rewriting on this site.

- **Enable Feeds**: Optionally, you can specify the syndication feeds related list, which is created and manages syndication feeds for the users on your sites.

- **Clickjack Protection Level**: This specifies the type of framing allowed. If same origin framing is selected, site pages can only be framed by the other pages on the same domain name and protocol security (HTTP or HTTPS).

- **Require Secure Connections (HTTPS)**: If you select this checkbox, it redirects all HTTP site requests to HTTPS.

6. Click on **Save**.

Now, you will be redirected to the **Site Detail** page, which is as follows:

Site Details
ELeave

Help for this Page

« Back to List: Sites

Site Detail   Edit | Public Access Settings | Login Settings | URL Redirects | Deactivate

Site Label	ELeave	Site Name	ELeave
Site Description		Site Contact	Chamil Madusanka
Active	✓	Login	Not Allowed
Active Site Home Page	UnderConstruction [Preview]	Site Favorite Icon	
Inactive Site Home Page	InMaintenance [Preview]	Site Robots.txt	
Site Template	SiteTemplate [Preview]	Enable Feeds	☐
Analytics Tracking Code		URL Rewriter Class	
Clickjack Protection Level	Allow framing by the same origin only (recommended)	Require Secure Connections (HTTPS)	☐ [i]
Created By	Chamil Madusanka, 12/26/2014 8:54 AM	Last Modified By	Chamil Madusanka, 12/26/2014 8:54 AM

Edit | Public Access Settings | Login Settings | URL Redirects | Deactivate

Custom URLs   Custom URLs Help (?)

Action	Domain Name	Path	Site Primary Custom URL
Edit	Del	View	Preview as Admin	eleaveportal-developer-edition.ap1.force.com	/	☐

Site Visualforce Pages   Edit   Enabled Visualforce Page Access Help (?)

Visualforce Page Name	AppExchange Package Name	
BandwidthExceeded		💬 Chat

Once you have created the site, the next move is to configure the site on the site detail page.

Assigning Visualforce pages to the site

Force.com sites use Visualforce pages as the site pages. After you create the Force.com site, you can create many Visualforce pages and assign them to the Force.com site, which can be displayed according to your requirements. All the pages that you want to expose in your Force.com site must be listed under your Force.com site. Click on the **Edit** button under the **Site Visualforce Pages** related list to manage Visualforce page to the Force.com site, which is shown in the following screenshot:

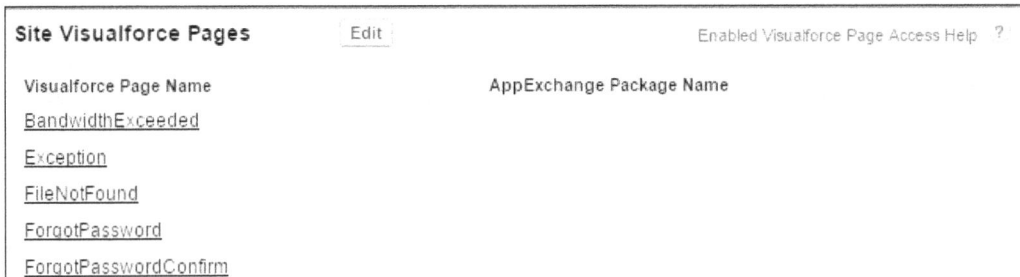

Site Visualforce Pages	Edit	Enabled Visualforce Page Access Help ?
Visualforce Page Name		AppExchange Package Name
BandwidthExceeded		
Exception		
FileNotFound		
ForgotPassword		
ForgotPasswordConfirm		

On the next page, you can add/remove the Visualforce pages that you want to make accessible at this Force.com site, which is shown in the following screenshot:

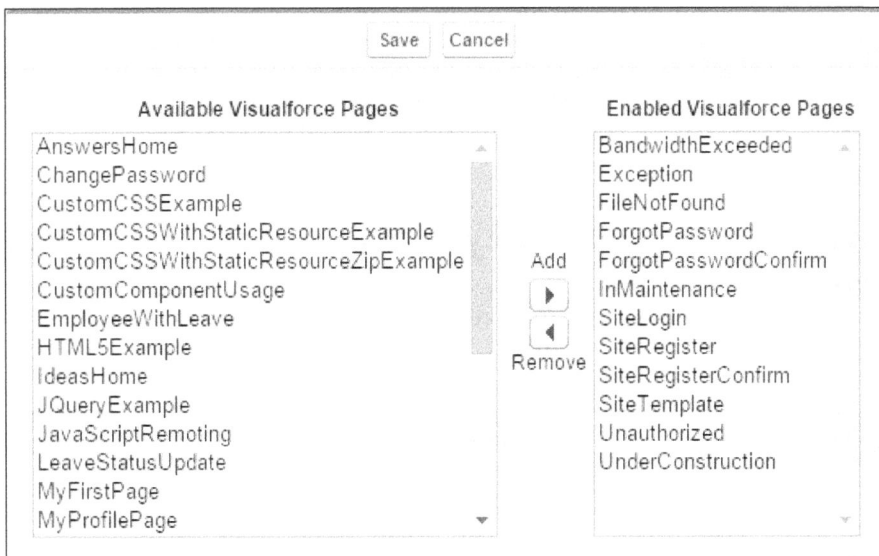

Save Cancel

Available Visualforce Pages

AnswersHome
ChangePassword
CustomCSSExample
CustomCSSWithStaticResourceExample
CustomCSSWithStaticResourceZipExample
CustomComponentUsage
EmployeeWithLeave
HTML5Example
IdeasHome
JQueryExample
JavaScriptRemoting
LeaveStatusUpdate
MyFirstPage
MyProfilePage

Add ▶ Remove ◀

Enabled Visualforce Pages

BandwidthExceeded
Exception
FileNotFound
ForgotPassword
ForgotPasswordConfirm
InMaintenance
SiteLogin
SiteRegister
SiteRegisterConfirm
SiteTemplate
Unauthorized
UnderConstruction

You have learned more about Visualforce developments in *Chapter 8, Building Custom Pages with Visualforce*.

As with Visualforce page adding, you can expose standard pages and error pages to the Force.com site, which is shown in the following screenshot:

Site Standard Pages	Edit		Site Standard Pages Help ?
Name	**Description**		
Home Page	Page associated with the Home Tab		

Error Pages	Page Assignment		Error Pages Help ?

Action	Error Condition	Site Page Name	Site Page Description
Preview	Authorization Required Page (401)	Unauthorized	Default Force.com Authorization Required page
Preview	Limit Exceeded Page (509)	BandwidthExceeded	Default Force.com Limit Exceeded page
Preview	Maintenance Page(500/503)	InMaintenance	Default Force.com In Maintenance page
Preview	Page Not Found Page (404)	FileNotFound	Default Force.com Page/Data Not Found page
Preview	Generic Error Page	Exception	Default Force.com page for post-authentication errors

> Additionally, you can add a Visualforce page called My Profile Page, which is associated with a customer portal or site user profile. Users can log in to either your Force.com site or the customer portal, and can update their contact information. These updates are reflected on the corresponding portal user and contact record in the organization.

Setting up the security access permissions

Once you create the Force.com site, you can configure the security settings for the site from the **Site Details** page. There are two types of security settings in a Force.com site:

- **Public Access Settings**
- **Login Settings**

The preceding points are shown in the following screenshot

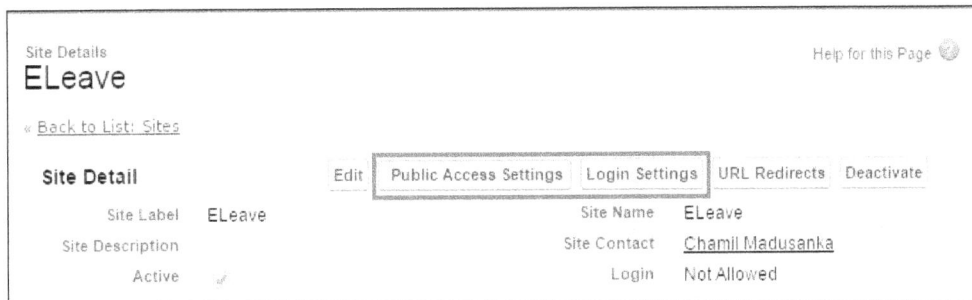

Security options in the Force.com site

Public Access Settings

With the creation of the particular Force.com site, the corresponding user profile is created with the same name of the site. For example, we created the ELeave site and the name of the site profile is ELeave. By clicking on the **Public Access Settings** button, you can customize the particular profile of the Force.com site, including **Standard Object Permissions**, **Custom Object Permissions**, **Login hours**, **Login IP ranges**, **Page Layouts**, **Record Types**, **Tab Settings**, **Field-Level Security**, **Administrative Permissions**, and **General User Permissions**. This Force.com site profile reflects the permissions that are assigned to the guest users, which is shown in the following screenshot:

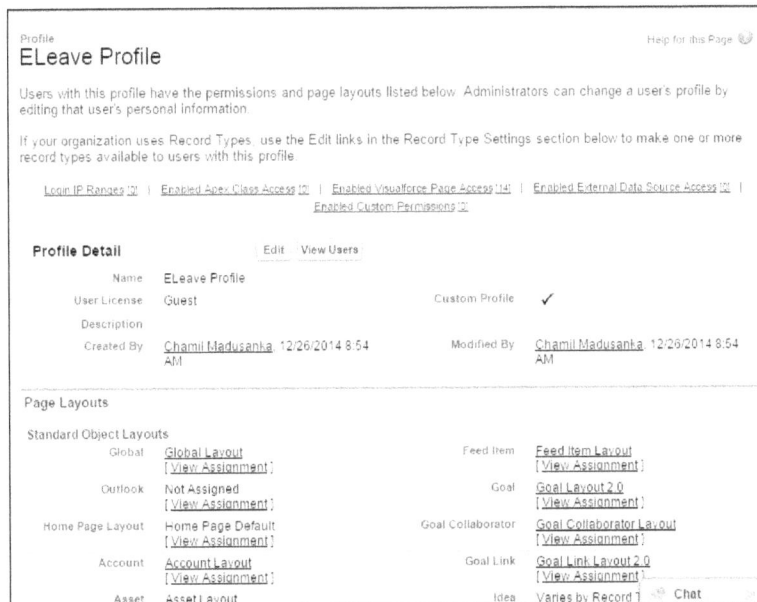

> **Products**, **Price Books**, and **Ideas** standard objects are always exposed to the Force.com site as read only.

We discussed further details about the profile settings in *Chapter 4, Designing Apps for Multiple Users and Protecting Data*.

> By restricting **IP Ranges** on the user profile, you can create a site for only internal employees (corporate intranet). To use IP restrictions, HTTPS is required. You must use the secure URL associated with your Force.com domain to access your site.

Login settings

Click on **Login Settings** to enable users to log in to an existing portal from your site. It also allows you to implement the login and registration logic, quickly and seamlessly. Optionally, you can replace the built-in login and registration pages with your own custom pages.

The following are the built-in login and registration related pages:

- SiteLogin
- SiteRegister
- SiteRegisterConfirm

The built-in login process checks whether the site is enabled or not for logins, the validity of the logging user, and allows users to reset their expired passwords. The built-in registration process checks the new user information to the existing user records for the customer portal associated site and also checks for an existing contact record for the new user or creates a new contact record.

Before enabling the **Login Settings** options, your customer portal must be enabled in the organization. To do so, perform the following steps:

1. Navigate to **Setup | Customize | Customer Portal | Settings | Edit**.
2. Select the **Enable Customer portal** checkbox.
3. Select the **Login Enabled** checkbox.
4. Optionally, you can select **Administrator** of the portal.
5. Specify **Portal Default Settings**, including **Login URL**, **Logout URL**, and **HTML Messages Default Language**.

Through the translation workbench, Force.com sites are supported for multilanguage.

6. Specify **Email Notification Settings**, including **From Email Address, From Email Name, New User Template, New Password Template, Lost Password Template, New Comment Template**, and **Change Owner** to **Portal User Template**.

7. Under the **Look and Feel** section, you can select the **Header, Footer, Logo,** and **Login Message** option of the portal.

JavaScript and CSS will be removed from any HTML file selected as the portal **Login Message**.

8. Under the **Self-Registration** settings, select the **Self-Registration Enabled** option. It allows existing contacts to register themselves for accessing your **Customer Portal**. If you select the **Self Registration Enabled** option, you need to specify **Default New User License, Default New User Role,** and **Default New User Profile**.

9. Optionally, you can specify **New User Form URL** and **Registration Error Template**.

10. Click on **Save**.

After enabling the login credentials in the customer portal, you can enable users to log in to an existing portal from your site by performing the following steps:

1. Navigate to **Setup | Develop | Sites |** Click on your Site name **| Login Settings | Edit**.

2. Select the appropriate customer portal from the **Enable Login For** option.

3. Select the **Change Password Page** and **My Profile Page** for the portal login.

4. Select **Require Non-Secure Connections (HTTP)** to override your organization's security settings and exclusively use HTTP when logging into the customer portal from your site. **Warning: HTTP connections aren't secure, so use of this setting isn't recommended**. When this option isn't enabled, the **Require Secure Connections (HTTPS)** setting under **Setup | Security Controls | Session Settings** controls your organization's security level. In that case, if **Require Secure Connections (HTTPS)** is enabled on the **Session Settings** page, the users logging into the associated customer portal from the Force.com site will see the site's preferred HTTPS domain, which may be a subdomain of `secure.force.com`.

[💡 To allow registration, enable login and registration for a portal, then add the appropriate Visualforce pages to the site.]

5. Click on **Save**.

[💡 You can set up Force.com Sites' URL redirects to inform users and search engines that site content has moved. You cannot implement the following in Force.com Sites URL Redirects:

- Error pages
- CSS files
- URLs that include the `LastMod` parameter]

Best practices on Force.com sites

There are a few best practices that you need to consider while creating and authenticating users with a Force.com site:

- If users interact with private data on the Force.com site, then always use the portal authentication process for tracking the users on the Force.com site. For example, if you are building a private shopping cart, you should use customer portal authentication.

- According to your requirements, try to build a lightweight process in the Force.com site.

- Always use custom objects for guest applications.

- Do not prompt the request for a username and password and do not store that information inside the application.

- Always try to set up the sharing setting as private for the objects that you grant read access to on the Force.com site. From that practice, you can ensure that users can view and edit only the data related to the Force.com site.

- Set the visibility of all list views for certain user groups but do not set the **Visible to all users** option.

- The cache control of the static resources that are used in the Force.com site must be set to public.

The Force.com site imposes two daily limits, which depend on the organization type.

Organization Type	Bandwidth Limit (per day)	Service Request Time (per day)
Developer Edition	500 MB	10 minutes
Sandbox	1 GB	30 minutes
Production	40 GB	60 hours

- If you plan to use a field for searching purposes, index the field and avoid the use of long text fields because these indexed fields are stored in a separate table to improve performance.
- If you are planning to use large video and audio files in your Force.com site, store them in a third-party system to avoid exceeding the daily bandwidth limit.
- Use **CAPTCHA** for public form submissions to avoid spam.

Summary

In this chapter, you learned to extend the Force.com application to the outside organization with limited access permission using the Force.com sites. You learned to create a simple Force.com site.

In the next chapter, you will learn to deploy the Force.com application to another organization.

12
Deploying the Force.com Application

Now, we have finished developing the Force.com application. It's time to deploy the developed application to production organizations or any other organization, or distribute onto AppExchange. In traditional software development, the deploying process is more complicated and more iterative because applications are developed offline and then the deployment process is done. However, the Force.com platform is a little bit different from traditional software developments because the changes in the application are immediately available. The deployment methodology of the Force.com platform is one of the powerful features. It allows developers and administrators to complete the deployment process quickly, and create prototypes for customers.

This chapter covers the options available to you to deploy your Force.com platform applications and components from a development environment to a production environment.

The following is the list of topics that will be covered in this chapter:

- Application development methodology and architecture
- Migrating configuration changes
- Sandboxes
- Change sets
- Packages
- Managed packages
- Unmanaged packages

- Creating and uploading a package
- Simple deployment with the Force.com IDE
- Distributing Force.com applications onto AppExchange

Application development methodology and architecture

Typically, application development is a process that directs the phases from requirements gathering to deployment of the application. There are different kinds of development methodologies, which are currently used in the software development industry, for example, **Rational Unified Process** (**RUP**), waterfall model, spiral model, and agile methodology. You are allowed to use any of these methodologies for the Force.com application development.

According to the complexity of the application, your development methodology can be simple or complex. However, we can use the following typical development cycle for Force.com application development:

- Create a development environment
- Develop using Salesforce web and local tools
- Test within the development environment
- Replicate production changes in the development environment
- Deploy what you have developed to your production organization

The Force.com platform provides the facility of creating Force.com organizations as isolated environments for the development, testing and migrating changes between these environments. This isolation is considered as the core of the implementation of the Force.com application development methodology. In a large enterprise, developers must have private environments within which they can do the initial development. After that, the application must be tested through integration, functional, regression, QA, and user acceptance testing. After the successful testing cycles, we are allowed to deploy the application to the production. There can be slight changes due to the team size and release formalisms in place. However, you need to protect the core of the implementation, which we have explained earlier.

Migrating configuration changes

As organizations make changes to one environment, those changes often need to be carried over to another environment. Configuration definitions are stored as metadata. During the development life cycle, you might want to repeatedly migrate the configurations to move or sync the changes. Migration can be done in the following two ways:

- **Manual Migration**: The components that are not available in metadata API need to be migrated manually in each environment. Modifications must be repeated in every organization.

- **Metadata Migration**: The components that are available in the metadata API, can be migrated automatically from one organization to another. There are a few automated ways to move metadata from one organization to another organization, which are as follows:
  - Change sets
  - Force.com IDE
  - Force.com migration tool

Sandboxes

One of the main Force.com application development methods with an isolated environment is Sandboxes. On the Force.com platform, a sandbox is a copy of a particular precaution organization, which is used for development, testing, and training purposes. Since sandboxes are totally isolated from a particular production organization, you can perform the tasks without disruption to the production and vice versa. Overall, there are four types of sandboxes available in the production organization, which are as follows:

- **Developer Sandbox**: This is used by individual developers to develop and test an application on Force.com. A Developer sandbox can be shared by multiple developers, but its not recommended. Because you cannot gain the actual purpose by sharing the same sandbox among multiple developers. The primary use of a Developer sandbox is that it is used to perform developmental-related changes and are kept until those changes are ready to be shared with other developers. Developer sandbox includes a copy of the metadata and setup data of a particular production organization.

- **Developer Pro Sandbox**: The only difference between this and Developer sandbox is that it has larger storage limit. It can be used for more robust test data sets.

- **Partial Copy Sandbox**: This is used to create test environments such as integration testing and user acceptance testing and training. Partial Copy sandbox includes a copy of the metadata, setup data of a particular production organization, and a subset of the production data, which is defined by a sandbox template.

- **Full Sandbox**: It is used to perform full performance testing and load testing because full sandboxes are a replica of a particular production organization, including all the data and metadata.

The following table concludes the features against the type of sandbox. These limits can be changed in the future releases:

Feature	Developer Sandbox	Developer Pro Sandbox	Partial Copy Sandbox	Full Sandbox
Refresh Interval	1 day	1 day	5 days	29 days
Storage Limits	200 MB of data storage and 200 MB of file storage	1GB of data storage and 1GB of file storage	5GB of data storage and 5GB of file storage	Same as the production organization
Data Copy	Metadata only	Metadata only	All metadata and sample of object data	All metadata and data
Sandbox Templates	Not included	Not included	Required	Available

To create a sandbox in your production organization, perform the following steps:

1. Go to **Setup | Data Management | Sandboxes**.
2. Click on **New Sandbox**.

> For the examples of this book, you have probably been using a free Developer edition organization in which the sandboxes are not available. For more details on the various license types, refer to the Salesforce.com company website www.salesforce.com. Sandboxes are available in Enterprise, Unlimited, and Performance Editions. With the Unlimited and Performance Editions, you can create multiple sandbox copies of different types.

3. Enter a name and description for the sandbox.
4. Select the sandbox type of environment.

> If you select the Partial Copy sandbox, you need to specify the Sandbox template, which defines the data for your sandbox. You can select a sandbox template for Full sandbox as well.

5. Click on **Create**.

In the sandbox list page, you can refresh the sandbox according to the sandbox refresh time period.

> The login URLs of production and the sandbox are as follows:
> *   Production: `https://login.salesforce.com`
> *   Sandbox: `https://test.salesforce.com`

Change set

Change set is a means by which move configuration changes (metadata) between related organizations using a point-click interface. For example, you create a new object in a sandbox and send it to a particular production organization using a change set. In a change set, you can include only the customizations, which were created through the **Setup** menu. Customizations to existing or new components can be included in a change set, but a change set cannot be used to delete or rename components. A change set is used to transfer only the metadata not data.

In the change set terminology, there are two types of change sets, which are as follows:

*   **Outbound change set**: This change set is created in the logged-in organization and you would want to send it to another organization
*   **Inbound change set**: This is the change set that has been sent from another organization to the organization in which you are logged in

To send the changes from one organization to another, we require a deployment connection. Change sets can only be sent between organizations that are related to a production organization. When you create a sandbox, a deployment connection is automatically created between the related organizations. Each organization must be authorized to send and receive change sets. The deployment connection list shows which organizations can upload changes to this organization, and which organizations allow this organization to upload changes to them. The following diagram illustrates the change sets and deployment connections:

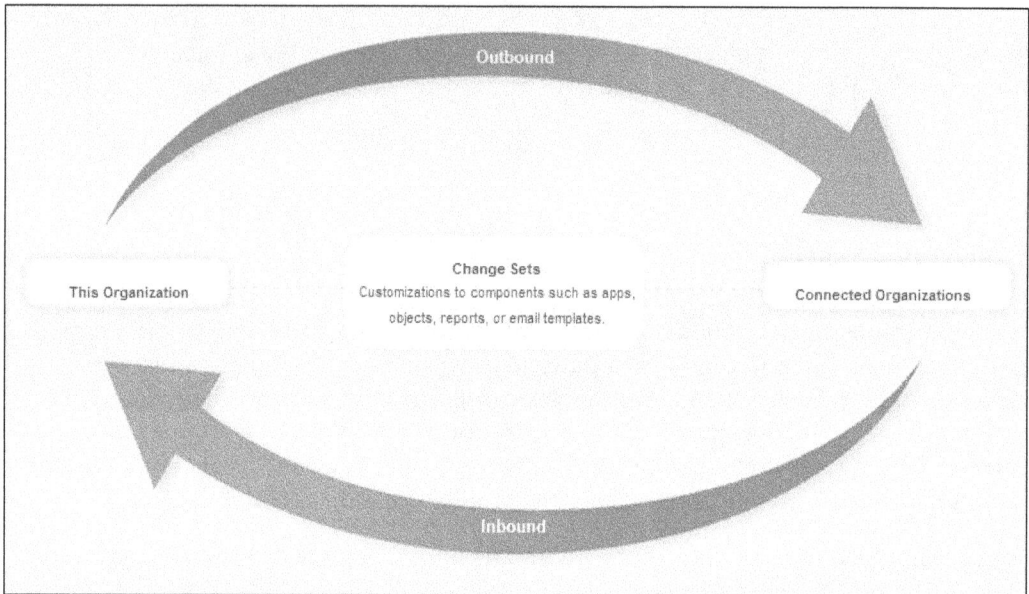

Change sets and deployment connections

Setting up deployment connections

Perform the following steps to deploy components using change sets. Suppose you have already created a sandbox for a particular production organization. When you create a sandbox, a deployment connection is automatically created between the related organizations:

1. Authorize the deployment connection. In order for another organization to send change sets to the organization you are logged into, you must authorize the inbound change set. Perform the following steps:

    1. Go to **Deploy** | **Deployment Settings** | **Deployment Connections**.
    2. Click on **Edit** associated to the organization that you want to authorize.

3. Select **Allow Inbound Changes**.

4. Click on **Save**.

2. To create the outbound changes set in the sandbox, perform the following steps:

   1. Go to **Setup | Deploy | Outbound Changes Sets | New**.

   2. Specify the **Change set** details and click on **Save**.

   3. Click on **Add** to add the particular components to be included in the change set.

3. Now, you have created the change set for the deployment and for before you deploy. By clicking on **View/Add Dependencies**, make sure that there are no dependencies for the particular component.

4. Click on **Upload**. The configurations that are contained in the change set will be added to the production organization and an e-mail notification will be sent to the sandbox administrator.

> A change set is deployed in a single transaction. If the deployment process is not completed, the whole transaction will be rolled back. In a successful deployment, all the changes will be committed and cannot be rolled back.

5. To log in to the production organization, navigate to the inbound change set to validate and deploy to the production organization. Perform the following steps:

   1. Go to **Setup | Deploy | Inbound Change Sets**.

   2. Click on the particular change set name.

   3. Click on the **Validate** button to make the changes, which will be made in the system after the deployment and it provides results. Use the **Validate** button as a best practice, which needs to be used before clicking on the **Deploy** button.

   4. If the validate result is successful, click on the **Deploy** button to deploy the change set to the production organization.

Best practices

When you use change sets to fulfill your deployment requirement, it is better to follow the following best practices:

- Limit the number of components per change set to 5000 components. If you are exceeding this limit, deploy the e-mail templates, reports, and dashboards in a different change set.
- Deploy all the dependent components within the same outbound change set.
- Validate the change set before deployment.
- View the XML representation of a component before uploading an outbound change set or deploying an inbound change set.
- Change sets cannot be used to delete or rename components. Therefore, use the web interface to delete or rename any component.
- Add permissions and access settings to outbound change sets.
- Plan the deployments with a maintenance schedule for production and sandboxes.
- Before change sets are deployed, Salesforce executes all the Apex tests in the organization. Therefore, write proper test classes with different scenarios, which will run in the target organization. After a successful Apex test run, you can deploy a particular change set quickly by clicking on the **Quick Deploy** button. It will not run for the test coverage again.

Packages

After you develop your application, you need to distribute this application to other organizations. There are scenarios where you need to deploy the same set of components (an application) to multiple organizations. Most probably, these many organizations are outside of your company and you have to access the source and target organizations with high-level permissions. Packages are the medium for this type of deployment. A package is a collection of the Force.com platform components such as apps, objects, reports, or e-mail templates. These packages can be uploaded to be shared with others privately or posted on the Force.com AppExchange to be shared publicly. Mainly, there are two types of packages:

- Managed packages
- Unmanaged packages

The following diagram illustrates the concept between managed and unmanaged packages:

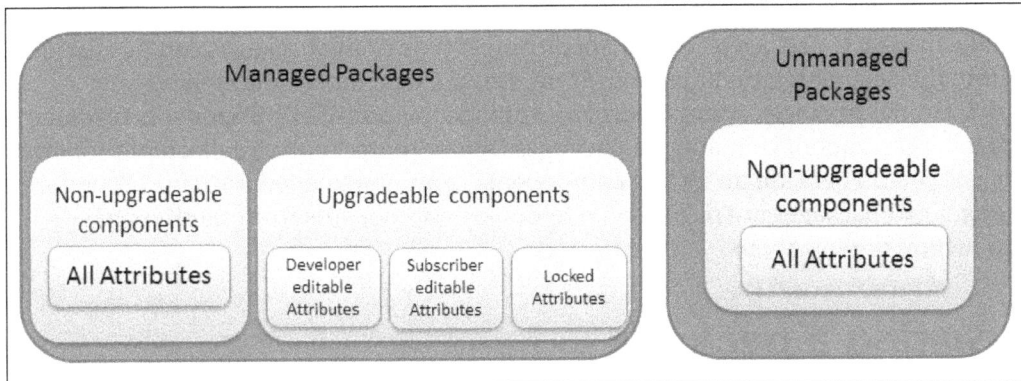

This diagram will be explained under the next two sub sections.

Managed packages

Managed packages allow us to create an upgradable distribution medium for Salesforce applications. After you install the particular package in another organization, you can push upgrades for the packaged application. There are some locked components in a managed package, for example, removing fields or objects, rename filed labels and so on. This type of packages are used to distribute and sell applications to customers. You can create managed packages in a development edition organization. Salesforce partners and developers can sell and manage user-based licenses to the application by using AppExchange and **License Management Application (LMA)**. In a managed package, you can see the following main features:

- Manage packages are fully upgradable. Therefore, you can push updates seamlessly.

- To ensure the nonconflicted app installation, you need to use a unique namespace for all components. You also need to register the namespace prefix when you are creating a package.

- Your Apex code is protected. No one can see the implemented logic, which are written in Apex code. It protects the intellectual property of the developer.

- Managed packages have built-in versioning feature, which supports for accessible components.

- You can branch and patch a previous version using managed packages.

Unmanaged packages

Typically, unmanaged packages are used to share the application in an open source manner as a building block of the application, which can be used by the developers. Unlike managed packages, the installed components of the packages can be edited within the destination organization. However, the developer who created and uploaded the package cannot control or upgrade the installed components from the source organization. Unmanaged packages cannot protect your intellectual property such as code. There are no locked components in an unmanaged package. Therefore, unmanaged packages are not suitable to deploy components from sandbox to production organizations.

Creating a package

To create a package, perform the following steps. In this case, we are creating an unmanaged package:

1. Go to **Setup** | **Create** | **Packages**.
2. Click on **New**.

Package Edit	Save Cancel	
Package Name	eLeave	Managed
Language	English ▼	
Configure Custom Link	--None-- ▼	
Notify on Apex Error	Chamil Madusanka 🔍	
Description		
	Save Cancel	

Create a package

3. Specify the **Package Name** and the **Language**. The selected language will be the default language of the package.

> For the managed packages, you need to specify a unique namespace prefix. It must begin with a letter, can contain 1-15 alphanumeric characters and cannot contain two consecutive underscores.

4. Optionally, you can select a custom link from the **Configure Custom Link** field, which displays the configuration information to the app installer.

5. **Notify on Apex Error**: Optionally, you can specify a user who receives an e-mail notification on Apex exception of your package. If you leave this field blank, notifications will be sent to Salesforce.

6. Optionally, you can specify a **Description**, which explains the package and the package content.

7. Click on **Save**. You will be redirected to the **Package** detail page.

> Apex can only be packaged from Developer, Enterprise, Unlimited, and Performance Edition organizations.

8. Under the **Component** tab, click on **Add** to add the particular package components such as apps, objects, reports, or e-mail templates. Select the particular components and click on **Add to Package**. Click on **View Dependencies** to check whether the added components rely on other nonadded components or permissions.

9. Under the **Versions** tab, you can view all the previous uploads of a particular package.

> For the managed packages (by clicking on **Push Upgrades**), you can push upgrades that automatically upgrades the subscribers to a specific version.

Now, let's upload the created package.

Uploading the package

After you create the package and add the particular components to it, you need to upload the package to prepare for the distribution of the package. Perform the following steps to upload a particular application:

1. On the **Package Detail** page, click on the **Upload** button.

Package							
eLeave							Help for this Page

« Back to Package List

Package Detail		Edit	Delete	Upload			
Package Name	eLeave				Type	Unmanaged	
Language	English						
Notify on Apex Error	Chamil Madusanka						
Description							
Created By	Chamil Madusanka, 1/11/2015 2:32 AM			Last Modified By	Chamil Madusanka, 1/11/2015 2:32 AM		

Components	Versions

		Add	View Dependencies		

Action	Name	Parent Object	Type	Included By	Owned By
	Age	Employee	Custom Field	Employee	
	All	Employee	List View	Employee	
	All	Leave	List View	Leave	
	All	Leave Type	List View	Leave Type	
	All	Leave	List View	Leave	
	All	Leave Category	List View	Leave Category	

Upload the package

2. Provide the following details about the particular package before upload. These settings determine what requirements must be met in order to install this package.

3. **Version Name**: Name of the version. As a best practice, use a simple and short description and the date, for example, Spring 2015.

4. **Version Number**: A number with the format of `majorNumber.minorNumber`. The version number represents the release of a package, for example, 1.0, 1.1, and so on. **Version Name** and **Version Number** are required for both managed and unmanaged packages.

> For the managed packages, managed released upload corresponds to the version number and the same version number is used for all the beta uploads until the next managed released upload.

5. Only for the managed packages, you need to select **Release Type**. There are two options:

    ° **Managed – Released**: Choose this when you are going to upload an upgradable version. The locking attributes mechanism will be applied.

    ° **Managed – Beta**: Choose this when you are going to upload a sample of your package for testing purposes. The locking attribute mechanism will not be applied. You can upload more beta versions using it. With this, releases can only be installed in Developer editions or sandbox organizations and cannot be pushed to the production organizations.

6. Optionally, you can specify the **Release Note URL**. This link will be available during the installation process and from the package detail view after installation.

7. Optionally, you can specify the **Post Install Instructions** as a URL or a Visualforce page. These instructions will be shown after the installation and will be available from the package detail view after installation.

8. Optionally, enter and confirm a password to protect the package. It will allow you to share the package privately. Leave it blank if you do not want a password.

9. **Package Requirements**: Specify to notify installers of any requirements and incompatibilities with this package. The selected requirements will be displayed to the administrator prior to download. The administrators will not be allowed to install this package if their Salesforce.com configuration does not meet the requirements specified (some requirements have been automatically detected as part of the sharing process).

10. **Object Requirements**: Specify to notify installers of object requirements for this package. The selected requirements will be displayed to the installer prior to download. The users will not be allowed to install this package if they do not meet the requirements specified (some requirements have been automatically detected as part of the upload process).

11. Click on **Upload**.

12. You will receive an e-mail specifying the success or failure. The installation link will be included in a success notification.

> Before uploading the package, the required Apex code coverage must be fulfilled. Otherwise, you will get errors while you upload the packages.

Simple deployment with the Force.com IDE

There are two interfaces for the Force.com application development, which involves metadata: Setup menu and Force.com IDE. Declarative configurations are easy to develop through the setup menu and Apex code, Visualforce pages are easy to develop through the Force.com IDE. All the previous deployment methods are executed through the setup menu. If you want to deploy the configurations from one organization to another, regardless of the related organizations, such as production and sandbox, you can use the Force.com IDE. The Force.com IDE uses the metadata API to perform its functionalities. When you want to deploy Apex from a local project in the Force.com IDE to a Salesforce organization, use the **Deploy to Server** wizard.

Before performing the deployment, you need to prepare the development environment through the Force.com IDE. To create a Force.com project in the Force.com IDE, use the following steps:

1. Open the Force.com IDE.

2. Go to **File | New | Force.com Project**.

3. Click on **Next** and specify the **Project name**, **Username**, and **Password** of the source organization, **Security Token** of the log in user.

Creating a new project in through Force.com IDE

4. Click on **Next**.

5. Choose metadata components from your organization to include in this project. You'll be able to change this after you create the project. For this example, we will choose **Classes**, **Pages**, **Applications**, **Triggers**, **Layouts**, **Tabs**, **Object – Custom**, **Object – Standard**, **Reports**, **Dashboards**, and **Static Resources**.

6. Click on **OK** to add the selected components to the request list.

7. Click on **Finish** to download the components to your new project.

8. Now that your project is loaded into your Force.com platform IDE workspace, you can deploy the project to another server.

9. In the **Package Explorer**, right-click on the src folder and navigate to **Force.com | Deploy to Server**. You will see the wizard as shown in the next screenshot:

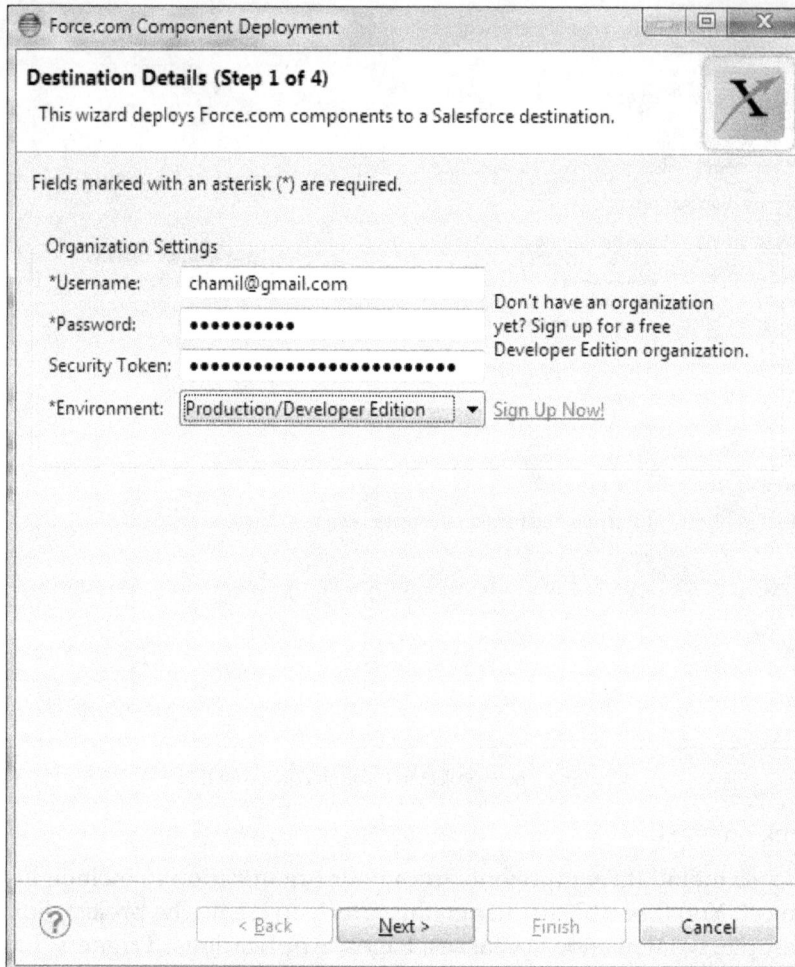

Preparing to save a new project

10. In that wizard, specify the **Username**, **Password**, and **Security Token** of the destination organization. Select the type of environment. Click on **Next**. The IDE logs into the target organization and verifies your permissions.

11. In the next step, you are presented with options for creating archives of the project and destination Force.com components. Archiving is a good idea not only because you can remember when you've made changes, but also because, if the archives are needed at any time in the future, you might want to reverse one or more of the changes. Prior to deployment, it is recommended to create an archive (zip) of the project and destination Force.com components.

12. Select a directory for the destination archive and click on **Next**.

13. In the next panel, the deployment payload will be calculated, generated, and displayed, as shown in the following screenshot:

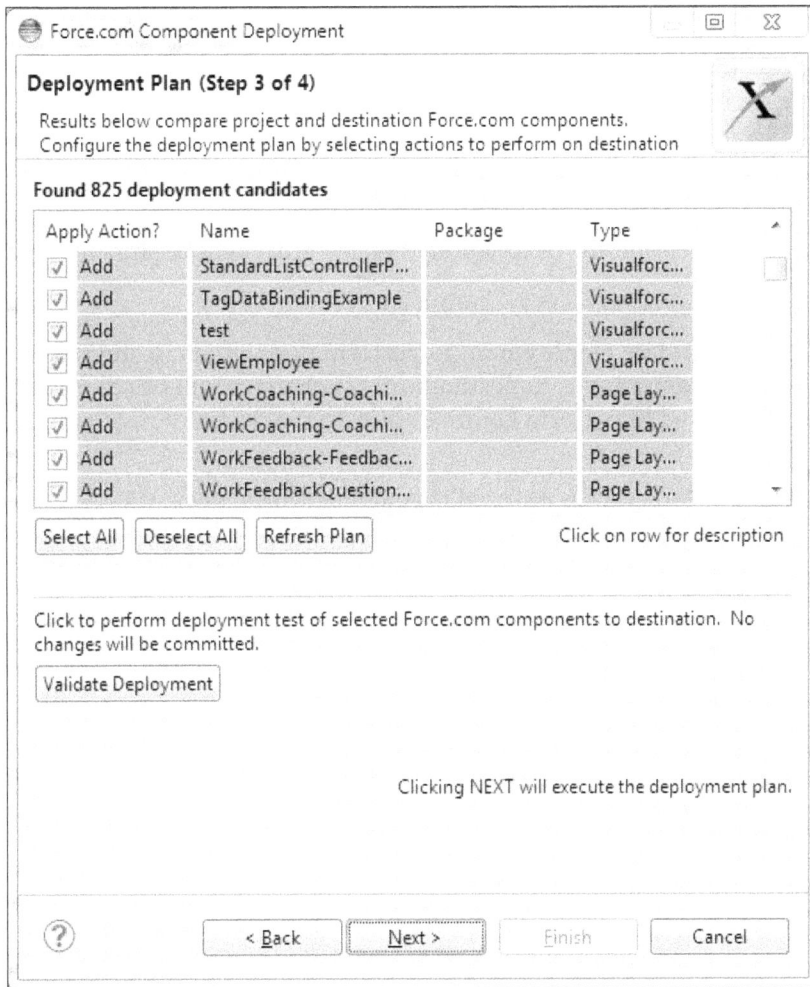

The results of the calculation of the deployment plan

14. The results in the preceding screenshot show the comparison of the source project and destination Force.com components. Configure the deployment plan by selecting the actions to perform on the destination Force.com components. Each component is shown in one of the four colors:

    ° **Green**: If a particular component is not present in the destination organization (including newly adding components), then the entry will be shown in green color.

    ° **Yellow**: If a particular component is present in the destination organization and the metadata of that component is different in the source and the destination (including overwritten with the new metadata), then the entry will be shown in yellow color.

    ° **Red**: If a particular component is present in the destination organization but not present in the source organization, then the entry will be shown in red color.

    ° **Gray**: If a particular component is present in the destination organization and the metadata of that component is identical in the source and the destination, then the entry will be shown in gray color.

15. Select the components to be deployed.

16. Click on **Validate Deployment** to perform deployment testing of the selected Force.com components to destination. No changes will be committed. This is recommended to perform before deploy to the destination organization.

> If Apex code is included in your deployment plan, you cannot deploy to the production organization without a successful test method execution. An appropriate test coverage must be there.

17. Once the validation of the deployment is successful, click on **Next** to start the actual deployment.

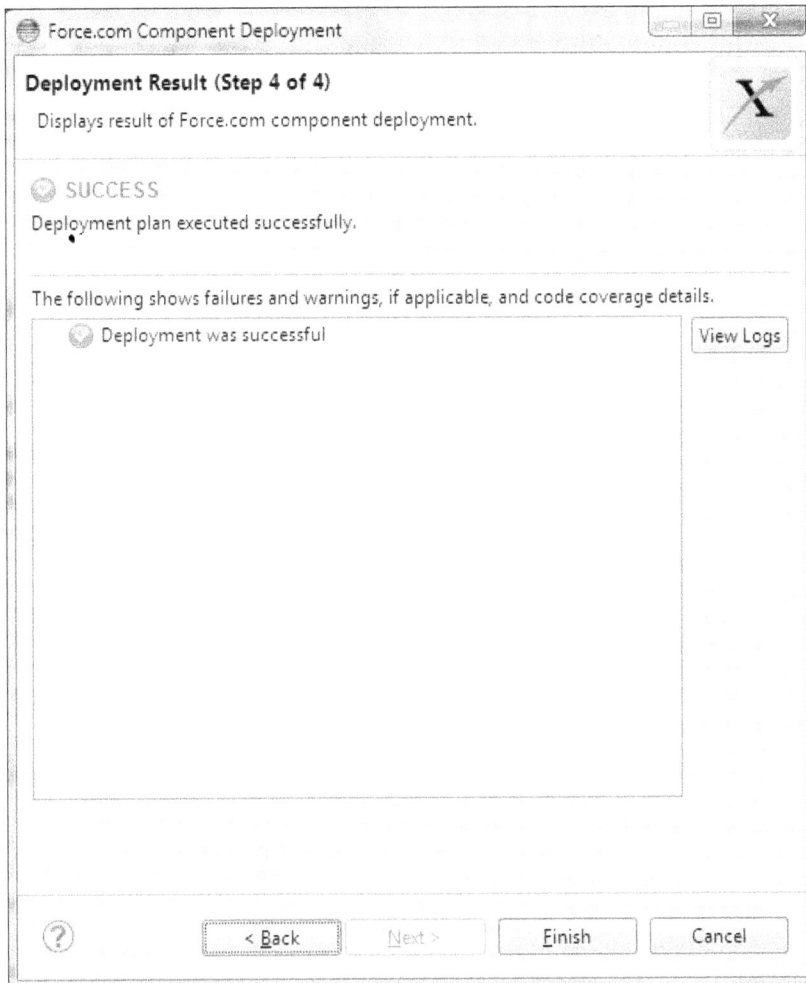

The final page of the Force.com IDE Deployment wizard

If the deployment is successful, you will get the preceding panel and the changes are saved in the destination organization. Log in to the target organization and check out the results of the deployment.

Distributing Force.com applications onto AppExchange

You have learned to build different kinds of applications and have also learned to build packages to distribute them. We can distribute the applications privately to specific users as well as list it publicly on AppExchange. Commercial and free applications (both managed and unmanaged packages) are listed on the AppExchange. In this section, we will discuss a high-level overview of distributing a Force.com application onto AppExchange. The AppExchange framework provides the following features, which add additional functionality rather than distributing applications:

- **Listing**: The things that appear in AppExchange, including marketing aspects are considered as the particular application's listing. Any customer can study your application by reviewing the whitepapers, watching the demo, and test driving. A good application listing will convince the customer to click on the **Get it Now** button for installing the application.

- **Test Drives**: Test drives are provided by the AppExchange for a particular application listing. This is the best way to facilitate the customer to try out the application functionalities in a controlled environment. A good test drive will explain the powerful features of the application to the customer.

- **License Management**: The License Management Application (LMA) provides the facility to track the installation and upgrades of the managed packages, which are created by your organization. You can control the number of users who are allowed to access your package and the accessing duration by applying the licensing on managed packages.

Becoming an AppExchange publisher is a long process. The following are the steps to become an AppExchange publisher and publish applications on AppExchange:

1. **Registering as a Salesforce.com Partner**: Sign up as a Salesforce partner via `http://www.salesforce.com/partners`. Fill in the request form and submit your request. Your partner portal username will end with `@partnerforce.com`. Salesforce has the following two partner programs:

    ◦ **ISVForce**: The **Independent Software Vendor (ISV)** program is for partners who want to build and sell apps.

    ◦ **Force.com Embedded Edition (the OEM model)**: The Force.com Embedded program is for partners who plan to deliver services related to Salesforce.com.

2. **Start building your Application**: You can develop your application in either a free developer organization or **AppExchange Publishing Organization** (**APO**). Free developer organizations are not ideal for a managed application, which is going to publish on AppExchange. APO can be obtained after you registered as a Salesforce partner. After you become a Salesforce partner and log in to the partner portal, you can create an APO by clicking on the **Create a Test Org** button and selecting the org type **Partner Developer Org**. The APO is the ideal organization for a managed application, which is going to publish on AppExchange. In an APO, the number of user licenses, data limits are higher than a regular developer organization. Plan and manage your development and upgrade the life cycle in a suitable way.

3. **Becoming an AppExchange publisher**: Once you are signed up as a partner, you can create an APO as we discussed in the previous point. You will receive the credentials for the organization and you can move on to the development aspect. The purpose of an APO is to help you publish app listings on AppExchange.

4. **Signup for AppExchange checkout**: This step is only applicable for the paid applications. If you are going to publish your application as a free app, you can skip this step. With this feature, customers can pay for your application directly through AppExchange.

5. **Start and complete your security review**: This is a very important step because this is the main process to ensure your application has followed the best practices and developed a secure and quality app. This is mandatory for both ISVForce and Force.com Embedded partner programs. The scope of the security review depends on the composition of the application. The scope can be categorized into Native (Force.com), Composite (Web Applications), and Client/Mobile. The following high-level tests and reviews will follow within the security review (according to the scope):

   ° **Native (Force.com)**: In this type of review, there will be automated code scans, manual code review and black box testing, Client-side components (flash and JavaScript), Integrations and web services

   ° **Composite (Web Application)**: In this type of review, there will be automated code scan, manual code review and black box testing, Client-side components (flash and JavaScript), Integrations and web services, Architecture review and web server testing

- ° **Client/Mobile**: In this type of review, there will be manual hands on testing of the application, Integrations and web services, Architecture review and web server testing

6. **Go Live**: Once your application has passed the security review, your application is ready to be listed on AppExchange. Click on **Make Public** to list your app on AppExchange.

Summary

In this chapter, you have learned deployment methodologies available in the Force.com platform. We introduced sandboxes, change sets, packaging, and explained a simple deployment with the Force.com IDE. Finally, we explained high level steps for distributing the Force.com application onto the AppExchange.

The next chapter is an *Appendix, Force.com Tools*, and it will give you an overall idea about some tools, which are available on the Force.com platform and are related to the Force.com development/deployment environment.

Force.com Tools

In the Force.com platform, all the development and deployment can be done via the browser version. However, there are some tasks that can be easily completed using a tool rather than the browser version, for example, Data Loader for uploading bulk data, the Force.com IDE for developing Apex classes and Visualforce pages, the Migration tool for deploying the Force.com components from one organization to another, and so on. We can categorize the Force.com tools into the following categories:

- Development tools
- Data tools
- Cloud integration tools
- Language integration libraries
- Salesforce platform mobile services

In this chapter, we will provide a high-level description of these tools.

Development tools

Development tools are the tools that are used to develop the application, including some portion of declarative (point-click) development (creating objects and fields using metadata) and programming development (Apex classes, triggers, and Visualforce pages). The development tools are as follows:

- **Force.com IDE**: The Force.com IDE is an open source (you can download the source from `https://github.com/forcedotcom/idecore`) Eclipse-based tool, which can be used to create, modify, and deploy the Force.com application from a local computer. It provides a full-featured, collaborative development environment for coding, compiling and testing, and version controlling. The major features of the Force.com IDE are as follows:

  ○ Writing and managing Apex classes and triggers.

  ○ Unit tests can be executed with the Apex Test Runner and can provide the code coverage report.

  ○ Locating the syntax errors while you are writing the code and providing error messages and debugging output.

  ○ Creating, modifying, and downloading all the metadata components available in the metadata API.

  ○ Creating and editing Visualforce pages and Visualforce components.

  ○ The schema explorer allows you to execute SOAL queries and you can see all the standard and custom objects with their fields. You just need to pick particular fields to generate the SOAL query.

  ○ It deploys application components to the production organization or any other organization with the Deploy to Server wizard.

  ○ By integrating the Eclipse-enabled version control system, you can develop, test, and deploy your application in a collaborative environment.

  ○ The Force.com IDE can detect and resolve the conflicting changes between online and local versions of the application.

- **The Force.com migration tool**: The Force.com migration tool is a Java/Ant-based command-line tool that is used to move metadata between the local machine and the Force.com organization. This tool is based on the metadata API and is used in the following scenarios:

  ○ To prepare a test environment with enormous volumes of setup changes in a short time.

- ◦ Typically, in a development process, we maintain iterative development; testing phases and final release will be deployed to the production organization. Using the Force.com migration tool, you can maintain a scripted retrieval and deployment process, which is more efficient. More details about the migration tool can be found at `https://developer.salesforce.com/page/Force.com_Migration_Tool`.

- **The Developer console**: The Developer console is an online tool, which is available in your organization. It is a compact tool for Force.com application development to create, edit, debug, and test your application. The Developer console can be found at **Your Name | Developer Console** or **Setup | Develop | Tools | Developer Console**. The developer console allows us to perform the following tasks:

  - ◦ Create Apex classes, triggers, Visualforce pages, Visualforce components, and static resources.

  - ◦ Edit Apex classes, triggers, Visualforce pages, and Visualforce components. There is an in-built code editor in the developer console.

  - ◦ Open Apex classes, triggers, Visualforce pages, objects, Visualforce components, packages, and static resources.

  - ◦ Debugging and troubleshooting through viewing logs, set and view checkpoints in Apex code.

  - ◦ Executing the anonymous code.

  - ◦ Testing and validating the performance of the code by testing the Apex code and inspecting logs for performance issues.

  - ◦ Executing SOQL and SOSL queries via the in-built query editor and viewing the query results.

  - ◦ For more details visit `https://help.salesforce.com/apex/HTViewHelpDoc?id=code_system_log.htm`.

> The Force.com IDE, the Force.com migration tool, and the developer console are Salesforce supported tools.

- **The Force.com Explorer**: The Force.com Explorer is a .NET-based (cross-platform AIR application) tool. It is a lightweight tool for inspecting schema and building and testing SOQL queries. In order to install the Force.com Explorer, you have to install the Adobe AIR. You can download the Force.com Explorer from `http://developerforce.s3.amazonaws.com/media/forceexplorer/ForceExplorer.air`. Currently, static resources cannot be managed through the Force.com Explorer. For more details refer to `https://developer.salesforce.com/page/ForceExplorer`.

- **Workbench**: The Workbench is one of the most powerful tools for interacting with the particular organization via the Force.com APIs. It is a web-based tool for both administrators and developers. The workbench supports the following APIs:
  - Bulk API
  - Streaming API
  - Rest API
  - Apex API
  - Metadata API

  This tool is used to manipulate, query, and migrate data and metadata in a particular organization. It provides more advanced features for testing Force.com APIs such as backward compatibility testing, customizable SOAP headers, providing debug logs for API traffic, and SSO) integration. For more details, visit: `https://developer.salesforce.com/page/Workbench`.

- **Force.com CLI tool**: This is a command-line interface to Force.com. You can directly interact with the Force.com platform via this tool. It allows you to manage custom objects, execute Apex code, and execute SOQL queries. You can download the Force.com CLI tool from `https://github.com/heroku/force`.

Data tools

Tools that are used to manipulate data in a particular organization are categorized as Data tools.

Force.com Data Loader: Data Loader is a client application for the bulk import or export of data. It is used to insert, update, delete, or extract Salesforce.com records. The Apex Data Loader can move data in or out of any type of Salesforce.com record, including opportunities and custom objects. When importing data, it reads, extracts, and loads data from comma-separated values (CSV) files. When exporting data, it outputs CSV files.

The Force.com API is required to perform operations in Data Loader. A wizard interface that is easy to use and an alternative command-line interface are available in Data Loader. It is a support for all the custom and standard objects and it provides detailed success and error log files after every functionality. You can download the Data Loader from **Setup** | **Administer** | **Data Management**. More details about the Data Loader can be found at `https://developer.salesforce.com/page/Data_Loader`.

Cloud integration tools

Tools that are used to integrate with other cloud platforms are categorized as cloud integration tools. The tools available are as follows:

- **Force.com for Google App Engine**: This allows the developer to create web applications that access both the Google cloud platform and Salesforce.com. Both Java and Python versions are available. The toolkit allows us to build consumer-oriented web apps on the Google App Engine that can easily leverage data and execute logics on the Force.com platform.

- **Force.com toolkit for Azure**: Windows Azure is another cloud platform that has been launched by Microsoft. The Force.com toolkit for Azure leverages the Force.com platform from Windows Azure. It allows you to integrate Force.com and existing Azure projects and it is easy to call back the API to the Force.com platform.

- **Force.com for Amazon Web Services**: This allows us to integrate Force.com applications and the Amazon Web Services (AWS). There are two services that support this toolkit, namely, Simple Storage System (S3) and EC2. The access methods are wrapped by the Force.com Apex code and it can be used directly within the Force.com platform. You can manipulate S3 objects based on the workflow or data changes. You can use Amazon Machine Image to kick-start integration development via EC2.

- **Force.com for Facebook**: This toolkit allows us to access the Facebook API within Force.com Apex code and lets us create new social graph applications. Using this toolkit, you can build business applications for Facebook.

Language integration libraries

Language integration tools are used to integrate with other applications, which are developed using other software development languages, for example, Java, .Net, PHP, and Ruby, which are as follows:

- **Java and .Net**: Using the Force.com SOAP API, you can integrate Java applications. It uses the standard WSDL and SOAP to fulfill the integration requirements.

- **PHP toolkit**: This toolkit provides a way to integrate a PHP web application and the Force.com application using SOAP API. You can invoke SOAP API methods within the Force.com platform.

- **Force.com toolkit for Ruby**: This toolkit allows you to integrate the Force.com application with Ruby. In this integration, you can directly manipulate Force.com data within the Ruby application.

Salesforce platform mobile services

The following tools are used to interact with mobile devices and mobile applications:

- **Salesforce platform mobile services in Force.com**: This service provides a way to access enterprise data by leveraging standard web protocols (REST API). It allows you to expose business data across any device. Salesforce platform mobile services include Mobile SDK, identity services, social engagement, geolocation services, Analytics API, mobile design templates, REST API, and JavaScript frameworks.

- **Salesforce Mobile SDK**: This is an open source pack of familiar technologies such as REST API and OAuth 2.0. It allows you to build rich mobile applications that use Force.com and Database.com as the backend. It supports the building of HTML5, native, and hybrid applications.

Summary

In this chapter, you learned some important tools that can be used in Force.com application development. You gained an overall idea about these tools.

Every start has an end, and thus, we have reached the end of the book. We have covered the most important topics that will help you improve your knowledge of Visualforce development. Further, you can use Force.com resources such as the Force.com discussion board (where you can seek help on technical issues), by using `#askforce` on Twitter and `https://developer.salesforce.com/blogs/`.

May the force be with you!

Index

Force.com site
about 325, 326
best practices 336, 337
creating 326
creating, domain name used 328-330
customizing 326
domain name, registering 327, 328
security access permissions,
    setting up 332, 333
Visualforce pages, assigning to 331, 332
FOR loop 200
formats, report
joined reports 288
matrix reports 287
summary reports 285, 286
tabular reports 284
formatted text data types
about 43
creating 43-45
Email 43
Phone 43
URL 43
free developer edition account
signing up for 11, 12

G

general user permissions 112
getRecord() method 271
get request, Visualforce page 274
getter methods 266
groups
about 116
personal groups 116
public groups 116
scenarios 116

H

HTML5 255-257

I

ID field
15 digit 29
18 digit 29
IF statements 200
inbound change set 343

InboundEmailHandler interface
implementing 306, 307
inbound e-mails
e-mail service, setting up 309-312
handling 305, 306
InboundEmailHandler interface,
    implementing 306, 307
inheritance syntaxes, Apex
abstract 204
extends 204
virtual 204
interfaces
syntax, defining 205
ISVForce 358

J

Java
versus Apex 194, 195
Java Database Connectivity (JDBC) 179
JavaScript
callbackFunction 251
controller 250
escape 251
method 251
namespace 250
params 251
JavaScript, Visualforce pages
about 248
for Apex controllers 250-252
Visualforce components,
    accessing with 248-250
joined reports 288

L

language integration libraries
about 366
Force.com toolkit for Ruby 366
Java and .Net 366
PHP toolkit 366
leave management application
creating 60-64
example 24-31
License Management
    Application (LMA) 347
limited option data types
about 48

W

Web Service Definition
      Language (WSDL) 194
web services, Apex code 194
web tab
  about 71
  creating 71-73
while loop 201
without sharing keyword 193
with sharing keyword 193
Workbench
  about 364
  APIs 364
  URL 364

Work.com Only User license 87
workflow process
  and approval process, comparing 160
workflow rules
  about 135
  creating 138-146
  elements 137
  time-dependent action, creating for 146
  time triggers, creating for 146
workflows
  used, for automating business
      process 136-138

[PACKT] PUBLISHING enterprise
professional expertise distilled

Thank you for buying
Learning Force.com Application Development

About Packt Publishing

Packt, pronounced 'packed', published its first book, *Mastering phpMyAdmin for Effective MySQL Management*, in April 2004, and subsequently continued to specialize in publishing highly focused books on specific technologies and solutions.

Our books and publications share the experiences of your fellow IT professionals in adapting and customizing today's systems, applications, and frameworks. Our solution-based books give you the knowledge and power to customize the software and technologies you're using to get the job done. Packt books are more specific and less general than the IT books you have seen in the past. Our unique business model allows us to bring you more focused information, giving you more of what you need to know, and less of what you don't.

Packt is a modern yet unique publishing company that focuses on producing quality, cutting-edge books for communities of developers, administrators, and newbies alike. For more information, please visit our website at www.packtpub.com.

About Packt Enterprise

In 2010, Packt launched two new brands, Packt Enterprise and Packt Open Source, in order to continue its focus on specialization. This book is part of the Packt Enterprise brand, home to books published on enterprise software – software created by major vendors, including (but not limited to) IBM, Microsoft, and Oracle, often for use in other corporations. Its titles will offer information relevant to a range of users of this software, including administrators, developers, architects, and end users.

Writing for Packt

We welcome all inquiries from people who are interested in authoring. Book proposals should be sent to author@packtpub.com. If your book idea is still at an early stage and you would like to discuss it first before writing a formal book proposal, then please contact us; one of our commissioning editors will get in touch with you.

We're not just looking for published authors; if you have strong technical skills but no writing experience, our experienced editors can help you develop a writing career, or simply get some additional reward for your expertise.

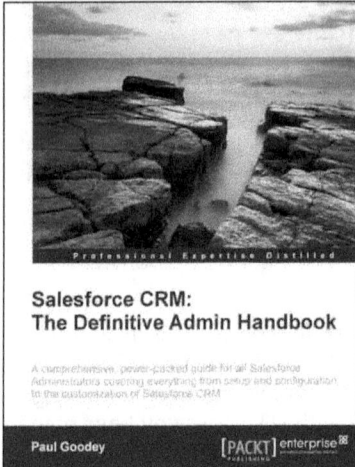

Salesforce CRM: The Definitive Admin Handbook

ISBN: 978-1-84968-306-7   Paperback: 376 pages

A comprehensive, power-packed guide for all Salesforce Administrators covering everything from setup and configuration, to the customization of Salesforce CRM

1. Get to grips with tips, tricks, best-practice administration principles, and critical design considerations for setting up and customizing Salesforce CRM with this book and e-book.

2. Master the mechanisms for controlling access to, and the quality of, data and information sharing.

3. Take advantage of the only guide with real-world business scenarios for Salesforce CRM.

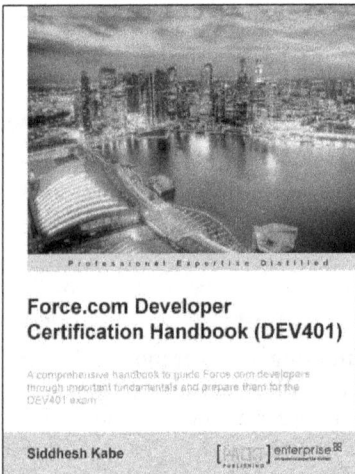

Force.com Developer Certification Handbook (DEV401)

ISBN: 978-1-84968-348-7   Paperback: 280 pages

A comprehensive handbook to guide Force.com developers through important fundamentals and prepare them for the DEV401 exam

1. Simple and to-the-point examples that can be tried out in your developer org.

2. A practical book for professionals who want to take the DEV 401 Certification exam.

3. Sample questions for every topic in an exam pattern to help you prepare better, and tips to get things started.

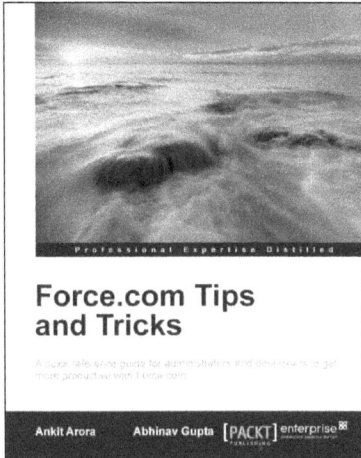

Force.com Tips and Tricks

ISBN: 978-1-84968-474-3   Paperback: 224 pages

A quick reference guide for administrators and developers to get more productive with Force.com

1. Tips and tricks for topics ranging from point-and-click administration, to fine development techniques with Apex & Visualforce.

2. Avoids technical jargon, and expresses concepts in a clear and simple manner.

3. A pocket guide for experienced Force.com developers.

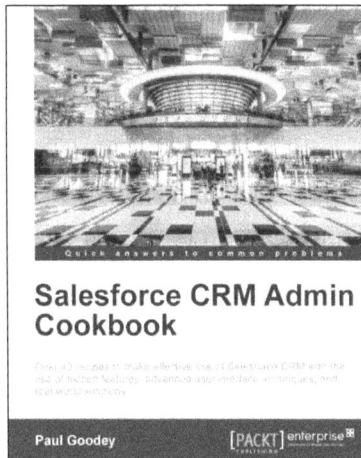

Force.com Tips and Tricks

Ankit Arora   Abhinav Gupta   [PACKT] enterprise ⊠

Salesforce CRM Admin Cookbook

ISBN: 978-1-84968-424-8   Paperback: 266 pages

Over 40 recipes to make effective use of Salesforce CRM with the use of hidden features, advanced user interface techniques, and real-world solutions

1. Implement advanced user interface techniques to improve the look and feel of Salesforce CRM.

2. Discover hidden features and hacks that extend standard configuration to provide enhanced functionality and customization.

3. Build real-world process automation, using the detailed recipes to harness the full power of Salesforce CRM.

Salesforce CRM Admin Cookbook

Paul Goodey   [PACKT] enterprise ⊠

Please check **www.PacktPub.com** for information on our titles

www.ingramcontent.com/pod-product-compliance
Lightning Source LLC
Chambersburg PA
CBHW080657220326
41598CB00033B/5242